THE
ECONOMIC BASIS
OF PEACE

THE ECONOMIC BASIS OF PEACE

Linkages Between Economic Growth and International Conflict

WILLIAM H. MOTT IV

Contributions in Economics and Economic History,
Number 187

GREENWOOD PRESS
Westport, Connecticut • London

Library of Congress Cataloging-in-Publication

Mott, William H.
   The economic basis of peace : linkages between economic growth and
international conflict / William H. Mott.
      p.   cm. — (Contributions in economics and economic history,
ISSN 0084–9235 ; 187)
   Includes bibliographical references and index.
   ISBN 0–313–30366–5 (alk. paper)
   1. Economic development.   2. International economic relations.
3. International relations.   4. Peace—Economic aspects.   I. Title.
II. Series.
HD82.M595   1997
337—dc21   96–51138

British Library Cataloguing in Publication Data is available.

Library of Congress Catalog Card Number: 96–51138
ISBN: 0–313–30366–5
ISSN: 0084–9235

First published in 1997

Greenwood Press, 88 Post Road West, Westport, CT 06881
An imprint of Greenwood Publishing Group, Inc.

Printed in the United States of America

The paper used in this book complies with the
Permanent Paper Standard issued by the National
Information Standards Organization (Z39.48–1984).

10 9 8 7 6 5 4 3 2 1

Contents

vi   Contents

Preface

This is not a book about economic growth, prosperity, or wealth. Nor is it a book about international conflict, peace, or war. It is a book about the relationship between these two most salient features of the global human experience in recent times: economic growth and international conflict. It begins with an essay in comparative political-economic history, and shifts in Chapter 3 to a survey of theoretical approaches—or indifference—to any growth-conflict relationship. The final section is an effort to pool comparative and historical analyses of how or whether economic performances of several selected countries can be related to their international conflict behaviors.

The unusual nature and form of this book calls for some explanation. Reflecting my deep interest in the conjunctions between the orthodox domains of politics and economics, this book had its genesis in the years 1981-1986, which I spent as Chief of the U.S. Office of Defense Cooperation in London. My duties involved me deeply in both government efforts to avoid and pursue international conflict and the actions of industry that generated economic growth. Both sectors agreed generally on broad goals of avoiding conflict and promoting growth and each pursued its own course, usually trying to avoid the other. Yet both industry and government were quite ready on some occasions to cooperate in sacrificing both peace and growth (the Falklands War occurred in 1982). So long as politics and economics remained visibly separate, government and industry might follow their own independent paths toward peace and prosperity. When, however, politics and economics merged or mixed (as in war), growth and conflict also changed, as did policy—both government and corporate.

The international order in which I had spent my career had historically isolated economic growth as a purely national phenomenon—the business of industry, while dealing with conflict as an international dynamic—the business of government. These bifurcations may have been taxonomically suitable, realistic, and effective in explaining the world in which economists and political scientists had formed the respective premises of their disciplines, and defined their domains of interest and expertise—their *magisteria*. My experiences in London, however, left some doubt about the autonomy of growth and conflict as separate phenomena, of business and politics as distinct activities, and of economics and political science as nonoverlapping *magisteria*. This traditional separation did not seem to be a natural phenomenon. Nor had humanity merely been extraordinarily clever in adjusting its thought and behavior to some fortuitous series of countless past experiences of growth and conflict. The relationship—or separation—between growth and conflict and the international system within which it operates are nothing more nor less than parts of a structure of ideas, created in human minds, and operated by human beings. They are neither immutable and unknowable nor unpredictable and unexplainable.

I left London with the vague intention of finding some way to understand, and possibly to change, the ways in which humans related growth and conflict in the international system. Prior to the formidable difficulties of ever changing human behaviors, the challenge had several aspects—philosophical, historical, empirical, and theoretical. It was necessary to determine how humankind had related growth and conflict over the centuries of historical time. It was necessary to appreciate how thinkers have thought about, understood, and explained the growth-conflict relationship. It was necessary to discern how modern societies and countries actually behaved as they grew, stagnated, competed, cooperated, and fought with each other. And finally, it was necessary to try to explain all of this in some way that might be useful to real people living real lives in real societies facing real problems.

This book does not propose or imply ways of dealing with all of the perennial problems that arise across the growth-conflict relationship. It contains a theory about that relationship, as human thought has developed and refined it over time. Preparation of the book was an almost empirical process, involving examination of many societies, from ancient Uruk to modern Europe. Despite the theoretical survey of Chapter 3, this book does not seek to be accepted into the academic literature of reinterpretations of originally robust interpretations of thought about economic and political philosophy and human affairs. It is not a book about theory; it builds and presents a theory.

The broad scope and unusual nature of the book make it clear that different people will read it for different purposes. Some will find a broad, focused historical and theoretical survey of the relationships between economic growth and peace or war. Others, intent on developing policy or models of "world systems," may find few tools for their particular work, but cannot ignore the implications suggested in Chapter 6. Those interested in only prevention or resolution of conflict, or in generating economic growth, may be disappointed. The book offers, and refers to, a wealth of material about both growth and conflict, which may be useful to those who seek to make generalizations about political or economic social behaviors. It does not, however, overcome the dual problem, intrinsic in trying to blend historical inquiry with empirical analysis, that historical evidence is always so diverse that "hard" scientific conclusions are impossible (or at least unreliable), and empirical examples are always disputable as "case-specific" anomalies.

The book's novel concept of "lawlike regularity" may satisfy neither historians nor scientists. Nevertheless, if one abandons any *a priori* theoretical perspective and observes history over millennia, it is clear that some generally valid conclusions may be drawn about growth and conflict. Qualification of such generalizations as lawlike regularities, as rigorously defined in Chapter 4, may avoid the trap of economic (or political) determinism. Development of a theory—even as a hypothesis—based on a set of lawlike regularities seems also to avoid the banal explanations, "it depends primarily on exogenous factors," or "that problem lies beyond the scope of the study," or "we don't have enough evidence," or "the methodology lacks rigor."

Even though the book's concluding hypothesis, as presented in Chapter 6, may strike incisive readers as liberal, behavioralist, structuralist, or perhaps recall some other theoretical approach, its essential features transcend all of these, and—I would suggest—not only provide a new perspective on a set of old ideas, but offer some additional new thoughts. While the hypothesis was not constructed by synthesis, it seems impossible to think about economic growth and international conflict without referring to these familiar concepts. This book contains a novel structure of ideas and attitudes—necessarily in the traditional languages of political science and economics—presented as a hypothesis, as a possible foundation for explaining and managing growth and conflict. I accordingly invite the cooperation of readers through comment or criticism. Especially fruitful might be contributions of relevant material, thoughts, or examples, either as references to additional sources of both theory and history, as well as experiment and analysis, or as sharing of personal insight and experience.

Behind my specific intent in writing the book lay a broad aim of exploring the wonderfully complex intersections of economics and politics along their common magisterial border. Many of the deepest questions of each discipline can only be addressed by crossing the border, and creating some sort of hyphenated political-economic *magisterium* as an analytical and philosophical structure for political-economic ideas. This hyphenated political-economy is more than what all humanity has come to know as global interdependence. It involves not only policy and theory, but thoughts and attitudes, not only about growth and conflict but about how we think about them, and about other things, and what it all means. As modern interdependence progresses into its fourth phase (the first three were mutual strategic deterrence brought by nuclear weapons and ballistic missiles, economic interdependence based on global production, and environmental interdependence due to global pollution and human transformations of the Earth), far-sighted leaders and thinkers have already called for a novel sort of global vision of the world and life. It is my hope that this book may make a small contribution to illumination of this fourth horizon of human understanding. I shall be satisfied if my exploratory thoughts and theories generate more profound thoughts about the growth-conflict relationship, which could sharpen humanity's skills at managing each.

The manuscript was completed in 1995. No alterations or additions have been made to account for the many important political or economic events that have occurred since.

Acknowledgments

Whatever weaknesses readers may find in this book, they would have found many more without the kind and patient help, understanding and support of my mentors, family, and friends. George Mitchell, Scott Thompson, and Denis Simon waded through several versions of the entire manuscript, raising difficult questions of both theory and philosophy, and guiding me toward useful answers. My Fletcher colleague Bob Filippone insisted repeatedly on bringing me back to contemporary reality after my jaunt through history in the first two chapters. Jeswald Salacuse and Michael Klein inspired the formulation of Chapters 4 and 5, and endeavored (I fear with only partial success) to make my comments on international law and foreign investment a bit less crude. Many scholars and students have heard and read my papers on subthemes in this book, and have provided references and ideas, much-needed criticism, and encouragement.

The libraries and staffs of the Fletcher School of Law and Diplomacy, Tufts University, were not only of immeasurable assistance, but often made special arrangements to accommodate my peculiar research techniques. Katie Chase has been a meticulous and patient editor, tactfully convincing me to refine my stylistic idiosyncrasies for the benefit of the general reader.

My family has been patiently understanding over the many years that I took to organize a cloud of nebulous thoughts and feelings into a theme that made some sense. The result of a very special relationship, this book is dedicated to my wife, Donna, to whom I owe so much.

1

Introduction

For most of the twentieth century the most salient features of the international political-economy have been the chiaroscuro of international conflict and the panorama of economic growth. Any connections between them, suggested occasionally by observers since at least Aristotle, have seemed vague, intermittent, and probably situation-specific. Following centuries of epistemological tradition, modern analysts continue to note, and orthodox economic and political-scientific theories allow, some mildly causal, or at least stimulative, relationship between economic growth and international conflict. "Economic objectives, resources, and instruments of foreign policy have always been significant elements in the struggles between political groups."[1] Beyond broad aphorisms and intuitive assertions of this sort, and occasional interesting speculations about human nature, orthodoxy has simply accepted that some natural relationship exists between economic growth and international conflict. Secure within their own disciplines, historians, economists, and political scientists have largely ignored the cross-disciplinary question of how and why such a relationship works, or even what it is.

Beyond the obvious insight that there seem to be some parallels between politics and economics, between conflict and growth, or between trade and war, neither empiricism nor theory has produced general explanations of what those relationships are, or how they work. Only by combining, selecting, or compromising among various sets of data and integrating convenient bits of various theories has orthodoxy been able even to approach a weak, ambiguous, highly conditional generality, the same that was deduced three millennia ago by Socrates, Plato, and Aristotle (see sources in Notes to Chapter 2): growth could sometimes lead to war.

The ancients and the classicists seem to have been comfortable with this sort of vapid, ambiguous separation between the essential processes of international relations. Contemporary analysts and decision-makers, however, need more in confronting political-economic realities that confound traditional political or economic models of *either* conflict *or* growth. As the two disciplines begin to converge in a hyphenated international political-economy,[2] it is no longer enough to explain growth in economic terms, and conflict in political terms. Nor can analysts dismiss either as simply coincidental or exogenous; decision-makers must address both in a single policy. It becomes interesting and urgent, if not critical, to understand how growth (salutary, or at worst benign)—or perhaps its absence—can affect conflict (adverse, or at best uncomfortable); to explain political events in economic terms; and to understand economic growth as a political process. Rather than simply an interesting academic curiosity, the relationship between growth and conflict is crucial in the continuing struggle of modern peoples and their governments for lasting peace and continuing prosperity.

THE ARGUMENTS: CONFLICT, GROWTH, AND THE RELATIONSHIP

The fundamental features of any theory are the dependent and independent variables and the relationship between them. The independent variable, economic growth in this study, is presumed to affect, through some predictable relationship, the dependent variable, international conflict. Empirical observations of the two variables allow either statistical correlations or logical deduction, which indicate the nature, strength, causality, and limitations of the relationship.

Dependent Variable: Conflict

War is a profound agent of historical change, but it is not the fundamental driving force of history, Whatever causes war—economic factors, class conflict, human nature, modes of production, technological change, divine will—is by definition a more basic causal agent than war itself. No matter how ubiquitous or profound the effects of war may be, war itself is a derivative and secondary phenomenon, never a prime moving force. By the same token, war should never be seen as an exogenous force that acts on states and societies from without; it derives rather from within them.[3]

Human propensities to engage in both conflict and cooperation with other humans are probably as ancient as civilization. The fourth chapter of the Christian Bible records humanity's first murder. The ancient Hindu saga, *Bhagavad Gita*, begins by chronicling the "heroic warriors, powerful archers . . . and the chariots of war" of two great armies facing each other to resolve in battle some unknown conflict between forgotten nations.[4] Political science, history, sociology, and even psychology have analyzed conflict and cooperation since the dawn of history. Large databases and powerful theories measure and explain both, yet humanity remains unsure about whether, when, or where to expect war or peace, conflict or cooperation. That neither individuals nor their national governments agree on any universal set of values would seem to require no demonstration. Struggle and conflict around various values are indeed the substance of politics. Nor is it necessary to explain that international relationships involve as much disagreement and competition as concord and cooperation.

Whatever the pragmatic, logical, or apparent geneses of cooperation and conflict, the range of international relationships extends from the former to the latter. It includes agreement and collaboration among nations with similar values, combinations of cooperation and conflict, total opposition, and war. As in a rainbow, the spectrum presents no clear boundaries between conflict and nonconflict, or between acrimonious discord, nonviolent conflict, and military war, the extreme violent end of the spectrum.

A "normal" political-economic equilibrium allows international competition within a relatively narrow range of choice in national policies or objectives on controversial issues. Conflict arises in reaction to efforts at revision of this *status quo*; to expansion of one nation at the expense of another; to waves of nationalism, resurgence of historical disputes, or various racial, religious, ethnic concerns; or simply to policy differences around current issues. At least one of the nations is "happy with the *status quo* and is drawn into the conflict by a demand for change from someone else." National feelings in either nation can involve dissatisfaction, insecurity, frustration, vulnerability, or desperation.[5]

From such premises this study's design shares Bruce Porter's focus[6] on Kenneth Waltz's well-known "second image" of war (the origins of war lie in the internal structures of states),[7] but eschews deeper speculation about the causes or socio-political effects of war. In contrast to Porter and Waltz, the primary interest here is not war itself, but the relationship between economic growth and international conflict, with war as a major hyponymn and nonwar conflict as its other. Common, historical usages of such terms as war and international conflict are broadly imprecise, but indicate the relationship "between at least two national states in which at least one state chooses to resist efforts by at least one other state to induce change in its policies or actions, or when two nations wish to take actions that are mutually inconsistent."[8]

Within Michael Nicholson's definition violent conflict involves military mobilizations, combat operations, and war. Nonviolent international conflict can involve diplomacy, negotiation, litigation—arbitrated, mediated, or adjudicated—commercial and trade disputes, disputes over borders and shared resources, and nonviolent or civil force.[9] In the vague interstices between nonviolence and violent conflict lie such things as arms races, assembly of allies, establishment of foreign bases, or foreign deployments for training. The analytical difference between the two types is of degree, rather than kind.

Decisions to begin, continue, and end conflict, or to escalate from nonviolence to violence, involve national political choices about style, intensity, or technique, based on perceptions of cost, risk, benefits, and rewards. Both resistance and actions resisted may be passive or active; violent or nonviolent; political, military, or economic; but all inherently involve confrontation. A single broad purpose—victory—pervades the entire family and chronology of issues that adhere to an international conflict. These generate periodic "crisis points" of confrontation until the conflict ends, usually with victory for one of the opponents. Usable as indicators of conflict, crisis points appear in history as wars; "diplomatic incidents"; disputes over borders, trade, or something else; and even international litigation or piracy. These are the "event-interactions" from which timeseries and databases are built (see section on "Nonwar Event-Interaction Data" in Chapter 4).

Conflict, then, includes a variety of confrontational relationships between national states, such as military aggression and defense; political-diplomatic competition over market shares or sources of resources; national claims to the same territories; discriminatory barriers to trade, investment, or migration; extraterritorial assertion of sovereignty; or violation of international law. International conflicts involve national governments in confronting, with the intent of defeating, other national governments, the "enemy." Conflict is what Anatol Rapoport has called a "friend and foe" situation.[10]

Independent Variable: Economic Growth

In its simplest sense, and in common usage, economic growth is any increase of output. In a world of autonomous national states supporting their own populations, the common indicator of growth and economic performance is total national output—appropriately measured as gross domestic product (GDP), gross national product (GNP), or *per capita* income (PCI). Continuing support for growing populations without reducing standards of living implies growth only in a simple sense of increasing aggregate capacity to produce. Since the eighteenth century most countries, with slow parallel growth of both population and production, have experienced this simple sort of economic growth, with appropriate annual increases in various elements of their national accounts. Short-term changes in *per capita* income or production are small, although an era of what Lloyd Reynolds calls "extensive growth" may be quite long (as much as six centuries for Mayan Yucatán or imperial China).[11]

From an orthodox neoclassical perspective, growth appears as a rise in output consequent to accumulating and concentrating the right sorts of physical and human resources (capital, labor, technology) within a national state, and using them efficiently for economic production. Shifts in supply or demand, expansion and penetration of new markets, and reallocation of resources are incidentals of growth, since marginal returns to capital and labor are seen as equal for all uses. Neoclassical theory assumes Pareto optimality over time in allocating resources, and the impossibility of increasing aggregate production through forced reallocation of resources, which occurs naturally as a result of growth, and only as the economy expands or contracts. Simple neoclassical economic growth increases the economy's capacity for output, or creation of wealth, in balance with increases in the requirements of the population, and appears as an increase in gross national product.

A more modern perspective—the structural approach—considers growth as only one aspect of modernization, which transforms the structure of production "to meet changing demands and to make more productive use of technology."[12] This perspective does not consider general equilibrium as axiomatic, or economic structure as rigid; reallocation of resources assumes a primary role in generating economic growth. Reallocation of factors of production (capital or labor) from less productive to more productive sectors can accelerate growth, as can diversification of an economy into new sectors, or even expansion into new markets. Growth appears as an increase in *per capita* gross domestic product, or *per capita* income. For the structuralist, an inevitable effect of the growth process is fundamental change in the structure of a national economy.[13]

Immediately after World War II, the world's economies began a period of spectacular growth unprecedented in history. Growth rates have become multiples of premodern rates, and explosive growth has affected most of the world, if only briefly in some countries. So dramatic is the emergence of the modern growth era that economics has developed a specialized subdiscipline—development economics—to deal with this epiphenomenon. Development-economic growth models, which allow manipulation of the "engines of growth" to manage growth, range from intuitive aphorisms to excruciatingly arcane computer simulations, each based on its own unique set of assumptions and parameters.

Even the most sophisticated concepts of economic development retain the traditional sense that growth is reflected in an increase in national output —aggregate and *per capita*—as a dependent variable in some effort to generate or manage growth by manipulating something else. Yet, beyond prescriptions for liberal "fundamentals" of macro- and microeconomics, economics has little more to say about growth than "it depends," and virtually no comments at all about international conflict, or many of the other effects of growth.

The Relationship

Until the late twentieth century, orthodoxy did not find especially interesting any apparent relationship between growth and conflict—or even between economics and politics—and had not gone much beyond observation and speculation. Any growth-conflict relationship that may have existed was apparently positive, and possibly causal, although the direction and strength of causality were not clear.[14] Economists and political scientists tended simply to dismiss any such connections into the realm of the exogenous, as they explored other issues that seemed more relevant, interesting, or fashionable.

Orthodox realist political science seems to be predicting that international conflict will continue much as humanity has experienced it for at least half a millennium, although cooperation may increase somewhat. In some contrast to the past, however, economics suggests that the growth explosion is just beginning, that humanity has entered a new age of rapid economic growth, and that—whatever the political dimensions—the international political-economy is profoundly different from what it was. More pragmatic pundits of "policy science" offer a less sanguine view of increasing—if lower intensity—conflict, and economic stagnation in most of the world, despite rapid growth in a few dozen countries. For perhaps the first time in history, understanding the dynamics of a political-economic growth-conflict nexus may justifiably assume a priority on a level with those of identifying viable growth strategies and determining the fundamental causes of international conflicts.

The imponderables of the growth-conflict relationship go well beyond the vagaries of growth rates, elections or referenda, international incidents, battle casualties, and even commerce. They entail numbers and kinds of states involved, diverse ideas held in different societies about preferable outcomes and ways of achieving them, and the nature of the international system itself. The very richness of the relationship imposes a further layer of complexity involving myriad exogenous issues of power and influence, commerce and industry, understandings and beliefs about appropriate behaviors, expectations about reciprocities and responsibilities, and various notions of obligation or privilege.   These sorts of issues have linkages to and among political, economic, commercial, and security issues, and extend into the future and the past through memories, expectations, and aspirations.

In the spirit of a hyphenated, cross-disciplinary political-economy, this investigation tries to converge two historically diverse intellectual traditions: conflict analysis and economic development theory. The former centers on efforts by political scientists to identify the origins of international conflict— including, but not limited to, war. The latter focuses on economic growth. A putative relationship between international conflict and economic growth—its existence, nature, direction, and strength; how it affects and is affected by international relations—is the object of this inquiry.

The broad purpose is to move toward a political-economic theory of the dynamics between economic growth and international conflict. Such a theory would account for absence or presence of war, and of significant nonmilitary conflict, in conditions of sustained rapid economic growth— positive or negative (recession, depression)—and possibly in absence of growth —stagnation (see Appendix A). Of primary interest are not the "ultimate causes" of peace and war, or the "original engine" of growth. Rather, the study examines the possibility of promoting and sustaining growth without provoking conflict: of enjoying *both* peace *and* prosperity.

NOTES

1. Robert Gilpin, *The Political Economy of International Relations* (Princeton, New Jersey: Princeton University Press, 1987), 3-4.

2. Adam Smith used the term "political œconomy" to designate the

> branch of the science of a statesman or legislator, [which] proposes two
> distinct objects: first, to provide a plentiful revenue or subsistence for the
> people, or more properly to enable them to provide such a revenue or
> subsistence for themselves; and secondly to supply the state or
> commonwealth with a revenue sufficient for the public services. It proposes
> to enrich both the people and the sovereign. Adam Smith, *An Inquiry into
> the Nature and Causes of the Wealth of Nations* (New York: Modern Library,
> [1776] 1937), p. 397.

Modern use of the term "political economy" implies some integration of the
traditional disciplines of economics and political science, especially in dealing with
issues that are not purely economic or political. The hyphenated term "political-
economy," as used here, implies an even deeper and broader synthesis of the two
disciplines that stresses the interdependence and cross-disciplinary influences of political
and economic processes, structures, and phenomena.

3. Bruce F. Porter, *War and the Rise of the State* (New York: The Free Press, 1994), 3.

4. *The Bhagavad Gita* (New York: Penguin Books, 1962), 43-47.

5. L. N. Rangarajan, *The Limitation of Conflict* (New York: St. Martin's Press,
1985), 212, 227.

6. Porter's concern is with the effects of war on development of states after their
initial establishment. In casting war as an independent variable in a causal relationship,
with various aspects of state development as dependent variables, he examines the
effects of war on the origins, evolutions, and power of states. For Porter's purpose,
economic growth is simply one of many indicators of state development and not a
primary analytical concern. His interesting analysis of industrialization and war
provides useful insight into the relationship between preceding war and subsequent
industrial-economic growth. *War and the Rise of the State*, esp. ch. 5, 149-196.

7. Kenneth N. Waltz, *Man, the State and War: A Theoretical Analysis* (New York:
Columbia University Press, 1954).

8. Michael Nicholson, *Conflict Analysis* (London: Oxford University Press, 1970), 2.

9. Among the most common nonviolent diplomatic techniques are expulsion or
recall of diplomats, denial of formal recognition, rupture of diplomatic relations, and
suspension of treaties. Common economic techniques of conflict include boycott,
embargo, trade-investment controls, commercial subsidies and protection, and nontariff
barriers or discriminatory incentives. "Force short of war" includes blockade, reprisal,
retorsion, extraterritoriality, piracy and terrorism, as well as military demonstrations.

10. Anatol Rapoport, *Fights, Games, and Debates* (Ann Arbor: The University of
Michigan Press, 1960), esp. ch. V, 166-179.

11. Lloyd G. Reynolds, *Economic Growth in the Third World, 1950-1980* (New
Haven, Connecticut: Yale University Press, 1985).

12. Hollis B. Chenery, Sherman Robinson & Moshe Syrquin, *Industrialization and
Growth* (New York: Oxford University Press for the World Bank, 1986), 13.

13. Over historic time, the two most important structural changes have been the
rising share of industry in national product, and an increasing proportion of the
population living in cities. In addition, the nation's age structure changes dramatically,
and consumption patterns change as consumption shifts to consumer durables, and
leisure products and services.

14. Few orthodox thinkers would quibble with a causality from growth to conflict. But for a dissenting view see A. F. Mullins' "Feedback" hypothesis (See Chapter 3, "Feedback" section, esp. Figure 3.7).   In addition, a perverse extension of A.F.K. Organski and Jacek Kugler's "Power Transition Theory" (see Chapter 3, section on "The Power Transition Model") could envision the massive defense-industrial bases necessary for modern war as "sufficient" conditions for economic growth.

2

Historical Perspectives

Through most of human history, any growth-conflict nexus that may have existed was neither interesting nor even noticed, as both analysts and politicians have found it convenient to separate these persistent features of social intercourse along two separate paths of human progress—economic and political. International relations have involved the specialized interactions of governments dealing in the "high politics" of diplomacy and war, power and sovereignty. Whatever else that humans did to, with, or for each other was done by other groups (churches, companies, parties, families, *etc.*). In the real world of real people, however, economics and commerce, often relegated to low-status groups (Jews, Moslems, gypsies, foreigners, slaves), happened outside "high politics." Occasional academic forays into the "low politics" of other human concerns (economics, business, religion, philosophy, biology, physics, *etc.*) were left to the human and physical sciences. Liberal, realist, and idealist traditions of political and economic thought all adopted this perspective, albeit with different views and conclusions, and have been disposed to neglect any excursions across disciplinary boundaries.

Although conflict is as ancient as humanity, and every civilization has experienced some sort of economic growth—usually oppressively slow and best measured in 100-year growth rates—any sort of rapid sustained growth occurred only sporadically before about the seventeenth century. Speculations about connections were in the domains of philosophers, rather than the realms of kings, and indicated a positive relationship, not very strong, not very predictable, and not very important. For premodern humanity, conflict was simply an unpleasant, but inevitable, aspect of living; economic growth was usually little more than a hope that one's grandchildren would not starve.

The appearance of rapid economic growth on the wings of science and knowledge in seventeenth- and eighteenth-century Europe, and Napoleon's invention of "total war," blurred distinctions between what governments do and what happens to their societies, between economics and politics, between diplomacy and commerce, between peace and war. Historians recalled that major economic and political events had often occurred together, or at least in succession.   Political scientists and economists—as well as politicians and businessmen—began to find ever more realities that did not conform to unidisciplinary political or economic constructs.

As theories of international relations, political science, and economics abandoned premodern metaphysical and moral models, empirical measurement continued to suggest, and occasionally emphasized, some relationship between growth and conflict. Even in the Age of Enlightenment, however, scholars found little interest in a positive, direct relationship, which was simply another "given" feature of life.   Characteristically they accepted Socrates' judgment as definitive (see note 4). For post-Renaissance man in a world that involved both rare economic growth and routine international conflict, the growth-conflict relationship, still not particularly interesting or even important, was easily and naturally explained by intuition, inherited wisdom, and fashionable prototheories.

As reporting gained statistical sophistication, such things as trade, national output, battle casualties, and military budgets gained prominence as convenient data, and it became possible to quantify both growth and conflict. While empty lands and backward peoples remained, and growth was not too high or too low, both realism and liberalism, as well as most radical ideas, could confirm the power of their theories with apposite supporting data. Even polished empirical findings linking growth and conflict, however, have not been well explained by any single theoretical concept, yet each explains some evidence. Nor is any single theory or approach supported by all the figures, yet each set of data supports some particular theory quite well. The actual occurrence of sustained rapid economic growth—Industrial Revolution in Europe, military expansion throughout the world, and the analytical techniques of modern social science—made this jejune equivocal ambiguity at best annoying to analysts and irrelevant to policy-makers.

ANCIENT PERSPECTIVES

For as long as people have cooperated to satisfy their needs, they have disagreed over who gets how much of what. Quarrels over distribution of resources have always been features of politics: interpersonal, familial, national, international. Relying on memories and experiences of earlier civilizations, ancient philosophers simply noted and accepted that competition for scarce resources brought humans into conflict with each other. As they tried to accumulate stores, to improve their living conditions, or simply to consume more, ancient peoples learned to cooperate in war for mutual economic gain, defensively by protecting what they had already accumulated for themselves and aggressively by taking what others possessed. In ancient subsistence economies, resource-based conflict was a normal, expected part of social life, and the "inevitable" result of economic growth.

In about 2700 BC, Gilgamesh, king of Uruk took a military expedition to obtain cedar wood to sustain Uruk's economic growth.[1] Although obscured by the haze of time, it is clear that a linkage between growth and conflict existed nearly five millennia ago. By the time of Naram Sin (2260–2223 BC), Uruk had been expanded by his grandfather, Sargon of Agade, the world's first emperor. His inherited Sumerian empire, which had been generating wealth and refining the practice of war for some five centuries, became the most important political-economic fact in the developing civilization of Mesopotamia. "Its wealth was a magnet to jealous predators living beyond the magic circle, among whom, nevertheless, some elements of its civilization took root, as a result partly of war, partly of trade."[2]

By about 2000 BC the Sumerian Empire was surrounded by a coterie of less wealthy protosocieties experiencing their own growth. These peoples were refining ancient pastoralism into a horse-breeding military mobility to carry the waves of conquerors—Gutians, Hurrians, Kassites—that drowned the wealthy, stable, and sedentary civilizations of Sumeria over the next thousand years.[3]

The first millennium BC shifted the focus of protocivilization to the subsistence-economy city-states of Greece, where resource-based conflict was a normal feature of life, an "inevitable" result of growth.[4] The ancient Athenians of classical Greece may have been the first to try to invert this hapless relationship between conflict and growth. In the two centuries after about 700 BC, Athens had evolved along a path of political progress and economic growth that brought the city to place critical importance on maritime commerce, and created strategic dependence on its naval fleet.

> While Sparta had maximized the military advantages supplied by its exclusive social order to make itself pre-eminent in the Peloponnese, Athens, impelled in part by the difficulty it found in feeding its population off its poor soils, had turned itself into a trading, and increasingly a political, empire with allied or dependent cities as far away as Asia Minor.[5]

This system brought growth, as well as security. With as many as 150 allied or dependent cities as far away as Asia Minor bound together by its superb battle fleet,[6] Athens pursued a dual policy of "armed trading" on dictated terms and active political-military intervention. It was primarily for profit, but also for the benefits of local hegemony, that Athens became the world's dominant naval power, and led the Delian League to victory over Persia in 448 BC.[7]

After the costly debacle of the First Peloponnesian War, Pericles led the city in what finally (the Sicily campaign of 415 BC) became a strategy of desperation for a city that had enjoyed unprecedented growth for three centuries. Athens concentrated its vast wealth and sophisticated naval and military resources on continuing commercial-political expansion, successfully challenging the other large commercial cities. Completely dependent on foreign trade by about 430 BC, Athens was forced into

> effectively abandoning its rural population and surviving on maritime imports, particularly those brought down the route from the grain centers around the Black Sea. When Sparta in 424 BC sent an army to capture the Thracian ports by which this route was maintained, Athens was driven to seek a truce.[8]

Classical historical thought has suggested that Roman imperial growth, in striking contrast to Athenian cupidity, did not include economic motives. While Rome never needed foreign goods or food to survive, as had Athens, Roman wealth grew through conquest. At least initially, Romans enthusiastically acquired land and the resources on or under it: Roman citizens quickly settled agricultural colonies in conquered lands, and most prospered. Despite weak arguments about looting, slaving, mining, and simple theft, "it was scarcely possible for a Roman to disassociate the expectation of gain from the expectation of successful war and conquest. . . . Economic gain was . . . an integral part of successful warfare and of the expansion of power."[9]

The growth-conflict relationship seems not to have been limited to civilizations of the "fertile crescent" and Mediterranean basin. The enigmatic Anasazi of the Colorado Plateau in North America showed no indication of organized warfare during the Archaic period (5500–100 BC) of low growth as a poor hunter-gatherer culture. The arrival of maize from Mesoamerica (1000 BC) brought the possibilities of agriculture and growth. As some Anasazi adopted a sedentary lifestyle, careful selection of maize cultivars and diligent irrigation produced dramatic increases in yields.   Introduction of new technologies (bow and arrow) from the south not only increased population but in good years even generated surpluses. Apparently to protect surpluses from less successful nomads, some Anasazi migrated southward to large settlements that gradually assumed political-economic roles like those of Greek city-states. Some evidence suggests that by the Pueblo II period (AD 700–900), sustained growth and cyclic maize surpluses "also led to increased conflict and warfare: hunter-gatherers rarely stored surpluses beyond their short-term needs, but hoards of maize made attractive targets for looters and pilferers."[10]

Even the Mayan civilization, "one of the least warlike nations who ever existed,"[11] could not avoid a growth-conflict nexus and wars over resources. Archaeologist David Webster has shown that warfare and organized "international" conflict were features of the development of the Maya lowlands.[12] Jeremy Sabloff's sophisticated work reinforces Webster's view:

> warfare was a result of population pressure, which led to competition for [economic and natural] resources in the lowlands as early as the Late Preclassic period (about 300 BC). . . . Competition for resources and labor, and perhaps for markets for goods, probably incited conflict throughout ancient Maya history."[13]

"By the Late Classic [AD 600–800] such conflict may have been rampant."[14]   Apparently unable to manage the combination of sustained growth, continuing population increases, and "problems created by the mushrooming urban, agricultural, and military demands,"[15] in the Post-Classic (AD 1250–1450), Mayan civilization shrunk to a few cities in northern Yucatán with massive walls "to protect [them] from attack during the many conflicts between the cities of the confederacy that characterized the period."[16]

Reflecting other ancient societies, the truncated histories of the Maya and the Anasazi suggest that growth, initially as agricultural development, transformed far more than a society's diet. Emergence of agricultural surpluses seemed to favor a society that included artists and warriors, rulers and artisans, whose primary pursuits had little to do with the struggle for survival. While economic growth generated surpluses that led to flowering of material culture, it also imposed significant social costs through stratification, urbanization, intermittent or regional famine, and warfare. Ancient societies of both the old world and the new seemed unable to cope with these changes.

As massive barbarian migrations in the Dark Ages emptied lands beyond the Rhine into the contracting Roman Empire, the Scandinavian threat was diverted eastward.   By the late eighth century, land hunger, population growth, and envy of wealthier southerners shifted the interests of pagan northerners again toward Europe for colonization, loot, and profitable "trade on dictated terms."[17]   By the tenth century, Vikings (from Norse *Viking*, piracy) had adopted a way of life reminiscent of the Athenian approach to growth and conflict: "armed trading." Unlike the Athenians, the Vikings did not intervene politically in societies with which they "traded," but they did enjoy the prosperity of growing economies. In wide-ranging expansion across the Baltic and down Russian rivers, they came into violent conflict, as well as profitable commerce, with Islam and Byzantium.   In the west armed Viking "traders" stormed into Central Europe, where in AD 911 they forced Charles the Simple of France to cede several provinces to the Viking leader Rolf, who became a duke of France. From Rouen, the Vikings continued their economic-military expansion into England, southern France, Italy, and Germany.[18]

Deterioration of the vestiges of Roman and Carolingian feudal empires left rich kingdoms, fiefs, and individuals prey to aggression and robbery. Conflict seemed to Augustine—or Mohammed, Tamerlane, Genghis Khan— as to the ancients, the normal fate of mankind, not related to anything else that anyone might do.   Even in Platonic idealizations of "perfect community," considerations of whether enough economic growth to end scarcity would also reduce intersocietal conflict simply did not arise.   Nor did notions that insufficient growth or economic stagnation—the normal condition—might create scarcity and throw societies into conflict occur to thinkers more concerned with survival or justice. Any growth-conflict linkage seemed even less relevant to medieval European societies bent on physical survival of their "brutish" existence in a grim earthly life, salvation for a better in heaven, and escape from a worse in hell.

Only with the Ming Dynasty in Asia, the European Renaissance, and the age of global exploration did humanity begin to experience notable improvement of its lot through economic growth. Even after Europe's Enlightenment and Asia's reluctant collisions with European traders, absence of growth and persistent conflict allayed concerns about any growth-conflict nexus. As humanity approached modernity, growth seemed (as Socrates had observed) to bring unpredictable competition for resources that often led to intersocietal and international conflict, not a particularly interesting, or surprising, observation. People seemed simply to accept the association of growth with conflict as immutable.

PREMODERN LINKAGES—COMMERCE AND CONQUEST

While the Romans were struggling to contain their huge empire in Europe, and Americans were learning about the growth-conflict nexus, China had begun to expand westward as early as the fourth century. By the tenth century, however, when Europe was in the depths of the Dark Ages, and ancient American civilizations had collapsed, the S'ung Dynasty had deliberately refocused China's interests inward at a regional level. Only with the Ming Dynasty did China again in the fifteenth century revive its ancient interests in extension beyond the "Middle Kingdom."

In Europe and the Levant, a religious version of Athenian and Viking "armed trading," the European Crusades, marking with their violence and fervor the end of feudalism, associated growth with conflict, perhaps causally. With the decline of unprofitable feudalism, European industry and commerce spread quickly beyond the municipal limits of feudalism to local protonational economies that generated surpluses for both agriculture and urban business. As trade followed the armed cross, profit became wealth to pay for the wars of the Middle Ages.[19]

Crusading Europeans reestablished Middle-Eastern trading links, while Chinese merchants penetrated Indian, African, and occasionally European markets. Burgeoning trade in Europe and sinification of the Mongols in China—both in the wake of battle—brought growth that the world had not known for centuries. In parallel with market extensions and armed trading, territorial expansion by conquest was a principal engine of growth and consolidation of power, especially in premodern Europe.[20]

Although China had developed a substantial, peaceful, trade with India, Arabia, Persia, and Africa by the ninth century, the first post-medieval European essay at expansion beyond Europe only began in the last years of the fifteenth century, just as China was also rediscovering the world beyond its own borders. In the historic Greek, Roman, and Norse traditions, Europeans again combined commerce with conquest in and beyond Africa in a modern version of "armed trading" as Portugal attempted, until an embarrassing defeat at Jiddah (1511), to develop a sixteenth-century spice monopoly.[21]

After Jiddah, European seafarers established military bases in the East Indies, India, and China. From these issued demands, "first, for trading rights, then for land on which to build trading posts, finally for exclusive trading-rights enforced by military control."[22] By the century's end, cannon-armed, soldier-manned forts, and ports filled with European battle cruisers, along the coasts of Africa, Asia, and the Americas, had become military nuclei of commercial empires to generate growth in the next era of human history.

In contrast to earlier Chinese expansion, European merchant-traders seeking profit were invariably accompanied by armies and navies seeking conquest and plunder. From their own erstwhile impoverished nations Europeans arrived seeking wealth and resources in comparatively rich Asian and African lands at the height of local prosperity. Europeans were soon fighting not only backward, overseas societies, but each other, for valuable resources and rich markets, both at home and throughout the world.[23] As Dutch and Portuguese fleets yielded to British naval and maritime ascendancy in the eighteenth century, naval and military power seemed necessary adjuncts of commercial expansion, and prerequisites for economic growth.

In contrast to squalid medieval Europe, the Ming China that sent Zheng He to Africa in the fifteenth century was the center of the world with gold, wealth, people, and resources in more than plenty.[24] Rather than the European vision of foreign lands with unimaginable riches filled with benighted souls awaiting salvation, the Chinese wanted only a few rare spices and animals in tribute. As Philip Snow remarked, "Zheng He and his captains surveyed Africa from far too lofty a standpoint to think of disrupting the flow of African life."[25] For Ming China, nothing in Africa, South Asia, or Europe was worth war. China had no need for either growth or conflict; it had already grown and fought under Sung and T'ang Dynasties. Europe at the time was just beginning its era of growth and conflict, and anything that Europeans could find was a legitimate object of conquest, plunder, and appropriation.

Eventually populations, and governments, began to notice that some were doing better than others, that wealth was being shifted, concentrated, accumulated. The phenomena of growth and recession gradually condensed into competition between national states. Individuals and groups hurt by economic stagnation sought relief from embryonic national governments. Progressive Europeans sought to shift the social costs of growth onto other countries,[26] and to protect populations and wealth from the pernicious effects of growth. The predictable results were foreign retaliatory discord and eventually costly conflict. Somehow, despite increases in national wealth, growth and expansion—or perhaps "negative growth" and stagnation—were still bringing nations into conflict with each other.

German Peasant Revolution

Weakness of central government in Germany shunted postfeudal growth onto a different track, with a different sort of growth-conflict relationship. In his study of the German Peasant Revolution, Friedrich Engels noted a temporal linkage between *uneven* economic growth and conflict.[27] In the fourteenth and fifteenth centuries German industry experienced unprecedented expansion, as primitive, feudal rural industry was superseded by urban guild production. Textile weaving had become a well-established industry, as well as the artistic crafts (gold- and silver-smithing, sculpture and carving, etching and engraving, *etc.*). Local commerce had kept pace with industry, as the cities of upper Germany—Nürnberg and Augsburg—became centers of opulence and wealth. Aggregate growth of the several local German economies fell behind those of other countries experiencing integration around strong central governments. German agricultural production lagged behind that of England and of Holland; local industries were not able to compete with Italy, England, or Flanders; Dutch merchants dominated commerce by the early sixteenth century. No German Edward III appeared to galvanize a German economy for growth. As the feudal empire slowly collapsed, German vassals became independent princes while cities and knights formed petty coalitions and alliances against each other.

In the rest of Europe monarchies began to coalesce around concentrations of wealth and power in nascent urban capitals—Paris, Madrid, Lisbon, London, Stockholm. Outside Germany, emerging nationalism absorbed the violent energy exposed in the German Peasant Revolution. Uneven increases of wealth in the midst of decreasing imperial authority brought conflict among the many protostates and principalities, which eventually erupted in the Thirty Years War. Like later analysts, Engels simply noted the relationship, accepted it as a "given" of capitalism, not really interesting, and followed other paths of research and thought.[28]

The Protestant Reformation

A century after Engels, sociologist Mancur Olson noted the same relationship in a supranational mass movement. The Protestant Reformation, involving substantial conflict, clearly followed some two centuries of growth. By about the fifteenth century, the church had developed into a vast, economic empire, the largest landowner in Europe. Rising monarchies were accumulating wealth, discovering the insatiable financial needs of government and war, and experimenting with Edwardian theories about trade and industry as the fundamental sources of wealth. A new, wealthy middle class of merchants and producers brought a powerful pattern of capitalist economics into profound conflict with both historic Roman Catholic dogma and traditional religious economic privilege.[29] Ruthless capitalist merchants and producers demanded "profits," not merely wages for socially useful work.

Introduction of commercial banking outside Jewry and Islam in the fifteenth century, as Christian kings and merchants accumulated and required wealth, exacerbated the gap between the past and progress.

The resulting explosion of growth occurred over some two centuries in parallel with the implosion of decaying feudal political-religious structures. While scholars may debate details and historians quibble over timing,

> there can be little doubt that the pace of economic change quickened well before the Protestant Reformation became a major mass movement. . . . Nor can there be any doubt that the Reformation was a profoundly destabilizing movement . . . before and during the popular religious controversies [of the fifteenth, sixteenth, and seventeenth centuries] there had been a great deal of rapid growth.[30]

The combined effects formed a direct link between late Renaissance growth and two centuries of war culminating in the Thirty Years War in Europe and English Civil War. Writing in response to modern assertions that "economic development is one of the keys to stability and peace in the world,"[31] Olson argues from a sociohistorical perspective that "rapid economic growth is a profoundly destabilizing force."[32]

In the premodern glow of industrial promise,[33] the lesson of European history was clear, at least for historians, traders, and monarchs, that just as Socrates had observed, growth and war were somehow related. Conflict seemed a tedious part of the process of generating wealth; but when nations went to war, growth quickly slowed or stopped. Such truths seemed almost self-evident, and not at all interesting for pundits examining the new phenomenon of rapid growth or the ancient scourge of war.

TRADE-RELATED CONFLICT

Trade was probably the earliest continuing direct contact between nations, and far more relevant to the lives of ancient and Renaissance common people than either diplomacy or war, which generally interrupted trade. At least since Henry VII, nations and their governments have felt some connection, either positive ("mercantilism" and "economic nationalism") or negative (liberal "free traders," interdependence theorists), between trade, economic growth, and conflict.

English Protectionism

Among slowly coalescing postfeudal national autarkic economies, several states learned to benefit through specialized production and concentrated industry; these were to become liberal capitalist economies. Others relied on traditional methods of territorial conquest and local accumulation of resources; most of these developed later through mercantilism along an authoritarian path. Under either approach, growth emerged from expansion through commerce or conquest.

In protocapitalist England commerce grew faster than agriculture. By the fourteenth century, industry was exploiting all of England's known coalfields, and most of its industrial minerals. In massive restructuring, the woolen industry shifted ever more land from agriculture to sheep grazing. After the innovative Import-Substitution-Industrialization strategy of Edward III, who imported weaving technology and labor from Flanders in 1331, the Crown established severe protectionist trade controls. By about the end of the fifteenth century, England's textile industry had aroused a commercial revolution, and become the primary source of England's wealth and sustained economic growth.

Aggressive commerce and voracious mills generated trade disputes with foreign suppliers and buyers. As Portuguese, Spanish, and Dutch traders tried to monopolize the riches of Asia, Africa, and America, resourceful British merchants, under royal license and support, sailing in British-built ships, pushed British exports (metals and textiles) into growing economies of the North Sea, the coastal Atlantic, and the Mediterranean. Italian (especially Genoese) and Hanseatic merchants resented loss of market share in their traditional regional and local markets. The ensuing international conflict, embodied in embargoes, piracy, and a few naval battles, led Henry VII to bring English commerce under royal naval and diplomatic protection. His network of commercial agreements operated as a primitive international security regime for managing conflict, and allowed English "merchant adventurers" to generate sustained national growth by dominating the North Sea and much of the northeastern Atlantic.[34]

Edward's technology transfer and industrial protection in the fourteenth century, and Henry's threat of trade (if not military) war and use of English power to impose trade agreements on continental markets in the fifteenth, set a powerful precedent for export-based growth. Both monarchs acted to sustain growth in a stagnating economy; each transferred some of the costs of English growth to other economies through controlled trade. Henry's imposed trade agreements increased English market share through decreases in competitors' shares. Edward's industrial concentration and commercial expansion became engines of growth, with trade as a vehicle, and protectionism, the fuel. A powerful central government could transform growth into concentrated national power and intimidate competitors through the threat, and sporadic actuality, of war to obtain the resources and markets to sustain national growth through commercial and industrial expansion.

The English "zero-sum" strategy of trade-based growth at the expense of foreign economies reflected the increasing influence of commercial-industrial capitalism and relative decline of traditional medieval thought (see note 29). As later British mercantilist and imperial governments adopted it as overt foreign policy, international conflict became a necessary, but perhaps not causal, concomitant of growth. Based on a powerful direct relationship between growth and conflict, this growth strategy was magnificently effective.

Virtually every developing nation over the next five centuries has adopted variants of these approaches as fundamental elements of some trade-based development strategy.[35]

Mercantilism

Based on Machiavellian politics and accumulation of resources, mercantilism was the first coherent concept that related politics and the state systematically to economics and wealth. To increase the wealth of their domestic communities, which was stored in states' treasuries, from the sixteenth through the nineteenth centuries, states actively accumulated gold and silver bullion, colonized new lands, promoted exports, and limited imports to generate trade surpluses.

Mercantilism was a major force behind the development of European empires as sources of precious metals, labor, and raw materials. Colonies also became captive markets for the metropole's goods and products. Home governments subsidized export industries and provided infrastructure to complement their colonial empires, emphasizing export goods that were cheap to ship and commanded high prices in foreign markets. In the resulting zero-sum mercantilist economy, commercial profits for a competing state—perceived as losses at home—led to fierce interstate competition for markets. The importance of international commerce in generating wealth made naval forces as important as military forces in providing national security. Legitimate grounds for war expanded from disputes over territory, populations, and religion to questions of market shares and commercial privileges. The historical result of mercantilism was to concentrate physical wealth in a few European nation-states, and create a network of global economic interdependence whose vestiges remain today.

Mercantilism evolved in two related but separate forms: Colbertian varieties supporting absolutist courts; and entrepreneurial forms oriented toward the private sector. The former appealed to continental European states—France, Prussia, Russia, Austria, Spain, Portugal—sustaining economic bases for powerful, but declining, monarchies unresponsive to commercial or industrial pressures. The latter developed in Scandinavia, Holland, England, and America under liberal political structures that showed concern for the "public weal" and national wealth, and sought private profit as allowed by the market and protocapitalist morality.

For both English and continental versions of mercantilism, trade was a powerful strategic element of national competitive advantage, rather than simply profit-seeking interactions between firms. Universal mercantilist orthodoxy asserted that national trade policies should create opportunities for production and exports, and discourage imports. Modern versions emphasize a country's aggregate balance of trade, exchange rate, or annual rate of economic growth, as indicators of the current state of confrontation in the economic war with the rest of the world.[36]

In denouncing mercantilism generally, Adam Smith introduced Colbertism as a devious ploy "imposed upon [Jean-Baptiste Colbert] by the sophistry of merchants and manufacturers".[37]   In contrast to Smith's shallow misrepresentation, Colbert sincerely felt that state regulation of commerce was necessary to "ensure that such activities redounded to the greater wealth, and hence power and glory, of France."[38]

The socialist spirit of Colbertism is embodied in his conservative approach to manufactures as France faced the Industrial Revolution. Colbert used various techniques to stimulate and revive France's traditional manufacturing and trading base: subsidies, tax exemptions or reductions, protective tariffs, population growth to keep wages low, privileges for critical firms and industries, and state-owned factories (*manufactures royales*) to produce import-substitutes.   The necessary regulation and control for managing such a Procrustean task required an elaborate Code of Commerce, detailed technical specifications and standards, state inspections of production facilities and products, and rigid organizational structures for labor.

Colbertian mercantilism provided massive state financing for the great monopolistic French trading companies—as well as traditional industries and firms—which suffered from lack of commercial interest, enthusiasm, or investment. Colbertism was not at all democratic or parliamentary, and involved explicit state control of both production and trade, wholly absent from English versions of protocapitalist mercantilism.[39]   Anachronous and conservative even in the seventeenth century, Colbertism affected the economic development of modern France in three profound ways.   It was

> a continuation and codification, a new ordering of old practices; it was part of an *étatisme* with medieval roots.   Second, at the time that Colbert was imposing these measures on the French economy, their English counterparts were withering away; the last legislative attempt at general regulation of the English cloth industry failed in 1678.   Third, Colbert's regulative achievements were continued after his death: Colbertism brought many more detailed regulations in the seventy years after 1683.[40]

The Colbertian legacy was unprecedented French growth based on state trading monopolies in a ponderous global commercial empire closely controlled from Paris, but relatively unresponsive to markets or technology. Ultimately it could not compete with more flexible, decentralized English, Dutch, and American trading networks oriented toward free trade, and increasingly brought the diverging systems into political and military conflict. France's economic growth of the eighteenth and nineteenth centuries, "though owing something to Colbert's initiating stimuli, continued despite, rather than because of, the perpetuation of Colbertism."[41]

In contrast to the continental conservative drift toward socialism, English mercantilists since Edward III have eschewed heavy state involvement, relied heavily on market capitalization, promoted new ways of doing business, and ensured state protection for trade through a democratic parliament. Like the Dutch and later the Americans, this sort of democratic mercantilism encouraged innovative, new industries that were expected eventually to export and penetrate new markets.

Thus, England negotiated a relatively brief, albeit traumatic, transition to capitalism under Victoria, while France remained an economic anachronism until well into the Fifth Republic. In addition to the international conflicts inherent in mercantilism of any sort, these fundamentally different styles of mercantilist economic growth kept the two systems in continuing conflict over several centuries.

Economic Nationalism

Under utilitarian and liberal influences, mercantilism mellowed into a patriotic sort of politics linking national interest to state promotion of industry and protection of trading advantage. In a refinement of Edward III's technology transfer and Colbert's industrial patronage, Alexander Hamilton's economic nationalism stressed trading within and between capitalist economies to improve national competitive advantage and generate growth. Less severe than Tudor militancy, his concepts for using tariffs to protect "infant industries" and manipulate national trade reflected the shift in economic thought from mercantilism toward industrial capitalism. Hamilton argued strongly for state protection of American trade from "unfair" foreign competition, and for government promotion of domestic industries.

The success of Hamilton's ideas in the adolescent United States led to German adoption of economic nationalism as explicit policy, even as both Americans and Britons were shifting toward Liberal capitalism. Otto von Bismarck's addition of *Realpolitik* brought conflict throughout Europe as German industrial growth captured market share, and "set every continental power on the search for security and self-sufficiency."[42] After Bismarck, imperial Germany extended economic nationalism into foreign and trade policy, creating political rivalries that spread beyond Europe in intense imperialistic conflict. The spread of economic nationalism after the Depression of the 1870s had the paradoxical effect of deepening international economic interdependence through political-military power [the major powers forced Japan, Korea, Siam, and China to accept trade with the West], while erecting protectionist tariff barriers to economic relationships.

A neo-Hamiltonian school arose briefly in the United States before World War I, which "combined Bismarckian *realpolitik* in foreign policy with support for progressive reforms [and growth] at home." Theodore Roosevelt was the *beau idéal* of neo-Hamiltonianism, uniting "progressive nationalism in domestic policy with an assertive realism, based on military power, in foreign affairs."[43] Roosevelt's "jingoism" was adopted after the war by a wing of the Democratic Party, which embraced only the progressive nationalism of Hamiltonianism.

After World War II, the architects of the Asian economic miracle took inspiration from both American Hamiltonians and some of their European disciples (Friedrich List, William Roscher, Gustav Schmoller, *etc*.[44]), albeit perhaps overstressing Hamilton's approach to trade and industry.   Like Wilhelmine German policies, the eminently successful Japanese combination of protectionism, subsidies, and industrial targeting was, by the late 1970s, generating conflicts over trade with most of the world. Emulation of Japan in export-oriented growth strategies has spread the phenomenon throughout the modern world.

The enduring appeal of economic nationalism is clear in historic European and Asian concerns about protectionism, the modern American obsession with a "level playing field," and the prevalence of strategic trade diplomacy. The popular contemporary notion of competitiveness—of nation-states competing as if they were huge collective commercial enterprises in a global marketplace—"greases the rails for those who want confrontational, if not frankly protectionist, policies."[45]   The inevitable result seems again to be Socrates' growth-based conflict.

Commercial Liberalism

As market power surpassed that of the church in the seventeenth and eighteenth centuries, mercantilism lost credibility as a national philosophy and policy to a liberalism that included not only individualism and political rights, but capitalism and economic freedom. Peace and prosperity after Waterloo, the chaotic economic situation following the demise of mercantilism, and the rise of European economic empires of controlled trade seemed to indicate the path toward human progress that mercantilism had lost. A short way along this path lay "a strong and systematic relationship between commerce and war,"[46] which is powerfully negative or inverse, and operated by or through trade.

Farther along this path was the rise of "big business," recognition of private enterprise as the engine of economic growth, and discovery of the "global marketplace." The paradoxical precondition seemed to be high tariffs— but not the state dominance—inherited from mercantilism.   Especially in North America and imperial Britain, commercial liberalism tempered *laissez-faire* policies with state intervention through tariff protection, great public works, regulation of infrastructure and utilities, and trade-based foreign policy.

Neomercantilism

Conjunction of political liberalism, deteriorating colonial empires, the Industrial Revolution, and American efforts to liberalize the global economy brought heavy popular pressure to generate and sustain growth. Governments were drawn to fundamentally mercantilist premises linking wealth and power—as refined by Hamilton and List. As states increasingly defined their national interests in terms of industries and trade, governments justified both domestic and foreign policies to promote particular aspects of national growth, often at the expense of other nations. While not overtly protectionist in any Tudor sense, or even "illiberal," many sophisticated trade regulations, monetary policies, and investment codes have brought clear mercantilist or economic nationalist effects. This Machiavellian claim of liberalism, while practicing economic nationalism, has come to be known as neomercantilism.

Neomercantilism accepts the realist position that the international system is in the Hobbesian anarchic state of nature. In addition, however, to the realist political struggle, each state is necessarily involved in an economic struggle to benefit as much as it can from market forces and commercial transactions. It is the responsibility of the state to provide not only national security but also national welfare. Modern indirect versions of early preliberal direct linkages between wealth and power involve political efforts to create and maintain economic advantages for domestic industries, and to destroy any advantages that competing states may provide for their own firms. Neomercantilism tempts states to intervene actively not only in its domestic economy, but in the international economy, and even foreign economies, to accumulate and protect national wealth and power.

As economists were discovering the intricacies of proactive fiscal policy, and business was exploring capitalism, political science dealt with the implications of sovereignty, democracy, revolution, and the new moralities of imperial and industrial politics. Neither discipline found much interest in asking why or how growth caused or was caused by conflict, nor were politicians or capitalists much bothered about it. The relationship—whatever it was—seemed intuitive, and not very important anyway, since growth was again falling to late feudal levels—but beginning to recover in a few liberal countries—and war was brief and sporadic. At the dawn of the industrial age, the "enlightened" world seemed content with Socrates' saturnine findings.

INDUSTRY, REVOLUTIONS, AND AMBIGUITY

As Europeans began to burst from premodern "enlightenment" into a modern industrial age, the century between about 1750 and 1850 saw a renewal of economic growth and conflict. Europeans were aggressively extending both around the world as they built several versions of political-economic empire. The national state emerged as the central focus for political power, and began slowly to influence economic affairs, as well. The world's modern political-economic, military-commercial empires (Spanish, Portuguese, British, French, Dutch, Belgian, American) coagulated in political, scientific, military, ethical, and philosophical revolutions. While many such revolutionaries debated the ethics and moralities of empire, fashionable attitudes seemed to accept inevitable conflict as the price of imperial growth.[47] The persistent salience of both growth and conflict blurred any clear nexus between them, while reinforcing ancient predictions of some unclear, but positive, linkage. Economics and politics, trade and war, growth and conflict seemed to be connected somehow, despite whatever else was happening.

Far more interesting than this Socratic syllogism were the powerful new forces of technology and industry, and their profound effects on how people really lived. The combination of ancient truth and new technical power formed a potent element of European political-economic dogma that commerce and empire ineluctably dispersed to Asian, Indian, African, American, and Islamic cultures. It figured prominently in fashioning durable international institutions and processes, as well as national attitudes and policies, under Western dominance as European thought expanded from fifteenth-century local feudalism to twentieth-century global capitalism. "The legacy of Western dominance includes the main institutions of the states-system today, such as diplomatic practices and international law, the United Nations, and other global organizations, and international commercial and financial procedures."[48]

The words "Industrial Revolution" conjure images of technology and factories. Most historians have defined the phenomenon from macroeconomics and focused their analyses on domestic patterns of capital formation and production, supply and demand, income distribution, or economic fluctuations.[49] Few have extended their analyses to the international level, and fewer still, beyond economics. Although recent analyses have shifted to quantitative approaches, the absence of good statistical data has left the field primarily to social historians. Orthodoxy suggests that the Industrial Revolution began in England in about 1780, and simply abandons the earlier eighteenth century as an uninteresting appendage of preindustrial history. It has been primarily radical and socialist analyses, drawing on historical economic approaches of the earlier twentieth century, that have dwelt upon the earlier years of the Industrial Revolution. Although their attempts to merge economics and history subsequently fell from fashion as post-1945 growth claimed the world's attention, these earlier analyses had delved deeply into some aspects of preindustrial manufacturing and the early Industrial Revolution.[50]

Industrialization and Innovation

It is probably impossible to identify with any precision the political-economic origins of the host of innovations that accompanied the European Industrial Revolution. Dramatic increases in productivity, which led to higher aggregate output, arose from both technical innovation and organizational change. New techniques, machines, tools, and skills cannot, however, be separated from the structures of the production processes in which they are implemented. Improvement of industrial organization, with or without technological change, could often affect production as much as new technologies. In addition to purely technical advances, various forms of increased efficiency in exploiting labor forces, rationalization of commercial and mercantile networks, and simple increases in the amounts of input all generated their own increases in aggregate productivity and output.

Industrialization seems to have been seen by its implementers in the eighteenth and nineteenth centuries as a single collective innovation that led to one-way progress. For firms it involved a single dramatic effort; for nation-states, however, it could be spread over generations as successive industries and firms shifted separately, and across countries as regions industrialized at their own rates.[51] Even to those who lived through it, a sharp contrast appeared between two models and approaches to production—"one associated with innovation, machinery and the factory, the other with backwardness, hand techniques and the domestic system."[52] Modern factories involved, even early in the eighteenth century, innovative exercises in division of labor, standardized mass production, order and discipline, formal job specification, and deliberate use of as much cheap, unskilled labor (and as few skilled artisans) as possible. Backward firms were those that had, for some reason, not yet adopted these modern innovative approaches. Since, as Maxine Berg emphasizes, both systems lived "side by side" and "intermingled" for some two centuries, it was difficult, except in hindsight, to designate a particular firm or industry as modern or backward, and virtually impossible to relate such a contrast to the greater political-economy in which all existed.

Much more clear over a long period are the profound, traumatic changes in the ways that people lived and worked. Both apocalyptic and evolutionary views of the Industrial Revolution rely on new technologies and dynamic innovation as dual engines of growth and transformation. Innovation occurred not merely in technology, but in the forms of industrial organization—the factory system, "putting-out," artisanship, subcontracting; the structure of the labor force—recruitment and training, mobility; types and applications of technology—manual and mechanized, task-specific and general, techniques and work practices. The most traumatic innovation involved, perhaps, the shift over nearly two centuries toward large, capital-intensive factories replete with mechanization of every possible human task. This innovation brought another that transformed entire societies: the division of labor. Mechanization through new technologies and imaginative combinations of division, specialization, and greater exploitation of labor established completely new ways of working and producing. Increasing reliance on capital and innovative reorganization of networks of marketing, sales, and distribution brought creativity to commerce. Powerful combinations of technology and innovation transformed the premodern sixteenth-century world into the commercial-industrial twentieth-century world.

Industrialization, Trade and the State

The Industrial Revolution, symbolized by James Watt's invention of the separate-condenser steam engine in 1776, was a necessary condition for increase in industrial efficiency and productivity. Growth arose with new production methods, which removed mercantilist constraints on availability of, or access to, resources (see previous section, "Mercantilism"). The constellation of inventions, applications, and novel organizations arising from steam power (and electricity, steel, and the internal combustion engine) brought vast increases in both human productivity and efficiency of capital. The Industrial Revolution shifted the base of wealth from labor, agriculture and trade to technology, industry and manufacturing. Growth no longer depended solely on access to physical resources, labor, and capital. Technology was a new, added factor into every nation's production function, with profound effects: "economic relations became a decreasing source of conflict. One nation's economic gain was not necessarily another's loss; everyone could gain from international trade; albeit not in equal measure."[53]

The course of history did not, however, reflect Robert Gilpin's happy prospect. Beginning first in Britain and France, in the latter decades of the eighteenth century, indigenous industrialization was, like its predecessor, commercialization, a slow process. It involved creation of new knowledge, not simply learning what someone else already knew, or doing "more of the same." With no foreign precedents, Britain's "economy was modernized and changed *relatively* [emphasis in original] slowly and steadily. . . . Britain's Industrial Revolution followed in the path broken long before by its commercial revolution."[54]

In industrializing England, liberal influences of "Smithian" and "Ricardian" economics, and "Lockean" politics, and the large economic benefits and commercial profits for successful industrial competitors "permitted a relatively small role for the state" in early domestic British industrialization and growth.[55] Later industrializations, following the British lead with due respects to Colbert, were quicker. "Government involvement in the economy was crucial for France, Sweden, Germany, and even the US and England earlier in their histories."[56] Other countries also relied on active industrial and fiscal policy, and on various sorts of support or protection for national enterprises, as well as foreign military interventions. "The result of this active state participation in the struggle between monopolies could only be discharged in open conflicts, such as occurred in the two world wars from which the North American hegemony over the world-economy emerged."[57]

After Westphalia and even after Waterloo, Whitehall stressed the "high politics" of diplomacy and war, and provided naval and military support for British trade. In an England heavily reliant on foreign trade, it was almost instinctive to extend Edwardian trade-based strategies, with compliments to Louis XIV, into the politics of empire. The Victorian version of Henry VII's trade agreements extended through diplomatic coercion and beyond military intervention to military conquest, political empire, and hegemony. "The use of gunboat diplomacy, informal rule, and, where necessary, actual political control were frequent occurrences during the era of 'free' trade. In the words of Lord Palmerston, the government's business is to 'open and secure the roads for the merchant.'"[58]

After hesitant emergence in Britain, industrialization slowly diffused through Europe, across the Atlantic to America, and through the empires to the rest of the world. Dramatic increases in production brought requirements for markets and raw materials, which could only be met through expanding trade. As they had followed London into mercantilism, Paris, Madrid, Lisbon, Amsterdam, and later Berlin, Rome, Washington, Tokyo, and Moscow followed the British lead into their own competitive trading empires. The only European anomalies were the Nordic countries—Finland, Sweden, Norway, Denmark—which experienced rapid, sustained economic growth without empire, and seemed to avoid much of the incident conflict.

Industrialization and War

A separate, parallel, geopolitical process began with Napoleon's invention of total war. Industrializing nations felt a need for military superiority not only to achieve victory in the competitive scramble for resources and markets, but to avoid the huge costs of defeat in war. Sustained growth seemed to require both intimidation and deterrence, conflict and cooperation. This need happily coincided with the appearance of engineering skills and technological capabilities for modern weaponry, firepower, and strategic mobility through the diffusing process of industrialization.

The obvious solution was a large, expensive, high-technology military force permanently poised in combat readiness. Peacetime military power, resting firmly on its own national arms industry, could both deter and intimidate. Should deterrence fail, victory would be quick and cheap. The Industrial Revolution had spawned a new sort of military power that could both win wars and prevent them, exploit conflict and control it. To use this new sort of power, however, required sustained economic growth. Industrial military power seemed to have its own peculiar relationship with growth and conflict.

Few would argue that the fundamental discoveries, inventions, and innovations of the Industrial Revolution arose primarily to meet military requirements. Only the myopic, however, could fail to notice the historical association between technological-industrial progress and surges of militarism. As has occurred in other places and times, scientific and industrial progress in modern Europe were spurred by contemporary innovation in military doctrines, logistics, and strategic concepts that exploited emerging industrial capabilities, exemplified by the rise of Germany before World War I.

Before Bismarck, the German states enjoyed initial rapid growth and an Industrial Revolution that laid a foundation for development based primarily on economic and industrial strength. After Bismarck, unified Germany, under Wilhelm II, actively sought a position among the Great Powers of the time (1890–1915) through creation of a large modern army, a powerful blue-water navy, and a global commercial-industrial presence. European ineptitude in accommodating German growth and development into a powerful nation—economically, militarily, industrially, politically—led to global war.[59]

Territory and population had been the measures of power through the eighteenth century. After Waterloo, armaments and industry became more important. States learned to increase their own wealth and power without decreasing the power of other states, simply by increasing or improving their weaponry and manufacturing industries. Growth, industrialization, and trade provided readily available resources, and technology offered superior combat effectiveness. Governments assembled costly navies and armies in peacetime hoping to avert or to win war. Resulting parallel increases in armaments led to a growth-fed, unstable equilibrium among the major powers.[60]

Raymond Aron, among others, has argued that the Industrial Revolution, and the accompanying tremendous increases in both quantity and quality of weaponry available in the several national arms industries, created a powerful positive relationship between economic growth and war. "A traditional conflict [World War I] was amplified into a superwar because of the weapons that industry placed at the disposal of combatants."[61] Paradoxically, the same relationship seems also to have operated in reverse after the war. Reversion to controlled trade, military self-sufficiency, and economic isolation in the 1930s re-established a conflict-prone international system. "Such a structure is not favorable either to peaceful international trade, or to the peaceful coexistence of empires."[62]

AMBIGUITY AND PARADOX

Anecdotal historical evidence implies a weak causal, direct, positive relationship from growth to conflict: growth and conflict have tended to occur together, with dramatic conflict—usually war—usually occurring after rapid growth. Orthodox historical wisdom saw growth as either inviting invasion or enabling aggression. Both phenomena were the "natural" course of history; the best that humanity could do was to be aware of them. Even in isolated American societies, the salutary effects of growth on cultural development seemed to bring inevitable social costs of conflict and war.

In addition to the specifically trade-based links forged by Henry VII, linkages through technology transfer and military-industrial establishments became apparent as industrialization progressed and diffused. While the aggregate effect still seemed positive, the Industrial Revolution introduced political-economic and technological novelties that began to inhibit conflict through unfamiliar negative relationships with growth. Victorian and colonial refinements of Renaissance trade-based growth strategies, albeit with powerful sophistications of industrial technologies, brought the same direct relationship between growth and conflict that the fifteenth and sixteenth centuries had shown. Just as medieval societies had faced the limits imposed by local, or domestic, resources, industrial nations faced the limits of global markets and global resources. Like Henry VII, Victoria found it necessary to engage in conflict and war over national market shares.

In parallel with the direct relationship, and with increasing force as they cumulated over time, the novel technology-based effects seen by Gilpin operated in an inverse growth-conflict relationship. Trading partners really did experience reciprocal, shared, parallel, "positive-sum" benefits. These salutary relationships between growth and conflict seemed most significant within, rather than between, the controlled trading regimes. But they could never balance the more powerful trade-based direct relationships that led eventually to both war and decolonization.

A third sort of relationship emerged as technology brought the several competing national military-industrial complexes into prominence. Although operating in a predominantly direct relationship, military industrialization also brought new salience to the deterrent effects of arms races—especially through the enormous costs of modern sophisticated weaponry—and introduced financial limitations to national military establishments and operations. Just as with the commercial versions of the growth-conflict relationship, the military versions were at best ambiguous, although the direct, positive effects continued to predominate until at least the late-twentieth-century Cold War.

The paradox within Gilpin's observation about universal, but unequal, gain from economic relations became apparent in the decades preceding World War I. New technologies brought high productivity and output, which could indeed moderate Socrates' observations about economic growth and conflict (see note 4), by severing the connections between growth and expansion. Growth could, presumably, be sustained by continuing technological progress and increasing productivity, which would continue to obviate any need for expansion and conflict. Rapid progress and diffusion of technology, thus, become critical to separating growth from conflict.

Traditional growth based on continuing commercial expansion through controlled trade, rather than technological advance, meant that growth could continue without conflict only if national governments continued to expand their political control over additional markets and sources. When further expansion faced political or physical limits, the only results were increasing conflict, decreasing growth, or a new strategy. The global empires made technically possible by the Industrial Revolution now required diversion of its potentially unlimited energies away from sustaining economic growth into ever-expanding trade, which was paradoxically limited by the politically bounded size of controlled markets.

By the end of the nineteenth century, when virtually all territory had been occupied and claimed as controlled markets, industrial nations faced two apparent options for continued growth. Expansion of trade still required increasing national share in existing markets, at the expense of another nation, to ensure availability of traditional resources (land and population) and markets. Once again, as in the fourteenth and fifteenth centuries, this approach held substantial risk of conflict.

Unlike the commercial revolution of the fifteenth century, the Industrial Revolution provided a new, more agreeable, option: development of an economic power base through intense application of the new factor of production—technology—that had appeared during the century. This option could minimize risk of conflict by creating new markets for new products based on new industrial technologies. The same factor that created the problem was paradoxically a solution: technology.

The fundamental power of the Industrial Revolution was not in the additional factor of production (technology) that it introduced. The critical feature of industrialization (as of commercialization) that could separate growth and conflict was innovation, the ability to create new knowledge and use it to achieve valuable purposes. This ambiguity and paradox have evolved into the still controversial issues of "guns or butter," "national competitiveness," "economic security," "managed trade," and "industrial policy." The evolution, however, has not much elucidated the fundamental relationships between growth and conflict. Nor has it exposed anything more effective than knowledge and human reason for managing either growth or conflict, and understanding the relationships between them.

NOTES

1. William H. McNeill, *A World History* (New York: Oxford University Press, 1961), 5.

2. John Keegan, *A History of Warfare* (New York: Alfred A. Knopf, 1994), 135.

3. Keegan, *A History of Warfare*, 135; McNeill, *A World History*, esp. 34.

4. In Book II of Plato's *The Republic*, Socrates posits a state that grows "beyond the necessaries of which I was first speaking, such as houses, clothes, and shoes. ... Then we must enlarge our borders; for the original healthy State is no longer sufficient. ... gold and ivory and all sorts of materials must be procured." To Glaucon's ultimate assent that this would be the natural consequence of economic growth, Socrates raises the issue of conflict and war by asking,

> "Then a slice of our neighbors' land will be wanted by us for pasture and tillage, and they will want a slice of ours if, like ourselves, they exceed the limit of necessity, and give themselves up to the unlimited accumulation of wealth?"
> "That, Socrates, will be inevitable."
> "And so we shall go to war, Glaucon. Shall we not?"
> "Most certainly," he replied.
> "Then, ... this much we may affirm, that now we have discovered war to be derived from causes [growth & accumulation of wealth] which are also the causes of almost all the evils in States, private as well as public."
> "Undoubtedly."

Plato, *The Dialogues of Plato*, trans. by J. Harward (Chicago: Encyclopedia Britannica, 1952), 318-319.

5. Keegan, *A History of Warfare*, 256.

6. Keegan, *A History of Warfare*, 256.

7. "Where Athenian intervention sometimes provided revolution to install Athenian-style democracy, the combined effects of Athenian extortion, political subversion, and widening strategic and commercial dominance eventually turned first Corinth, and eventually one city after another, against Athens and provoked an outbreak of hostilities" (Keegan, *A History of Warfare*, 256).

8. Keegan, *A History of Warfare*, 257.

9. William V. Harris, *War and Imperialism in Republican Rome: 327-70 BC* (New York: Oxford University Press, 1979), 54-67.

10. Michael J. Balick & Paul Alan Cox, *Plants, People, and Culture* (New York: Scientific American Library, 1996), 80. The apogee of the Anasazi culture was the Pueblo III period (AD 1100–1300) when animal husbandry and turkey ranching appeared. The combination of epidemic disease in dense urban communities, total dependence on a single hybrid crop (maize) with the ever-present specter of drought and famine, and unrestricted warfare over maize surpluses, doomed the Anasazi to only brief prosperity. Twenty-three years of relentless drought in the fourteenth century destroyed the culture and forced migration of the few survivors to better drainage areas in modern Mexico.

11. Jeremy A. Sabloff, *The New Archaeology and the Ancient Maya* (New York: Scientific American Library, 1990), 84, quoting a 1937 comment of Thomas Gann expanding on his pivotal work with Eric Thompson: Thomas Gann & J. Eric S. Thompson, *The History of the Maya from the Earliest Time to the Present Day* (New York: Scribner's, 1931).

12. David L. Webster, "Warfare and the Evolution of Maya Civilization," in R. E. W. Adams, ed., *The Origins of Maya Civilization* (Albuquerque: University of New Mexico Press, 1977), 335-372.

13. Sabloff, *The New Archaeology and the Ancient Maya*, 91, 119-122.

14. Sabloff, *The New Archaeology and the Ancient Maya*, 143. Sabloff speculates that the combination of economic growth and population increase brought "two significant trends: conflicts among [population] centers increased as they began to compete for land, resources, and people, and large workforces were mobilized to undertake ambitious building projects" (139), which he sees as "critical factors in the development by about 300 B.C. of the first large towns and urban centers . . ." (140).

15. Sabloff, *The New Archaeology and the Ancient Maya*, 145.

16. Sabloff, *The New Archaeology and the Ancient Maya*, 148.

17. Keegan, *A History of Warfare*, 287.

18. Will Durant, *The Age of Faith* (New York: Simon & Schuster, 1950), 475.

19. Although economic growth had, perhaps, little to do with the motivations for the Crusades, it was closely associated with their results:

> They [the Crusades] re-established the presence of Latin (Roman Catholic) states in the eastern Mediterranean, not only in Palestine and Syria but more lastingly in Greece, Crete, Cyprus, and the Aegean, through which staging-places the northern Italian cities, notably Venice (where town life and commerce had never wholly died), were enabled to reopen a prosperous trade with the Middle and eventually Far East, and to revive the safe transportation of goods between ports throughout the Mediterranean itself; the money they made thereby fuelled most of the wars fought during the fifteenth century between themselves and later by France against the Hapsburgs of the Holy Roman empire for dominance south of the Alps.

Keegan, *A History of Warfare*, 296.

20. Robert Gilpin, *War and Change in World Politics* (Cambridge: Cambridge University Press, 1981), 112, 132.

21. Local inferiority of naval and military power doomed this effort to failure after brief success. With naval supremacy in the Indian Ocean after victories at Ormuz (1507) and Diu (1509), "the Portuguese learned at Jiddah, in the Red Sea . . . that it was too dangerous to close with a local (in this case Mameluke) fleet supported by cannon on shore, and their attempt to block the maritime spice route into the western Islamic lands therefore failed." Keegan, *A History of Warfare*, 339; see also J. Guilmartin, *Gunpowder and Galleys: Changing Technology and Mediterranean Warfare in the Sixteenth Century* (London: Cambridge University Press, 1974), 8-11.

22. Keegan, *A History of Warfare*, 339.

23. Dealing with this period in depth, Keegan summarizes the seventeenth century quite neatly:

> Dutch dominance of Atlantic maritime trade in the early seventeenth century matured into challenges for Portuguese influence elsewhere. Dutch traders and warships arrived on the Coromandel coast of India in 1601, and the English in 1609. Soon both were fighting the Portuguese in the Indian Ocean — the Dutch fought them also off Brazil in 1624-9. England and the Netherlands then fought each other over trade in the English Channel and North Sea in three naval wars (1652-74). Both nations also challenged Spain over trading-rights in the Caribbean which later became the richest colonial area in the world. Finally the tardy French entered the fray with all of their neighbors by establishing armed trading-forts in India, West Africa, Indochina, and America by the mid-17th century.

Keegan, *A History of Warfare*, 340.

24. In 1405 Zheng He, grand eunuch of the Three Treasures, brought his first Chinese fleet to ports of Indochina, Indonesia, India, and Ceylon. After two more short voyages, he arrived at Bengal in 1414 with 62 galleons, 100 auxiliary vessels, 26,000 soldiers, and a huge staff. His fifth (1417), sixth (1421), and seventh (1431-1433, the final) voyages touched in Mogadishu, Mombasa, Tanzania, Mozambique, and Madagascar, and possibly rounded the Cape of Good Hope into the Atlantic. Undoubtedly the most formidable naval forces of the world, the pacific mission of these "Star Rafts," bringing the "starlike" radiance of an imperial ambassador of the celestial emperor, was simply to accept the allegiance of distant peoples. Fei Xin, *Xing cha sheng lan [Triumphant Tour of the Star Raft]*, edited by Feng Chengjun (Peking: Zhonghua Shuju [China Bookshop], [1436] 1954). "By trading with the fleet the African coastal states were paying the Ming emperor the homage they owed him as sovereign of the world." Philip Snow, *The Star Raft, China's Encounter With Africa* (London: Weidenfeld and Nicholson, 1988), 27.

25. Snow, *The Star Raft, China's Encounter With Africa*, 30.

26. While they probably did not recognize the modern concept of social costs, and were certainly unaware of the prices that were being paid by Mayan and Anasazi civilizations for the benefits of economic growth, contemporary policy-makers (perhaps instinctively) realized the inabilities of their still feudal societies to absorb such costs. The emergence of modernism, allowed Europeans—unlike the Mayans and Anasazi—to shift some of those costs, albeit at the risk of international conflict.

27. The first serious rebellion of the peasants was the "Great Revolt" in England in 1381, quickly suppressed. On the continent, the first *Bundschuh* (Peasant Revolution) occurred in 1493 in Alsace and southwest Germany. The movement erupted again in 1502 in Speyer, and in 1513 in Württemberg and the Black Forest. Following the

Revolt of the Knights in 1522-1523, the final, most violent, peasant uprising in 1524 also included urban laborers. After engulfing most of Germany, this Peasant's Revolt was suppressed after a year of chaos, trials, and executions, although the final battle of the Peasant Revolution was not fought until 1534 when the final "lunatic fringe of the movement" was destroyed at Münster. Edward McNall Burns, *Western Civilizations*, 7th ed. (New York: W. W. Norton, 1969), 469-472.

28. Friedrich Engels, *The Peasant War in Germany* (New York: International Publishers, [1850] 1926).

29. A sophisticated refinement of Aristotle's doctrine of the Golden Mean, medieval economic theory reflected the ascetic flavor of medieval Christianity: absolutely everything in life was subordinate to the salvation of one's soul. Wealth, luxury, and comfort were obstacles to salvation. The resulting doctrine pervaded Pre-Renaissance economics, politics, religion, and business, and life generally:

- the purpose of economic activity is to provide goods, services, security, and freedom from want for the general community, not for the individual;
- every commodity has a "just price," a "true economic value": cost of production + expenses + "reasonable" profit;
- no individual is entitled to a larger share of worldly goods than is necessary for reasonable needs — any surplus belongs to the general community;
- no individual has a right to economic reward unless for socially useful labor or acceptance of actual risk.

Burns, *Western Civilizations*, esp. 343-350 and 462-464.

30. Mancur Olson, Jr. "Rapid Growth as a Destabilizing Force," *Journal of Economic History* 23(4) (December 1963): 529-552, 548; see also J. U. Nef, "The Progress of Technology and the Growth of Large Scale Industry in Great Britain, 1540-1640" & "Prices and Industrial Capitalism in France and England, 1540-1640" in E. M. Carus-Wilson, ed., *Essays in Economic History* (London: Edward Arnold, 1954), 88-134.

31. Eugene R. Black, President, World Bank, quoted in Grant S. McClellan, ed., *US Foreign Aid*, (The Reference Shelf, Vol. 29, No. 5) (New York: The H.W. Wilson Company, 1957), 90.

32. Olson, "Rapid Growth as a Destabilizing Force," 531.

33. Orthodoxy suggests that the Industrial Revolution began in England in about 1780, and simply abandons the earlier eighteenth century as an uninteresting appendage of preindustrial history.

34. Will Durant, *The Reformation* (New York: Simon & Schuster, 1957), 38, 109.

35. The simplistic elegance of this strategy encouraged innumerable successors of many nationalities to assume that the unadorned techniques of Edward and Henry, which were truly innovative creations in the fourteenth and fifteen centuries, were immutable keys to economic development and growth, regardless of the rest of the world. Most failed to recognize, however, that the "key" was not simply in protectionism and trade, but in the innovative creativity of Edward and Henry in using them. Sedulously adopting an analogous Import-Substitution-Industrialization strategy six centuries later does not use the "key" (innovation), and can vitiate the power of trade-based growth strategies.

36. Martin Wolf suggests two more sorts of competition that emerge from mercantilism: "overall cost level of a country, given its productivity," and "the fate of particular firms or enterprises." Martin Wolf, "Cooperation or Conflict? The European Union in a Liberal Global Economy," *International Affairs* 71(2) (April 1995): 329.

37. Adam Smith, *An Inquiry into the Nature and Causes of the Wealth of Nations* (New York: Modern Library, [1776] 1937), 434.

38. D. C. Coleman, "Colbertism," in John Eatwell, Murray Milgate & Peter Newman, eds., *Problems of the Planned Economy* (New York: W. W. Norton, 1990), 51.

39. Cunningham's fetching description of English economic policy (1689-1776) as "Parliamentary Colbertism" was not only misinformed and inaccurate, but oxymoronic. W. Cunningham, *The Growth of English Industry and Commerce*, 3 vols. (Cambridge: Cambridge University Press, 1907), Vol II, 403-468). Like Marx he seems to have accepted Smith's generalization from English mercantilist practices with neither question nor data. In many ways Colbert bears the same relationship to orthodox Fabian socialism that Adam Smith bears to orthodox liberal capitalism, and Karl Marx to orthodox communism. Each was the prophet of a separate, powerful, radical (at least when introduced) approach to modern political-economy.

40. Coleman, "Colbertism," 52.

41. Coleman, "Colbertism," 52-53.

42. John Condliffe, *The Commerce of Nations* (New York: W. W. Norton, 1950), 233.

43. Michael Lind, "Hamilton's Legacy," *Wilson Quarterly* 18 (Summer 1994): 45.

44. Friedrich List, *National System of Political Economy* (London: Longmans, Green, 1928); see also Condliffe, *The Commerce of Nations*.

45. Paul Krugman, "Competitiveness: A Dangerous Obsession," *Foreign Affairs* 73(2), (March/April 1994): 41-42.

46. Edward D. Mansfield, *Power, Trade, and War* (Princeton, New Jersey: Princeton University Press, 1994), 122.

47. Despite the prevalence of ancient realist traditions that "barbarians" have no rights, liberal Spanish theologians (Suarez, Las Casas, Vitoria) began, as early as the sixteenth century, to advocate rights of property and conscience for indigenous peoples. Martin Wight has noted that even liberals (Wight's rationalists) justified imperialism and colonization of the "barbarian" (non-European) world, primarily for economic reasons. Ascription to barbarians of incomplete rights—"not full rights, not equal rights, but appropriate rights"—also justified the concepts of "trusteeship" for Wilson, rebellion for Locke, empire for Burke, and "protectorate" for Hitler. Martin Wight, *International Theory: The Three Traditions*, edited by Gabriele Wight & Brian Porter (Leicester & London: Leicester University Press for the Royal Institute of International Affairs, 1991), 79.

48. David S. Yost, "Political Philosophy and the Theory of International Relations," *International Affairs* 70 (1994): 282.

49. For example: Arnold Toynbee who originated the term "Industrial Revolution"—"The essence of the Industrial Revolution is the substitution of competition for the medieval regulations which had previously controlled the production and distribution of wealth": Arnold Toynbee, *Lectures on the Industrial Revolution in England* (Boston: Beacon Press, [1884] 1961), 85; and Peter Mathias — "The concept [of "Industrial Revolution"] implies the onset of a fundamental change in the structure of an economy; a fundamental deployment of resources away from agriculture": Peter Mathias, *The First Industrial Nation: An Economic History of Britain 1700-1914* (London: Methuen, 1969), 2.

50. T. S. Ashton, Paul Mantoux, & Charles Wilson specifically analyzed the eighteenth century: Thomas S. Ashton, *An Economic History of England: The 18th Century* (London: Barnes & Noble, 1955); Paul Mantoux, *The Industrial Revolution in*

the Eighteenth Century: An Outline of the Beginnings of the Modern Factory System in England rev. ed. (Methuen, New Jersey: University Paperbacks, 1964); Charles Wilson, "The Other Face of Mercantilism," in D. C. Coleman, ed., *Revisions in Mercantilism* (London: Methuen, 1969). A. P. Usher intended his monumental study (*An Introduction to the Industrial History of England* [London: G. G. Harrap, 1921]) as a critique of socialist economic history. Although their attempts to merge economics and history subsequently fell from fashion as post-1945 growth claimed the world's attention, these earlier analyses had delved deeply into some aspects of preindustrial manufacturing and the early Industrial Revolution. They remain useful, despite overtly socialist overtones.

51. David Landes' industrial revolution was the apocalyptic "bold sweep of technology's advance." Like a republican army, confident in its own morality, principles, and preordained triumph, technology, machinery, and new sources of power and energy dramatically overwhelmed all social, historic, and economic barriers. The other classic analyst of early industrialization, J. H. Clapham, saw a Darwinian, evolutionary "industrial revolution in slow motion." Clapham emphasized structural and cultural continuity, persistence of traditional forms of work and organization, and traced labor-intensive techniques well into the twentieth century. Maxine Berg has absorbed both visions (apocalyptic changes of technology and stubborn persistence of traditional society) in her view of industrialization as parallel microeconomic growth and macroeconomic "development." David Landes, *The Unbound Prometheus. Technological Change and Industrial Development in Western Europe from 1750 to the Present* (London: Cambridge University Press, 1969), esp. 41-43; J. H. Clapham, *An Economic History of Modern Britain*, 3 vols. (Cambridge: The University Press, 1938); Maxine Berg, *The Age of Manufactures: 1700–1820*, (New York: Oxford University Press, 1985), esp. 23-24.

52. Berg, *The Age of Manufactures: 1700-1820*, 40.

53. Robert Gilpin, "Economic Interdependence and National Security in Historical Perspective" in Klaus Knorr & Frank N. Trager, *Economic Issues and National Security* (New York: National Security Education Program of New York University, 1977), 33.

54. Olson, "Rapid Growth as a Destabilizing Force," 549.

55. Bertha K. Becker & Claudio A. G. Egler, *Brazil: A New Regional Power in the World-Economy* (Cambridge: Cambridge University Press, 1992), 8.

56. Paul Wallich & Elizabeth Corcoran, "The Analytical Economist, Don't Write Off Marx," *Scientific American* 264 (February 1991): 135 (interviewing Professor Stephen Marglin).

57. Becker & Egler, *Brazil: A New Regional Power in the World-Economy*, 8.

58. Donald Gordon, *The Moment of Power: Britain's Imperial Epoch* (Englewood Cliffs, New Jersey: Prentice-Hall, 1970), 87.

59. Raymond Aron, *The Century of Total War* (Boston: Beacon Press, 1955); Simon Kuznets, *Modern Economic Growth* (New Haven, Connecticut: Yale University Press, 1966).

60. See Samuel P. Huntington, "Arms Races: Prerequisites and Results," in Robert J. Art & Kenneth N. Waltz, eds., *The Use of Force: Military Power and International Politics*, 3rd ed. (Lanham, Maryland: University Press of America, 1988), 637-670; see also Aron, *The Century of Total War*, esp. 17-22.

61. Aron, *The Century of Total War*, 72.

62. Aron, *The Century of Total War*, 72.

3

Theoretical Approaches

Modern theory and empiricism have both consistently analyzed growth and conflict along the traditional paths of political and economic thought—realism, liberalism, idealism, materialism—and focused their analyses on one or the other, but rarely, or only incidentally, on both or on any connection between them. Gradual divergence of realism and liberalism in the Renaissance crystallized two orthodox approaches to understanding any growth-conflict relationship: realist irrelevance and liberal trade-related independence. Orthodoxy designated any other sort of relationship, or theories suggesting a different approach, as radical.

GENERA, SPECIES, AND MODELS

Classical realists averred that growth was fundamentally irrelevant to conflict: international relations revolved around politics and war, conflict was endemic in international anarchy, and economic pressures could be released in acquisition of empty territories and subjugation of backward peoples. The realist approach does not easily accommodate nonpolitical or nonmilitary factors in international relations, and is uncomfortable with the purely internal processes and motivations that condition, but do not cause, foreign policies.

More flexible neorealist, or structural, theories expanded and enriched the concept of nationalism, and later recognized some weakly positive relationship that could allow growth to generate conflict. Some approaches relied on political structures, operating as intervening variables between growth and conflict, as the primary explanation of international behaviors. Other explanations included a weak growth-conflict relationship as one of several dynamics, each contributing the influence of a separate structure or process.

Accepting that international economic behaviors and political conduct could affect each other, trade-related classical mercantilist analyses had reflected powerful positive relationships between growth and conflict, reminiscent of "armed trading," "privateers," and "merchant adventurers." Commercial liberalism argued later that both conflict and growth were dependent variables of trade. Trade would both minimize conflict and maximize growth: growth and conflict were independent of each other, but related through their respective relationships with trade. Political scientists found broadly negative correlations of trade with international conflict—most analyses limited observations to military war. Economists happily linked more trade with increased output, and defined it as growth. Mathematicians then constructed various growth-conflict relationships that depended on the data: the relationship could be either positive or negative. It seemed that particular levels or types of trade could generate either sort of relationship between variables—conflict and growth—that were definitely not irrelevant, even if they were independent and did not determine each other.

In a perverse sort of convergence with neorealism, some neoliberals later found certain economic variables—early analyses limited observations to particular sorts of trade—in a broadly negative relationship with war, and generalized a similar relationship between growth and conflict. As liberal thought and policies gradually elicited neorealist refinements, trade became a comfortable euphemism for growth, and the liberal syllogism was complete. Growth was not irrelevant, but could either inhibit or promote conflict; the relationship and its causality depended on how trade was involved, and the effects of any exogenous variables. Like both neorealists and neoliberals, various integrated theoretical-empirical neo-approaches have concluded that the relationship is ambiguous. Even modern behavioral empiricism can only conclude that it is indeterminate until mediated by intervening systemic variables (structuralism), or determined jointly by domestic attributes of the relevant nations and the dynamics of their other international relationships (interdependence theory, status theory, status-field theory, etc.).

In parallel with orthodox theorizing, observation, and analysis, radical thought observed and analyzed the same phenomena, but developed different theories and conclusions. Radicals found several sorts of explicit relationships between growth and conflict—positive and negative, causal and incidental—unadulterated by either politics or economics. Idealists and utopians argued that conflict prevented growth, and developed a group of theories based on an inverse-negative relationship. Materialism postulated that growth caused conflict—a direct-positive relationship—and evolved along Marxian lines.

A second genus of growth-conflict relationships—powerful and positive, but not related to trade—emerged in the nineteenth and twentieth centuries with the several species of quixotic, materialistic political-economic theories. Marxism and its Leninist derivatives seem unique in predicting an unequivocal positive causal nexus between growth and conflict; other approaches saw conflict as a technique for achieving growth. For these radical thinkers, economic growth became a proximate cause of international conflict, which could be eliminated simply by repressing capitalist growth, and establishing a peaceful socialist (or Nazi, or Fascist, or some other visionary) world.

The third genus—unrelated to either trade or politics, and usually nonmaterialistic—took shape in utopian visions of conflict as an obstacle to growth. These idealists found the relationship powerful and negative, and urged that conflict be eliminated. (Martin Wight has collected these materialistic and idealistic approaches into his "revolutionist" tradition, including "soft," "hard," and "inverted" versions[1].)

Historical and classical analyses of growth and conflict have favored simple explicit explanatory relationships between them. Even arcane trade-related concepts are epistemologically succinct. Modern approaches, with more data and increasing technical sophistication, often lead to less parsimonious explanations, involving intervening variables. The most useful fall into two broad groups: "structural" variables imported from political science, and "process" variables borrowed from economics.[2]   Each type transmutes economic growth into the political phenomenon of conflict, either by disrupting the political structures of international relations, or by converting an economic process into a political process.

As quantitative analysis migrated from physical and natural science into economics, political science, and sociology, analysts discovered a new world of sources for conflict: human behavior. In addition to structural and process variables of intervening-variable relationships, these contributory behavioral linkages may involve national attributes, their international differences, and changes in those differences.   Some of these several types of contributing independent variables seem to generate conflict from growth with powerful positive immediate effects.   Others act as intervening variables, while yet others seem to create additional secondary independent variables that generate conflict. Some operate to inhibit conflict, and others seem to prevent growth, with heavy negative effects.

With the prominent exception of classical realism, with its insistence that international relations are purely political, most orthodox approaches—liberal, neorealist, structural, behavioral—as well as the radical doctrines, recognize that some economic behaviors of some people could significantly affect some political behaviors under some conditions at some points in history. For liberals and neorealists, what that effect is depends on the situation, and on other exogenous factors; indeed it may change over time. For radicals, the growth-conflict relationship is either positive or negative, in accordance with a preferred ideology, morality, worldview, religion, or interpretation of history.

The generic growth-conflict relationship has remained an incidental artifact for both political science and economics, inherently unstable and unpredictable, systemically unclear, situation-dependent, ambiguous, and not very interesting. Neither economics nor political science—nor even the ever fashionable and presumptuous discipline of "policy science"—can confidently predict either whether conflict or growth will occur, or if one occurs how it will affect the other.

Modern analyses and theories of growth and conflict have absorbed virtually all aspects of classical thought—ancient, moralist, realist, liberal, radical, idealist. Some three millennia of history, much speculation, ample theorizing, and some research have, however, served only to confuse the three broad genera of growth-conflict relationships with several of their species:

UNRELATED-IRRELEVANT = growth and conflict are unrelated and do not affect each other; predicted by classical realist and patron-client dependency;

DIRECT-POSITIVE = growth and conflict rise and fall in parallel; any mathematical relationship between them is positive; high growth is associated with high conflict and low growth, with low conflict;

growth causes conflict or conflict causes growth; predicted by uneven growth theories and radical approaches (Marxism-Leninism, "feedback" theory *dependencia*, modern-world system theory, *etc.*);

trade allows growth and causes conflict; growth and conflict may be positively, but not causally, related; predicted by mercantilism, economic nationalism, long wave theory, and hegemonic stability theory;

growth affects conflict through distinct intervening variables; predicted by Kuznets' triad, hegemonic stability theory, long wave theory, power redefinition theory, core-periphery dependence, redistribution of power, and structural approaches;

growth is one among many independent variables that affect conflict separately; predicted by theories of national attributes, status inconsistency, power transition theory, and interdependence approaches.

INVERSE-NEGATIVE = growth and conflict rise and fall inversely; any mathematical relationship between them is negative; high growth is associated with low conflict and low growth, with high conflict;

conflict prevents growth or growth prevents conflict; predicted by idealist or utopian approaches;

trade causes growth and inhibits conflict; predicted by liberal approaches, business cycle approaches, long wave theory, hegemonic stability theory, and some structuralist interdependence approaches;

growth affects conflict through intervening variables; predicted by hegemonic stability theory, power redefinition theory, redistribution of power, patron-client dependency, and structural approaches;

growth is one among many independent variables that affect conflict separately; predicted by national attributes theory, status inconsistency, and some interdependence approaches.

For convenience in comparing the specific growth-conflict relationships, this analysis presents several archetypal species of theory within each genus. Each theory implies a separate model of the growth-conflict relationship, and a separate set of relevant features for the predicted relationship. With each species of theory appears a diagram of its model. A table comparing analogous features of the several species within each genus allows intragenus comparison, and a final cross-genus table completes comparative analysis of the family of growth-conflict relationships.

KEY TO PRESENTATION IN MODEL DIAGRAMS

☐	. . . . Independent Variable
▨	. . . . Intervening Variable
▣	. . . . Contributing Variable
▬	. . . . Dependent Variable

$\Rightarrow, \Leftarrow, \Uparrow, \Downarrow, \Updownarrow$ . . . . Causal Dynamic

$\searrow, \nearrow, \nwarrow, \swarrow, \uparrow, \downarrow, \rightarrow, \leftarrow, \leftrightarrow$ . . . . Incidental Dynamic

$+$ . . . . Additive Dynamic

IRRELEVANCE BETWEEN GROWTH AND CONFLICT

In the premodern protorealist world, which brought nations together only periodically through war, migration, and trade, national growth could occur independently in each country, first by concentrating domestic resources as factors of production, and later by exploiting foreign resources obtained through exploration and discovery, conquest or commerce. So long as a nation had, or could obtain, additional resources for production, it could continue growth, independently of the rest of the world, and generally irrelevant to international relations, which involved other parameters. Indeed, so long as a nation was content with its particular situation in the world, with growing—or stagnating—within its own resources and territory, it had no need, or even incentive, to deal with other peoples at all. Conflict, whenever it occurred, seemed an annoying nuisance of international society.

Historically unequal distribution of power, resources, wealth, and population led eventually to the Westphalian system of national sovereignty, territoriality, whose inexorable logic obliges states to assert autonomy, ensure self-preservation, pursue some national version of justice, provide national security, and pursue national prosperity. Its powerful "realistic" mystique gives preeminence to state-centered concepts of common good, and reinforces every nation's convictions of its own excellence.[3] Each state adopts national interests that are inherently self-centered and focussed on the state as an institution, and do not permit reliance on any other state. Growth is explicitly a domestic phenomenon, unrelated to international conflict, which is explicitly an external phenomenon.

UNRELATED-IRRELEVANT GROWTH-CONFLICT LINKAGE MODEL

ENGINE OF GROWTH is accumulation of resources within an autonomous domestic economy.

DOMESTIC POLITICAL-ECONOMY is hierarchic (feudalism, monarchy, autocracy, bureaucracy, *etc.*), with substantial state involvement in economic affairs.

INTERNATIONAL POLITICAL-ECONOMY involves only national states or protostates and their extensions; private firms trade and invest outside their home countries only at the sufferance of, or in partnership with, national states.

INTERNATIONAL RELATIONS are political, and establish structure for intereconomy relations limited to trade and equity investment.

ECONOMIC GROWTH is quantitative, based on increases of factors of production, and limited by availability of resources.

INTERNATIONAL CONFLICT occurs as polities seek to impose values on each other, to record change in an international balance of power, but only rarely as economies reaching limits of resources seek to continue growth by expansion.

LINKAGE between economic growth and international conflict may be strong and positive, but operates only rarely, since growth occurs within polities without approaching political limits.

INTERNATIONAL SECURITY REGIMES control or contain international conflict; failure of security regimes bring catastrophic war; lesser conflict is chiefly political and endemic to the system.

POWER RESOURCES are population and territory.

Realism

The predominant species of the genus, classical realism was the earliest coherent approach to both conflict and growth. Emerging during the Renaissance, realist explanations of international relations stressed political-military forces, and held that "conflict among states over economic resources and political superiority is endemic in a system of international anarchy."[4] In the realist world, economic processes operated outside the range of importance in explaining conflict—military war or nonmilitary dispute. A dependent variable of distribution and use of power, conflict was not systematically affected by trade, investment, growth, depression, or other economic factors. Realist analyses continue to emphasize political and military variables,[5] and argue that any relationship between political and economic processes is dramatically weakened by the permanently dominating effects of political-military variables on both commerce and international relations.[6]

The realist model, which has informed both practice and analysis, condenses reality into two primary determinants of foreign policy: interstate geopolitics and distribution of power.[7] Realist stress on national security leads inevitably to its neglect of domestic and economic factors.[8] Realism accepts, parenthetically, that growth may sometimes be destabilizing and could in some situations lead to conflict, but only incidentally, rarely, and always in conjunction with other political forces. In the very condition of independent nationhood, each state faces the paradoxical dilemma of sovereignty: "it must grant every other state the same freedom and independence, yet it cannot really trust anyone but itself. . . . absolute security is possible only if it controls more power than the remainder of the world combined."[9]

When economic growth, military aggression, political expansion, or anything else moves a state even slightly toward this goal, the security of other states decreases proportionately. In a Richardsonian action-reaction syndrome, self-interest obliges each either to oppose change or to seek a corresponding advantage to reestablish its own security. The product of this anarchic system is the universal aspiration of each state to increase its power and wealth, relative to all others, a sort of "Red Queen's Race"[10] as the entire world glides inexorably toward conflict.[11] Introduction of the Westphalian nation-state system as a realist political-economy made conflict at least as likely in international relations—actual, apparent, potential—as cooperation.

The intractable paradox of sovereignty, inherent in the Westphalian system, abates only when conflict is contained within a larger consensus to allow some, but not all, conflicts. Acceptance of a "legitimate" international order by nations promotes adherence to norms and procedures that reduce tendencies toward, and incidence of, unacceptable conflict. An international security regime imposes an accepted set of limits on conflicts, regulates noneconomic international relations, and even allows some changes in the international hierarchy of nations. It may be robust or weak as it constrains national states in their uses of power, but it provides some common level of individual national security. Several international security regimes may operate simultaneously, nested in each other, in parallel or series, or locally. Familiar international security regimes have included hierarchy, feudalism, hegemony, empire, balance-of-power, collective security, polarity, and alliance.

Even constrained by a powerful international security regime, the sovereign national state system is inherently competitive, and conflict has become a habitual, if intermittent, feature of world politics. States whose interests lie within the parameters of the security regime generally engage in milder forms of conflict, and even make minor adjustments to their international influence and stature. Nations may increase national power or domestic wealth in small increments within the agreed parameters of the security regime. In a realist international system populated solely by national states, only a consensual international security regime holds the political-economy together, and prevents national expansion from exploding the system. So long as the security regime is legitimate and efficient, nations prefer cooperation to conflict, and growth does not matter.

When, however, a nation believes that the regime no longer supports its interests, and that it has enough power to do so, it can defect from, or simply ignore, the regime. Other states, driven by ideology, irrationality, or rejection of some aspect of the prevailing international political-economy, tend impulsively toward conflict, aggression, and violent rejection of the international security regime. Primary forces of expansion, unrestrained by the security regime, can provoke uncontrolled conflict, often in the form of world war. Lesser conflicts, even within the constraints of a security regime, also arise from purely political disputes, primarily over power, and marked changes in the distribution of power.

The availability of ample resources for continued growth obviated Socrates' visions of conquest or conflict over economic issues (see note 4, Chapter 2). As domestic supplies of resources reached physical limits, however, a government might seek growth outside the national economy. This, however, was a political matter, and only incidentally related to growth. In the realist world, economic growth was neither sufficient nor necessary to generate international conflict. Only when political decisions allowed economic growth to increase national political-military power sufficiently to change the distribution of power, or brought nations into conflict over resources to sustain it, could growth lead through politics to conflict.

Classical realism explained conflict and growth well in a finite world with too few states to fill it. So long as parts of the world were unclaimed, and not incorporated into some sovereign jurisdiction, nations faced few political constraints, physical limits, or even competition in obtaining resources. Since, in a realist world, states generated national power from little more than population and territory, both resources and power, as well as growth, were, in effect, unlimited. States could simply claim some more territory, including any resources and population on it, and thereby increase resources and power, and continue resource-based growth.

Accumulation of wealth and power was a major national goal in a system whose chief concern was security and whose dominant dynamic was geopolitical expansion. In the absence of political or physical limits on resources, national efforts to expand power or increase wealth only rarely brought conflict over economic issues: they were irrelevant. Classical realism banished into the irrelevant such issues as the results of sustained rapid growth, any consequences of subjecting all peoples, lands, and waters everywhere to national sovereignty; or whether political conflict could be affected by economic cooperation: they were not part of the realist system.

In cleverly avoiding the apparent historical and empirical association between growth and conflict, neorealism inserted between them a structural filter—distribution of power—and a dynamic damper—an international security regime. Structural variants of the "irrelevant" genus deemphasize process variables of any sort, and relegate growth to an obscure role among various minor processes that may influence distribution of power. Nor do structural arguments allow international economic structures even to season the ultimately determinant forces of politics in generating, managing, and resolving international conflict. Structural arguments do not recognize a systematic relationship between growth and conflict, "since (to the extent that they exist at all) relationships between features of the global economy and war are likely to be by-products of the distribution of capabilities on both international conditions and war."[12]

The obvious primacy of political and military processes and institutions in the relationships among nations necessarily condemns other influences and factors to insignificance, random coincidence, or irrelevance.

> Because of the dominance of military and political factors in determining the use of force, the impact of economic structure on international security is anyway subordinate. Within that subordinate position the choice between liberalism and mercantilism offers no decisive direction. Benign and malevolent features attend both options, but their effects are not strong enough to determine the basic character of international relations. . . . the effect of either a liberal or a mercantilistic economic structure is too heavily influenced by the particularities of other historical conditions to have, by itself, a predictable impact on the stability of international relations.[13]

Even in its most modern and sophisticated renderings, realism would argue that growth and conflict are only weakly and randomly related. Other variables, structures, and processes determine international behaviors. Growth is at best a feeble, incidental stimulus. Realism expects, but would not try to predict, occasional random associations between growth and conflict, which would, of course, be notable and anomalous, and clearly not causal in any credible sense. Realist or neorealist theory would expect growth to be normally uncorrelated with conflict; correlation coefficients would be generally low and statistically insignificant. Realists would not rely on the predictive power of any imputed growth-conflict relationship to explain international behaviors (see Diagram 3.1).

Diagram 3.1: Irrelevance Between Growth and Conflict

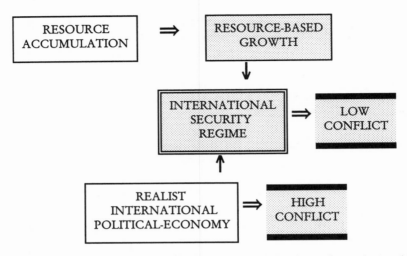

It is an artifact of realist logic that any growth-conflict relationship is at best metastable, and can persist for only so long as political-military variables permit. With perverse confidence born of what Professor James Robinson has termed "primary certitude," realism bestows on its dogma of irrelevance or ambiguity a quality of "perfect obviousness,"[14] and dispenses with any need to adduce or demonstrate evidence of "first principles," or logical deductions of effects from causes.

Patron-Client Dependency

In his extensive study of modern Africa, A. F. Mullins notes a significant difference between the modern world and the historical realist Europe upon which he based his radical "Feedback" model of the direct-positive relationship (see "Feedback" section of this chapter): the tremendous impact—military, political, economic—of preexisting advanced countries on the development process (there were none during European development). Mullins suggests a patron-client relationship between pairs of advanced and developing countries. Economic dependency and political protection involving military assistance, economic aid, or collective security balance trade and investment preferences. This dependency brings political protection and economic support that insulate a client country from the international environment, and break the "normal" direct link between war and growth. This self-serving intervention of a powerful patron allows a client country to proceed with growth, or any other agenda, well insulated from obstacles, costs, and diversions of international conflict. Patron-client relationships sever any systematic growth-conflict linkages, and imply irrelevance between growth and conflict, with at best only a weak, insignificant, or coincidental linkage (see Diagram 3.2).

Diagram 3.2 Patron-Client Dependency

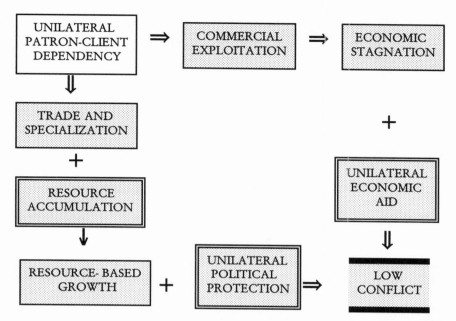

Mullins concludes that patron-client dependency between developing-country elites and militarily powerful advanced countries removes any threat of invasion. Absence of pressures for defense allows dependent nations to develop (or not) in response to domestic pressures. In addition to insulating a client from the threats of the realist world, development aid and military assistance from a patron could be expected to reduce the need to extract resources from a reluctant population. Mullins' scheme presumes a realist world of states that are—at least potentially—self-sufficient, autonomous, and distinct. Patron-client dependency theory would expect an increasingly ambiguous linkage as the international political-economy shifts from classical realist anarchy, with its feedback between growth and conflict, toward more liberal or hegemonic models of interdependent peoples and states.

Not only do growth and conflict neither stimulate nor hinder each other within a patron-client relationship, but they do not require, or even affect, each other: Mullins' feedback model simply fails. For the dependent nation, low conflict becomes an imposed norm, rather than a result of its own activities. (Mullins notes cryptically that Singapore and Malaysia are exceptions to his conclusions. He did not analyze other Asian situations.)

Although each has spawned various minor or purely imaginative subspecies, classical realism and patron-client dependency are the major species of the genus of irrelevant growth-conflict relationships. Their basic features are, as expected, quite similar (see Table 3.1).

Table 3.1 Orthodox Growth-Conflict Relationships—Irrelevant

THEORY   DETERMINANT SIGNIF (t-stat) STRENGTH (R²) DELAY

IRRELEVANT	POLITICS	INSIG (<2.0)	WEAK	?-?
Patron-Client Dependency	Patron Insulation	Insignif (<2.0)	Ambiguous (??)	??
Realism No Linkage	Political Power Security Regime	Insignif (<2.0)	Weak (<0.4)	Volatile Unclear

DIRECT POSITIVE RELATIONSHIP

Several mature species of the "direct-positive" genus rely on trade to transmute the economic process of growth into the political effect of international conflict. The first trade-related approach, classical mercantilism, was succeeded by more mellow versions in various economic forms of nationalism. So long as growth remained unusual and restricted to a few countries, it also fell conveniently into place in radical models of the international political-economy, which did not rely on trade to mediate a direct-positive growth-conflict relationship, and routinely rejected the realist irrelevance of growth to conflict. As growth became more salient, various structural and behavioral methods sought to explain its role in political-economy, and orthodox analysis broadened its focus to include both growth and war. Most approaches—mercantilist, economic nationalist, radical, behavioral, structural—have explicitly linked them with some sort of positive causality: growth causes conflict or conflict causes growth.

DIRECT-POSITIVE GROWTH-CONFLICT LINKAGE MODEL

ENGINE OF GROWTH is exogenous to the growth-conflict relationship, but usually involves national accumulation of resources, addition of technology to production processes, increases in national political power, and expansion of national economy through commerce or conquest.

DOMESTIC POLITICAL-ECONOMY is capitalist and hierarchic (variations of feudalism, monarchy, democracy, socialism, etc.), with substantial state involvement in economic and commercial affairs.

REALIST INTERNATIONAL POLITICAL-ECONOMY involves national states or protostates and their extensions, and international organizations, often with a primary focus on economic or nonpolitical issues; private firms trade and invest outside their home countries only at the sufferance of, or in partnership with, national states; one state often dominates as hegemon; hegemony or multilateral agreement impose some regime of free trade and international security.

INTERNATIONAL RELATIONS are primarily political, and a establish legal-political structure for inter-economy relations limited to trade and investment; trade is a significant political issue.

ECONOMIC GROWTH is predominantly quantitative and resource-based, measured in terms of national aggregates, based on increases of factors of production, limited by availability of resources, capital, and technology to national economies (labor is abundant), and sustainable through expansion of a national economy.

INTERNATIONAL CONFLICT occurs as polities seek to impose their values on each other, or protect their national advantages, through exercise, or projection of national political power; to register changes in an international balance of power; and as growing economies reaching limits of ready resources seek to continue growth by economic expansion.

LINKAGE between economic growth and international conflict is expected to be positive and strong, with rising internal pressures toward national expansion, as economic expectations rise beyond historic political limits; linkage may be weak or ambiguous, since some other variable often overwhelms any direct effect by generating a primarily political source of conflict or cooperation.

INTERNATIONAL SECURITY REGIMES control and contain international conflict (through collective security agreements, deterrence, crisis management, multilateral sanctions, coercion, and suppression by the great powers); lose effect periodically as hegemons rise and fall, as economic pressures increase, and as social-economic forces erupt; failure of a security regime brings catastrophic war; lesser conflict is both political and economic, and may be endemic to the prevailing international system.

POWER RESOURCES are levels of aggregate production, technology, productive population and productive national resources located on national territory; most important factors of production are capital and labor; larger territory, population, and military strength are less salient, and may be deemed disadvantageous in the pursuit of some national interests.

Mercantilism

Based on realist politics, materialist concepts of wealth, and absolute advantages among competing trade partners, mercantilism regards trade specifically, and economic interactions generally, as the dynamic foundations of distribution and levels of national power. National power rests on economic productivity and the ability of the state to apply it as force. Nations use power in a zero-sum political-economic game "in which the gains of one country (primacy) are seem as canceling out the losses of another (subordination) even if both achieve growing prosperity."[15]

Economic growth is a domestic process resulting from internal activities powerfully reinforced by trade. Only insofar as it involves trade is growth even related to international conflict: growth and conflict are both consequences of trade. Mercantilism looks to *both* economic *and* political sources to explain war and conflict, but does not see national economic growth as a very potent explanation.

Primitive mercantilism—Colbertian or Smithian—quickly identified the interests of producers with the national interest, and the economic wealth and growth of industry with the political-military power of the state. It was the responsibility of industry to generate wealth through efficient production, and of commerce to increase it through advantageous trade. The role of political-military power was to control the trade that energized the wealth-power spiral of national growth, and to manage the inevitable conflicts with other states doing the same. Classic mercantilists, and their neomercantilist descendants, see the free trade system as "a cause of conflict and insecurity."[16] The anarchy of international commerce is the primary venue for conflict at all levels and intensities.

Trading relations are the dynamic basis of political relationships, distribution of power, and absolute levels of national power, the issues that most often lead to conflict.[17] "Fair" competition and total war are extremes on a scale of conflict, along which particular combinations of industry and arms provide national advantage at various points. Higher levels of trade confer higher, disproportionate, economic gains on potential national adversaries, and render states vulnerable (not merely sensitive) to international economic fluctuations or economic manipulation by trading partners. The mercantilist prediction is that a high level of trade, but not necessarily growth, brings close interdependence that "means closeness of contact and raises the prospect of at least occasional conflict"[18] (see Diagram 3.3).

Diagram 3.3 Mercantilism

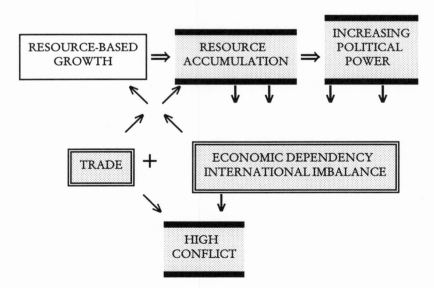

These mercantilist beliefs merge comfortably with classical realism in the presumption that conflict between self-interests of states is inherent in any sort of orderly international trading system. "Both of these closely related perspectives reflect the view that trade is naturally a form of war, though one fought by peaceful means."[19] Reducing trade reduces dependency on foreign sources and markets, and decreases vulnerability of national power to attack.

Mercantilism would expect growth to be positively correlated with trade, itself positively correlated with conflict. Any constructed relationship between the two dependent variables—growth and conflict—would be positive, unstable, unpredictable, and only coincidental. Some mercantilist thought could also support a self-reinforcing causality arising from particular kinds of growth or conflict through trade.

Economic Nationalism

In correctly anticipating the industrial nature of Ricardian comparative advantage, Alexander Hamilton originated the concepts of economic nationalism, which incorporated both trade protectionism and industrial development.[20] Hamilton began with the mercantilist linkage between trade and conflict, and argued that the infant United States should limit its foreign trade, and promote development of domestic industries through active protection from foreign competition:

> The aggregate strength of a nation . . . would be increased in every essential respect. The United States, by developing a diversified economy, would enjoy enhanced "security from external danger *less frequent interruption of their peace with foreign nations,* and what is more valuable, *an exemption from those broils and wars* between the [several] parts, if disunited, which their own rivalships, fomented by foreign intrigue . . . would inevitably produce."[21]

Hamiltonian nationalism developed a dynamic approach to economic growth based on restructuring a national economy to prefer manufacturing over agriculture. By authoritatively transferring factors of production and reallocating resources between economic sectors, and between national economies, national governments might thereby deliberately transform their economies and improve their trading positions in the international economy. More pragmatic than imperious, Hamilton advocated state protection of "infant industries" until they were able to maintain market share against mature foreign competitors, and reciprocity in opening and closing national markets. This simple premise has evolved into the modern conviction that a growing nation must protect all its industries—infant, disadvantaged, dominant, or mature—from unfair competition by changing the conditions of trade to benefit them. Hamilton felt that "economic policymakers should be guided by results rather than by dogmas in promoting state interests, such as national security and the diversification of the national economy."[22]

Extension and refinement of Hamilton's ideas in Germany and Austria during the nineteenth century (Johann Fichte, Georg Hegel, *etc.*[23]) led to the German Historical School (Friedrich List, William Roscher, Gustav Schmoller, *etc.*). These thinkers developed simple mercantilism into a sophisticated political-economic approach that gave primacy not to wealth, but to the power of producing wealth.[24] List's perception of developing countries' need to "catch up to" modern industrial countries complemented Hamilton's concept for protecting infant industries in rediscovery of Edward III's import-substitution-industrialization (ISI) development strategy, favored for the first stages of economic development by many modern economists and politicians. Inevitable cross-fertilization with Marxism, Colbertism, and continental realism eventually bloomed in the socialist branches of economic nationalism, as well as various theoretical explanations of the glide of Europe into World War I.

Working within the orthodox neoclassical paradigm, American economists and politicians expanded these ideas in a liberal direction, and defended free trade with "the new trade theory" (itself "little more than a recycling of the old Hamilton-List theory of tariff-driven industrial policy").[25] A subtle shift from "free" trade to "fair" trade, however, brought profound implications for both growth and conflict. For modern Hamiltonians, and economic nationalists, "free" trade is of less value than "fair" trade that promotes national interests. For Hamilton, however, both foreign policy and trade policy were simply means for establishing a strong, unified infant United States and a competent national government. National priorities of economic growth, political development, and national security always had first priorities, even at the expense of "free trade," or at the cost of international conflict.

Unlike the realist and the mercantilist, the economic nationalist has a narrow perspective, and focuses on a single country's interest. From the global realist perspective "the gains of one country (primacy) are seen as canceling out the losses of another (subordination) even if both achieve growing prosperity."[26] For individual states, however, "unequal gain is frequently more important than mutual gain. In order to increase their own relative gains, other nations seek to change the rules which tend to benefit the dominant industrial power(s)."[27] As market shares and competitive advantage change, losing nations can be expected to retaliate, usually in "unfair" ways that lead to disputes.

Like mercantilism, economic nationalism does not explicitly address the growth-conflict relationship, but sees both as results of trade. Growth flows not only from trade, but from industrialization, which increases a nation's trading advantage (see Diagram 3.4). Like realism and mercantilism, economic nationalism posits a zero-sum world of national rivalry mediated through trade—"free" and "closed." Economic nationalism would expect a strong positive correlation between the respective dependent variables. Since economic nationalism advocates an active government involvement in trade —through focused industrialization and protectionism—it might expect some stability and predictability in the relationship, arising from government's role.

Diagram 3.4 Economic Nationalism

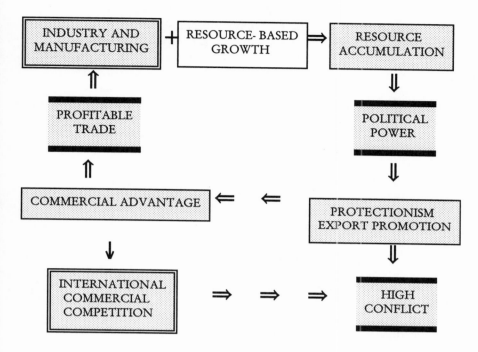

Marxism and Neo-Marxism

To Marxist thinkers, economic growth was both a dependent variable generated by capitalism and the proximate cause of international conflict. This latter could be eliminated by repressing, sharing, or diffusing growth, and establishing a peaceful socialist world, in which growth would benefit all society, not just capitalists. Marxism proposed violent revolution to achieve this happy state. Karl Marx not only explains the ills of society, but provides a remedy. Societies would be innately peaceful, eschewing conflict—both within and among themselves—if they were not capitalist. The plethora of "internal contradictions" surrounding private ownership and a free market condemns capitalist economies to competitive expansion in search of resources, profits, and markets. This unrelenting pressure to expand forces nations into ever more conflict with each other. While Marx's own analysis was focused at a national level, Lenin, and later neo-Marxists, expanded and refined it into a global concept to explain nineteenth-century imperialism, and to justify twentieth-century Soviet foreign policy.

The first serious hint that any links between growth and conflict may be more than incidental in human affairs came with V. I. Lenin's extension of Marxist materialism into international relations. His internationalism reflected

John Hobson's theories linking nineteenth-century European conflicts over African and Asian territories to an irrational "search for outlets for surplus which could not be sold at home."[28] Lenin transmuted Hobson's "irrationality" from a behavioral feature of international political decision-makers into a powerful, systemic element of international political-economy, which permeated all political decision-making, regardless of the personalities of individual decision-makers.

In Lenin's system, Marx's prediction of a falling profit rate as capitalism developed fit comfortably with Rudolph Hilferding's 1907 theory for integration of bank finance and industrial capital. Large cartels and monopolies gave a few capitalists controlling influence over governments, and changed the capitalist battle for markets into a political struggle for territory. The inevitable result was military confrontation and, ultimately, war. Uncontrolled *capitalist* growth led to imperialist expansion through deliberate conflict with other nations and oppression of their peoples. Lenin expanded Hobson's concept of imperialism to encompass "the entire set of unequal economic relations between capitalist countries—between rival mature capitalist countries fighting for markets as well as between mature countries and developing economies which become their markets."[29]

Presented first in *Imperialism: The Highest Stage of Capitalism*, Lenin's theory accounts for much of the pre-1914 commercial and colonial conflict in terms of capitalist growth in Europe, but focuses uniquely on the economic consequences of growth and industrialization. He simply accepts conflict and war as integral parts of the process, and chooses to deemphasize the profound sociopolitical effects of industrialization on the distribution of power among national and colonial states. Nor does he consider in any depth the proposition that uneven growth—on a global scale—shifts the distribution of power. The process of economic growth as it occurred in Europe and diffused through empires would lead to political conflict—international and domestic—when:

> The rate of growth falls below a level politically acceptable to all interest groups and population, and sufficient to maintain legitimacy of the regime and political-economic system (insurgency, revolution, *coup d'etat*, etc.); or
> Additional resources are no longer available without expansion of the economy beyond its political borders (capital through markets or raw materials; labor through populations; technology through nationalization or technology markets) (territorial war, aggression, colonization, trade war). *This would also follow in a realist anarchic "self-help" world.*

In subtle contrast to realism, Marxism-Leninism found the primary motives and means for imperial expansion to be economic and commercial —albeit under a political-military aegis, and always accompanied by armies and navies. As national economies sought both sources and markets through controlled trade, expansion brought conflict between expanding Europeans and indigenous peoples, and among Europeans themselves as they escalated commercial competition to military confrontation.

The incorporation of the periphery into the world economy frequently meant imposition on these areas and peoples of onerous restrictions, and heavy discrimination. Extraterritoriality privileges for Europeans and Americans and denial of tariff autonomy were common. Where local rulers opposed opening their countries to trade and investment, Britain and the other industrial powers felt few qualms about forcing them open to establish "law and order."[30]

Rosa Luxemburg, Nicolai Bukharin, Immanuel Wallerstein, and several generations of Soviet leaders and theorists developed and refined Lenin's theories on imperialism to reflect their perceptions of the modern world. Several strands of the materialist Marxist-Leninist approach include anti-imperial neocolonialism (after exploitation as colonies many countries are still exploited through nonpolitical, but efficient, economic techniques); *dependencia* (poor countries are inherently disadvantaged, and kept so by the world trading system dominated by the industrialized countries); modern world system (poor countries are essential to prosperity of core countries, but condemned to the periphery by rich, powerful core countries preserving their own privileges and wealth). A few common threads of Lenin's central idea form the essential strands of continuity through them all:

a capitalist economy cannot absorb its own production, because of its contradictory structure, and is ineluctably impelled toward conflict;

territorial, commercial, and geopolitical expansion and escalation into conflict are the ultimate consequences of economic competition, as capitalists seek raw materials, markets, and additional investments for their surplus capital; and

war results from political, economic, or military expansion through imperialism; "their real stake is the division of the planet. . . . They are accelerated by the growing disparity between the mother countries and the colonial empires—by the advent of the era of the closed world."[31]

The common prediction of both orthodox Marxism and the derivative neo-Marxist and Leninist approaches is that all countries cannot grow simultaneously; growth and political-economy are immutably zero-sum. Nor are mere people able to decide which countries are to grow and which are to stagnate. Those countries that grow *must* exploit those that do not through trade and investment in accordance with Marx's eternal materialistic forces of production. Imperialism and war are the immutable consequences of capitalistic expansion and economic exploitation. Revolution is the only way to break historic patterns of exploitation. The only rational course is to accept this condition, since humanity cannot change it. The only moral thing to do is to accelerate the course of history through active, violent revolution.

Diagram 3.5 Marxism-Leninism

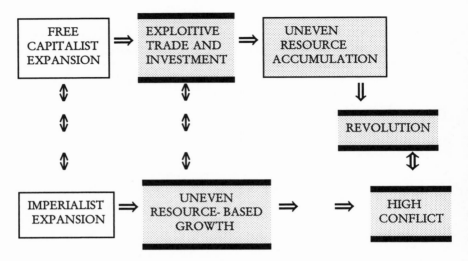

Marxism would expect—and even define—growth to be directly and positively associated with conflict. The growth-conflict relationship would be strong and causal, stable and predictable, and not subject to human manipulation (see Diagram 3.5).

Although these materialistic approaches all have some intuitive credence and ideological credibility, they contradict substantial evidence of sporadic, scattered growth in the eighteenth, nineteenth and early twentieth centuries and massive, sustained, worldwide growth since World War II. Many countries have overcome imperial exploitation (Canada, Malaysia, Indonesia, Australia), reversed their dependency (Brazil, Mexico, Japan), and ascended in the global hierarchy (South Korea, Finland, Israel, Singapore) without either catastrophic international conflict or violent domestic revolution, and little more than commercial competition. "[T]he breakdown of the international economy and the outbreak of war were the results of political rivalries among nation-states and not of economic conflicts among capitalists and foreign investors."[32]

Although Marxism, like other approaches, provides some intellectual satisfaction in its ability to explain some conflicts, its champions have not been able to demonstrate a robust relationship

> between the purely economic need for expansion, such as should have obtained according to the theory, and the actual facts of colonial expansion. . . . Neither the First nor the Second World War originated directly in a conflict over colonies. . . . None of the colonial undertakings that caused important diplomatic conflicts in Europe was motivated by the quest for capitalist profits; they all originated in political ambitions that the chancelleries camouflaged by invoking "realistic" motives.[33]

"Feedback"

Virtually all modern analysis of the economic development process places economic growth as the dependent variable, and seeks to identify a relationship to achieve or accelerate growth through manipulation of domestic policy variables. In a departure from convention, A. F. Mullins,[34] citing William McNeill[35] and Samuel Finer,[36] suggests that state creation and economic growth in a realist, anarchic world require significant military activity, both domestic and external. As national power coalesces in response to external threats or opportunities, emerging nations' involvements in international conflict have a powerful impact on their development strategies, growth paths, and their respective successes or failures.

For European countries in the seventeenth, eighteenth, and nineteenth centuries, striving for military capability in a hostile, anarchic world was the driving force in creating the modern state. National armies and navies were keys to survival in the Hobbesian world of international anarchy. As they grew, they became more expensive. Leaders of European protostates learned to use their armies for increasing penetration into their own domestic economies to extract resources to pay for their increasingly necessary military forces. The result was a "feedback" circle, both "vicious" and "virtuous." Larger armies and navies not only provided security and expansion, but enabled greater internal penetration and extraction of domestic resources, which permitted greater military power. National security was necessary for political survival, and economic expansion was required for economic survival. Each required national economic growth, which permitted accumulation of military power, which enabled and required, more economic growth.

Mullins does not analyze his "feedback" dynamic in the modern world of total war—the Napoleonic wars, World War I, World War II, and the Cold War—and the subsequent rapid economic growth in much of the world. His "feedback effect" operated under two implicit "state-of-the-world" conditions, which characterized the era of European history that he analyzed:

> military capability is equally useful for external security and internal policing; and
>
> the extant international political-economy is anarchic; only national military power can provide security.

Mullins' concept suggests—in an odd sort of "reverse Leninist" argument— that growth naturally arises *from* international conflict, which is itself caused —or at least stimulated—by economic growth. "Feedback" theory would expect strong positive correlation between growth and conflict in realist Europe of the fifteenth through eighteenth centuries, but, like mercantilism, would have difficulty in assigning any direction of causality (see Diagram 3.6). Since everything seems to lead to, and flow from, everything else. Like Marxism, feedback theory suggests that it is all inevitable.

Diagram 3.6 "Feedback"

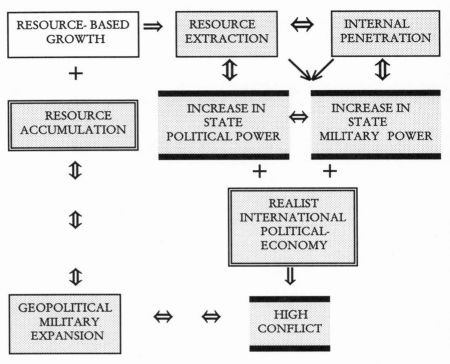

The period of relative peace and obvious prosperity in the late twentieth century intuitively suggests—as Mullins implies—that industrialized "total" war may mutate his "state-of-the-world" preconditions. The emergence of deterrence as a prominent national strategy during the Cold War seems necessarily to destroy his model. Feedback theory would continue to lose explanatory power as reality diverged from Mullins' realist "state-of-the-world" parameters. Further, Mullins argues that because his prerequisite conditions do not hold, this "European model" does not apply to the modern world, and has been replaced by a different model of patron-client dependency (see section on "Patron-Client Dependency" earlier in this Chapter).

In a world of political-economic interdependence and deterrence, the political-military features that dominate a realist world may evolve to become purely industrial-economic conditions that leave huge gaps between industrial supply and consumer demand. Commerce and trade may replace diplomacy and war as the definitive processes for international relations. Under such conditions, the feedback dynamic could operate through international commerce, while governments, well provided with tax revenues or official aid, would be left to deal with political things, as commercial liberalism urges.

Long Waves, Hegemony, Trade, and War

Nicolai Kondratieff's controversial results,[37] Fernand Braudel's sweeping epochal judgments (see Appendix C), and many subsequent analyses confirm the observations of previous historians of some linkage at a global level between growth and conflict, but do not adduce causality. Commonly known as "the Kondratieff War Generalization," these analyses stress correlation of war with upswing-rise phases of cyclic growth. Comparison of the list of wars generated for the Correlates of War project (1816-1914) with Kondratieff's waves indicates clearly that

> not only the most severe wars but also most of the interstate wars of the 1816-1914 period were initiated during the long wave's upswing. Of thirty-five wars, as many as twenty-eight (80%) began during the upswing. . . . Kondratieff's war generalization is readily substantiated, at least as a descriptive statement for the era between the Napoleonic Wars and World War I.[38]

Raimo Vayrynen's variant[39] of the Kondratieff War Generalization (see Appendix C) refines a trade-related link between Kondratieff waves and conflict by broadening the political-economic context. Deemphasizing trade as a sufficient—but not necessary—variable, Vayrynen introduces, instead, political contextual change as the necessary—but not sufficient—intervening variable for generation of war. Following Joseph Schumpeter's four-phase long-wave dating scheme (prosperity, recession, depression, recovery), Vayrynen focuses explicitly on phases of global economic growth as an independent variable. Assuming that hegemonic predominance discourages challenges and brings stability, Vayrynen suggests that hegemonic maturity is most peaceful, and that ascension is most bellicose.[40] Although Vayrynen's argument seems inherently sound, and intuitively appealing, its additional complexity predicts history no better than any other model, and adds little to Kondratieff's War Generalization.[41]

In the spirit of liberalism, various modern analyses have linked aggregate global growth to international relations through trade by combining Kondratieff's results, and Vayrynen's insights, with hegemonic stability theory. In close parallel evolutions, the global economy experiences two long waves for every four phases of the political hegemonic cycle: each phase of the cycle, with its accompanying "open" or "closed" international trade regime and hegemonic security regime, is associated with either an upswing or a downswing in the parallel Kondratieff cycle. Hegemonic ascension and maturity phases occur with upswings; hegemonic victory and decline phases occur with downswings.

In the maturity phase the commercial competitive and economic superiority of modern hegemons have led them generally toward free trade policies and an open trading system, national economic growth focused on domestic resources, and expansion until supply exceeds demand. Stephen Krasner has shown that these periods of open trading systems, which coincide with hegemonic ascension and maturity (Kondratieff upswings), have included more wars than periods of closure.[42] Edward Mansfield has verified the conclusion,[43] although the data sets of Lewis Richardson or the analyses of Melvin Small and David Singer indicate the reverse. For all data sets, moreover, "the incidence of war tends to be higher during the last half of openness than during the first half."[44] Nevertheless, he finds virtually no evidence that "whether the trading system is open or closed helps to account for variations in the outbreak of war."[45]

Despite some ambiguous results in his own, and other, analyses of Kondratieff cycles and war (both domestic and interstate), Mansfield suggests that "the outbreak of wars may be correlated with long-term movements in the global economy."[46] When war data include only interstate wars, however, "the results are not quite so robust."[47] Further refining his broad analysis, Mansfield finds that "the mean number of wars tends to decline during transitions from upswings to downswings (in three out of five cases); and the incidence of war also tends to be lower during the first half than the last half of both types of periods."[48] Focused in Mansfield's work, Kondratieff's generalization, Vayrynen's variant, and several derivative theories, incorporate hegemonic stability theory into international political-economic relations, and agree broadly that changes in hegemonic leadership involve instability—political and economic—which generates conflict.

Diagram 3.7 Hegemonic Stability and Long Waves

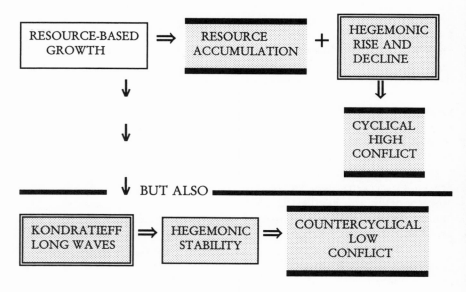

These theories collectively suggest that growth can generate conflict, but only when political change is also occurring anyway. Long-wave hegemonic-stability theories would expect a parallel, but not causal, relationship between growth and conflict (see Diagram 3.7). Economic growth of a rising state increases its ability and aspiration to challenge a dominant hegemon, especially when the hegemon is in decline. Conversely, growth of a dominant or rising hegemon allows it to assert dominance through threatened or actual conflict, to devote its energies to continuing its commercial and economic advantages, or even to maintain a judicious case-specific combination of both techniques.

Core-Periphery Interdependence

In a generalization of Mullins' bilateral patron-client structure, Robert Gilpin has put the core-periphery concept in a context of interdependence theory. Refining earlier skepticism,[49] he has extended both far beyond Immanuel Wallerstein's stable modern world system or the theory of hegemonic stability. In contrast to concentration of wealth and power in either a hegemon or the core states, as interdependence increases between core and periphery, growth spreads and wealth diffuses. In an inverted generalization of hegemonic decline, growth is faster in the less developed periphery, as its economic power increases relative to that of the advanced core nations. Rising expectations and appreciation of its growing strength and power—economic and political—generate dissatisfaction and ambition, rather than violent revolution, with periphery dependency on the core.[50] Sustained by the set of materialistic and social contributing variables intrinsic to core-periphery dependency, rapid growth in the periphery activates Marxism's immutable, positive growth-conflict relationship.

Departing from orthodox Marxian approaches, Gilpin's political-economic analysis concludes that "as the periphery grows in strength the tendency is for it to break away from the core"[51] (see Diagram 3.8).

Diagram 3.8 Core-Periphery Dependence

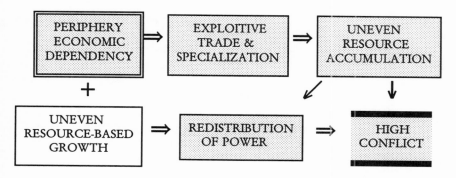

While focusing on the economic effects of uneven growth within a system of interdependence, Gilpin predicts international conflict through "undermining of the economic and political order . . . as [peripheral nations] seek to reorganize the world economy in order to advance their own economic and political interests."[52] Even though tempered by the effects of interdependence and sustained growth in the core, conflict arises from uneven economic growth, as growing periphery nations use their increasing wealth to redistribute international power.

Core-periphery interdependence theory would expect a high correlation between peripheral growth and international conflict, although some threshold growth rate—increasing for periphery growth and decreasing for core growth—may trigger any causality. The critical causal factor, however, is not simply growth in the periphery, but depends on what is occurring in the core. The strength and stability of the growth-conflict relationship depend on various factors other than growth, including Vayrynen's ambiguous changing political context. While Gilpin does not expound, and Wallerstein seems content to describe the modern world system with few predictions, the rates of divergent growth between core and periphery, and their respective degrees of dependence and interdependence seem intuitively critical.

Uneven Growth

Simon Kuznets' seminal work on modern economic growth leads inescapably to the suggestion that uneven growth would operate through his triad of intervening variables to pull an international system ineluctably toward conflict. He speculated that high rates of economic growth, and wide differences in rates of growth, "cumulated rapidly into marked shifts in relative economic and political power among nations—a situation usually provocative of international strain and conflict."[53]

From a historian's perspective, Paul Kennedy found a similar phenomenon in *changes in national wealth relative to other powers* (see "Power Position" section). He suggested that this particular sort of growth (uneven) was a causal process variable in the path from growth to conflict.[54] Like Kuznets, Kennedy seemed content simply to note an apparent relationship; he did not speculate about its effects on international relations.

Accepting the historical record uncritically and taking much previous work at face value, Robert Gilpin's early work simply asserted, in expansion of Kuznets' thinking, that "emergence of several large economically developed countries is the necessary, if not sufficient, condition for the occurrence of world wars."[55] He later generalized a more focused positive relationship around Kennedy's observation about uneven growth. Accepting—apparently as a premise for his theories about political economy—that "uneven economic growth tends to lead to political conflict," he refined the argument even more by asserting that even shifts in location of economic activity (which might lead to uneven growth) can generate conflict.[56]

Diagram 3.9 Uneven Growth

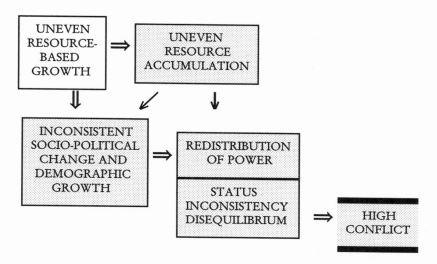

In a significant project that brought needed focus to the field, Michael Wallace pointedly adopted uneven growth as an independent variable, and continued along the line of thought that flowed from Kuznets through Gilpin. Wallace defined unevenness in terms of quantitative rates of growth (population, economic, military). His work extended across both structuralism and behavioralism, and suggested that differences in national growth rates were "closely associated with status inconsistency"[57] (see later section, "Status-Field Theory"). For Wallace, this was the critical intervening variable which could lead from growth to international war and conflict (see Diagram 3.9). Neither absolute growth nor uneven growth were sufficient in themselves to generate conflict. Wallace's great insight was, however, that uneven growth generated status inconsistency, a necessary intervening variable in the causal path.

Wallace tested several hypotheses with a variety of other contributing and independent variables, as well as other intervening variables between uneven growth and conflict. His conclusions pointed clearly to uneven growth and status inconsistency as a critical pair of variables. He did not, however, prefer a particular causal path from uneven growth through status inconsistency to conflict. While they do not allow generalization or specify status inconsistency in any rigorous way, his results suggest that

> wide discrepancies which exist between national rates of economic development and population growth have the effect of sharply intensifying international violence by increasing the level of status inconsistency in the international system and perhaps by directly inducing the polarization of international alignments as well.[58]

Like Kuznets and Kennedy, Gilpin was not initially trying to explain any relationship between growth and conflict, but to argue that conflict is not inherent to international politics.   The intrusion of growth into these arguments seems almost incidental.   Arguing in parallel with Kuznets, and extending Kennedy's observation, Gilpin's later work adopted Wallace's perspective on growth as an independent variable. He suggested that uneven growth could stimulate conflict by undermining the international *status quo*, but only through some other additional intervening political-military power-based variable. "The resulting redistribution of power and its effect on the standing and welfare of individual states accentuate growth-based conflict, and may also introduce purely political issues as nations struggle for dominance."[59]

Unlike orthodox liberal, behavioral, and structural theories, and in dramatic contrast to realist premises of irrelevance, these analysts recognize the salience of growth-related conflict between rising and declining states, and attribute it to "unevenness."   Insertion of an intervening variable—change in distribution of wealth and power among states, change or inconsistency in national status, or purely political issues—completes the "uneven growth" syllogism.   Uneven growth theories would expect any relationships between growth and conflict to be positive, dependent on some other critical intervening variable, and not very predictable.   Uneven growth was a necessary, but not sufficient, condition for international conflict.

Kuznets' Triad

Like other analysts, Simon Kuznets noticed an *apparent correlation between growth and war*, but merely speculated about it, suggesting various influences that may affect the relationship. He observed that following early British growth, the growth of other European countries, especially Germany after 1870, shifted the distribution of power, led to conflict, and eventually brought what Lenin conceived as hegemonic, or imperialistic, war. Kuznets speculated that "[m]any wars in the second half of the nineteenth and in the early twentieth century, appear to have been due indirectly to shifts in economic and related power."[60]

Kuznets inferred a clear positive linkage between growth (which he defines explicitly) and increase in power (whose definition he leaves to insight), which rests more on a nation's economically productive use of its resources, than on military might. Growth would increase political influence and economic advantage. These would create parallel disadvantage and decreases in other nations' power, which would tend toward conflict. He suspected that rapid growth in some nations, consequent to industrialization, paired with stagnation in others could vitiate the security regime binding the global community together.

Kuznets formulated his analyses within a broad, inchoate integration of liberalism and realism with several bits of materialism. Recognizing the complexity of any such nexus, he introduced a powerful triad of intervening political and economic variables and suggested several dynamic linkages.

Rising Expectations = In a murky brew of fear, threat and perception, growing nations' aspirations to wealth and advantage, and others' efforts to retain theirs, would generate conflict.

Concentration of Power = While causality remained vague, capital accumulation and technology development before World War I concentrated power and increased military capabilities, and enabled nations to conduct larger wars.[61]

Redistribution of Power = In a spirit of structuralism, with overtones of materialism, Kuznets suggested that increasing economic differences among national economies (and hence, disparities in power and status) would disrupt the distribution of power.

In a bold departure from orthodox ambiguity, Kuznets predicted frequent shifts of economic, and military, power in an age of rapid, continuous growth; and frequent conflicts to test such changes.[62] Suggesting that "major wars were associated with the emergence in the course of modern economic growth of several large and developed nations,"[63] he finally concluded that

the spread of modern economic growth to a number of large developed countries constituted a necessary, if not sufficient, condition for world wars and for the increasing strain of backwardness which forced the powerful central governments to take a more active part in the initiation of economic modernization[64] (see Diagram 3.10).

Diagram 3.10 Kuznets' Triad

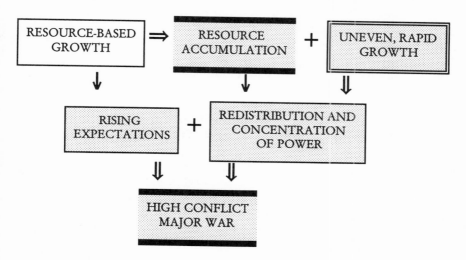

Power Position

In his formidable historical analysis of Europe during its modern growth and modernization, Paul Kennedy linked economic growth (and possibly economic decline), through a dynamic international system of power and status, to conflict and war that seemed to operate within—or at least in parallel with—Kuznets' triad (see Diagram 3.11).

Diagram 3.11 Linkage Through Power Position

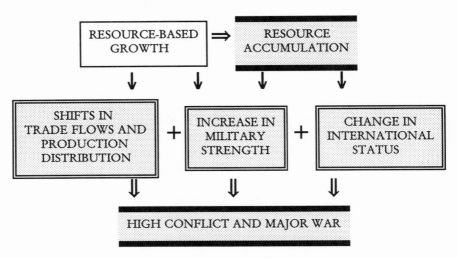

Kennedy's analytical intent—like those of so many other analysts—did not lead him to much more than observation of the intervening structural and process variables, and some broad speculation about them. Incidental to his primary historical focus, however, he corroborated other quantitative results of emerging status theory (see later section, "Status-Field Theory") and detected: "a causal relationship between the shifts which have occurred over time in the general economic and productive balances and the position occupied by individual Powers in the international system."[65]

Kennedy suggested that shifts in trade flows (a process variable) and distribution of production (a structural variable) have "heralded the rise of new Great Powers," and found a "very clear connection" between a power's economic growth (a domestic process) and its rise as a military power (an international status), albeit with noticeable "lag time."[66]

L. N. Rangarajan's earlier suggestion that change in a country's military "status" brings conflict completes the growth-conflict linkage through power position.[67] Kennedy further noted (in parallel with Rudolph Rummel's quantitative field-status-theory work) that the pivotal feature of the relationship between wealth and power—and hence between growth and conflict—is not a change in *absolute* wealth over time, but change in wealth *relative* to neighboring powers: uneven economic growth.

The Power Transition Model

Reflecting the increasing salience of economic factors in international relations, an alternative to the classical models of balance-of-power and collective security emerged during the Industrial Revolution. This approach recognized that nonpolitical, economic factors—but not just trade—were exerting as much influence on international behaviors as were traditional political-military structures; the nature of power was in transition. In addition to considerations of population, territory, and military might, the relevant aspects of national power were economic, social, and political. Rather than the unstable balance of political-military power resources inherent to an anarchic realist world, the emerging set of economic power resources would converge around a stable political-economic "imbalance of power."

The growth-conflict linkage operates through two intervening variables: change in the imbalance of power and differences in growth rates that accelerate such change. Change in the imbalance of power is affected not only by uneven growth, but by reinforcing contributions of several other important power resources (both economic and political-military). Further, fundamental changes in the nature of power resources allow them to intensify the effects of economic growth on the imbalance of power, and moderate traditional effects of political-military power.

What A.F.K. Organski and Jacek Kugler have called the "power Transition" model predicts low conflict within a large imbalance of power, which discourages conflict. Less powerful, upwardly mobile, dissatisfied countries would tend to be aggressors, rather than more powerful nations. Conflict would become likely as a stable imbalance became a metastable balance, and would erupt when ignited by a "routine" crisis.[68]

Power Resources

In predominantly agrarian premodern economies the power resources were population and territory—bases for taxation, food production, and military forces—and ultimately some form of self-sufficiency. Small countries had to grow through geographic expansion. For large, populous countries (Spain, France, China, India) able to dominate their regions of the world, even in purely economic terms, "it was cheaper to seize another's territory by force than to develop the sophisticated economic and trading apparatus to derive benefit from commercial exchange with it."[69]

Emerging hesitantly in the nineteenth century, new forces of economics, nationalism, and technology began to reduce the salience of territory, geography, and raw materials—geopolitical resources—even as indices of national power. In addition to dramatic increases in financial costs of military operations, nationalism severely inhibited the governments' capacities to mobilize foreign populations in weaker states. Technology extended the scope and range of international relations from diplomacy and war to all sorts of global relationships between groups of people, including mutual annihilation and commercial monopoly. Ruptures in trade relationships began to create high "opportunity costs" that could be unacceptable. The maturation and expansion of Lockean-Jeffersonian democracy generated powerful worldwide public opposition to prolonged, expensive military conflicts. Finally, the entire territory and population of the world were nationalized.[70]

Richard Rosecrance has suggested a twentieth-century world teetering in transition between the older territorial system and a modern commercial, trading system. In the latter, states recognize any sort of self-sufficiency as illusory and fleeting, and perceive national power in behavioral terms as the ability to influence world affairs of all sorts, not just peace and war. Economic-commercial linkages have become at least as important as diplomatic and military relationships in each nation's power calculus. Many international relationships that would have been expected to generate war in past epochs are patently inappropriate as *causae belli* in the modern world,[71] and others erupt unexpectedly into international violence.

Under the power transition model, gross national product (GNP) or gross domestic product (GDP) are parsimonious gauges of national physical capabilities, while population (reflecting size of the workforce and human resources) indicates less tangible resources. The value of populations is less as soldiers than as workers, and highest as a source of technology and solidarity. *Per capita* income measures productivity well, and taxes serve as a suitable indicator of government ability to mobilize resources.

Assessments of national power are no longer limited to military force structures, political will, and military industries. Strategic analysts stress technology, intellectual capital and knowledge, education, productivity and trade, political stability, and capacities to gain and hold global market share —commercial resources all associated with growth. These national attributes (not military forces, weapon inventories, or alliance networks) determine the imbalance of power. Military power cannot overcome differences in socioeconomic, demographic, and political attributes of nations. "Most important are economic productivity and the efficiency of the political system in extracting and aggregating human and material resources into pools available for national purposes."[72]

In the paradox suspected by Percy Bysshe Shelley and Reinhold Niebuhr, power resources arm the "goodness" of growth, but bring the "pestilence" of conflict.[73] The same variables are, paradoxically, both necessary preconditions of growth, and contributors to the power imbalance, operating as an intervening variable linking growth to conflict.

Difference in Growth Rates

The power transition model makes differences in growth rates—not simply uneven growth—another intervening variable in disturbing a stable imbalance of power. In a refinement of the uneven growth syllogism, power transition theory accepts growth as a necessary, but not sufficient, independent variable, *which does not necessarily lead to conflict*. The additional presence of uneven growth *rates* across countries as an intervening variable *does lead to conflict*.

As the economic aspects of power supplant the political-military foundations of international politics, "growth is the source of power. The distribution of power and shifts in that distribution shape the evolution of conflicts."[74] The changing nature of power implies that rapid, uneven economic growth—the result of differences in growth rates—leads to major shifts in the distribution of power. These shifts include powerful tendencies toward conflict *both* as nations migrate from one level of power to another *and* as the stable imbalance degenerates to unstable parity. If growth across countries is slow and proportional, shifts in relative power will be small, and can be accommodated without conflict. Rapid uneven growth is the result of differences in growth rates, and a necessary, but not sufficient, condition for international conflict.

A combination of a necessary, but not sufficient, independent variable (economic growth) and a powerful contributing variable (changing power resources) with a pair of sufficient, but possibly not necessary, intervening variables (power imbalance and differences in growth rates) links growth positively to conflict. Power transition theory expects no link between low growth and conflict, but strong positive correlation between uneven, rapid growth and international conflict (see Diagram 3.12).

Diagram 3.12 Power Transition

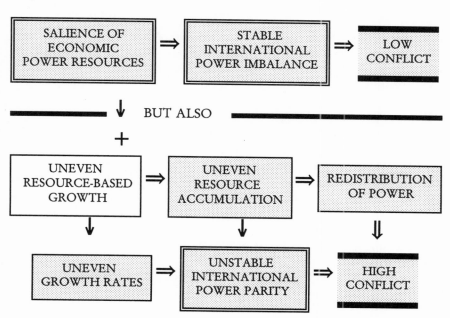

Growth is not a sufficient or causal agent, and may not even be a necessary variable. In the absence of *both* intervening variables growth may be irrelevant to conflict. In the absence of other power resources, growth may not occur, but conflict may arise anyway from purely political sources. While growth may not affect a stable imbalance of power, uneven growth can readily disrupt an unstable power parity. Like other theories of uneven growth, power transition theory emphasizes not absolute growth, but rates of growth. Nations with different growth rates would show parallel, proportional growth-conflict correlations. The interaction of growth rate and power resources

> determines the power available to a country. . . . Power and development go together, and as one changes so does the other . . . the manner and speed of national growth and development change the pools of resources available to nations, . . . such changes create the conditions in which international conflicts occur. . . . It is in the relative size and the patterns of growth of the members of a system that the rules governing behavior in international military conflicts are to be found.[75]

Status-field Theory

Status-field theory, developed by Rudolph J. Rummel, relies on quantitative and statistical methodology to integrate the behavioral status approach into field theory. Whereas field theory sees "distances" between entities as determinants of their behaviors, status theory uses "stratification" as a determinant. By redefining status of states as the distance between specific attributes, or groups of attributes—many of which involve economic growth— status-field theory unites both concepts. Status disequilibrium generates cognitive dissonance that leads states to restore balance to their status, often into conflict with other states. Pairs of states showing incongruent or inconsistent statuses tend to be uncertain about how to deal with each other, and drift into unstable relationships. Both inconsistency and disequilibrium seem to be associated with international conflict.

Status Theory

Status theory posits two distinct generators of international conflict: status disequilibrium and status inconsistency. Each can be activated by economic growth (as well as by other processes) and can lead to international conflict. The general concept of which Kennedy's "power position" dynamic is a specific single-variable application (see Diagram 3.11), status theory locates every nation relative to others in a hierarchy of status based on relative values of national attributes. Each nation's position in the hierarchy determines its "status" along any single attribute or dimension (group of attributes), relative to other nations.[76]

Status inconsistency arises when nations have different statuses, or show significant divergence, along a single attribute or dimension (growth rates for population or GDP, military strength, international influence, *etc.*), and present incompatible attribute profiles. Status disequilibrium arises where a nation's attribute profile is internally unbalanced across relevant dimensions, or where different nations are unbalanced across different dimensions.

In his early work on status theory, Johann Galtung[77] observed that many aggressive national states, especially in modern times, seemed to show inconsistency between their "achieved" dimensions of national status (military strength, industrial capacity, GNP, *etc.*) and their "ascribed" international status (recognition, prestige, influence, *etc.*).[78] Rapid economic growth relative to another nation immediately increased the "achieved" status of the growing nation (especially under Organski and Kugler's concepts of the changing nature of power; [see "Power Transition Model" section]). It also created between the growing nation's own high "achieved" and the low status still "ascribed" to it by the rest of the world a destabilizing disequilibrium, which dissipates only after significant delay, as other nations accept the new distribution of power. Galtung implies that this growth-based combination of disequilibrium and delay is a sufficient condition for international conflict.[79]

Status theory predicts that cooperation should be inversely proportional to differences between states on the relevant status dimension: states with compatible, balanced, consistent attribute profiles should be most cooperative. Conflict arises from status disequilibrium or inconsistency as each tries to balance its status upward, and threatens the dominance or challenge of the other.[80]

Field Theory

With origins in physics, and adapted into the social sciences through Kurt Lewin's contributions in psychology,[81] field theory analyzes the total situation or "life space" of an entity-in-environment as an integral constellation of interdependent factors, influences, and attributes. Quincy Wright, and other international field theorists, placed states within a geographic-social field defined by time-space coordinates overlaid with national values and capabilities. Wright's field was a description of the real world, with its distributions of people, resources, production, and power, and changes in these distributions over time.

By locating each state along each of these several dimensions, and identifying it with a multidimensional coordinate, Wright sought both to describe the international field at any moment, to explain the past, and predict the future.[82] International field theorists argued that states change their field positions over time and form new relationships with each other. The behavior of states was, thus, relative to their respective positions in the multidimensional field-space along dimensions of attributes, values, capabilities, and external influences.

Status-field Theory

Three complex research projects in the 1970s—Dimensionality of Nations (DON),[83] Correlates of War,[84] and Comparative Research on the Events of Nations (CREON)[85]—began to weave strands of status theory into those of field theory. The results indicated that national status, as reflected in attributes, exerted significant influences on conflict behaviors. Not limited to growth, attributes included several measures of economic—industrialization, wealth, levels of trade, *etc*. Dependent variables involved many aspects of international relations, including war, nonwar conflict, and cooperation.

Rudolph Rummel began the formidable DON project by investigating whether a single attribute—internal conflict—was associated with international conflict.[86] In expanding Raymond Cattell's work on war and domestic conflict,[87] Rummel's factor analysis confirmed Cattell's results and showed that, for a single state,

> *there are no common conditions or causes of domestic- and foreign-conflict behavior* . . . rapid industrialization, underdevelopment, totalitarian regimes, or unstable political systems cannot be the general cause of both, as is often asserted. Such conditions may serve as *necessary* causes, producing the required atmosphere for conflict behavior, but the *sufficient* condition setting off the [conflict] behavior differs as one goes from internal to external conflict behavior [emphasis in original].[88]

Nor was a subsequent refined hypothesis that related levels of national economic and technical development to foreign conflict confirmed by the results of the DON project. "not one of the foreign conflict measures had as much as ten percent of its variation associated with the [economic development] dimension. . . . [T]he most variation the economic development variables have in common with foreign conflict is 12.2 percent."[89]

Rummel's findings supported Brian Berry's factor analysis, whose correlations of a "technological dimension" (energy consumption, electricity *per capita*, and fiber consumption *per capita*) were near zero.[90] Both results suggested that "magnitudes within the two systems [attributes and behaviors] are not related. In other words, nations' characteristics do not predict their intensity of foreign conflict."[91]

Refining Quincy Wright's field theory, and the psychological work of Kurt Lewin, who had influenced Wright,[92] Rummel surmised that field differences, rather than attributes *per se*, influenced national behaviors,[93] and argued that "nation attribute similarities and differences are field forces creating space-time motion; attribute distance between nations cause [*sic*] international behavior."[94]

Refining the relative-values principle (see note 78), Rummel proposed that the relevant explanation of conflict behaviors is not a nation's absolute of power "but its relative power *vis-à-vis* some explicit other nation."[95] Rummel used attributes to measure states' field distances, and posited that

> crucial concepts within the two systems deal not with magnitudes, but with distance between nations in the attribute system and directed behavior between nations in the behavioral system. . . . the position of a dyad along the conflict dimension is a function of the distance between the two nations on value, economic development, power, and geographic dimensions.[96]

In parallel with Wallace's emphasis on uneven growth rates as generators of conflict (see section on "Uneven Growth") in a test of Rosenau's linkage hypothesis,[97] Rummel found that changes in relative levels of national income, energy consumption, and political orientation explained more of conflict-cooperation behavior than any other factors.[98]

From a perspective of status theory, Rummel suggested that economic growth (or development) and political power bases were the primary and largest dimensions of attribute space, "and can be considered the two status dimensions of wealth and power."[99] His status-field concepts sharpened status theory and focused field theory by suggesting that conflict seemed most likely when two nations had high power status (power parity), and were far apart, or diverging, in economic status. "Power, then, provides the resources for conflict; differences in economic development supply many of the issues for conflict."[100]

Rummel's results that *increasing difference* between national capabilities (Galtung's "achieved attributes" [see section, "Status Theory"], indexed by GDP) *increases tendency toward conflict*,[101] helped to confirm uneven growth, and discredit level of national wealth, as a determinant of conflict. His propositions about effects of national attributes on international behavior indicated that growth affects all international relations in some way; differences in economic status and growth rates inhibit cooperation and encourage conflict; differences in technology, politics, and culture encourage conflict; differences in strategy and national power discourage conflict.[102]

James Rosenau and Gary Hoggard found that countries' relative status along dimensions of size, economic development, and type of polity correlated highly with cooperation (-0.952) and with conflict (0.928).[103] In a more elaborate analysis, within the CREON project, Maurice East and Charles Hermann refined Rosenau's and Hoggard's results. They measured national size as a dichotomous dimension based on four attribute indicators: population, GNP, land area, and usage of electricity (KWH). Including significant elements of economic growth, East and Hermann seemed to be measuring national status along a dimension of general economic capability, including attributes of both economic growth (GNP) and industrialization (KWH). They concluded that size, with its economic content, was the only significant status variable. With the *caveat* that their index of size includes economic elements, they conclude that size, type of polity and development interacting with type of polity are the most important predictors of diplomatic and economic events, but—in parallel with Rummel's results—that neither the separate attributes nor any measure of status explained military events.

In refining this work, James Kean and Patrick McGowan obtained mixed and inconsistent results implying that national resources (measured by GDP) and national "need" (*per capita* level of trade) determined international behavior.[104] These attributes could be absorbed into a national status variable in analogy to model of individual political participation developed by Sydney Verba and Norman Nie.[105] Richard Mansbach and John Vasquez integrated this insight with sociological and political-economic research in an effort to develop a general, unified explanation of international political participation.

> Although groups such as nations do not have a socioeconomic status the way an individual does, a status hierarchy does exist among global actors, and there is an extensive literature on the effect of status on global behavior.[106]
>
> Size, development, resources, and needs can be seen as different aspects of the overall capacity that determines the status of actors.[107] . . . [There are] criteria of status, and these are related to overall political capability, which in turn seems to be based on such objective criteria as size (both demographic and territorial, including resource base), economic capability, and military strength.[108]

Others had argued, from different theoretical perspectives, that *increasing differences* between capabilities, the results of uneven growth, *generate conflict* by threatening the distribution of power,[109] or by increasing vulnerability of downwardly mobile nations.[110]   Organski had perversely suggested that *decreasing differences* due to different rates of growth, may challenge the international *status quo* and *increased conflict*.[111] As for its precursor theories, for status-field theory the independent variable is not simply growth at some absolute level, but the cross-country difference in growth rates (see Diagram 3.13). Status-field theory also depends on intervening variables for linkage.

Diagram 3.13 Status-Field Theory

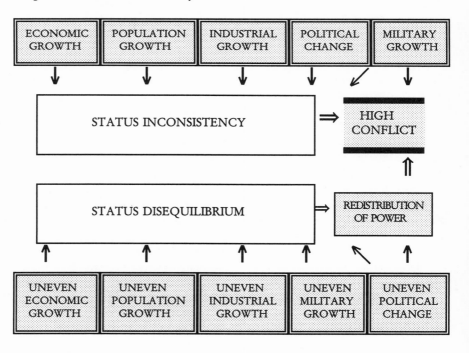

Although the dynamic is unclear, all of these various approaches support the status-field position that changes in differences in national capabilities, which arise through economic growth, may be causally connected with conflict. Some combination of national capabilities operating through both actual and perceived international distributions of power leads to conflict.

While allowing various paths, status-field theory would expect a strong, positive, causal growth-conflict link involving status disequilibrium or inconsistency. Refined versions of status-field theory would predict that the fastest growing countries would be the most involved in conflict. A tentative, untested, corollary might be that countries within a defined region could *all grow rapidly and simultaneously without intraregional conflict.*

Change in National Attributes

Bruce Russett has refined status-field theory and power transition theory around the dynamics of redistribution of power and national development. He has shown modest, but statistically significant, negative relationships between relative decline in *per capita* production, as an indicator of national power, and a nation's propensity for diplomatic disputes involving threat or use of military power.

Russett combined population, gross domestic production, and energy consumption as an index of "total capabilities," or national power. While he did not specify growth as a discrete variable, it is clear that changes in the attributes that he did consider all reflect accepted concepts of national economic growth. In addition to subsuming growth into the analysis, his emphasis on changes in national attributes as indicators of diplomatic-military behavior implicitly accepts the Kuznetsian premise that political-military power rests on an economic foundation.

For nondemocratic states, Russett showed a "militarized dispute" to be most likely two years after economic expansion (a lagged positive result). His general results emphasize the increased flexibility in international relations that wealth and power bring to larger states through higher relative status. "[S]tatus in the international system made a substantial difference: major powers have the greatest freedom of choice about whether, and when, to engage in international conflict. (As Thucydides' Athenian orator said, 'The strong do as they will, the weak do as they must.')."[112]

Critical to the argument is the premise that shifts in distribution of power—expressed as changing status—arise in changing demographic-economic attributes. Various sets of contributing independent variables—structural attributes and procedural features of both polities and economies—may form a critical status dimension, along which both growth and conflict occur. Intervening variables—distribution of power, unevenness of growth, differences in growth rates, status inconsistency or disequilibrium—mediate within an inherently complex nexus. Its intricacy might attenuate, or intensify, the significance of growth—or any single attribute—as an individual variable.

While pointedly discounting any monotonic causality, Russett confirms linkages between attributes—including growth—and conflict, and provides a firm theoretical structure for analyzing the specific relationship between growth and conflict:

> Economic attributes (Russett uses population, production, energy consumption), rather than political-military capabilities, seem consistently associated with conflict.
>
> Total capabilities seem consistently associated with wars, but not with disputes, or militarized disputes.
>
> Total capabilities of nations that engage in war are more equal than the norm; among dyads with equal capabilities a higher proportion engage in conflict than is the norm for all nations.
>
> For dyads with relatively equal total capabilities, those that engage in war show more rapidly converging or diverging capabilities, and higher rates of relative change in total capabilities than those that avoid war; the linkage between convergence-divergence and war is not limited to relatively equal dyads; rate of change in capability is more important than relative parity.
>
> Nation-states seem most likely to engage in war when their own total capabilities are rapidly increasing, but unlikely to do so when they are precipitously declining.[113]

Theories like Russett's that involve changing national attributes allow many paths between growth and conflict and involve many disparate variables (see Diagram 3.14). While analysis can readily focus on a specific variable, it would seem difficult to isolate a particular process or relationship within the intrinsic complexity of the nexus. Regardless of the individual or separate effects and influences of particular variables, these sorts of integrated theories would expect a positive, perhaps even causal, aggregate relationship, but would probably have difficulty with predictions or explanations arising from changes in particular attributes.

Diagram 3.14 Changing National Attributes

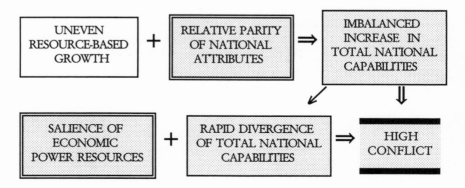

While Russett's results are sharply specific in addressing only particular dyadic relationships, and grandly universal in his amorphous concept of "total capabilities" as a dependent variable, they collect several useful strands of classical and modern thought about growth and conflict. To achieve balance between a "theory of everything that tells us nothing" and the "narrow truth that misses the point," any useful integration of status-field theory and power transition theory would require some premises to focus analysis, define terms and parameters, or control for contributing and intervening variables. Through extending and focusing Russett's results, selective borrowing from others' concepts, and concentrating the effects of several contributing variables in *per capita* income, a set of corollaries focused on growth as an attribute emerges:

> Nations are more likely to engage in conflict when their PCI (combining population and production) are relatively equal and converging or diverging. [This corollary addresses adjustment to new relative realities, redefinitions of power, the awkward dichotomy of both balance and imbalance of power, uneven growth, and changes in status.]
>
> A Nation is more likely to engage another nation in conflict when its PCI is rapidly growing. [This corollary refines the Kuznets-Gilpin thesis that rapid changes in PCI are destabilizing.]
>
> Nations seem more likely to engage in conflict when their PCIs are nearly equal; rival states (with similar PCIs and acceptable proximity) are more likely to engage in conflict with each other than are states that are merely contiguous. [This corollary refines Kautilya's famous theory that contiguous states are natural enemies, but discounts Leninist "core-periphery" models.]

Uncertainty and Disagreement

Thinkers who have found a direct-positive growth-conflict nexus have relied on facts, philosophy, a bit of speculation, and statistics to argue in five generally incompatible ways:

> growth causes conflict (Lenin);
> growth causes conflict and conflict causes growth (Mullins);
> trade causes growth, which causes conflict (Hamilton, List, Condliffe);
> trade causes conflict, which occurs in parallel with growth (Colbert, Viner);
> conflict and growth occur in parallel (Kondratieff, Thomsen, Mansfield, Kuznets, Kennedy).

If the growth-conflict relationship is, indeed, positive and direct, the bevy of factors affecting it seems to determine both direction of causality and its power. While classical realism and patron-client dependency are the major species of irrelevant growth-conflict relationships, the genus of direct relationships includes several species, and possibly many subspecies (see Table 3.2).

Table 3.2 Orthodox Growth-Conflict Relationships—Irrelevant and Direct

THEORY	DETERMINANT	SIGNIF (t-stat)	STRENGTH (R²)	DELAY
IRRELEVANT	**POLITICS**	**INSIG (<2.0)**	**WEAK**	**?-?**
Realism No Linkage	Political Power Security Regime	Insig (<2.0)	Weak (<0.4)	Volatile Unclear
Patron-Client Dependency	Patron Insulation	Insig (<2.0)	Ambiguous ??	???
DIRECT	**ECONOMICS**	**SIGNIF (>2.0)**	**STRONG**	**?-?**
Marxism	Wealth	Signif (>2.0)	Strong (>0.6)	Moderate
Long Waves	Global Economy	Signif (>2.0)	Strong (>0.6)	High
Hegemonic Cycles	Trade and Hegemonic Intervention	Signif (>2.0)	Moderate (0.4 – 0.6)	Moderate
Mercantilism	Trade and Power	Insig (<2.0)	Moderate (0.4 – 0.6)	Low
Nationalism	Managed Trade Wealth	Signif (>2.0)	Strong (>0.6) Strong (>0.6)	Moderate Low
Core-Periphery Dependence	Core Dominance Uneven Growth	??	Moderate (0.4 – 0.6)	Volatile
Power Position	Trade Flows Work Shares Change in Military Status	??	Strong (>0.6)	High
Uneven Growth	High, Different Growth Rates	??	Moderate (0.4 – 0.6)	??
Kuznets' Triad	Rising Expectations Redistribution of Power	??	Strong (<0.6)	High
Status-field Theory	Powr-Wealth Dist Uneven Growth	??	Strong (>0.6)	High
Power Transition	Powr-Wealth Dist Uneven Growth	??	Strong (>0.6)	High
Change in Attributes	Power and Wealth Development	Insig (<2)	Moderate (0.4 – 0.6)	Volatile
Feedback	Growth and Politics	Signif (>2.0)	Strong (>0.6)	Low

The basic features of the direct-positive species show considerably more diversity than do the two irrelevant species. Even so, the direct genus shows notable consistency across species. In contrast to the irrelevant genus, the primary determinant of the direct growth-conflict relationship is economics —for the irrelevant genus the determinant is politics. Further, the direct relationships are generally expected to be significant and strong—irrelevant relationships are expected to be weak and insignificant. Any positive-relationship theory would expect growth to be highly correlated with conflict; correlation coefficients would be positive, large, and statistically significant. The confusion and contradiction among the theoretical explanations, however, suggests that both levels of correlation and values of coefficients would be too unstable to allow confident prediction of behaviors.

The direct-positive relationship seems no better at explaining or predicting than the ambiguity of realism. Both radicals and liberals seem to agree with realists that something else, probably more important, may be involved: human psychology, national attributes, global trends, or even exogenous processes like technology or trade. It may be that every case is unique —although realists, liberals, and radicals alike have claimed universality, none have been able to generalize sufficiently to avoid confounding special cases. Only the Braudelians and the Marxists suggest the salience of any universal community of mankind operating under eternal principles.

INVERSE NEGATIVE RELATIONSHIP

In what Martin Wight has called the "rationalist" tradition of international relations (see Appendix B), growth and conflict were both subsumed in a "natural-law connection between all nations . . . [which] involved a system of mutual social rights and duties."[114] Recognizing that economic activities extended beyond simply possessing and enjoying property, and that humanity seemed to aspire at least as much to prosperity as to security, rationalists gave particular weight to economic factors. Rationalism accordingly deemphasized political-military features in assessing relations among nations, and stressed the effects of scientific progress, moral development, and material growth. Denis Healey noted this shift in emphasis when he observed:

> In the past it has only been possible to make a big change in the balance of power by gaining resources in territory outside one's frontiers. The sputnik has demonstrated with spectacular effects that it is now possible to produce great changes in the balance of power by making better political and scientific use of the resources inside one's own territories.[115]

As trade and industry brought rapid economic growth to communities, and private prosperity and wealth to more people, commerce became an inherent and "customary" part of international society. Rationalists took this as evidence that conflict was an "unnatural" product of perverted politics. Trade was one of several proofs that "the greater part of the totality of international relationships reposes on custom rather than on force."[116]

Drawing inspiration from Adam Smith's "invisible hand," idealists and liberals have held that international commerce could improve living conditions and deepen "material interdependence" among nations.   Prosperity and interdependence would bring salience to "moral suasion" and rationality in public opinion and government policy, and reduce violent conflict to what Richard Cobden called the "silent and peaceful aggrandisements [n.b. Cobden uses the term to mean "growing greater," not "aggression"] which spring from improvement and labour."[117]

Like radicals, Wight's "rationalists" reject realist irrelevance between growth and conflict.   Their notion that growth and conflict need not be associated also, however, rejects radical pessimism. Like liberalism, some forms of idealism suggest that economic growth can actually prevent conflict. This third genus—inverse-negative—of the growth-conflict relationship links the dependent conflict variable with an independent growth variable in a negative relationship.   Causality is even less clear than in the direct-positive relationships, and is usually through other economic or political variables.

INVERSE-NEGATIVE GROWTH-CONFLICT LINKAGE MODEL

ENGINE OF GROWTH is concentration and accumulation of resources through trade and commerce, national specialization in economic production in sectors of comparative commercial advantage, and economic interdependence among polities linked primarily through trade with each other.

DOMESTIC POLITICAL-ECONOMY is open-market, free-trade capitalist variation of democracy, with state involvement in economic and commercial affairs limited to issues of national security.

LIBERAL INTERNATIONAL POLITICAL-ECONOMY involves national states and their extensions, alliances, and international organizations, often with a primary focus on economic or nonpolitical issues; private firms trade and invest outside their home countries freely, but in the national interest of their home countries; one national state often dominates as hegemon; hegemony or multilateral agreement impose some regime of free trade and international security.

INTERNATIONAL RELATIONS are primarily political, and establish a legal-political structure for intereconomy relations limited to trade, lending, and equity investment; primary relationships between governments are diplomacy and war; primary intereconomy relationship is commercial trade in goods and services; trade is a significant political issue in both domestic politics and diplomacy, although political intergovernmental relations are separate from economic international relations.

ECONOMIC GROWTH involves national structural change, and shifts in allocation of resources and economic activity; some innovation and new knowledge are applied through technologies to generate commercial advantage; economic growth occurs predominantly within national economies.

INTERNATIONAL CONFLICT occurs as polities seek to impose their values on each other, or protect their national advantages, through exercise, or projection of national political power; as governments seek to combine economic and political power to generate additional national advantages and prevent diffusion of national technology; and as growing economies reaching limits of ready resources seek to continue growth by expansion.

LINKAGE between economic growth and international conflict is negative, constructed, and not causal; both growth and conflict are affected by trade and commerce; linkage may be weak or ambiguous, since some other variable often overwhelms any direct effect by generating a primarily political source of conflict or cooperation

INTERNATIONAL SECURITY REGIME to control and contain international conflict is based on trade and economic interdependence; collective security agreements, balance-of-power arrangements, multilateral sanctions are preferred to crisis management, coercion, unilateral deterrence, and intervention by great powers.

POWER RESOURCES are levels of aggregate production, technology, productive population and national resources located on national territory; most important factors of production are capital, technology, and labor; larger territory, population, and military strength are less salient, and may be deemed disadvantageous in the pursuit of some national interests

Idealism

Idealists have appeared periodically since humans began to think and dream about the future. The political idealism that briefly dominated global political theory coalesced only in the late nineteenth century. In analyzing his "soft revolutionist" tradition (see Appendix B), Martin Wight speaks of "a series of waves . . . [or] disconnected illustrations of the same politico-philosophical truths. . . . It is characteristic of Revolutionism . . . to deny its past, to try to start from scratch, to jump out of history and begin again."[118]

While intellectual origins of political idealism are obscure, the ethnodoctrinal arrogance implicit in the Old Testamentary concept of a "chosen people" to inherit the earth, and the concept of global empire introduced in the *Aeneid*, seem to contain germs of idealist prescriptions for universalism.   A second pillar of idealism seems to have emerged from Alexander the Great's invention of the "brotherhood of man," refined by Stoic philosophers (Zeno, Marcus Aurelius, *etc.*), and dogmatized in most of the world's great religions.[119]

Influenced in many ways by medieval Christian moralism, much modern idealism—Richard Cobden, John Bright, Immanuel Kant, Alexander Hamilton, Thomas Jefferson, Woodrow Wilson, Cordell Hull—has drawn economic inspiration from Adam Smith's "invisible hand." Grafted onto various ancient concepts (democracy, brotherhood of man, religious belief, *etc.*), political-economic idealism found structure in Grotian concepts of international law.

Arnold Toynbee, in his monumental work, *A Study of History* begins to collect these ideas, and predicts peace only through exhaustion of violence and subjection of national states to some law of universal government. Disappointingly, and unusual among idealists, Professor Toynbee offers no scheme for achieving this goal.

The optimism of late nineteenth-century Europe and North America found it easy to believe that peace and prosperity had finally been able to illuminate mankind's path into the future. Like Andrew Carnegie, who used much of his fortune to promote world peace, many politicians and academics convinced themselves that development and industrialization were so increasing the costs and risks of war that conflict would inevitably fade into a history best forgotten.[120] As a powerful political force in populist reaction to World War I, idealism could lead Vice-President Henry Wallace to argue a generation later that "the true purpose of the wartime alliance was not merely the elimination of fascism from the world but also the establishment of freedom for all peoples, the triumph of democracy, and the elimination of poverty and hunger everywhere."[121]

Vastly divergent across morality, ideology, ethics, and philosophy, idealism accepts as "universal" several premises about reality, humanity, and politics. With overtones of moralism, universalism, and religion, the idealist *weltanschauung* asserts that:

> human nature is essentially "good" and tends toward mutual aid, collaboration, and altruism;
>
> progress through "improvement" of civilization is made possible by fundamental human concern for other humans;
>
> "bad," selfish behaviors are products of bad institutions, not natural acts of evil people; revelation of institutional secrets to people and introduction of "outsiders" to institutional activities expose their "badness";
>
> war and conflict are not inevitable; occurrences can be reduced by destroying the institutions that cause them; democratic institutions are inherently peaceful;
>
> any solution to the problem of international conflict requires collective, multilateral (rather than national) effort; nationalism must be subordinate to humanitarianism or universalism; free trade must replace protectionism; and
>
> global society must be reorganized to eliminate institutions that breed war; self-determination to place political borders on natural lines is essential for peace.

This idealist perspective of humanity and the world differs significantly from that of both realists and radicals—and many liberals. They observed different data and reached different conclusions about growth and conflict. Prone to see history and progress as linear (rather than cyclical) and moving ineluctably toward some apocalyptic *denouement*, some messianic fulfillment (political, religious, economic, or something else), idealists have been attracted to imperative prescriptions. Concluding that conflict was the independent variable that explicitly prevented growth, idealism deduced that the correct approach to human progress, rather than trying to manage growth, was to eliminate conflict; growth would naturally follow. Even for Kant or Toynbee, as for Marx and Hamilton, however, the growth-conflict relationship, once noted, was inconsequential to primary purposes, and not intrinsically interesting: simply a logical artifact of the argument.

One branch of idealism (the "optimistic nonintervention" of Kant, Cobden, Bright, *etc.*) has called for global institutions to prevent wars and provide social justice. Expecting peace and prosperity to emerge through the operation of human nature, this sort of idealism was embodied in the League of Nations and the United Nations. A second sort of idealism relies on law among nations. "It called for the use of legal processes, such as mediation and arbitration, to settle disputes and inhibit recourse to war,"[122] as illustrated in the Kellogg-Briand Pact, or the International Court of Justice. Many religious variants of idealism stress arms control and disarmament (Washington and London Naval Conferences, Strategic Arms Limitation Treaty, *etc.*). What Martin Wight has labelled the "messianic interventionism" of Giuseppe Mazzini, Woodrow Wilson, and V. I. Lenin, and an "inverted revolutionism" of pacifism constitute a more radical sort of idealism. Historically conspicuous with powerful rhetoric and emotional appeal, and often politically uncomfortable, most idealist prescriptions—with the exception of replacing economic nationalism with free trade—have never been tried, and even fewer have been achieved.

Diagram 3.15 Idealism

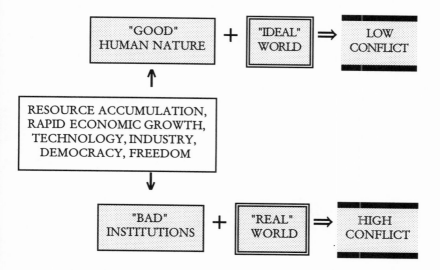

Idealism would expect conflict to show a strong, negative, stable pressure on growth, and would expect causality to flow from conflict to growth: high conflict would prevent growth (see Diagram 3.15). High growth, however, would not necessarily ensure low conflict. Nor would low growth necessarily lead to conflict. As an independent variable, growth would influence conflict only weakly through an ambiguous, negative relationship sensitive to numerous other variables.

Commercial Liberalism and The Manchester School

By the nineteenth century, commercial international relations had ceased to be a realist-mercantilist zero-sum game and source of recurring conflict. Instead, many thinkers accepted Kant's idealism, combined it with the modern capitalism introduced by Adam Smith and David Ricardo and came to see trade and international commerce as powerful sources of both economic growth and international peace. Liberal economics emerged slowly from the materialistic thinking of the eighteenth-century physiocrats into a world ready for both commerce and peace.

For national states, as well as for individuals, the right to possess, accumulate, and enjoy property was, obviously, the necessary precondition for any viable existence. Like the physiocrats, liberals argued that economic health of individuals and community depended on the ability of both to acquire property without political restraint. Like the idealists, liberals decried war and conflict as at best a nuisance, and usually a crippling obstacle in the path of human progress. The proper role of government was to create and protect the private and public ability to prosper, and to remove any political impediments to commerce, trade, and prosperity.

Commercial Liberalism incorporated Ricardian comparative advantages involving costs of production and prices, and included a dynamic concept of wealth as expandable, in addition to the traditional sort of static wealth that could only be transferred and accumulated. Liberals accepted that mutual trading interdependence could be economically beneficial to both trading partners. Growth could involve both expansion of each nation's wealth through comparative advantages, and accumulation of domestic wealth by concentrating factors of production. Trade was the critical process in both mechanisms, and conflict an annoying obstacle.

In the half-century after Waterloo, with peace and prosperity in Europe, the Manchester School developed a set of commercial liberal tenets identifying trade with peace. Trade created the preconditions for peace, which increased trade, which brought domestic growth and national prosperity, which obviated the political tensions that lead to war. In this happy situation, economic self-interest was the real engine of growth: capitalism was its highway; trade and industry were its ready vehicles carrying society into a virtuous spiral. In the unfortunate absence of trade, however, conflict would dominate international relations and inhibit growth in a vicious vortex (see Diagram 3.16).

Diagram 3.16 Commercial Liberalism

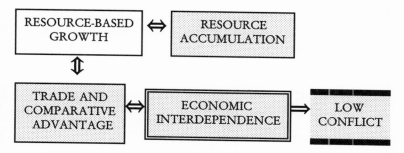

Nations could gain security, welfare, power, and growth through trade and commerce, rather than military conflict;[123] the result was international peace and national prosperity. Commercial liberals, before and after the Manchester School, "believe that the mutual benefits of trade and the expanding web of interdependence among national economies tend to foster cooperative relations."[124] For commercial liberals, trade—free trade was best—was the critical dynamic of both growth and strength.

Theories of this genre suggest that as commerce and trade among states increase, political tensions that lead to conflict and war decrease. Commerce is far more efficient and effective than war or conflict for national economies to gain access to resources and markets, which generate economic growth. Further, economic dependence generated by high trade discourages governments from interrupting commerce to wage war, or to initiate even nonmilitary conflict.[125]

Commercial liberal theories suggest that low levels of trade and commerce, as well as periods of relative closure of the international economy, should reflect *both* lower economic growth *and* more international conflict and war than would stable high flows of trade in an open economy. Although any causality in the relationship is unclear—despite commercial liberals' visions of a virtuous spiral—growth and conflict should show a high negative correlation.

Orthodox "Free Trade" Liberalism

Like classical realism, orthodox liberalism recognized a finite world, completely filled with sovereign national states acting in their own self-interest. European growth occurred independently in each country, first as populations concentrated domestic resources as factors of production, and later as conquest or commerce brought additional foreign resources. So long as a nation had, or could obtain, more resources as factors of production, it could continue this sort of resource-based growth.

Sovereignty's exclusive paradox (see "Realism" section) bestowed the economic privileges of population and territory on each nation within its own jurisdiction, and imposed substantial political constraints on all others. For liberals, economic self-interest is the primary inherent force behind both interpersonal and international relations. Accumulation of wealth is not only the primary individual aspiration, but also the primary dynamic of the international system. Based ultimately on resources within a nation's boundaries, populations could increase national wealth through economic relationships with other nations, through military conquest, or through more intensive and efficient exploitation of domestic resources.

Economic self-interest, in combination with political constraints imposed by sovereign nations, brings nations to establish interdependencies, linkages, and other economic relationships among themselves. The most powerful and self-beneficial of these is free trade, which accumulates and concentrates resources, which generate domestic growth. This trade-growth process is independent of politics, so long as the international political-economy allows free trade among nations.

A free trade regime, the core of liberal thought, is a powerful deterrent to conflict. Trade links, ancillary foreign investment (see Appendix D), and derivative economic interdependencies, acting as an international security regime, obviate any other structure or process to contain conflict. So long as a nation participates actively, honestly, and "fairly" (as defined by the hegemon operating the regime) in the regime of free trade, its "opportunity costs" of conflict would be greater than any benefits that it could gain through conflict.[126] In these circumstances the economic costs of conflict (through severance of commercial relations) are likely to be high, or even unacceptable. States go to war when opportunity costs of foregone trade are low: since opportunity costs would be lowest in periods of least trade, conflict would be more desirable. In conditions of high trade, the high opportunity costs of severing trading ties allow an open, liberal international economic order to make "a substantial and positive contribution to the maintenance of international security."[127] Other weaker linkages, with complementary ideological or political-functional foundations—democracy and human rights; religion, race, or culture; non-governmental, transnational, international organizations; international law; multinational enterprises—strengthen the power of trade to bind the system together and constrain international conflict within the limits of economic self-interest.

For liberals, politics contributes little to human progress, beyond ensuring that the free trade regime and other complementary international relationships remain in place. It is economics and self-interest, not politics and power, that hold the system together. Political efforts to manage economic affairs seem generally ill-conceived and counterproductive, particularly at the global level: politics and economics are best conducted separately.

Even, however, while dogmatically eschewing "externalities" created by political intervention, liberal thought, in a single great exception, unabashedly allows government to intervene in economics wherever national security is involved. Adam Smith devoted much of his Book V to "[t]he first duty of the sovereign, that of protecting the society from the violence and invasion of other independent societies, [which] can be performed only by means of a military force."[128]

While acknowledging a positive relationship between economic growth, military strength, and the national power to wage war, orthodox liberals discount the importance of political-military power, and stress the stronger negative effects of free trade and profitable commerce. International political-military relationships are often dysfunctional in their tendencies to generate costly conflict, which inhibits trade and weakens the economic interdependencies that bind the system together. National political-military efforts to increase national power, often at the expense of that of other nations, can also dangerously weaken interdependence and generate conflict, as economic ties, frayed by conflict, ultimately lose their power.

Not a normal element of the liberal system, international conflict emerges when nations allow political issues to intrude into economic relationships, or shift priorities toward ideological or power-based concerns. When rising national expectations make growth a political issue, or when other nations impede the free-trade regime, the fundamental forces of self-interest, unrestrained by interdependence, bring uncontrolled conflict, often in the form of war (see Diagram 3.17). Further, "a smaller global market may lead to new, and exacerbate existing, tensions."[129]

Diagram 3.17 Free-Trade Liberalism

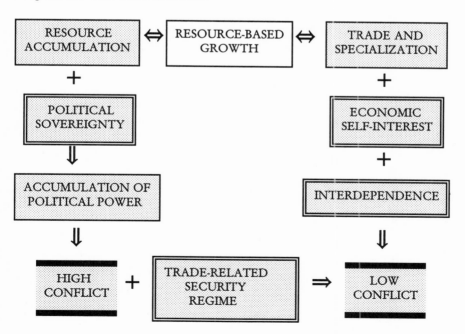

In the liberal world, economic growth is neither sufficient nor necessary to generate international conflict. Conflict and growth are both separate dependent variables of trade, and associated with each other only through trade and domestic economic policy. Trade brings interdependence, accumulation of wealth, high opportunity costs of conflict, prosperity, and peace. Obstacles to trade inhibit these processes, and lead to poverty and war. Although not caused by trade, economic growth occurs naturally and easily within the free-trade regime, which generates international cooperation. Absence or deterioration of trade-based interdependence weakens the restraints imposed on international conflict by economic self-interest.

In contrast to realism, mercantilism, and economic nationalism, liberalism would predict a constructed correlation between growth and conflict to be *negative*, weak, and not especially significant or stable. In parallel with economic nationalism, liberalism would expect the relationship to be predictable and responsive to government economic policy, protectionism, industrial policy, or managed trade.

Business Cycles and Long Waves

The urgent pragmatism of policy science deals more with the annual growth rates, trade disputes, and short business cycles reported by financial journalists than with the epochal changes analyzed by Kondratieff, Kuznets, or Fernand Braudel (see Appendix C). Stressing immediate, visible effects of growth on employment, trade balances, and elections, policy science can combine trade theory with business-cycle analysis in a crude growth-conflict linkage. Orthodox trade analyses accept that the short-term business cycle influences trade, since changes in income are assumed to change both demand for imports and supply of exports.[130]

From this perspective, the business cycle should also influence both growth and conflict not only through its effects on trade, but through its influences on domestic politics. Gilpin has reversed this position in his suggestion that the rate of economic growth determines the political effects of trade, which then generate conflict or cooperation with other nation-states.

> Although it is true that the decline of protectionism and the enlargement of world markets stimulates economic growth, the corollary is also true; a rapid rate of economic growth leads to increasing trade and economic interdependence. By the same token, a slowdown in the rate of economic growth makes adjustment difficult, intensifies international trade competition, and exacerbates international political relations.[131]

This "Gilpinesque" analysis implies a negative growth-conflict relationship operating through a complex nexus of trade, business, and national politics. The power of the relationship depends on the responsivity of politics and trade to each other, which is determined by another set of independent, contributing variables (see Diagram 3.18).

Diagram 3.18 Business Cycles

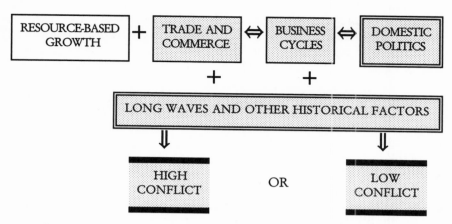

Like Gilpin's political-economic approach, historical "Braudelian" analyses imply (in contrast to direct-positive conclusions [see previous section "Long Waves, Hegemony, Trade, and War"]), a negative relationship at the global level in parallel with long waves of growth. Unlike Gilpin, historical approaches say little about growth at a national level.   None of the interpretations of waves and cycles suggest that growth and conflict are mutually irrelevant (realism), or independent (liberal contention).

Like positive linkages, the negative connection seems subject not only to mediation through trade but to hegemonic intervention.   It is unstable at a national level, and infected by political volatility.   The strength and stability of any such wave-related relationship—positive or negative—seem dependent on several exogenous variables: hegemonic cycles, trade levels, Kondratieff waves, hegemonic policy preferences, business cycles. Further any wave-related linkage seems to be permanently captive to domestic politics in any of the states involved in an international relationship. The complexity of any putative growth-conflict nexus through waves or cycles, and the plethora of relevant variables and dynamics are summarized in Mansfield's findings of virtually no evidence that "either the Kondratieff cycle or short-term fluctuations in the business cycle are related to the incidence of major-power wars."[132]

Interdependence Theory

Several theorists have begun to integrate the structural power of realism with the behavioral pragmatism of liberalism in a synthesis of both orthodox traditions.[133]   Under the rubric of interdependence, they recognize that a *combination* of (1) distribution and levels of power, *and* (2) international trade and economic interactions and flows creates the conditions of conflict and cooperation, war and peace.[134] To realist convictions that the proximate causes of conflict are predominantly political, interdependence joins the idealist tenet that the proximate causes of cooperation are economic. In broad consonance with both liberalism and realism, interdependence theory avers that "*both the distribution of capabilities and trade help to explain the outbreak of war, and that the relationship between trade and the frequency of major-power war is inverse*."[135]

Trade-related interdependence theories accept positive liberal linkages between trade and growth, but add the important prediction that growth cannot continue without trade. Interdependence argues that trade has, in addition to its symbiosis with growth, important political effects. These become an indirect relationship between growth and conflict. Unlike either liberalism or realism, however, interdependence imputes some causality to the relationship.

Accepting with realism growth as a domestic phenomenon, interdependence also accepts the liberal view that two economies can grow faster than one. Growth in one economy leads to trade between economies, which generates growth in each, which increases trade. Interdependence extends the liberal syllogism to increase national sensitivity to both economic opportunity costs of war and domestic political costs of recession, depending on the distribution of power, the current security regime, and other structures of the international system. The result is a complex independent variable involving both economic processes (growth and trade) and political structures (domestic linkages between economics and politics). Whether the independent variable is trade-based growth, growth-based trade, or domestic political sensitivity to economics is not relevant.

Diagram 3.19 Interdependence

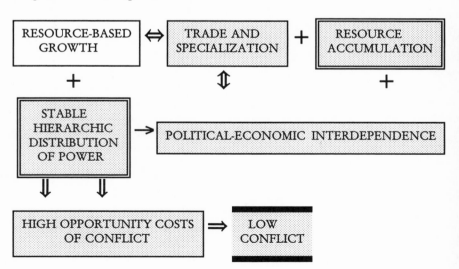

While recognizing the possibility of perverse relationships, trade-related interdependence theory predicts a negative, highly significant, growth-conflict relationship, with lower levels of conflict in close association with higher trade-based growth (see Diagram 3.19). With firm liberal foundations, interdependence theory would explain any unpredicted positive relationships as consequences of unwarranted intrusions of political affairs into economic life. Interdependence theory recognizes that evolving international structures and processes, in a neorealist sense reflecting power transition theory, would seem to improve stability of the growth-conflict relationship and the predictive power of the interdependence model. The effects of many other relevant variables—both contributing and intervening—would, however, weaken it, and decrease its elegance. In some contrast to Bruce Russett's tight focus on specific dyadic pairs, much interdependence theorizing tends toward an idealistic Braudelian "theory of everything that explains nothing."

Focused Uncertainty and Ideological Disagreement

Like those who have determined the growth-conflict relationship to be direct and positive, the thinkers who have found an inverse-negative connection have used diverse arguments and different evidence, and speculated freely. Relying heavily on trade, morality, and hope, the theories of the inverse-negative genus generally include the powerful influences of human nature and self-interest to inhibit conflict and promote growth. Explanatory weaknesses arise not from bad theory, but simply from the uncertainties of human behavior. Faulty predictions reflect not soft analysis or incomplete data, but sincere disagreement and uncertainty about why humans do what they do—their moralities, their purposes, and their ideologies.

In contrast to this sort of rational optimism about humanity and its activities, realists and discoverers of a positive growth-conflict relationship see a more contentious humanity that either cannot avoid conflict (realism, Marxism) or deliberately uses conflict to achieve its purposes (hegemony, mercantilism, feedback). If the growth-conflict relationship is positive, it seems to be natural, and even immutable. If the growth-conflict relationship is truly negative and inverse, it seems to be humans and their natural characteristics—rather than some intrinsic feature of the relationship itself—that make it so. When humans prefer prosperity and peace, they arrange their affairs to produce high growth and low conflict. When other things seem more important (ideology, religion, politics, power), they seek other paths toward progress and allow nature, history, or circumstance to work its way with growth and conflict.

The focus of uncertainty seems to suggest at least three distinct genera of the growth-conflict relationship. Smaller than the genus of positive relationships, and larger than the small genus of irrelevant growth-conflict relationships, the genus of inverse growth-conflict relationships includes several major species, each of which certainly has several subspecies (see Table 3.3).

Table 3.3 Orthodox Growth-Conflict Relationships: Irrelevant, Direct, and Inverse

THEORY	DETERMINANT	SIGNIF (t-stat)	STRENGTH (R²)	DELAY
IRRELEVANT	**POLITICS**	**INSIG (<2.0)**	**WEAK**	**?-?**
Realism No Linkage	Political Power Security Regime	Insig (<2.0)	Weak (<0.4)	Volatile Unclear
Patron-Client Dependency	Patron Insulation	Insig (<2.0)	???	???
DIRECT	**ECONOMICS**	**SIGNIF (>2.0)**	**STRONG**	**? - ?**
Marxism	Wealth	Signif (>2.0)	Strong (>0.6)	Moderate
Long Waves	Global Economy	Signif (>2.0)	Strong (>0.6)	High
Hegemonic Cycles	Trade and Hegemonic Intervention	Signif (>2.0)	Moderate (0.4 - 0.6)	Moderate
Mercantilism	Trade and Power	Insig (<2.0)	Moderate (0.4 – 0.6)	Low
Nationalism	Managed Trade Wealth	Signif (>2.0)	Strong (>0.6) Strong (>0.6)	Moderate Low
Core-Periphery Dependence	Core Dominance Uneven Growth	??	Moderate (0.4 – 0.6)	Volatile
Power Position	Trade Flows Work Shares	??	Strong (>0.6)	High
Uneven Growth	High, Different Growth Rates	??	Moderate (0.4 - 0.6)	??
Kuznets' Triad	Rising Expectations Power Redistribution	??	Strong (<0.6)	High
Status-field Theory	Power-Wealth Distribution Uneven Growth	??	Strong (>0.6)	High
Power Transition	Power-Wealth Distribution Uneven Growth	??	Strong (>0.6)	High
Change in Attributes	Power and Wealth Development	Insig (<2)	Moderate (0.4 – 0.6)	Volatile
Feedback	Growth and Politics	Signif (>2.0)	Strong (>0.6)	Low
INVERSE	**ECONOMICS**	**???**	**???**	**??**
Idealism	Natural Law	Signif (>2)	Strong (>0.6)	High
Long Waves and Hegemony	Hegemony Trade	Signif (>2)	Unclear	Volatile

Table 3.3 continued

THEORY	DETERMINANT	SIGNIF (t-stat)	STRENGTH (R²)	DELAY
Commercial Liberalism	Free Trade Self-interest	Insig (<2)	Strong (>0.6)	Low
Orthodox Liberalism	Self-interest Interdependence	??	Strong (>0.6)	Moderate
Business Cycle	State Intervention	??	Unclear	Volatile
Interdependence	Power-Wealth Distribution Self-interest	Signif (>2)	Strong (<0.6)	Moderate

THEORETICAL DIVERGENCE

After three centuries of analysis, political-economic orthodoxy remains equivocal about the relationship between economic growth and international conflict. Various approaches adopt different sets of precepts, principles, and assumptions; and naturally reach different conclusions, and unique predictions. The ambivalence of orthodoxy seems not so much epistemic as paradigmatic.

Nonradical orthodoxy did *not* expect high correlation between growth and conflict, in the absence of dominant effects of some other variable. With clear realist origins, this expectation became fashionable and acceptable as expanding liberalism separated economics from politics. With this expectation, the challenge for analysis was not to examine growth and conflict in terms of each other, but to identify the intervening variables. Just such an epistemological paradigm seems to have guided nonradical researchers, politicians, and analysts over more than three centuries:

> economics and politics are separate, should not be mixed, and can only be connected through something else;
>
> since it is good to avoid conflict, and good to grow, policy should manipulate the connecting variable (whatever it may be) to allow, or even stimulate, growth, but to prevent growth from "leaking" out of the economic sector, destabilizing politics, and generating conflict;
>
> thus, the common task of analysis and policy is to identify the dominant intervening variables and learn how to manipulate them.

The broad liberal and classical realist paradigms rest on separation of economics from politics: growth is an economic matter, while conflict is a political phenomenon. Any linkage between them is either coincidental or an artifact, and definitely not explicit or causal. Any relationship between economic growth and political conflict would imply at least an illiberal perspective, and probably a violation of fundamental liberal principles. Indeed, the approaches that suggest such relationships are commonly labelled "radical."

Orthodox views of the growth-conflict relationship defy a neat summary. They have few common ideas—or even variables or results—across the various approaches. They can usefully be compared in terms of predicted effects of any growth-conflict relationship, the process and structural variables involved, and its strength or stability (see Table 3.4). Even such a crude comparison, however, accentuates the persistent and ubiquitous theoretical ambiguity that continues to generate new approaches.

Table 3.4 Orthodox Growth-Conflict Relationships: Comparative Profiles

THEORY	PROCESS	STRUCTURE	STRENGTH	STABILITY
IRRELEVANT				
Realism	Domestic Politics	Hierarchy International Security Regime	Weak	Volatile
DIRECT-POSITIVE				
Marxism and Neo-Marxism	Economic Expansion	Capitalism Empire	Strong	Stable Increasing
Feedback	Self-reinforcing	Anarchy Dual-use Military Power	Strong	Unstable Decreasing
Hegemonic Cycles	Hegemonic	Hegemony Anarchy	Moderate	Unclear
Mercantilism	Power Based on Wealth	Free Trade Hierarchy	Moderate	Stable
Nationalism	International Competition	Managed Trade Economic Power	Strong	Stable
Long Waves and Hegemony	Trade and Hegemonic Intervention	Hegemony	Unclear	Volatile
Power Position	Change in Military Status	Hierarchy Balance-of-Power	Moderate	Stable
Kuznets' Triad	Rising Expectations Shifting Power Concentration of Power	Balance-of-Power Distribution of Power	Strong	Unclear
Core–Periphery Dependence	Redistribution of Power	Core Dominance Uneven Growth	Moderate	Volatile
Long Waves	Unclear	Hegemony Global Growth	Unclear	Volatile
Long Waves and Hegemony	Redistribution of Power Global Growth Phases	Hegemony and Political Change	Moderate	Volatile

Table 3.4 continued

THEORY	PROCESS	STRUCTURE	STRENGTH	STABILITY
Field-status Theory	Status Inconsistency and Disequilibrium	Distribution of Power based on Economic Traits	Strong	Stable
Power Transition Theory	Change in Power Resources and in Power Imbalance	Distribution of Power based on Economic Traits	Strong	Stable
Change in National Attributes	Redistribution of Power	Distribution of Power based on Demographic-Economic Traits	Moderate	Volatile
INVERSE-NEGATIVE				
Commercial Liberalism	Trade	Free Trade Economic Self-Interest	Strong	Stable
Orthodox Liberalism	Opportunity Costs Domestic Policy	Economic Self-Interest Interdependence Sovereignty	Strong	Stable Responds to Domestic Policy
Business Cycle	Political Effects of Trade	Integration of Trade and Politics	Unclear	Volatile
Interdependence	Political Effects of Trade Opportunity Costs	Distribution of Power Economic Self-Interest Integration of Trade and Politics	Strong	Stable
Patron–Client Dependency	Insulation from Threat	Anarchy Dependency	Unclear	Dependent on Patron

Although orthodoxy includes no universally accepted recognition of any systematic relationship between growth and conflict, most approaches suggest that a relationship, if it exists, is probably positive. Growth and conflict would increase or decrease in parallel; growing economies would be associated with quarreling polities. Only idealism and some of the trade-related approaches imply a negative relationship. From these perspectives, growth could lead not to conflict, but to cooperation, trade, and peace. Doctrinaire realism denies any influence of growth on conflict, which is a purely political phenomenon. Many nonradical approaches also involve various other variables that have more power than either growth or conflict.

From their different sets of values and initial conditions, different concerns and purposes, and different perspectives, most radicals, and some "neoliberal-realists," have developed and accepted a broad counterparadigm:

> economics and politics are the same, and cannot be separated;
>
> since it is good to avoid conflict, and good to grow, and since growth can cause conflict, policy must ensure that growth is contained or diffused, and that neither conflict nor any of the other variables involved destroy society;
>
> thus, the common task of analysis and policy is to identify sources of conflict-producing growth, and learn to manipulate them for social progress.

One sort of "neo-approaches" has inserted various intervening variables —processes and structures—between growth and conflict. Another has associated eclectic selections of additional contributing variables, and relegated growth and conflict to minor roles within a complex socioeconomic-cultural-political relationship. Yet another has created new independent variables with new features or changed old ones to increase their relevance.

Each approach stresses a particular combination of process and structural variables upon which economic growth acts. The salience of processes involved in any linkage seems to have shifted from early mercantilist emphases on the transmutation of wealth into power, through classical references to balances and redistributions of political power, to modern recognition of a fluid interdependence between economic changes, political dynamics, and various exogenous factors.

Most approaches presume a fundamental realist international structure of anarchy and self-reliance. More sophisticated and complex concepts impose hegemony, an international security regime (balance-of-power or collective security have been most favored), and some sort of trade regime. The result is some international hierarchy or equilibrium with both political and economic aspects, changes in which bring either conflict or peace, and allow or hinder growth. Structural analyses suggest that the critical intervening variable is the international distribution of power, and that the critical process is some destabilizing effect of national economic growth on that distribution. Many approaches stress the power of uneven growth to disrupt an existing international equilibrium and hierarchy of power.

The strength, stability, and predictability of any species of any genus of the growth-conflict relationship do not enjoy majority consensus among the approaches. While radical approaches rely on a strong, constant, positive relationship as a fundamental tenet, "interdependence" approaches imply that neither strength nor effect are predictable, except possibly in specific cases. Even, however, in a specific situation, nonradical approaches hesitate to predict an effect of growth, but refer to some other cause of conflict (trade, balance-of-power, political change, self-interest, anarchy, etc.). For the most sophisticated approaches, an eclectic set of intervening or contributing variables determines both the strength and effect of any growth-conflict relationship. Predictability, explanatory power, or stability would arise from the exogenous variables, not from the relationship itself.

The result of three centuries spent pondering these questions is an orthodoxy that is not sure whether there is a relationship between growth and conflict or not, that focuses narrowly on current policy, and seeks the causes of growth and conflict as separate, unrelated phenomena. While their respective disciplines have much to say, and many powerful theories and explanations to offer, about *either growth or conflict,* neither economists nor political scientists seem prone to answer clearly the many vexing questions about *both growth and conflict* that arise as nations struggle with the search for *both peace and prosperity:*

> If there is a growth-conflict relationship, what is it?
> If there isn't one, why not?
> If there is one, what can people do about it?
> If there isn't one, what should people do about it?
> Is some intervening variable really more significant than either growth, the independent variable, or conflict, the dependent variable?
> If so, what is it, and how can people manage it?
> How can analysts or policy-makers predict whether an action, policy, or phenomenon will bring growth, stagnation, conflict, or cooperation?

NOTES

1. Martin Wight, *International Theory: The Three Traditions,* edited by Gabriele Wight & Brian Porter (Leicester & London: Leicester University Press for the Royal Institute of International Affairs, 1991).

2. A third sort of intervening "behavioral" variables had some currency briefly after World War II. Reflecting sociological and psychological theories of individual behavior, these explanations offered little beyond noting that decisions depend on decision-makers.

3. At least one contrary strand of an inchoate "post"-neorealism is trying to resurrect David Hume's eighteenth-century concept of "moral sciences," which referred to efforts to understand the human condition and free humanity from ignorance, superstition, and oppressive social relations. See Peter Hamilton, "The Enlightenment and the Birth of Social Science," Stuart Hall & Bram Gieben, eds., *Formations of Modernity* (Oxford: Polity, 1992), 18-58. What Ken Booth has named "Global Moral Science" hopes to shift the focus of realism from "accumulating knowledge about relations between states . . . to thinking about ethics and applied ethics on a global scale . . . the study of security *and* the good life of the world." Ken Booth, "Human Wrongs and International Relations," *International Affairs* 71 (January 1995), 111.

4. Robert Gilpin, *The Political Economy of International Relations* (Princeton, New Jersey: Princeton University Press, 1987), 3-4.

5. John H. Herz, *Political Realism and Political Idealism* (Chicago: University of Chicago Press, 1951); Henry A. Kissinger, *A World Restored: Metternich, Castlereagh, and the Problems of Peace, 1812-1822* (New York: Grosset & Dunlap, 1964); Hans J.

Morgenthau & Kenneth W. Thompson, *Politics Among Nations: The Struggle for Power and Peace*, 6th ed. (New York: Alfred A. Knopf, 1985).

6. With obsessive compulsion toward brutal reality ("telling it like it is") realists find the modern world populated (or at least dominated) by civilized, moral, intelligent, rational, heroic people whose individual lives are not particularly fascinating. This "best of all possible worlds" gains color and interest, power and meaning, and a set of orderly processes and relationships, in its focus on war and conflict as the primary international relationships. Classical realism leans toward a subject matter revolving around national security, which Raymond Aron has called politics for "soldiers and diplomats." Mary Midgley has called the same thing "special lies that people tell themselves and each other to justify doing unjustifiable things." Mary Midgley, *Wisdom, Information and Wonder: What is Knowledge For?* (London: Routledge, 1989), 98.

7. Kenneth Waltz has argued powerfully for the primacy of the international system: Kenneth Waltz, *Theory of International Politics* (Reading, Massachusetts: Addison-Wesley, 1979), while Stephen Krasner convincingly applies realism to foreign policy analysis: Stephen Krasner, *Defending the National Interest* (Princeton, New Jersey: Princeton University Press, 1978).

8. Several analysts have ably exposed this weakness of realism: Richard Ashley, "The Poverty of Neorealism, " *International Organization* 38 (Spring 1984); Daniel Garst, "Thucydides and Neorealism," *International Studies Quarterly* 33 (March 1989).

9. Charles O. Lerche & Abdul A. Said, *Concepts of International Politics* (Englewood Cliffs, New Jersey: Prentice-Hall, 1963), 144.

10. Lewis Carroll, *Through the Looking Glass and What Alice Found There* (New York: Random House, 1946).

11. After finding the Red Queen in the spacious garden of Looking Glass House, Alice was mysteriously entered into an exhausting "Red Queen's Race." After catching her breath, she observed that

> somehow or other, they began to run. . . . The most obvious part of the thing was that the trees and the other things round them never changed their places at all: however fast they went, they never seemed to pass anything. . . . [After the race the Red Queen explained] it takes all the running you can do to keep in the same place. If you want to get somewhere else, you must run at least twice as fast as that.

Carroll, *Through the Looking Glass and What Alice Found There*, 30-32.

12. Edward D. Mansfield, *Power, Trade, and War* (Princeton, New Jersey: Princeton University Press, 1994), 232.

13. Barry Buzan, "Economic Structure and International Security: The Limits of the Liberal Case," *International Organization* 38 (1985): 623.

14. James H. Robinson, *The Mind in the Making* (New York: Harper & Brothers, 1939), 43.

15. Vincent Cable, "What Is International Economic Security?" *International Affairs* 71(2) (April 1995): 305-324; 308.

16. Gilpin, *The Political Economy of International Relations*, 57.

17. Jacob Viner, "Power versus Plenty as Objectives of Foreign Policy in the Seventeenth and Eighteenth Centuries," *World Politics* 1 (1948): 1-29; Albert O. Hirschman, *National Power and the Structure of Foreign Trade* (Berkeley: University of California Press, [1945] 1980).

18. Kenneth N. Waltz, "The Myth of National Interdependence," in Charles P. Kindleberger, ed., *The Multinational Corporation* (Cambridge, Massachusetts: MIT Press, 1970), 205.

19. Martin Wolf, "Cooperation or Conflict? The European Union in a Liberal Global Economy," *International Affairs* 71(2) (April 1995): 325-337; 326.

20. *Report on the subject of Manufactures* presented to House of Representatives, December 1791, cited in John Condliffe, *The Commerce of Nations* (New York: W. W. Norton, 1950), 240.

21. Cited in Edward Meade Earle, "Adam Smith, Alexander Hamilton, Friedrich List: The Economic Foundations of Military Power," in Peter Paret, ed., *Makers of Modern Strategy: From Machiavelli to the Nuclear Age* (Princeton, New Jersey: Princeton University Press, 1986), 235; emphasis added.

22. Michael Lind, "Hamilton's Legacy," *Wilson Quarterly* 18 (Summer 1994): 44.

23. Klaus Knorr, *The Power of Nations: The Political Economy of International Relations* (New York: Basic Books, 1975), esp. 235.

24. See Friedrich List, *National System of Political Economy* (London: Longmans, Green, 1928); see also Condliffe, *The Commerce of Nations*.

25. Lind, "Hamilton's Legacy," 49.

26. Cable, "What Is International Economic Security"? 308.

27. Robert Gilpin, "Economic Interdependence and National Security in Historical Perspective," in Klaus Knorr & Frank N. Trager, *Economic Issues and National Security* (New York: National Security Education Program of New York University, 1977), 42.

28. Meghnad Desai, "Vladimir Ilyich Lenin," in John Eatwell, Murray Milgate & Peter Newman eds., *Problems of the Planned Economy* (New York: W. W. Norton, 1990), 153.

29. Desai, "Vladimir Ilyich Lenin," 153.

30. Gilpin, "Economic Interdependence and National Security in Historical Perspective," 35.

31. Raymond Aron, *The Century of Total War* (Boston: Beacon Press, 1955), 57.

32. Robert Gilpin, "The Political Economy of Foreign Investment," *US Power and the Multinational Corporation* (New York: Basic Books, 1975), reprinted in Benjamin Gomes-Casseres and David B. Yoffie, eds. *The International Political Economy of Direct Foreign Investment, Vol. II* (Brookfield, Vermont: Edward Elgar, 1993), 274.

33. Aron, *The Century of Total War*, 58-59.

34. A. F. Mullins, Jr., *Born Arming: Development and Military Power in New States* (Stanford, California: Stanford University Press, 1987).

35. William H. McNeill, *The Pursuit of Power: Technology, Armed Force, and Society Since A.D. 1000* (Chicago: University of Chicago Press, 1982).

36. Samuel Finer, "State- and Nation-Building in Europe: The Role of the Military," in Charles Tilly, ed., *The Formation of National States in Western Europe* (Princeton, New Jersey: Princeton University Press, 1975), 84-163.

37. Nicolai D. Kondratieff, "The Long Waves in Economic Life," *Review of Economic Statistics* 17 (November 1935): 105-115; reprinted as Nicolai D. Kondratieff, "The Long Waves in Economic Life," *Review* 2 (Spring 1979): 519-562.

38. William R. Thompson, *On Global War: Historical-Structural Approaches to World Politics* (Columbia: University of South Carolina Press, 1988), 171.

39. Raimo Vayrynen, "Economic Cycles, Power Transitions, Political Management and Wars Between Major Powers," *International Studies Quarterly* 27 (December 1983): 398-418.

40. Hegemony refers to a period "in which one core power exceeds all others in the efficiency of its productive, commercial and financial activities, and in military strength." Research Working Group on Cyclical Rhythms and Secular Trends, "Cyclical Rhythms and Secular Trends of the Capitalist World-Economy: Some Premises, Hypotheses, and Questions," *Review* 2 (Spring 1979): 497.

41. A weakness of analyses linking Kondratieff long economic waves through hegemonic cycles or redistributions of national power, or any other intervening variable, to a tendency toward international conflict, lies in the inability to put the political concepts of hegemony or power hierarchy in quantitative, or even measurable, terms. Efforts to establish unequivocal quantitative indicators of comparative national power across countries or over time remain ambiguous. As a convenient default, analyses assume a close relationship between international politics and trade through interdependence theory, and use trade data as surrogates for growth, prevalence of great power war as an index of conflict, and historical impression as a discrete index of hegemony and power distribution.

42. Krasner identified three periods of openness (1820-1879, 1900-1913, 1945-1970) when tariffs fell, absolute and relative amounts of trade grew, and regional trading patterns lost salience, and two periods of closure (1879-1900, 1918-1939). Stephen D. Krasner, "State Power and the Structure of International Trade," *World Politics* 28 (1976): esp. 324.

43. Mansfield, *Power, Trade, and War*, Table 2.5, 56.

44. Mansfield, *Power, Trade, and War*, 53, see Table 2.6, 56.

45. Mansfield, *Power, Trade, and War*, 233.

46. Mansfield, *Power, Trade, and War*, 58.

47. Mansfield, *Power, Trade, and War*, 58, table 2.7, 59.

48. Mansfield, *Power, Trade, and War*, 58.

49. Gilpin, *The Political Economy of International Relations*.

50. Gilpin, "The Political Economy of Foreign Investment," 245-256.

51. Gilpin, "The Political Economy of Foreign Investment," 254.

52. Gilpin, "The Political Economy of Foreign Investment," 256.

53. Simon Kuznets, *Modern Economic Growth* (New Haven, Connecticut: Yale University Press, 1966), 344.

54. Like Kuznets, Kennedy did not consider the logical converse of the proposition: that economic decline, which also increases relative differences, is also associated with war. Both arguments rest on the effects of "increase" in a nation's power; they lose relevance when power decreases (See Appendix A). Paul M. Kennedy, *The Rise and Fall of the Great Powers: Economic Change and Military Conflict from 1500 to 2000* (New York: Random House, 1987), xxii.

55. Gilpin "Economic Interdependence and National Security in Historical Perspective," 47.

56. Gilpin, *The Political Economy of International Relations*, 54, also 23.

57. Michael D. Wallace, "Status, Formal Organization, and Arms Levels as Factors Leading to the Onset of War, 1820-1964," in Bruce M. Russett, ed., *Peace, War, and Numbers* (Beverly Hills, California: Sage Publications, 1972), 53.

58. Wallace, "Status, Formal Organization, and Arms Levels as Factors Leading to the Onset of War, 1820-1964," 68.

59. Gilpin, *The Political Economy of International Relations*, 47, 54-55; see also Robert Gilpin, *War and Change in World Politics* (Cambridge: Cambridge University Press, 1981).

60. Simon Kuznets, "Characteristics of Modern Economic Growth," in *Postwar Economic Growth: Four Lectures* (Cambridge, Massachusetts: Belknap Press of Harvard University Press, 1964), 57.

61. Kuznets, *Modern Economic Growth*, 344.

62. Kuznets, *Modern Economic Growth*, 344-345.

63. Kuznets, *Modern Economic Growth*, 345.

64. Kuznets, *Modern Economic Growth*, 500.

65. Kennedy, *The Rise and Fall of the Great Powers: Economic Change and Military Conflict from 1500 to 2000*, xxii.

66. Kennedy, *The Rise and Fall of the Great Powers: Economic Change and Military Conflict from 1500 to 2000*, xxii-xxiii.

67. L. N. Rangarajan, *The Limitation of Conflict* (New York: St. Martin's Press, 1985), 21.

68. A.F.K. Organski, *World Politics*, 2d ed. (New York: Alfred A. Knopf, 1968), 364-367; A.F.K. Organski & Jacek Kugler, *The War Ledger* (Chicago: University of Chicago Press, 1980), 19-20.

69. Richard N. Rosecrance, *The Rise of the Trading State: Commerce and Conquest in the Modern World* (New York: Basic Books, 1986), 160.

70. Joseph Nye has artfully and compellingly combined these forces over half a millennia, and noted the gradual shift in salience from political-military toward economic-commercial power resources:

Period	Hegemon	Major Power Resources
XVI Cent.	Spain	Gold bullion, colonial trade, mercenary armies, European dynastic ties
XVII Cent.	Netherlands	International and colonial trade, capital markets, navy and commercial fleet
XVIII Cent	France	Population and territory, agriculture and rural industry, public administration, national army, navy and commercial fleet
XIX Cent.	Britain	Domestic industry, political stability and cohesion, finance and credit, liberal values and institutions, navy and commercial fleet, easily defensible location (island)
XX Cent.	United States	Large economic scale of domestic market and industry, scientific and technical dominance, universally attractive culture, military forces and alliances, liberal international regimes, center of transnational communication, finance, transport

Joseph S. Nye, Jr., "The Changing Nature of World Power," in Demetrios Caraley & Cerentha Harris, *New World Politics: Power, Ethnicity, and Democracy* (New York: Academy of Political Science, 1993), Table 1, p. 45.

71. In 1853 American Admiral Matthew C. Perry could threaten, and intend, to bombard Japan if the emperor did not open Japanese ports for American trade and revictualing. A similarly bellicose threat by Washington in the 1990s over American exhortations to open Japanese markets is unimaginable.

72. Organski & Kugler, *The War Ledger*, 20; Nazli Choucri & Robert C. North *Nations in Conflict* (San Francisco: W.H. Freeman, 1974), 26-43.

73. Both Shelley and Niebuhr noted that power could paradoxically convert good to evil:

Power, like a desolating pestilence,
Pollutes whate'er it touches.

Percy Bysshe Shelley, *Queen Mab 1813* (Oxford: Woodstock Books, [1813] 1990), Canto III, 40.

Goodness, armed with power, is corrupted.

Reinhold J. Niebuhr, *Beyond Tragedy: Essays on the Christian Interpretation of History* (New York: Charles Scribner's Sons, 1937), 185.

74. Organski & Kugler, *The War Ledger*, 204.

75. Organski & Kugler, *The War Ledger*, 8-9.

76. Status theory developed the idea of "status dimensions" comprising several structural attributes of states. Attributes treated as dimensions have included GNP, area, population, government budgets, legal codes, political parties, riots and crimes, *etc.* Status dimensions could also involve process variables (trade, growth rates, structural shifts, political trends, *etc.*). Rudolph Rummel used two status dimensions (economic development indexed by energy usage, telephones, and GNP); and power bases (national income, population, land area, military strength, and military expenditure) to position states in a two-dimensional attribute space and determine their relative statuses in developing his status-field theory. See Rudolph J. Rummel, "U.S. Foreign Relations: Conflict, Cooperation, and Attribute Distances," in Bruce M. Russett, ed., *Peace, War, and Numbers* (Beverly Hills, California: Sage Publications, 1972), 71-113, esp. 78.

77. Johann Galtung, "A Structural Theory of Aggression," *Journal of Peace Research* 1(2) (1964): 95-119.

78. A major assumption implicit in the status inconsistency approach is that the principle of relative Values operates in the context of international relations, and especially in cooperative and conflictual national behaviors toward each other. Under this principle, behaviors and attributes of nation-states derive their importance primarily relative to other nations. The significance of some national attribute (wealth, military strength, population, *etc.*) rises not in its absolute value, but in its effect relative to a specific other nation. National power emerges from an aggregate of national attributes, and is seen as a relationship involving at least two nations. See Harold D. Lasswell & A. Kaplan, *Power and Society: A Framework for Political Inquiry* (New Haven, Connecticut: Yale University Press, 1950), esp 65; David Easton, *The Political System: An Inquiry Into the State of Political Science* (New York: Alfred A. Knopf, 1953), esp. 143-146; Hans J. Morgenthau, *Politics Among Nations*, 4th ed. (New York: Alfred A. Knopf, 1967), esp. 142.

79. Galtung discusses the converse inconsistency (high ascribed - low achieved) in Johann Galtung, "Rank and Social Integration: A Multidimensional Approach," in J. Berger *et al.*, *Sociological Theories in Progress*, Vol. I (Boston: Houghton Mifflin, 1966).

80. Rummel, "U.S. Foreign Relations: Conflict, Cooperation, and Attribute Distances," 87.

81. Psychological field theory argues that the determinants of human behavior are a single unified field, rather than separate individual traits. Lewin's field theory is similar in several respects to systems theory in its emphasis on the search for equilibrium in relation to the individual's environment. See Kurt Lewin, *A Dynamic Theory of Personality* (New York: McGraw-Hill, 1935); Kurt Lewin, *Field Theory in Social Science* (New York: Harper & Row, 1951); Morton Deutsch, "Field Theory," *International Encyclopedia of the Social Sciences*, David L. Sills, ed. (New York:

Macmillan and The Free Press, 1972), Vol. 5, 407-417.

82. Quincy Wright, *The Study of International Relations* (New York: Appleton-Century-Crofts, 1955), 524-569; Quincy Wright, "Development of a General Theory of International Relations," in Horace V. Harrison, ed., *The Role of Theory in International Relations* (Princeton, New Jersey: Van Nostrand, 1964), esp. 38.

83. Rudolph J. Rummel "Testing Some Possible Predictors of Conflict Behavior Within and Between Nations," *Papers I*, Chicago Conference, Peace Research Society (Chicago: Peace Research Society, 1963), 79-111; Rudolph J. Rummel, "Dimensions of Conflict Behavior Within and Between Nations," in *General Systems: Yearbook of the Society for General systems Research*, Vol. VIII (Society for General Systems Research, 1963), 1-50; Rummel, "U.S. Foreign Relations: Conflict, Cooperation, and Attribute Distances," 71-115.

84. Wallace, "Status, Formal Organization, and the Onset of War, 1820-1964," 49-69.

85. Maurice East & Charles F. Hermann, "Do Nation-Types Account for Foreign Policy Behavior?" in James N. Rosenau, ed., *Comparing Foreign Policies* (Beverly Hills, California: Sage Publications, 1974), 269-303.

86. Rummel, "Dimensions of Conflict Behavior Within and Between Nations"; Raymond Tanter, "Dimensions of Conflict Behavior Within and Between Nations, 1958-1960," *Journal of Conflict Resolution* 10(1) (March 1966): 41-64.

87. Cattell showed that domestic conflict had little relationship to foreign conflict, and that wars and nonmilitary conflicts (1837-1937) were statistically independent of economic growth and technological development, which were unrelated to war deaths and peacetime military expenditures. Raymond B. Cattell, "The Dimensions of Cultural Patterns by Factorization of National Characters," *Journal of Abnormal and Social Psychology* 64 (1949): 443-469; Raymond B. Cattell, B. H. Bruel & H. P. Hartman. "An Attempt at More Refined Definitions of the Cultural Dimensions of Syntality in Modern Nations," *American Sociological Review* 17 (1951): 408-421; Raymond B. Cattell & Richard L. Gorsuch, "The Definition and Measurement of National Morale and Morality," *Journal of Social Psychology* 67 (1965): 77-96.

88. Rudolph J. Rummel, "Dimensions of Domestic Conflict Behavior: Review of Findings," in Dean Pruitt & Robert Snyder, eds., *Theories of International Conflict* (Englewood Cliffs, New Jersey: Prentice-Hall, 1969), 226.

89. Rudolph J. Rummel, *The Dimensions of Nations* (Beverly Hills, California: Sage Publications, 1972), 364.

90. Brian J. L. Berry, "An Inductive Approach to the Regionalization of Economic Development," in Norton Ginsburg, ed., *Essays on Geography and Economic Development*, Department of Geography Research, Paper No. 62 (Chicago: University of Chicago Press, 1960), 78-107.

91. Rummel, *The Dimensions of Nations*, 373.

92. Lewin, *A Dynamic Theory of Personality*; Lewin, *Field Theory in Social Science*; Wright, *The Study of International Relations*, esp. 530-569; Wright, "Development of a General Theory of International Relations," esp. 38.

93. Rummel, "US Foreign Relations: Conflict, Cooperation, and Attribute Distances," 71-115; Sang-Woo Rhee, "China's Cooperation, Conflict and Interaction Behavior viewed from Rummel's Field Theory Perspective," in Rudolph J. Rummel, ed. *Field Theory Evolving* (Beverly Hills, California: Sage Publications, 1977), 371-403.

94. Rudolph J. Rummel, "A Status Field Theory of International Relations," in *Dimensionality of Nations Project Report No. 50* (Honolulu: Dimensionality of Nations Project, 1971), 5.

95. Rummel, "U.S. Foreign Relations: Conflict, Cooperation, and Attribute Distances," 77.

96. Rummel, *The Dimensions of Nations*, 374. Evidence for Rummel's hypothesis is in Ithiel de Sola Pool, *Symbols of Internationalism* (Stanford, California: Stanford University Press, 1951); Dina A. Zinnes, "Expression and Perception of Hostility in Inter-State Relations," PhD dissertation, Stanford University, 1963; Bruce M. Russett, *Community and Contention* (Cambridge, Massachusetts: MIT Press, 1963); Lewis Richardson, *Statistics of Deadly Quarrels* (Pittsburgh: Boxwood Press, 1960); Paul A. Smoker, "A Mathematical Study of the Present Arms Race," in *General Systems: Yearbook of the Society for General Systems Research*, Vol. VIII, 1963, 51-59; Paul A. Smoker, "A Pilot Study of the Present Arms Race," *General Systems: Yearbook of the Society for General Systems Research*, Vol. VIII, 1963, 61-76; Robert C. North, Richard A. Brody & Ole R. Holsti, "Some Empirical Data on the Conflict Spiral," *Peace Research Society, Papers I*, Chicago Conference, 1964, 1-14.

97. Rosenau suggested that a nation's foreign behavior is linked to attributes, specifically to economic development, size, and political orientation; differences in these national characteristics contribute most to the actions of one state toward another. James N. Rosenau, "Pre-Theories and Theories of Foreign Policy," in R. B. Farrell, ed. *Approaches to Comparative and International Politics* (Evanston, Illinois: Northwestern University Press, 1966), esp. 82-83, 97-98.

98. Rummel, "U.S. Foreign Relations: Conflict, Cooperation, and Attribute Distances," 78.

99. In three-dimensional attribute space, Rummel finds that "the three dimensions together—economic development, power bases, and political orientation—typically subsume over 40 percent of the variation of nations on their attributes." Rummel, "U.S. Foreign Relations: Conflict, Cooperation, and Attribute Distances," 78.

100. Rummel, "U.S. Foreign Relations: Conflict, Cooperation, and Attribute Distances," 88.

101. Rummel, "U.S. Foreign Relations: Conflict, Cooperation, and Attribute Distances."

102. Rummel, "U.S. Foreign Relations: Conflict, Cooperation, and Attribute Distances," Table 1, p. 94.

103. The negative correlation for cooperation reflects the test hypothesis that less-developed countries would be more cooperative than advanced wealthy countries. Their results show that developed countries are both more cooperative and more conflict-prone. James N. Rosenau & Gary Hoggard, "Foreign Policy Behavior in Dyadic Relationships: Testing a Pre-Theoretical Extension," in James N. Rosenau, ed., *Comparing Foreign Policies* (Beverly Hills, California: Sage Publications, 1974), 117-151). Kean and McGowan urged caution in accepting these results, because of their reliance on media sources in advanced nations, which may underreport actions of less developed nations. James Kean and Patrick J. McGowan, "National Attributes and Foreign Policy Participation: A Path Analysis," in Patrick J. McGowan, ed., *Sage International Yearbook of Foreign Policy Studies*, Vol. 1 (Beverly Hills, California: Sage Publications, 1973), p. 246.

104. Kean & McGowan, "National Attributes and Foreign Policy Participation: A Path Analysis," 226.

105. Sidney Verba and Norman Nie suggested that individuals of high socioeconomic status (job, education, income) tend to participate more than low-status people in politics. Sidney Verba & Norman H. Nie, *Participation in America* (New York: Harper & Row, 1972, esp. 13-22, 263-264.

106. Galtung, "A Structural Theory of Aggression"; see also Rudolph J. Rummel, "A Status-Field Theory of International Relations," in Rudolph J. Rummel, ed., *Field Theory Evolving* (Beverly Hills, California: Sage Publications, 1977), 199-255.

107. Richard W. Mansbach & John A. Vasquez, *In Search of Theory. A New Paradigm for Global Politics* (New York: Columbia University Press, 1981), 149.

108. Mansbach & Vasquez, *In Search of Theory. A New Paradigm for Global Politics*, 152. See also Rummel, "A Status-Field Theory of International Relations," 213; J. David Singer, Stuart Bremer & John Stuckey, "Capability Distribution, Uncertainty and Major Power War, 1820-1965," in Russett, ed., *Peace, War, and Numbers*, 25-26; J. David Singer & Melvin Small, "The Composition and Status Ordering of the International System, 1815-1940," *World Politics* 18(2) (January 1966): 236-282; J. David Singer & Melvin Small, *The Wages of War, 1816-1965: A Statistical Handbook* (New York: John Wiley, 1972), 19-30.

109. Morgenthau, *Politics Among Nations*.

110. G. Lagos, *International Stratification and Underdeveloped Countries* (Chapel Hill: University of North Carolina Press, 1963).

111. Organski, *World Politics*.

112. Bruce M. Russett "Economic Decline, Electoral Pressure, and the Initiation of Interstate Conflict." in Charles S. Gochman & Alan Ned Sabrosky, *Prisoners of War? Nation-States in the Modern Era* (Lexington, Massachusetts: Lexington Books, 1990), 123-140; 125.

113. Russett "Economic Decline, Electoral Pressure, and the Initiation of Interstate Conflict," 123-140.

114. Otto von Gierke, *Natural Law and the Theory of Society 1500 to 1800*, trans. Ernest Barker, (Cambridge: Cambridge University Press, [1913, 1934] 1950), 85.

115. Denis Healey, "The Sputnik and Western Defence," *International Affairs* 34(2) (April 1958): 154.

116. Wight, *International Theory: The Three Traditions*, 39.

117. Richard Cobden, *The Political Writings of Richard Cobden*, Vol. I (London: William Ridgway, 1868), 269.

118. Wight, *International Theory: The Three Traditions*, 12.

119. Wight, *International Theory: The Three Traditions*, passim, esp. 43-109.

120. Norman Angell, *The Great Illusion: A Study of the Relationship of Military Power in Nations to Their Economic and Social Advantage* (London: Weidenfeld & Nicholson, 1910).

121. Paul Seabury, "Realism and Idealism," in Alexander DeConde, ed., *Encyclopedia of American Foreign Policy: Studies of the Principal Movements and Ideas*, Vol. III (New York: Scribner's, 1978), 862.

122. Charles W. Kegley, Jr. & Eugene R. Wittkopf, *World Politics: Trend and Transformation*, 5th ed., (New York: St. Martin's Press, 1993), 21.

123. Gilpin, "Economic Interdependence and National Security in Historical Perspective," 39.

124. Gilpin, *The Political Economy of International Relations*, 56.

125. John Maynard Keynes, *The General Theory of Employment, Interest, and Money* (New York: Harcourt Brace Jovanovich, [1935] 1964); David Mitrany, *The Functional Theory of Politics* (London & New York: St. Martin's Press, 1975); John Mueller, *Retreat From Doomsday: The Obsolescence of Major War* (New York: Basic Books, 1989); Earle, "Adam Smith, Alexander Hamilton, Friedrich List: The Economic Foundations of Military Power."

126. An implicit liberal premise, of course, is that every country has, and is exploiting, its comparative advantage in relation to its various trading partners.

127. Buzan, "Economic Structure and International Security: The Limits of the Liberal Case," 598. Economic nationalism would argue that the increased competition of free trade can (by decreasing opportunity costs of lost trade) generate new, and exacerbate existing, tensions and escalate into international conflict and war. See Keynes, *The General Theory of Employment, Interest, and Money*; Jacob Viner, "Peace as an Economic Problem," in Jacob Viner, ed. *International Economics* (Glencoe, Illinois: Free Press, 1951); Nazli Choucri & Robert C. North, *Nations in Conflict: National Growth and International Violence* (San Francisco: W. H. Freeman, 1975); Robert Gilpin, *US Power and the Multinational Corporation: The Political Economy of Foreign Direct Investment* (New York: Basic Books, 1975).

128. Adam Smith, *An Inquiry into the Nature and Causes of the Wealth of Nations* (New York: Modern Library, [1776] 1957), 653.

129. Mansfield, *Power, Trade, and War*, 233.

130. Charles P. Kindleberger, *Foreign Trade and the National Economy* (New Haven, Connecticut: Yale University Press, 1966); Edward E. Leamer & Robert M. Stern, *Quantitative International Economics* (Boston: Allyn & Bacon, 1970); Wilfred Ethier, *Modern International Economics* (New York: W. W. Norton, 1983); Morris Goldstein & Mohsin S. Khan. "Income and Price Effects in Foreign Trade," in Ronald W. Jones & Peter B. Kenen, eds., *Handbook of International Economics*, Vol. II (Amsterdam: North-Holland, 1984).

131. Gilpin, *The Political Economy of International Relations*, 57.

132. Mansfield, *Power, Trade, and War*, 234.

133. Robert O. Keohane & Joseph S. Nye, Jr. "*Power and Interdependence* Revisited," *International Organization* 41 (1987): 725-753, esp. 747; see also Mansfield, *Power, Trade, and War*.

134. Viner, "Peace as an Economic Problem"; Robert O. Keohane & Joseph S. Nye, Jr., *Power and Interdependence: World Politics in Transition* (Boston: Little, Brown, 1977); Keohane & Nye, "*Power and Interdependence* Revisited"; Rosecrance, *The Rise of the Trading State: Commerce and Conquest in the Modern world*; Joseph S. Nye, Jr., "Neorealism and Neoliberalism," *World Politics* 40 (1988): 235-251.

135. Mansfield, *Power, Trade, and War*, 233 (italics in original).

4

An Empirical Approach

The causes of growth and conflict remain subjects of formidable research, but are of only incidental interest to this study, which deals specifically and only with the relationship between them: occurrence of rapid, sustained economic growth as an independent variable, and incidence of international conflict as a dependent variable. A perhaps implicit premise, which rejects the classical realist position, is that some relationship between growth and conflict does indeed exist, and can be discerned. The aim of the research is to identify any lawlike regularities that may exist in the relationship between international conflict and modern economic growth (see Appendix N). An additional desirable result would be any predictions about manipulating the variables for best efficiency in achieving desired policy effects; this result would arise from evaluating various elements of the variables for their individual power.

RESEARCH DESIGN

The analysis accepts growth and conflict as separate phenomena arising from causes that are presumed to operate whenever either phenomenon occurs. Causality may indeed flow through the relationship, and a set of robust lawlike regularities may even imply causality. Any investigation, analysis, or determination of such causality is, however, beyond the scope, depth, and intent of this research.

The analysis does not assume that any particular set of political-economic conditions determines the nature of the relationship. Any lawlike regularities would hold as powerfully in a world dominated by war as in a world of peace and prosperity. Nor does the analysis consciously include normative concepts of growth or conflict: neither is inherently good or bad, nor always a preferred policy goal.

To achieve generality commensurate with the concept of lawlike regularities, the analysis addresses long periods that span various sets of political-economic conditions, and enough countries to avoid artifacts of purely national features. It includes sufficient objective observations to constitute more than a set of selective case studies. To address the separate incidence of growth and conflict at different times, the analysis considers both temporal directions of the relationship: from earlier growth to later conflict and from preceding conflict to following growth.

An effective methodology for achieving the research goal is the search for lawlike regularities across a set of regressions on country time series, each of which constitutes a single observation of the growth-conflict relationship. Use of lags and leads allows some appreciation of directionality, but does not allow any deterministic conclusions about causality,[1] while standard statistical techniques allow both quantifying data and assessing individual significance of components of the variables. With time series for conflict as dependent variables and time series for growth as independent variables, the Weighted Ordinary Least Squares (WOLS) regression process describes the growth-conflict relationship for each country over the period 1930-1990.[2] The combination of adjusted correlation coefficient and stabilized regression equation specifies the growth-conflict relationship for each country and constitutes a single observation. The design of the analysis is to identify lawlike regularities among these observed relationships, to infer from them explanations, and to expose any anomalies or singularities that weaken the set of lawlike regularities.

Primary data are annual time series from 1930 through 1990 for indicators of conflict and growth for the 30 countries identified as having experienced periods of rapid economic growth at least once in the eighteenth, nineteenth, or twentieth centuries. For dependent-variable time series the primary data are national involvement in international war and national incidence of nonwar international conflict. Primary conflict data form time series for three sets of relationships between the indicators of growth and three distinct indicators of conflict: international war (W), nonwar conflict (NW), and total conflict (TC) (the sum of war and nonwar conflicts). One country-specific conflict time series appears directly as the dependent variable in each regression of the three regression sets. Weighting each dependent-variable country time series with its corresponding global time series—total global war (TOTWAR), total global nonwar conflict (TOTNWC), or total global conflict (TOTCNF)—generates an adjusted correlation coefficient as a primary indicator of the growth-conflict relationship.

Primary data for independent-variable time series are national population and national product. Data are not available for some countries for every year in the 1930-1990 period. Annual independent-variable time series, thus, include "best-estimate" interpolations between reliable direct observations. Extrapolation extends trends for short periods before the earliest data only for China, Korea, Taiwan, Russia, and Australia, only to allow the regression process to generate a statistic.

INTERNATIONAL CONFLICT

Between national adversaries conflict varies in intensity, quantity, and kind over time. Specific disputes may lie dormant for many years, emerge into awareness, escalate through diplomacy to war, find temporary resolution or recede from concern, and reemerge later in a different form or context. Historic patterns of enmity, rivalry, or discord, continuing over long periods, can solidify into institutions with powerful dynamics that may submerge original issues beneath misunderstanding, emotional ideology, or inertia, within one, or each, nation. Embedded in diplomatic and commercial relations between national adversaries, these sorts of disputes follow their own paths through generations and across cultures.[3] Many international conflicts are also interlocked over time, or across opponents, by the tendency of pragmatic decision-makers to establish precedents, or learn lessons, from past, or similar, conflicts. Such related conflicts thereby gain or lose salience and intensity in series or in groups.[4]

Use as a dependent variable requires some quantification and specification of international conflict, or at least determination of whether a nation is in conflict or not. Analysis must separate the innumerable occurrences of international conflict into discrete cases or observations. Conflict must be measured absolutely as a discrete countable event with a beginning, an end, and some distinguishing features. This sort of specification necessarily involves analytical discrimination, definite criteria, and judgment in converting behaviors into discrete data, but what the data may lose in richness the analysis gains in objectivity. While general and topical information in depth or in breadth often provides invaluable insight into relationships and processes, because reliable specific data provide more confidence in identifying lawlike regularities, the focus is on analysis of data, rather than on interpretation of information.

Conflict Databases

While studies on war, revolution, and other military conflicts are legion, fewer have dealt with the less violent, more mundane aspects of international conflict: troop movements, demonstrations, or mobilizations, border incidents, diplomatic accusations and protests; policy defiance, resistance, or formal threats. Information and data on international conflict have been collected in two broad forms: massive amounts of qualitative and historical information on war, with substantial quantitative data addressing incidence and intensity; and a few small sets of quantitative modern data on event-interactions involving both cooperation and conflict, supplemented by massive amounts of "current-events" analyses, "policy papers," and miscellaneous topical information about international relations. While databases for both war and nonwar involve various fields of topical data, both types include compatible data on frequency and intensity.

Quantitative historical war databases extend formally from 1475 through 1980, and have been extended through 1992 by several research projects; modern event-interaction databases extend from 1948 through 1990, and can be extended backward or forward by archival research and coding. The former deal exclusively with violent conflict; the latter, predominantly with nonviolent events. Although for dually reported modern periods the war data sets can duplicate some items in event-interactions sets, careful sorting can eliminate dual counting.

Because of the arrangement of conflict data, consideration of international conflict as a dependent variable must involve, at least initially, two separate analyses: relationships between war data and economic growth; relationships between modern event-interaction data and economic growth. Thus the initial focus of research and analysis is on war data sets and event-interactions data sets.

War Databases

The conflicts most often studied entail violence of some sort, military forces and operations, destruction, and death: international war and revolution. In many studies of violent conflict, scholars have generated a plethora of interesting theories, and several useful sets of empirical data about the incidence and intensity of wars. These sorts of violent conflict, at one limit of a multidimensional range of conflict, constitute a "war dimension" (proposed by Rudolph Rummel and Raymond Tanter) that also includes threatening military activities, mobilization, troop movements, blockade, occupations, or arms races. Violent international conflict, thus, can appear in analyses in two ways: war (combat between at least two national military forces) and militarized dispute (threat or unilateral use of military force).[5] War generally involves substantial troop strengths or battle casualties. Militarized disputes are incidents of explicit threats, displays, or uses of military power by one state against another.

Quincy Wright intended his large, comprehensive catalogue to include all military hostilities of any sort "which were recognized as states of war in the legal sense or which involved over 50,000 troops."[6] Lewis Richardson's criteria for inclusion involve combat casualties.[7] The Correlates of War Project, directed by J. David Singer, collected data on both wars and militarized disputes, which Bruce Bueno de Mesquita extended to 1974.[8] For Jack Levy war is "substantial armed conflict between the organized military forces of independent military units,"[9] but he limits his data to wars involving the great powers. In refining their earlier work, Melvin Small and J. David Singer list all wars and militarized disputes between 1816 and 1980 identified by Wright, Richardson, and several other sources, but then exclude those that disqualify for: (a) inadequate or ambiguous political status of the participants; or (b) failure to meet a minimum threshold of battle-connected casualties of troops in combat.[10]

Each war data set involves its own unique definition of war, and its own approach to quantifying war. Eight data sets are particularly useful both in ascertaining the distribution and incidence of wars over time and across countries and in identifying their features:

Lewis Richardson, *Statistics of Deadly Quarrels* (Pittsburgh: Boxwood Press, 1960)

Quincy Wright, *A Study of War*, 2d ed. (Chicago: University of Chicago Press, 1965)

J. David Singer & Melvin Small, *The Wages of War, 1816-1965: A Statistical Handbook* (New York: John Wiley, 1972)

Raymond Lyle Butterworth, *Managing Interstate Conflict, 1945-1974: Data With Synopses* (Pittsburgh, University Center for International Studies, University of Pittsburgh, 1976)

Bruce Bueno de Mesquita, *The War Trap* (New Haven, Connecticut: Yale University Press, 1981)

Daniel Frei, *Managing International Crises* (Beverly Hills, California: Sage Publications, 1982)

Melvin Small & J. David Singer, *Resort to Arms: International and Civil Wars: 1816-1980* (Beverly Hills, California: Sage Publications, 1982)

Jack Levy, *War in the Modern Great Power System: 1495-1975* (Lexington: University Press of Kentucky, 1983).

As might be expected, the several data sets show considerable variation and differences. Each investigator has adopted a different definition of war, a different analytical perspective, and a separate set of criteria for inclusion in the universe of relevant wars. A second pair of differences is level and intent of an investigation, which affect the process of separating war into units of analysis through the operational parameters of the hypothesis. A third difference is reflected in different techniques for dating duration of war. Consequently, an analytical "case" in one data set may not correspond to a particular perception of a specific war. A single case may represent, or involve, several different wars, while the international community—or anyone else—may collect several analytical cases into a single war. Further, when the international community has chosen to treat a series of related wars as a single issue (World War I, World War II, decolonization and independence in a country, *et al.*), those wars can become a single analytical case. A continuing war can also involve several cases when its course or content (diplomatic, strategic, political) changes over time. The structure of a case may, thus, not be constrained to a single set of disputants and issues at a particular time.

Edward Mansfield compared most of these data sets and found pronounced variation in details and only low correlation between sets.[11] Differences in detail may generate contradictions in the specific analyses of individual data sets. He found, however, that the several sets of data each fit the Poisson distribution well with no evidence of autocorrelation, although trending is ambiguous.[12] His results suggest that analysis can confidently aggregate data at the level of general conclusions, tendencies, and impressions, and may suggest lawlike regularities, without introducing obvious statistical artifacts.

In any aggregation of war data line entries, analysis must recognize and accept, however, that the data in different sets are not interchangeable, or even obviously complementary, except in a narrow and truly historical sense. Because they are at best supplementary, results involving each data set separately cannot be dismissed as invalid. Indeed a single analysis could probably frame questions appropriately and select a particular set of war data to "prove" or "disprove" virtually any hypothesis. Some regularity of gross results across the war databases may be the most that analysis can expect.

Use of an aggregate data set comprising any wars in any source set, but carefully avoiding multiple counts, avoids quibbles about definitions or criteria without degrading confidence in aggregate results or apparent lawlike regularities. A broad search of public and historical information, based on initial direct aggregation and integration of the eight data sets, identified a list of cases of international conflict that seem to meet some common criteria —implicit to all of the data sets—for war. Arranged in chronological sequence by year of emergence as an important international, public concern, the list of wars identifies each case by a title, the opposing countries, and its active dates. The master war list, which provides the dependent variable in one set of regressions, includes 760 wars and militarized disputes fought between 1480 and 1990, each listed in at least one source data set.

Nonwar Event-Interaction Data

Events data are words and deeds—verbal and physical actions and reactions—that nations direct toward their environments (see Appendix H). They are observations of the process, which record who says or does what to whom. An event is the result of political decision, and originates in the choices of decision-makers. An event is specified in terms of national initiator, action, and national target. Usage has collected events into three groups: cooperation, ambiguous-neutral, conflict.

Charles McClelland posits international behavior as a result of the flow of transactions and event-interactions among nations.[13] Subject to various disturbances, transactions are routine, aggregated, nonpolitical flows that do not involve *ad hoc* decision making: complying with regulations, implementing policy or strategy, and following precedent. Event-interactions (or events) are "turbulent, public, political flows such as threats, protests, and demands."[14] Events are major disturbances to the routine of international transactions that reflect some deliberate deviation from that routine. Reported by the public press, they reflect political, rather than administrative, measures; they are the actions of the higher levels of national government.[15] They determine whether and how nations pursue cooperation or conflict.

In developing the concepts and procedures of events data analysis, scholars, journalists, and analysts have generated a set of databases encoding international conflict in a variety of ways that allow quantification in both absolute and relative terms. Analysts have fashioned many coding schemes around Harold Lasswell's classic statement of the process: "who says what to whom, through what channels, with what effects."[16] Conflict events are coded in terms of initiator (who), recipient (whom), subject (what: recall of diplomats and breaking diplomatic relations, war, diplomatic protests, border incidents, nonmilitary confrontations, *etc.*), time (when), and mode of communication (channel). A conflict event occurs when each of the coding rules can be satisfied with sufficient information and specificity to generate an observation.

The events data bases used as primary sources to develop the time series for nonwar international conflict include:

WORLD EVENT INTERACTION SURVEY (WEIS): Charles McClelland; WEIS Project (1966-1969); Sources = *New York Times, Times* (London), *Los Angeles Times*, 18 other sources[17]

DIMENSIONALITY OF NATIONS (DON): Rudolph J. Rummel; codes only CONFLICT behavior[18]

CONFLICT AND PEACE DATA BANK (COPDAB): Edward Azar, University of North Carolina[19]

COMPARATIVE RESEARCH ON THE EVENTS OF NATIONS (CREON): Charles Hermann; Focus on internal, domestic influences on foreign policy (1957-1958); Sources = *Deadline Data* based on 46 other sources[20]

SITUATIONAL ANALYSIS PROJECT (SAP): Richard Rosecrance, Cornell University; 1870-1890; Sources = diplomatic histories (American Historical Association's *Guide to Historical Literature*), *Times* (London)[21]

LENG-SINGER EVENTS DATA TYPOLOGY: Singer-Small Ecological Correlates of War Project, University of Michigan; 1815-1965[22]

Additional data bases used as secondary sources include:

CONFLICT AND COOPERATION IN EAST-WEST CRISES: Walter Corson; Cold-War System 1945-1965; Sources = *Deadline Data, New York Times, World Almanac*; modification of WEIS categories (also in McGowan, CREON, FRIP)[23]

MIDDLE EAST CONFLICT AND COOPERATION ANALYSIS (MECCA): Robert Burrowes; 7 nations (ISR, LEB, JOR, KSA, IRQ, SYR, EGYPT) 1961-1967[24]

MIDDLE EAST PROJECT: J. Wilkenfeld 1969; 6 ME countries 1949-1967 intracountry interactions only, no external relationships; Sources = *New York Times Index, Middle East Journal, Keesing's Contemporary Archives, Facts on File*[25]

AFRICAN FOREIGN POLICY BEHAVIOR STUDY: Patrick McGowan; sub-Saharan regional only 1957-1969[26]

FOREIGN RELATIONS INDICATOR PROJECT (FRIP): Vernard Lanphier; Phase I = 7 nations over 6 months, Phase II = LATAM focus; Source = DOS operational traffic[27]

MODERN ECONOMIC GROWTH

Simon Kuznets established a profound distinction between simple economic growth, which has been occurring for millennia, and what he called modern economic growth (MEG), which only emerged in the eighteenth century.[28]   This restricted concept includes high growth rates of both population and *per capita* product, with the necessary result of enormous increases in aggregate product. Unlike simple annual increases in elements of national accounts, this intensive growth involves changes of such magnitude and rapidity that they can overwhelm low-frequency high-amplitude business cycles and economic swings, epidemics, catastrophes, and even minor political disturbances and wars. These evolutionary changes appear only over long periods, and allow identification of any sustained (more than a single generation) trend: periods of decades, rather than years.

Virtually everything that happens in a country affects its rate of growth, the actions of its people, or both. The concept includes any effects that people may introduce through irrationality, politics, learning, or something else, and allows expanding the analytical focus beyond purely economic factors. This sort of analysis subsumes the impacts of other interesting domestic variables that contribute to international behaviors, but restricts analysis to aggregate and external effects.[29]

High Growth Rates

With rapid increase in *per capita* output as its most prominent feature, modern economic growth involves high, sustained growth rates—significantly higher than those of previous periods, or those of the rest of the world—for *both* total national product *and* population. In the premodern past, economic growth involved increase in population and in product, but seldom in *per capita* product, which often grew only as a result of catastrophic reductions in population. Growth of this sort necessarily implies immense increases in aggregate national product, and shifts the focus of analysis from annual indicators to at least decadal measures.

For modern countries experiencing MEG, decadal growth rates have ranged between 14% and 28% in nineteenth-century Europe and North America, over 40% (United States, Canada, Japan, USSR), to more than 100% in modern East Asia. Decadal growth rates for *per capita* income have been well above 10%, and for many countries (Sweden, Japan, USSR), more than 20%. During the 1950s, European *per capita* incomes grew at decadal rates between 24% and 81%, with most around 40%; American growth was in the range 10% to 13%.[30] Such high growth rates allow small differences across countries to generate rapidly increasing absolute and relative differences in wealth and power, with corresponding dramatic effects on both economic relationships and distribution of political power among nations.

Independent Growth of *Per Capita* Income and Population

Human labor has been historically, and remains, a primary productive factor, upon which both survival and economic growth depend. Societies are, in principle, able to increase production, and thereby wealth, by exploiting increases in population. Population growth rates, however, have differed considerably among countries experiencing MEG and over time in a single country experiencing several periods of growth. During periods of rapid economic growth in both Europe and North America (nineteenth century, post-1950), national populations were growing rapidly, with decadal rates ranging from 2.5% for France through 6%–7% for United Kingdom, Italy, Sweden, USSR (1928-1958) to more than 20% for United States, Canada, Australia. Between about 1810 and 1900, while Britain experienced a second and third growth period, and France a second, Britain's population tripled, while France's increased by only a third.[31]

Although not intuitively apparent, it is empirically demonstrable that the size of a country—either in area or in population—is not significantly correlated with growth of aggregate production, however measured,[32] and inferentially that simultaneous growth of both is a distinctive feature of MEG. Further, Kuznets finds no apparent systematic association between rates of growth for population and *per capita* income—either over time or across countries—beyond the implicit high rates of increase in total product from about 20% to as much as 50% per decade for countries experiencing MEG.[33] Economies experiencing MEG have, perhaps coincidentally:

  increased access to natural and human resources through migration, colonization, and aggression;

  benefitted from disproportionately large increases in the productive cohorts of populations;

  capitalized on falling infant mortality to reduce economic waste involved in raising large families in expectation that only a few children would survive to productive adulthood;

  released females into the nation's labor force;

  increased labor productivity through reductions in morbidity and senescence;

  generated growing domestic markets, with larger economies of scale; and

  reduced risk of investment and encouraged business expansion through increasing confidence in the stability of large markets, low volatility of death rates, and continuing population growth.

Growth Rates Are Uniform and Increasing

Growth rates, especially for total product, in countries experiencing modern economic growth have been broadly uniform over long periods. Contributing factors include stable population growth (few epidemics, wars, catastrophes); scientific and technological progress based on discovery and innovation; increasing agricultural productivity and reduced risk of crop failure; expanded sources of supply and markets and rapid transportation; shift of production from resource-dependent agriculture to controllable industry and services. This capacity for sustained growth makes possible and likely high rates (at least averages over long periods) of growth.

Modern growth rates (population and *per capita* income) are substantially higher than premodern rates, and seem to be increasing.   Historical comparisons suggest that countries that began initial MEG periods later have grown faster than their predecessors.[34] It is easy to forget that sustained annual growth of 0.8% was seen as virtually impossible in the seventeenth century. As they grow and "catch up" or "close the gap," however, the annual growth rates for twentieth-century "late starters" seem to fall rapidly from very high to average. Given this long secular trend, modern countries starting growth from very low levels of production *per capita* can expect, and probably achieve, dramatically high initial growth rates as they accelerate into Kuznetsian MEG, but must also anticipate falling growth rates over time.

In addition to a secular trend toward higher rates, another, possibly phased, feature affects growth. The early years of industrialization appear to have little effect on current growth rates, but seem necessary preparation for commencement of MEG. Industrialization began in both England and France sometime between about 1690 and 1710, yet aggregate growth did not accelerate initially in either economy until the second quarter of the eighteenth century. Indeed most of the eighteenth century appears, in terms of aggregate economic indicators, as a period of little change, until the French Revolution. Nearly two centuries later, and over a similar period, Japanese industrialization probably began with Admiral Matthew Perry's visit in 1853, yet MEG did not commence until about 1870. Recognizing the necessary preparations for MEG places industrialization more in the context of a long period of cumulative innovation than that of a short apocalyptic spurt of technological dynamism. Post-1945 growth, which seems very rapid, even compressed, in these historical terms, seems either to be qualitatively different, or to be occurring in a different political-economic context.

Factor Inputs and Innovation

North America and Europe, and even Japan initially, faced the relatively primitive global economies of the eighteenth and nineteenth centuries. After centuries of premodern economies operating only slightly above subsistence levels, aggregate demand far exceeded available national, and even global, supply, and was the ultimate economic justification for increasing production. So long as demand remained higher than supply, economic self-interest, which liberal capitalism recognized as the "nature of mankind," pointed growing nations toward increasing the supplies of goods available for sale. The obvious challenge was to expand production capacity through application of more factor inputs (capital and labor), wherever and whenever they could be found. Growing economies extended Mercantilist, commercial, and political empires in search of population and territories, traditionally the most salient factors of production. The initial engine of resource-based growth was economic expansion of national political jurisdictions and influence to gain access to additional factors of production, and also to additional markets demanding even more production. This sort of economic expansion, as practiced two centuries ago, is no longer, however, the same powerful engine of growth. Indeed, it may not have been a very powerful engine even then.

A final feature of resource-based growth, even when it meets Kuznets' criteria for modern economic growth, is that it must end. Marx identified a critical limitation in noting that since this system—based on division of labor— had no foundation independent of the workers, capital would be constantly wrestling with insubordinate labor. He presented three fundamental socioeconomic weaknesses that prevent indefinitely continuing resource-based growth (see Appendix E):

> the necessary pyramidal hierarchies of skill, strength, and capability created by division of labor prevent infinite application of "The Babbage Principle" through merely increasing the amounts of unskilled labor applied to production;
> division of labor could only increase efficiency to some finite limit set by what a single worker was able to do; all parts must be made, and all tasks performed, ultimately by a single worker with limited human capabilities; and
> even through division of labor and technology, manufacturers could never overcome the physical, social, and political limitations on available labor time.[35]

In addition to these labor-related limits, the ever increasing requirements for raw materials and markets present another set of limits to resource-based growth. Growth can continue only so long as the economy can provide more raw materials for the production process, and markets for its products. Since both are finite—in either national or global terms—growth must end at some point. That point is, in the Westphalian system, determined primarily by national states in their international relations with each other.

In parallel with economic expansion through trade, the effects of new technologies, novel industrial organizations, and the division of labor, introduced in early MEG periods, were often well hidden by more obvious, and politically sensitive, changes in labor and capital. While national labor forces increased only slightly as a proportion of population in most countries during early growth periods, absolute hours worked declined substantially, and growth in aggregate output occurred with fewer work hours *per capita*.

For most of the eighteenth century, the structure of British and French output did not change much. Macroeconomic indicators suggest that MEG in the eighteenth century, and even well into the nineteenth, seemed little but "more of the same": more labor, more capital, more trade. Not until about 1780 (the orthodox beginning of the Industrial Revolution) did structural change even begin to appear. After the Napoleonic Wars, "a definite trend away from agriculture and in favor of manufacture became notable only from the 1820s."[36] Available data for Europe, North America, and Japan indicate that the ratio of capital to output actually declined as their economies expanded in the century-and-a-half after Waterloo.[37]

The eighteenth-century formula of "more of the same" didn't seem to fit facts, or even to work, as the twentieth century opened. A substantial increase in productivity, arising initially from eighteenth-century technological, organizational, and commercial innovation, had become essential to sustain growth. The technology-based view that MEG is a result of higher efficiency or improved factor productivity, rather than simply increased factor inputs, is familiar.[38] Modern economics has expanded the set of factor inputs to include technology, and some additional "residual."

Alternative Economies

Among the alternatives to these innovations of modern economic growth, artisan production, medieval guilds, colonialism, planned economies, state protection and political-economic stimulus developed their own dynamic systems in parallel, simultaneously, and in competition. Throughout modern Europe, and indeed through history, these alternative economic systems have proliferated and generated simple economic growth, but not Kuznetsian MEG. Nor were they always stagnant relics from the past in declining sectors. Alternative systems generally integrated social cooperation into economic production, to ensure sources of materials and stable, disciplined workforces, to accomplish complex production processes, or to provide ready markets in times of cyclical business fluctuations.

Particularly successful alternatives to MEG brought prosperity to Leiden and Lille, to Birmingham and middle England, and to southern Sweden, from the fifteenth to the nineteenth centuries. Market-oriented industries prospered and supported traditional urban societies. Vigorous competition and heavy investment were prominent economic features, which, at the same time, were rigidly circumscribed by certain firmly defended social values and institutions. Full employment, a "reasonable" standard of living, preservation of a monarchic social structure, complete political and economic autonomy for every producer, or rough equality among artisans and among workers, rather than macroeconomic growth and microeconomic profit maximization were the goals and results of these systems (see Appendix F).

In alternative systems, technological progress in devices, tools, and work techniques has usually been significant, ubiquitous, and flexible. Indeed, specific inventions, or improvements, were sequestered, rather than diffused, as guarantees of continuing the special skills or commercial advantages that they brought. Alternative systems generally involved encouragement, and even pressure, for innovation and change, *but did not allow change to transform society*. Rather, they were deliberately designed to generate sustained economic growth *without any other modification* of the ways in which people behaved.

Society's stubborn resistance to the power of the market has echoed over three centuries of wars, riots, strikes, crime, and conflict. Motivated or constrained by nonmarket forces, and mediated through various social, moral, political, or ideological values, these alternative systems were "not simply transitional or intermediate, but formed one of the 'obstacles' to the rise of capitalism."[39] Neither Marx's "manufactures" stage (see Appendix E) nor Franklin Mendels' "protoindustries" (see Appendix G) could "industrialize" spontaneously from any of these alternative systems; both concepts, however, included at least a spark of MEG, conspicuously absent from other alternatives. Modern economic growth itself is one of many alternative systems of production and growth. The power and viability of various approaches to innovation and change have been determined by their adaptability to the market.

The eighteenth century was not simply a confusing period of political-economic "alternatives" explainable only in case-specific exceptions to something, nor was it a static gap between the innovative insights of seventeenth-century mercantilists and the new economic orthodoxy of Adam Smith.[40] It laid a foundation for the emergence of modern economic growth as a robust, powerful phenomenon relying on the ultimate, unique capability of humanity to innovate, to invent, to create new knowledge, and to use those creations to change the conditions of human life, rather than to preserve obsolete forms. Whether from Marx's perspective of "capital accumulation," or from Mendels' of "protoindustrialization," initial periods of resource-based MEG must be "credited with creating the key changes in the use of land, labor, capital, and entrepreneurship which made the Industrial Revolution possible."[41]

Interdependence

Modern economic growth has markedly increased economic interdependence among nations—those experiencing MEG, others dominated by pre-MEG simple growth, and those not growing at all. Proportions of foreign trade and returns from foreign investments to aggregate production have risen significantly in all rapidly growing economies. *This increase appears to be a distinctive—even definitive—feature* of MEG.[42] Although technologies of transportation and communication have been critical, the political-economic dynamics of interdependence have overcome both space and time, "because the impressive attainments of economic modernization in developed countries set up ties of dependence and competition, of attraction and repulsion, of cooperation and latent conflict, which, in their universal reach and general intensity, are probably unmatched in the historical past."[43]

A powerful, cumulative—over time and across economies—effect of rapid growth seems to be aggravation of any imbalance between consumer purchasing power (aggregate demand) and productive capacity (aggregate supply). Unbalanced "demand-side" (consumption) or "supply-side" (industrialization) models often simply increase either production or domestic consumption. Other economies are left to deal with changes in markets, resources, and productivity, needed to accommodate additional demand or supply brought by growth. In contrast, however, to these "costs" of growth, the profound long-term "benefits" of additional investment, adoption of new technology, or increased employment often occur in other economies that are linked in either dependence or interdependence with a growing economy. "These international 'leakages' substantially weaken domestic economic policies. Stimulus in one country, if other economies remain stagnant, simply increases imports and immigration into the expanding economy."[44]

Modern economic growth seems to require policies that, at least, coordinate national growth with global or regional growth, which requires expanding demand in all economies, or at least in those that are closely linked to a growing economy. As interdependence increases, it is no longer enough to generate purely domestic growth. It may be that, unlike the fiercely nationalistic era of early MEG in Europe and North America, modern political-economic interdependence now obviates purely national versions of MEG.

Long-term Structural Change

Modern economic growth inherently brings—indeed requires and generates—significant, sustained political-economic structural changes over a long period. These are not merely fluctuations that increase briefly and then decline, or cycles around some static equilibrium or oscillating trend. Long-term changes are usually profound, self-reinforcing, and perhaps irreversible.

As new industries and institutions appear and old ones recede, cumulative, sustained rise in *per capita* product is almost inherently accompanied by a parallel shift in relative proportions of goods demanded and supplied, in patterns of living, and in the relationships between nations. Such changes in combinations of productive factors, and in productivity per unit of labor and capital input, are usually possible only through application of major innovations and new bodies of knowledge to some aspect of the processes of economic production. "Indeed, modern economic growth is, in substance, an application of the industrial system, i.e., a system of production based on increasing use of modern scientific knowledge."[45]

Timing

Virtually every economy has increased output rapidly at some time, and has experienced some brief growth in this simple pre-Kuznetsian sense. Many have also experienced growth in *per capita* income. Those, however, that have sustained parallel increases in *both* income *per capita and* population are few —probably no more than 40-50 of the hundreds of economies that mankind has operated. Virtually all of these have appeared in the modern era.

Modern economic growth appeared first in Britain in the second third of the eighteenth century, spread to France by the Revolution, and to the low countries and Switzerland by the battle at Waterloo. Austria, Germany, and North America began their growth a bit later, and by midcentury Scandinavia and Australia were beginning to feel its dynamics. Kuznets has estimated the median annual growth rate for these early-developing countries of Europe and North America at about 3%, or about 2% in *per capita* terms.[46]

The half-century before World War I seemed very favorable for beginning sustained economic growth. Noticeable Latin American growth began in Chile in about 1840 and in Argentina and Brazil by 1860. Ceylon, Burma, and Malaya emerged as growing colonial economies in the later nineteenth century. Canada, Russia, Thailand, and Italy were growing by the end of the century, as other Latin American countries, Japan and Southeast Asia were expanding. Economic growth can be dated from about 1910 in Korea. A few African colonial economies—Algeria, Nigeria, Ghana, Ivory Coast, Kenya, Uganda, Tanganyika, Rhodesia—experienced a brief episode of rapid growth before World War I.

In contrast, the interwar period brought growth to very few countries. While Poland and Czechoslovakia began to show slow growth in the 1920s, the rest of Southern and Eastern Europe did not begin sustained growth until after World War II. Economic growth can be dated from the 1920s in Zambia, Morocco, and Venezuela. The annual growth rate of world production fell from nearly 4% in the three decades before the War to less than 2.7% in the first postwar decade and to 1.3% in the 1930s; *per capita* growth fell even more sharply.

A final large group of countries, including India, China, Egypt, Turkey, the Arab countries, and Indonesia, has begun growth only during the postwar boom (1945 to 1973). These countries began their first experiences of rapid economic growth as the "developed" countries were entering their second and third periods of growth. After rising to a crest of 4.9% in 1973, the median annual aggregate growth rate for developed countries of the Organization for Economic Cooperation and Development (OECD) fell to 2.5% (the same level as 1870-1913). A dominating effect seemed to be a second acceleration of growth in countries that had earlier shifted into a pattern of sustained MEG.

Transition to sustained growth has often been associated with some prominent political occurrence, domestic or international. Several European countries began growth after the Concert of Europe (1815); Germany began to grow with unification (1850s). In many countries (Taiwan-Formosa, 1895) transition began with colonization, or (Cuba and the Philippines) after transfer to a new colonial power. Many such political events have been changes of government (coronation of Rama IV in Thailand in 1851, the Meiji Restoration in Japan in 1868, emergence of Kemal Ataturk as ruler of Turkey (1920s), independence of Iraq (1920s), installation of the Pahlevi dynasty in Iran in 1925, victory of Mao Tse-Tung in China in 1949, fall of the monarchy and installation of President Gamal Abdel Nasser in Egypt in 1956, President Suharto's replacement of President Sukarno in Indonesia in 1967, etc.). Transition in Latin America has often been marked by emergence of stable government after prolonged postindependence civil war (Argentina in the

1860s, Mexico in 1876, Colombia in 1885). After World War II, as the colonial empires dismantled themselves, reconstruction throughout the world was quickly completed and the largest period of global economic growth in history begun. In a few cases (India, Pakistan) transition occurred dramatically with decolonization and independence. Between 1960 and 1973, gross world product (GWP) rose annually by more than 5%, as more countries entered their first periods of modern economic growth.[47]

Most of the world's current countries have not yet begun an initial period of intensive growth—either premodern, simple growth or modern, Kuznetsian growth. These countries either remain in a stasis of slow, parallel growth of both production and population, with no significant rise in *per capita* incomes, or have fallen into maelstrom of rising population, decreasing production, deteriorating terms of trade, and *falling incomes*.

EXPANDING UNIVERSE OF MODERN ECONOMIC GROWTH

As many as 40-50 countries may have experienced MEG since the Industrial Revolution. Unreliability of data, or even good history, for many countries prevents assessment of growth rates, especially in earlier periods. For many countries, an initial spurt of growth quickly dissipated into stagnation (Ghana, Uganda, Zambia). For some, sustained growth later changed to decline (Britain, Argentina). Others' accelerating rates of growth (Japan, Taiwan, South Korea) are continuing into the present. Some have experienced intermittent periods of growth with idle periods between (Sweden, France, Norway, Canada, United States).

Units of Analysis

Many sociologists argue that subnational units—states, tribes, industrial sectors—are at least as significant as national units. While Gunnar Myrdal's "disequalizing" sectoral and individual differences are often extreme and traumatic in early stages of economic growth, they tend to shrink as economic cohesion and liberal macroeconomic policies operate to reduce inequality.[48] Some political theories—primarily neo-Marxist—argue, in contrast, that analysis dealing with growth is only relevant at the global level, that the relative position of a country within a modern world system determines its economic—and political—fate. The global booms of 1850-1914 and 1945-1973 presented innumerable opportunities for intensive national economic growth. Neither behavioral awareness nor globalist neo-Marxist approaches explain well how some countries were able to capture these opportunities while others did not do so.

Countries show predictable continuity in government and international relations, routine expectation of internal order, general recognition of peace or war, greater intensity of economic interactions within borders than across them, and significantly greater political-economic control within jurisdictions than externally. Even more significant than purely national attributes in analyzing growth and conflict is the increasingly national focus of any substantial political cohesion. In addition, virtually all historical data for either conflict or growth are arranged in national groups. With due respect for individualists and globalists, this study uses countries—both independent states and preindependence colonies—as the basic units of analysis; their national time series are the primary data.

The Course of Modern Economic Growth

Modern economic growth expanded from its appearance in eighteenth-century England in clear geographic leaps. Although early growth was confined to western Europe, by the nineteenth century it had clearly expanded to Scandinavia and North America. Since the War of 1812 in America and the Concert of Europe, North America and Europe have grown in tandem almost as a single entity. While MEG moved slowly eastward from Europe, American exuberance carried it to Asia and Latin America. After World War I Europeans brought growth to the Middle East and Africa, but not until the 1950s did Southeast Asia begin its dramatic growth. This pattern suggests seven regional groupings with some chronological consistency:

Europe (1690-1990)   Northeast Asia (1870-1990)
North America (1790-1990)   Middle East and Africa (1920-1990)
Scandinavia (1850-1990)   Southeast Asia (1950-1990)
Latin America (1870-1990)

Data and Measurement

An ideal database for analysis of growth and conflict would include long time series of economic and demographic magnitudes and indices of conflict —war and nonwar—for each country in the universe. The range of data would extend from well before transition into intensive growth until the present.[49] Actual data are, however, far from ideal. Pre-1930s data are at best fragmentary. What data are available relate to whatever governments chose to measure, primarily population, foreign trade, government finances, and agricultural information. Histories of individual countries tend to be qualitative, comparative, and subjective.

Since the 1930s economic data and national accounts are well and uniformly reported by the World Bank (International Bank for Reconstruction and Development), the International Monetary Fund (IMF), the OECD and other multinational organizations, as well as most governments. Historically, analyses of growth have centered on changes in gross national product (GNP), how much of what is produced for a country belongs to its citizens. A better measure of growth in a country's productive capacity is probably gross domestic product (GDP), which measures all that is produced within a country, regardless of who owns it.[50] This important distinction may be quite large, for countries that are large sources or recipients of foreign investment. That portion of production attributable to foreign-owned factors of production (capital, labor, technology) belongs to the source country's GNP, but to the host country's GDP. While changes in GNP reflect current changes in a country's standard-of-living quite well, changes in GDP reflect those evolutions of a national economy that seem to be involved in MEG.

For long periods—a quarter- to half-century is sufficient—decadal measures of structure can readily distinguish growth from transient volatility canceled by the expected short-term reaction. Observation of annual or short-term growth rates in output alone cannot identify this sort of growth.[51] A convenient, but gross, index is decadal growth-rate for *per capita* domestic product (GDP/population).[52] Shorter periods simply reveal short-term fluctuations, actions, and reactions that form the basis of classical equilibrium economics without growth. Although a few years of high annual growth may indicate the beginnings of MEG, they may also reflect a secular business cycle. In the absence of counterevidence, a substantial increase in this decadal growth rate over a long period seems to indicate the presence of MEG.

Conversion of *per capita* income, GDP, and population to annual, decadal, and tridecadal growth rates normalizes the data for changes, discontinuities, or inaccuracies in exchange rates, inflation, business cycles and short-term volatility, and carries information about aggregate productivity. It also helps control for changing components of national political-economic structure, various modes of technological innovations, cultural standards and value systems, and societal idiosyncrasies in adapting to change, or other incomparabilities across countries.

The only general methodological assumption needed for this approach is a similarity of human nature, wants, and motives over historic time and across countries. Use of decadal growth rates of *per capita* income as a primary independent variable, tridecadal growth rates as a confirmatory indicator, and annual rates of change as suggestions emphasizes sustained economic performance, while deemphasizing, yet not ignoring, short-term or long-term cycles and trends.

Criteria for Modern Rapid Growth

The universe of country episodes of such intensive growth would include countries that meet several basic quantitative criteria:

sustained decadal population growth rates that are larger than those of previous periods;

sustained decadal *per capita* income growth rates larger than those of previous periods, within a significant positive trend over the entire range of data;

decadal and tridecadal moving averages of *per capita* income growth rates as large as global means; and

sustained growth such that successive decades rarely show a fall in rate of *per capita* income growth below some high minimum.[53]

Quantitative analysis requires that a period of MEG have a definite beginning and an end. Countries enter MEG when beginnings of a "sustained rise in *per capita* output can be observed—sustained in the sense that, although year-to-year growth rates are uneven, *per capita* output does not fall back to its initial level."[54] A period of MEG continues so long as growth rates continue the trend, without encountering recession. These criteria can readily be specified in appropriate form for an objective determination of whether and when a country has experienced MEG.

Parameters

GDP = Gross Domestic Product
GNP = Gross National Product
POP = Population
PCI = Per Capita GDP or GNP
AGR = Annual Growth Rate of PCI

DGR = Decadal Growth Rate of PCI
3GR = 30-year Growth Rate of PCI
APG = Annual Growth Rate of POP
DPG = Decadal Growth Rate of POP
3PG = 30-year Growth Rate of POP

Start of Growth Period

PCI at local and Period minimum

AGR and APG are positive

Characteristics of Period

PRIMARY CRITERION: Mean DGR > mean DPG

Rapid growth of both Population and PCI
PCI grows faster than Population
Neither PCI nor Population return to previous levels
Mean DPG > 5 after 1815;
   > 2.5 before 1815
Mean DGR > 10 after 1815;
   > 4 before 1815
No more than two consecutive negative AGR in period; (3 negative AGR is Recession)

Mean DGR for the period > = mean DGR for range of data
No negative DGR after the sixth year of the period;
Mean 3GR for the period > mean for range of data
No negative 3GR after the tenth year of the period
Mean DPG for the period > mean DPG range of data
No negative APG or DGP in the period

End of Period

Negative APG or DPG
PCI at a local maximum and > = period maximum

3 successive negative AGR
DGR at a local maximum
3GR at a local maximum

Although many early reports of growth or growth rates are unclear or even contradictory, reliable data confirm 45 growth periods meeting these stringent criteria in 30 countries since about 1700. Two countries experienced three periods of MEG; 10 experienced two periods; 18 experienced, or are experiencing, their first period (see Table 4.1).

Table 4.1 Universe of Modern Growth Countries 1700–1992

(MEAN AGR > MEAN APG)
(MEAN DGR > MEAN DPG)
  (MEAN 3GR)

BRITAIN-1 1734-1764
(0.413 > 0.399)
(4.075 > 3.402)
(9.770)

SWEDEN-1 1861-1916
(2.01 > 0.7)
(22.7 > 6.9)
(76.7)

DENMARK-2 1918-1979
(2.65 > 0.88)
(26.67 > 9.89)
(87.17)

FRANCE-1 1739-1769
(0.48 > 0.42)
(4.46 > 4.37)
(11.62)

UNITED STATES-1 1864-1912
(2.95 > 2.07)
(24.48 > 24.2)
(81.76)

SWEDEN-2 1920-1974
(3.02 > 0.61)
(30.77 > 6.42)
(108.69)

BRITAIN-2 1820-1854
(1.31 > 1.30)
(14.59 > 14.41)
(46.85)

FINLAND-1 1871-1913
(1.47 > 1.3)
(16.26 > 12.06)
(51.59)

FINLAND-2 1932-1967
(3.13 > 0.81)
(32.45 > 8.47)
(108.92)

FRANCE-2 1823-1854
(1.24 > 0.52)
(15.43 > 5.76)
(40.03)

NORWAY-1 1871-1921
(1.31 > 0.85)
(12.4 > 8.45)
(38.2)

CANADA-2 1933-1988
(3.07 > 1.57)
(30.97 > 17.8)
(97.51)

GERMANY-1 1850-1912
(1.69 > 1.01)
(18.84 > 10.16)
(62.99)

CANADA-1 1872-1913
(2.29 > 1.79)
(28.87 > 17.34)
(82.49)

NORWAY-2 1934-1988
(3.6 > 0.7)
(41.0 > 7.43)
(161.00)

DENMARK-1 1856-1914
(1.55 > 1.09)
(14.62 > 11.43)
(44.61)

CHINA-1 1884-1939
(2.43 > 1.91)
(23.09 > 19.73)
(66.4)

NETHERLANDS 1935-1991
(3.08 > 1.08)
(31.61 > 11.63)
(111.12)

BRITAIN-3 1861-1902
(1.86 > 1.17)
(20.09 > 12.24)
(61.71)

JAPAN-1 1886-1938
(2.32 > 1.17)
(18.88 > 12.10)
(66.2)

MEXICO 1941-1979
(3.37 > 3.13)
(36.03 > 35.07)
(109.61)

RUSSIA-1 1861-1913
(2.33 > 0.9)
(24.2 > 11.3)
(57.5)

TAIWAN-1 1903-1936
(2.11 > 1.86)
(21.82 > 18.88)
(65.81)

UNITED STATES-2 1940-1991
(2.19 > 1.23)
(26.39 > 13.24)
(68.88)

Table 4.1 continued

ARGENTINA 1941-1975
(1.7577 > 1.7571)
(18.63 > 18.48)
(47.4)

RUSSIA-2 1946-1990
(4.17 > 1.4)
(62.0 > 12.4)
(288.72)

TAIWAN-2 1951-1987
(6.12 > 2.62)
(83.47 > 31.35)
(476.64)

IRAN 1943-1992
(10.57 > 2.84)
(206.99 > 29.45)
(1111.97)

JAPAN-2 1946-1992
(5.36 > 1.18)
(62.16 > 12.32)
(267.78)

CHINA-2 1952-1992
(5.65 > 1.81)
(56.85 > 19.92)
(147.2)

BRAZIL 1944-1980
(4.35 > 2.77)
(43.13 > 30.46)
(133.92)

PHILIPPINES 1947-1991
(11.00 > 2.75)
(168.2 > 30.88)
(954.73)

SOUTH KOREA 1953-1992
(8.10 > 1.05)
(97.72 > 13.99)
(484.42)

IRAQ 1944-1992
(5.86 > 2.97)
(70.15 > 32.67)
(339.28)

AUSTRALIA 1947-1992
(1.93 > 1.86)
(19.7 > 19.6)
(57.5)

INDONESIA 1954-1989
(4.04 > 2.25)
(43.5 > 24.21)
(89.23)

FRANCE-3 1945-1991
(3.23 > 0.96)
(40.57 > 7.64)
(155.28)

SINGAPORE 1948-1990
(10.23 > 1.78)
(201.21 > 26.68)
(1657.62)

NEW ZEALAND 1954-1989
(1.40 > 1.04)
(17.5 > 14.1)
(62.0)

GERMANY-2 1945-1991
(5.26 > 0.44)
(59.86 > 3.44)
(266.59)

MALAYSIA 1949-1989
(6.33 > 2.63)
(89.54 > 30.54)
(442.40)

THAILAND 1958-1990
(9.5 > 2.59)
(140.75 > 31.45)
(1300.15)

NIGERIA 1945-1992
(7.67 > 2.41)
(109.41 > 24.90)
(535.52)

ITALY 1951-1988
(3.97 > 0.54)
(52.72 > 6.07)
(170.28)

ISRAEL 1962-1992
(2.94 > 2.63)
(39.71 > 39.41)
(166.35)

THE MODEL AND THE METHOD

Stanley Hoffmann asked, "Can there *be* a theory of undetermined behavior, which is what 'diplomatic-strategic action,' to use Aron's terms, amounts to?"[55] Kenneth Waltz complained that theory has led to neither knowledge nor explanations. "Among the depressing features of international-political studies is the small gain in explanatory power that has come from the large amount of work done in recent decades. Nothing seems to accumulate, not even criticism."[56]

David Yost has noted the "severe limits" placed on prediction and explanation by "free wills, differing priorities and ultimately contingent choices of the many decision-makers."[57]   Raymond Aron has demonstrated that a theory of undetermined behavior can do little more than define concepts and note structures and features of some logic of behavior.[58]   Hedley Bull has observed that theory of international relations is "philosophical in character. It does not lead to cumulative knowledge after the manner of natural science."[59]   As the combined work of many scholars suggests, it may be impossible to formulate a model of sufficient depth, detail, generality, and flexibility to describe precisely just how economic growth and international conflict affect each other.   Perhaps within some set of broad uniformities, generalities, or "doctrine," *each case really is unique.*

The task of social-scientific analysis (unlike that of natural science) is not to draw clever, powerful universal conclusions, to produce precise multivariate models with high statistical "goodness of fit," or to specify "ultimate" or "fundamental" processes and factors in excruciating detail and unerring accuracy. The power of political-economic analysis arises from active inference of useful descriptions of the world from faint or indistinct patterns of human and national behaviors.   Such descriptions are reliable only insofar as the inferential processes that create them recognize and exploit empirical regularities. Social-scientific theory itself may not go much beyond discovery of relevant regularities and historical investigation of their power in guiding further inferences and policy responses.   Social science generally, and international political-economy specifically, resolves essentially to "a quest for truth in the form of general principles that are consistent, to the maximum extent possible, with historical accuracy.   Most generalizations, however, involve some simplification and hence some injustice to the complexity of a specific historical context."[60]

In contrast to the classical "scientific method," legitimate social-scientific analysis seems rather to be the search for general principles. While avoiding any Procrustean interpretations, the social scientist seeks to identify a set of "lawlike regularities" that describe complex phenomena "reasonably well," and provide some principles to explain the real world—historical and contemporary.

Observing the Relationship

Of primary interest are relationships between economic growth and international conflict over long periods, as well as the processes that link them. In addition to explanatory-predictive power, the primary features of the relationship are significance and effects of levels of national wealth and growth rates on conflict. Additional features of the growth-conflict relationship (GCR) are the power of unidentified or intervening variables, and any effects of the intensity of modern economic growth. An appropriate initial methodology for observing these features and identifying lawlike regularities in these relationships is that of Ordinary Least Squares (OLS) Regression over long time series.

Parameters

A generic equation relating the variables would be of the form:

$$International\ Conflict = F(Economic\ Growth).$$

Time series of international conflict, the dependent variable, reflect two broad types: violent and nonviolent. Violent conflict appears as war or militarized dispute (see previous section, "War Databases"); nonviolent conflict, as diplomacy, political confrontation, or commercial competition. Organization of historical data leads to a methodology that uses the national state as unit of analysis, and deals with each sort of conflict separately, in two parallel generic equations of the forms:

$$War = F(Economic\ Growth); \qquad Nonwar\ Conflict = G(Economic\ Growth);$$

and a third, which is their sum:

$$Total\ Conflict = H(Economic\ Growth).$$

Economic growth, the independent variable, is reflected in three sorts of indicators: wealth indicators, growth indicators, and an intensity indicator. Indicators of wealth are the quantities of total production (usually GDP), but also GNP or Net National Product (NNP) when GDP is not available) and individual income (PCI computed by dividing total production by population). The second set of indicators involves the growth rates of these fundamental values of wealth, conveniently combined in a set of growth rates for *per capita* income: annual, decadal, and tridecadal.[61] Of these growth-rate indicators, decadal growth rate (DGR) and tridecadal growth rate (3GR) of PCI are the most important for long-term observations.

With its focus on a relationship that involves not only the products of nations but primarily the actions and decisions of their populations, the analysis also considers the sociopolitical effect of Kuznets' modern economic growth, simultaneous growth of population and faster growth of wealth (see previous section, "Modern Economic Growth"). The third kind of indicator measures the presence of intensive MEG. Unlike wealth and growth indicators, which are continuous variables, this intensity indicator holds only discrete values in accordance with presence or absence of MEG in a nation.

The Regression Equation

Statistical time series for wealth, growth, and intensity indicators of economic growth are generated from two series of direct data: population and total product (continuous at constant domestic prices). With the observed-value national-product time series (GDP), the three calculated series (PCI, DGR, 3GR) and the "dummy" intensity variable (MEG) for each country constitute the five independent "growth" variables used to indicate and analyze modern economic growth.

The time series for national product appears directly as an independent "growth" variable in each regression; other time series used as independent variables are simple linear functions of population and product.[62] Inclusion of the two quantity variables (GDP, PCI) controls for possible thresholds of population or production that may affect the dependent variable, and allows observation of the significance and effects of absolute values of national economic attributes on international conflict. Inclusion of the two growth-rate variables (DGR, 3GR) indicates their effects and significance, while the dummy indicator variable (MEG) tests the null hypothesis that MEG does not affect international conflict. The zero-intercept (represented as a constant in a regression equation) reflects the effects of any additional or missing variables.

The generic initial regressive equations for analysis take the forms:

$$W = F(DGR, PCI, GDP, MEG, 3GR);$$
$$W = C + \alpha DGR + \beta PCI + \gamma GDP + \delta MEG + \varepsilon 3GR + \epsilon;$$
$$NW = G(DGR, PCI, GDP, MEG, 3GR);$$
$$NW = D + \zeta DGR + \eta PCI + \theta GDP + \vartheta MEG + \iota 3GR + \epsilon;$$
$$TC = H(DGR, PCI, GDP, MEG, 3GR);$$
$$TC = E + \lambda DGR + \mu PCI + \nu GDP + \xi MEG + o3GR + \epsilon.$$

Regression Analysis

For each country the Weighted Ordinary Least Squares process generates a "best-fit" time series regression relating the "growth" variables and the relevant "conflict" variable.[63] This "best-estimate" regression is that which best meets (or approaches) three criteria: parsimony (no more than three independent variables and the zero-intercept); robustness (at least two statistically significant independent variables [t-stat > 2][64]); explanatory power (high value of adjusted correlation coefficient). Each final observation of the growth-conflict relationship is the "best estimate" regression equation that includes the three most significant of the two "Growth-rate" (DGR, 3GR) variables, two "quantity" (PCI, GDP) variables, and the "dummy" growth-period variable (MEG), as well as the zero-intercept.

To allow for directionality in the search for lawlike regularities, each observation set (TC, NW, W) includes one subset with whole-year negative lag on the dependent conflict variable, and a second subset with positive lead. The negative lag allows the observation to specify the GCR between *preceding* (P) conflict and *subsequent* growth.[65] The positive lead specifies the GCR between *prior* growth and *following* (F) conflict. Each of the six subsets [total conflict preceding (TCP), total conflict following (TCF), nonwar conflict preceding (NWP), nonwar conflict following (NWF), war preceding (WP), war following (WF)] includes each "best-estimate" regression using the same dependent conflict variable with a single chronological relationship to growth (preceding lag or following lead). The "best-estimate" lag or lead is that which maximizes "goodness-of-fit" in a viable equation that meets the criteria for parsimony, robustness and explanatory power.

Each of the six subsets should contain 30 observations, each an observation of the GCR. Three countries (Singapore, Sweden, New Zealand), however, did not experience enough war to generate viable (at least 10 annual data points) dependent-variable time series; subsets WP and WF, therefore, each contain only 27 observations, while sets TCP, TCF, NWP, and NWF contain 30 observations.

The data base for analysis, thus, comprises the 174 observations in the six observation subsets across the three conflict variables with leads and lags: WP with 27 observations and WF with 27 observations; NWP with 30 observations and NWF with 30 observations; TCP with 30 observations and TCF with 30 observations. Each "best-estimate" regression represents one distinct observation of the GCR within the universal field of 174 observations.

The range of observation comprises 16 data fields, of which four (significances and effects of the two least significant growth variables within that observation) are blank for each individual observation. Each observation is across five features of the GCR: aggregate effect of growth on conflict; correlation level adjusted for degrees of freedom, or "goodness-of-fit"; lags or leads; significance and effects of each of the five "growth" variables (PCI, GDP, MEG, DGR, 3GR); features of the zero-intercept.

Each observation depicts the GCR and the related growth variables along five "dimensions," each with a set of salient features that characterize that particular observation, and which facilitate comparison and aggregation of individual observations:

EFFECT: aggregate effect of growth on the dependent conflict variable (high or low confidence; direct or inverse);

CORRELATION: level of correlation (high, moderate, low);

LAGS and LEADS: lag or lead between growth and conflict (high, moderate, low);

GROWTH VARIABLES: independent growth variables (t-stat $\geq$ 2 or t-stat < 2; positive or negative) that maximize the regression's adjusted correlation coefficient (R^2);[66] and

ZERO-INTERCEPT: significance (t-stat $\leq$ 2 or t-stat < 2); value (large or small); effect (positive or negative).

Each observation, thus, consists of 12 data points: adjusted R^2 (three possible values); lag or lead (three possible values); significances and effects of the three most significant growth variables (two possible values for each); most significant independent variables (one of five individual growth variables or a pair of growth variables), and significance, value, and effect of the Zero-intercept (two possible values for each feature).

For each dimension, the 30 (or 27) observations within each subset aggregated within dimensional features constitute a one-dimensional subset profile of the GCR. Each dimension shows six subset profiles, reflecting the respective features of the dimension.[67]   The salient features of dimensional subset profiles collect those of the individual observations:

> EFFECT: aggregate effect of growth on conflict;
> CORRELATION: mean of correlation coefficients of each regression showing the relevant feature of the profile;
> LAGS and LEADS: range and mean lag or lead by which conflict precedes or follows growth;
> INDEPENDENT VARIABLES: significance and effects of the independent growth variables that maximize the regression's adjusted correlation coefficient (R^2); and
> ZERO-INTERCEPT: statistical significance, size, and effect of the zero-intercept of the regression.

Regular features of the growth-conflict relationship across a dimension's subset profiles (or across a subset's dimension profiles) represent lawlike regularities within the subset or along the dimension.   More important, however, they suggest analogous regularities across the universe of generic superordinate relationships, of which each subset and dimension shows a hyponymic species.   Since dimensional subset profiles encompass and emphasize any regularities discoverable by "looking hard at" all of the 174 observations individually and collectively, it is equivalent in searching for regularities to examine the set of 30 (6 subset profiles for each of five dimensions) dimensional subset profiles, and only to refer to the set of seven regional profiles.

Singularities or irregularities may be reflected in constellations of significance or features along a single dimension of the GCR across one or two subsets, or involving only particular countries. These may be useful predictors or explanations of a specific *ad hoc* GCR under particular conditions of the growth variables. Anomalies may appear when a feature or variable is unique or unexpected in some way either within a subset, along a dimension, or across subsets and countries. Results that do not show regularities, singularities, or anomalies, but are predominantly country-specific, are simply ambiguous. These sorts of results can carry profound theoretical and practical meaning, but contribute little to the search for lawlike regularities.

DIMENSIONAL PROFILES

The five dimensional profiles of the growth-conflict relationship—effects, correlation levels, leads and lags, variables and dominance patterns, zero-intercept—provide convenient fields for seeking lawlike regularities.   In addition to searching the five dimensional profiles, the analysis searches for regularities in each of the seven geographic regions containing countries in the universe of modern economic growth.   An aggregate profile and a set of regularities, singularities, and anomalies complete the image of the growth-conflict relationship.

Presentation of Regularities

For convenience in analyzing the separate profiles, presentation along the "effects" dimension bifurcates each effect (direct and inverse) into high-confidence and low-confidence levels, but does not present a profile of the conjunct relationship (including *both* inverse and direct effects, with *both* high and low confidence levels). Presentations along the other dimensions omit levels of confidence and juxtapose conjunct and disjunct data in each table in a three-line format. The conjunct (or composite) GCR data (*both* direct *and* inverse) appear on an upper line, disjunct data for *only* the direct GCR appear on a lower second line, and disjunct data for *only* the inverse GCR appear on a lowest third line.

KEY TO NOTATION IN PROFILE TABLES

- ;	= range and mean of lags and leads;
SIG	= variable is significant in at least 2/3 of cases;
NS	= variable is significant in less than 1/3 of cases;
?	= significance, size, or effect of variable is country-specific;
+	= effect of variable is positive in at least 2/3 of cases;
-	= effect of variable is negative in at least 2/3 of cases;
LG	= zero-intercept is large (> 4) in at least 2/3 of cases;
SM	= zero-intercept is small or moderate (< 4) in at least 2/3 of cases (approximately 1/3 of the entire field of observations shows the zero-intercept as < 1, another third shows it a ≥ 1 and < 4; the other third shows the zero-intercept as ≥ 4);
GR	= growth-rate variables group (DGR, 3GR) is most significant with each growth-rate variable most significant in at least one observation;
QU	= quantity-variables group (PCI, GDP) is most significant with each quantity variable most significant in at least one observation;
DV	= dummy-variables group (MEG, zero-intercept) is most significant with each dummy variable most significant in at least one observation; and
Variable Indicator (3GR, DGR, GDP, MEG, PCI)	
	= A single variable is most significant with the other variable of its pair not most significant in any observation.

Effects Dimension

Measuring growth and conflict with reference to their respective sample means condenses the effects of the growth-conflict relationship to a simple dichotomy: direct or inverse. Each country's mean DGR is higher or lower than the mean DGR for the universe;[68] a country's mean for each conflict variable is similarly higher or lower than the universe mean for that variable. Where the country's values for both mean growth and mean conflict are the same (higher or lower than respective universe means), the effect of the relationship between them is direct (positive);[69] where values are opposite, the effect is inverse (negative).

Separating countries according to the type of GCR that each experienced most (direct, inverse) produces two groups of 15 countries each. Extraction of those countries for which neither type of GCR met the criterion for a lawlike regularity (predominance in five of six subsets) creates a third ambiguous group. Eleven countries experiencing predominantly a direct GCR showed associations between low growth and low conflict, and between high growth and high conflict:

Denmark	Italy	Argentina	Brazil
Indonesia	Mexico	Norway	Australia
Netherlands	Canada	Finland	

Ten countries had predominantly inverse GCR associating low growth with high conflict, and high growth with low conflict:

| United States | Malaysia | France | Nigeria | Thailand |
| United Kingdom | Philippines | Russia | Taiwan | Israel |

Nine countries experienced both direct and inverse GCR showing associations between low growth and both high and low conflict, and also associations between high growth and both high and low conflict:

Direct in 4 subsets	Inverse in 4 subsets		Direct in 3 subsets
Germany	Iraq	Korea	Japan
New Zealand	Iran	Singapore	
Sweden	China		

Any analysis of the dual effect of the growth-conflict relationship (see Table 4.3) is most useful in terms of confidence in the regression process, reflected in the residual variance of a regression. Comparison of the adjusted correlation coefficient with the zero-intercept (as an idiom of residual variance) allows crude high-low estimation of confidence in an observation of the GCR (see Appendix H). Analysis of the residual variance of each observation can characterize its effect as high-confidence direct, high-confidence inverse, low-confidence direct, or low-confidence inverse. Of the 174 observations, 89 show the expected contrast between correlation coefficient and residual variance, which provides high confidence, and 85 do not (see Table 4.2).

Table 4.2 Confidence Levels

89 Direct (POSITIVE)		85 INVERSE (NEGATIVE)	
43 HIGH (24.7%)	46 LOW (26.4%)	46 HIGH (26.4%)	39 LOW (22.4%)

Table 4.3 Effects Profiles

Total conflict following growth (TCF)

EFFECT	DELAY	R²	DGR	PCI	PROD	MEG	3GR	SIG	ZERO-INT
HiC Inv 9	0-11; 6	58	SIG +	SIG -	SIG ?	NS ?	? ?	?	SIG SM +
HiC Dir 5	0-9; 5	38	NS +	SIG -	NS +	NS +	NS -	GR	NS LG+
LoC Inv 8	0-10; 4	60	? -	SIG ?	? ?	NS +	SIG +	?	SIG LG ?
LoC Dir 8	0-14; 5	49	? ?	? -	SIG ?	? -	NS +	?	? ? -

Total conflict preceding growth (TCP)

EFFECT	DELAY	R²	DGR	PCI	PROD	MEG	3GR	SIG	ZERO-INT
HiC Inv 7	0-10; 7	64	? -	? ?	SIG -	NS ?	? +	GR	? SM ?
HiC Dir 8	1-17; 9	52	? +	SIG -	SIG+	NS ?	? -	?	SIG ? +
LoC Inv 9	1-15; 6	60	NS ?	SIG -	SIG ?	NS ?	SIG ?	?	SIG LG +
LoC Dir 6	1-13; 5	61	NS -	SIG -	SIG ?	NS +	? -	DV	SIG ? ?

War following growth (WF)

EFFECT	DELAY	R²	DGR	PCI	PROD	MEG	3GR	SIG	ZERO-INT
HiC Inv 7	0-8; 4	73	? ?	SIG+	SIG ?	NS -	? ?	GR	SIG SM +
HiC Dir 7	0-9; 5	62	? -	? -	? ?	SIG -	? -	INT	SIG SM +
LoC Inv 2	9-10; 9	58	SIG?	SIG ?	SIG ?	NS ?	NS ?	?	SIG ? ?
LC Dir 11	0-14; 7	32	? ?	SIG -	? +	? -	? ?	DV	SIG SM+

War preceding growth (WP)

EFFECT	DELAY	R²	DGR	PCI	PROD	MEG	3GR	SIG	ZERO-INT
HiC Inv 5	1-15; 8	73	NS -	? +	? +	NS -	? -	?	? SM +
HiC Dir 9	0-14; 8	66	SIG ?	SIG+	SIG -	NS -	? -	GR	SIG SM ?
LoC Inv 4	2-12; 6	76	? ?	? +	NS -	NS ?	SIG ?	GR	SIG LG ?
LoC Dir 9	0-14; 8	49	SIG ?	SIG ?	? ?	? +	? -	?	SIG SM ?

Nonwar conflict following growth (NWF)

EFFECT	DELAY	R²	DGR	PCI	PROD	MEG	3GR	SIG	ZERO-INT
HiC Inv 9	0-15; 5	60	SIG ?	? ?	SIG ?	NS +	? +	GR	? ? +
HiC Dir 7	0-14; 6	47	NS -	NS -	? +	NS +	? ?	?	SIG ? +
LoC Inv 8	0-14; 4	45	? +	SIG -	? ?	NS ?	? ?	?	SIG ? ?
LoC Dir 6	0-7; 3	40	? -	SIG +	SIG -	NS +	NS +	QU	SIG LG -

Nonwar conflict preceding growth (NWP)

EFFECT	DELAY	R²	DGR	PCI	PROD	MEG	3GR	SIG	ZERO-INT
HiC Inv 8	0-15; 6	70	? -	? -	SIG ?	NS +	SIG +	GR	? SM ?
HiC Dir 8	0-17; 7	62	? +	NS -	SIG +	? -	? -	?	SIG SM +
LoC Inv 9	0-15; 5	55	? +	? -	SIG +	NS ?	? -	?	? ? +
LoC Dir 5	0-11; 7	37	NS -	SIG ?	SIG ?	NS ?	? ?	GR	? ? ?

Although the distribution shows quantitative uniformity across both effects, and at each confidence level, the relationships show several notable features.   Across the six subsets the correlation levels of high-confidence inverse relationships are higher than those of high-confidence direct relationships.   In the direct GCR, PCI and 3GR are predominantly negative in the high-confidence relationships, but significant only at low confidence levels.   GDP is predominantly significant only in high-confidence inverse relationships, but neither effect is predominant.   The zero-intercept is predominantly significant and positive in high-confidence direct relationships, significant in low-confidence inverse relationships, and small in high-confidence inverse relationships.   A notable singularity is the significance of DGR at all levels of confidence in the direct GCR for WP (the only other instances of DGR significance are in inverse relationships) (see Table 4.3).

Of the 174 observations, 89 show direct (positive) relationships between growth and conflict; 43 of these show the expected contrast between correlation coefficient and residual variance, which provides high confidence of specification accuracy.   Of the 85 observations showing inverse (negative) growth-conflict relationships, 46 show the expected correlation-variance contrast, and deserve high confidence.   Of the 174 observations, 85 do not show the expected contrast between correlation coefficient and residual variance, and thus cannot provide high confidence of either specification accuracy or of the nature of the GCR. Like the high-confidence relationships, these low-confidence relationships are both direct and inverse, and occur across all 6 subsets.

The 174 observations comprise 43 high-confidence direct relationships, 46 high-confidence inverse relationship, 46 low-confidence direct relationships, and 39 low-confidence inverse relationships. The smooth effects profile across the six subsets does not suggest any immediately obvious lawlike regularities beyond the apparent ambiguities in both confidence levels and effects in every subset.[70] These results do suggest, however, that some missing variable not captured by the regression specification may operate to influence the effects of some particular relationships, but is absent in other situations.

Correlation-level Profiles

The second dimensional profile of the GCR is that of correlation levels across the six subsets. Analysis of this dimension is from three distinct aspects: a composite perspective of all observations, which disregards the effect of a particular observation; consideration of the set of all direct GCR; and examination of the set of all inverse GCR. The 174 observations show fewer country relationships with low correlation than with either moderate or high correlations.   The mean correlation level for all 174 observations in the field is 0.58; the median is 0.57. The range of correlation levels is nearly complete from 0.01 through 0.97, and shows a smooth distribution with no large gaps and two broad concentrations of relationships.   Over half (55%) of the relationships are in these two clusters: the larger (29%) is between correlation levels of 0.66 and 0.78; a smaller (26%) lies between 0.41 and 0.56.

The composite relationship—considering both direct and inverse GCR—shows few regularities between correlation levels and any of the independent growth variables. PCI tends to be more often significant at low correlations than at higher levels, while 3GR and the zero-intercept may be slightly more often significant at high correlations. Relationships with low correlation levels are consistently fewer than those with higher correlations.

The disjunct relationships show several notable differences. While the direct relationship is almost featureless, the inverse GCR shows a distinct, obvious profile. The sample shows no low-correlation inverse GCR at all in either war subset (WP, WF), and no inverse relationships at moderate correlations in WP. At high correlations each subset shows more inverse than direct relationships; at moderate levels four subsets show more direct GCR; low-correlation relationships are predominantly direct. In contrast to the smooth direct profile, the correlation-level profile of the inverse GCR shows positive DGR and GDP at low correlations, significant negative PCI at low and moderate correlations, 3GR positive at high correlations and negative at low correlations, and a significant positive zero-intercept at moderate correlations (see Table 4.4 and Table 4.5).

Lead and Lag Profiles

The third dimensional profile is that of leads and lags between growth and conflict. Across the six subsets, high lags and leads occur with lower correlation levels than do low lags and leads, except in NWP (0.58–0.58). For both effects, the product variable is more often significant at moderate lags and leads than at low or high lags and leads, and predominantly negative at low lags and leads. The zero-intercept seems most often significant at low lags and leads, and is insignificant only in NWF at very high leads. Predominantly positive, the zero-intercept seems to be smaller at high lags and leads (see Table 4.6).

Table 4.4 Correlation-level Profile Summary

INVERSE/DIRECT	Correlation	DGR	PCI	GDP	3GR	ZI
	High				+	
					-	
	Moderate		SIG -			SIG +
			? ?			? ?
	Low	+	SIG -	+	-	
		?	SIG ?	?	?	

Table 4.5 Correlation-level Profiles

Total conflict following growth (TCF)

R² LEVEL	LEAD	DGR	PCI	PROD	MEG	3GR	SIG	ZERO-INT
High (10)	0-11; 3	? -	SIG ?	? ?	NS +	? ?	GR	SIG ? +
Dir 2	0-7; 4	? -	? +	? -	? +	SIG -	GR	SIG ? ?
Inv 8	0-11; 3	? ?	SIG ?	? -	NS +	? +	GR	? ? +
Mod (12)	1-14; 7	? ?	? -	? ?	NS ?	? ?	GR	? ? ?
Dir 6	1-14; 5	? ?	? -	SIG +	? +	NS -	DV	? ? -
Inv 6	1-10; 8	? ?	SIG -	? -	NS -	SIG +	GR	SIG LG +
Low (8)	3-11; 5	? +	SIG -	SIG +	? +	NS -	DV	? ? +
Dir 5	0-9; 4	NS ?	SIG -	? +	? +	NS -	?	? ? +
Inv 3	3-11; 3	? +	SIG -	SIG +	NS ?	? -	DV	SIG LG +

Total conflict preceding growth (TCP)

R² LEVEL	LEAD	DGR	PCI	PROD	MEG	3GR	SIG	ZERO-INT
High (16)	0-15; 6	? ?	SIG ?	SIG ?	NS ?	SIG ?	?	SIG ? ?
Dir 5	1-13; 7	? +	SIG +	SIG ?	NS ?	SIG -	?	SIG ? -
Inv 11	0-15; 7	? -	SIG -	SIG ?	NS ?	SIG +	?	SIG ? +
Mod (9)	1-17; 5	? +	SIG -	SIG +	? +	NS ?	?	SIG LG +
Dir 7	1-17; 8	NS +	SIG -	SIG +	? +	NS -	?	SIG LG +
Inv 2	3-8; 5	? -	SIG ?	? ?	NS ?	? +	GR	SIG LG ?
Low (5)	3-11; 7	NS ?	SIG -	SIG +	NS ?	SIG ?	?	? ? +
Dir 2	7-11; 9	? -	SIG -	? +	NS ?	SIG +	?	? ? +
Inv 3	3-10; 7	NS +	SIG -	SIG +	NS ?	SIG -	GR	SIG SM +

War following growth (WF)

R² LEVEL	LEAD	DGR	PCI	PROD	MEG	3GR	SIG	ZERO-INT
High (11)	0-9; 4	? ?	SIG ?	? ?	NS -	? ?	INT	SIG SM +
Dir 3	0-8; 6	NS ?	NS -	NS ?	SIG ?	NS ?	INT	SIG SM +
Inv 8	0-9; 4	? ?	SIG +	SIG -	NS -	NS +	GR	SIG SM ?
Mod (10)	0-13;7	NS ?	SIG ?	? ?	? -	? -	DV	SIG SM +
Dir 9	0-13;6	NS ?	SIG ?	? ?	? -	? -	DV	SIG ? +
Inv 1	10; 10	SIG +	SIG -	SIG +	NS ?	NS ?	INT	SIG SM +
Low (6)	1-14;7	? +	SIG -	NS +	? -	NS +	DV	SIG SM +
Dir 6	1-14;7	? +	SIG -	NS +	? -	NS +	DV	SIG SM +
Inv 0								

Table 4.5 continued

War preceding growth (WP)

R^2 LEVEL	LEAD	DGR	PCI	PROD	MEG	3GR	SIG	ZERO-INT
High (17)	0-15;7	? ?	? +	? ?	NS -	? -	GR ?	SM ?
Dir 8	0-12;7	SIG+	SIG+	SIG -	NS ?	? -	GR SIG	SM +
Inv 9	1-15;7	NS ?	? +	NS ?	NS -	SIG -	? ?	? +
Mod (8)	0-14;10	SIG ?	? ?	? -	NS -	? -	GR ?	SM ?
Dir 8	0-14;10	SIG ?	? ?	? -	NS -	? -	GR ?	SM ?
Inv 0								
Low (2)	5-7; 6	SIG -	? +	? -	? +	NS ?	? ?	SM -
Dir 2	5-7; 6	SIG -	? +	? -	? +	NS ?	? ?	SM -
Inv 0								

Nonwar conflict following growth (NWF)

R^2 LEVEL	LEAD	DGR	PCI	PROD	MEG	3GR	SIG	ZERO-INT
High (9)	0-15;5	SIG -	? ?	SIG ?	? +	? ?	? ?	SM +
Dir 2	7-7; 7	? -	? -	? +	SIG +	? -	? SIG	? +
Inv 7	0-15;4	SIG -	NS ?	SIG -	NS +	? +	GR NS	SM +
Mod (13)	0-14;5	? ?	SIG ?	SIG ?	NS +	? ?	? SIG	? ?
Dir 5	0-14;4	? -	? +	? +	NS +	? -	? SIG	? -
Inv 8	1-11;5	? +	SIG -	SIG ?	NS ?	? ?	? SIG	LG +
Low (8)	0-8; 3	? ?	SIG ?	SIG ?	NS +	NS +	? ?	? ?
Dir 6	1-8; 4	NS -	SIG +	SIG -	NS +	NS +	GR ?	LG -
Inv 2	0-5; 3	SIG+	SIG -	? +	NS ?	NS -	? NS	? ?

Nonwar conflict preceding growth (NWP)

R^2 LEVEL	LEAD	DGR	PCI	PROD	MEG	3GR	SIG	ZERO-INT
High (15)	0-17;6	SIG ?	? -	SIG ?	NS ?	SIG ?	? SIG	? ?
Dir 4	1-17;8	? +	? ?	SIG ?	NS -	SIG -	GR SIG	SM ?
Inv 11	0-15;5	? -	? -	SIG -	NS +	SIG+	GR ?	? ?
Mod (9)	0-15;6	? +	? -	SIG +	? ?	? -	? ?	SM+
Dir 5	0-10;5	? +	NS -	SIG +	? ?	? -	? ?	SM+
Inv 4	2-15;7	NS +	? -	SIG +	NS ?	? -	QU NS	SM+
Low (6)	0-11;6	? +	SIG ?	SIG ?	NS ?	? +	? ?	SM ?
Dir 4	0-11;8	NS -	SIG ?	SIG ?	NS ?	? +	GR ?	SM ?
Inv 2	0-5; 3	? +	? ?	? ?	NS ?	NS ?	? NS	SM ?

Table 4.6 Lead and Lag Profiles

Total conflict following growth (TCF)

LEAD LEVEL	R²	DGR	PCI	GDP	MEG	3GR	SIG	ZERO-INT
Very High	49	SIG+	SIG -	NS +	NS ?	SIG ?	GR	SIG SM+
Dir 1	45	NS +	SIG -	NS ?	NS ?	SIG +	GR	NS SM -
Inv 5	49	? +	SIG -	? +	NS -	? -	GR	SIG LG+
Moderate	48	? ?	SIG ?	SIG ?	NS +	NS -	GR	? ? ?
Dir 7	44	NS ?	? -	SIG+	NS +	NS -	GR	SIG ? ?
Inv 5	59	? +	SIG -	? -	NS ?	? +	GR	? ? +
Very Low	65	? -	? ?	? -	? +	SIG +	?	SIG ? +
Dir 5	45	NS ?	? ?	? ?	? +	? -	DV	? ? ?
Inv 7	66	? -	SIG -	? -	NS +	SIG +	?	SIG ? +

War following growth (WF)

LEAD LEVEL	R²	DGR	PCI	GDP	MEG	3GR	SIG	ZERO-INT
Very High	40	NS +	? -	? +	? -	NS +	DV	SIG ? +
Dir 5	38	? +	? -	? +	? -	NS +	DV	SIG ? +
Inv 1	42	SIG+	SIG -	SIG +	NS ?	NS ?	INT	SIG SM +
Moderate	58	? ?	SIG ?	? ?	? -	NS ?	INT	SIG SM +
Dir 8	47	? ?	SIG -	? ?	? -	? -	INT	SIG SM +
Inv 6	73	SIG ?	SIG+	SIG -	NS -	NS +	?	SIG SM ?
Very Low	52	NS +	SIG ?	NS ?	? -	? ?	?	SIG SM +
Dir 5	42	NS +	? -	NS -	? -	? -	INT	SIG SM +
Inv 2	75	NS +	SIG ?	? +	NS ?	SIG ?	3GR	SIG SM +

Nonwar conflict following growth (NWF)

LEAD LEVEL	R²	DGR	PCI	GDP	MEG	3GR	SIG	ZERO-INT
Very High	51	NS +	SIG -	SIG +	NS ?	SIG ?	3GR	NS SM +
Dir 1	51	NS ?	NS -	NS +	NS ?	SIG +	3GR	NS SM +
Inv 2	51	? +	SIG ?	SIG ?	NS ?	? -	?	? ? +
Moderate	48	? ?	SIG ?	SIG ?	NS+	? ?	?	SIG ? ?
Dir 7	45	NS -	SIG -	SIG ?	? +	NS +	QU	SIG LG +
Inv 7	51	SIG +	SIG -	SIG +	NS+	NS ?	?	? ? +
Very Low	53	SIG ?	? ?	? ?	NS+	? ?	?	? ? ?
Dir 5	40	SIG -	NS+	? -	NS+	? -	?	? ? -
Inv 8	56	SIG -	? -	SIG -	NS+	? +	GR	? ? -

Total conflict preceding growth (TCP)

LEAD LEVEL	R²	DGR	PCI	GDP	MEG	3GR	SIG	ZERO-INT
Very High	60	NS +	SIG ?	SIG ?	NS+	SIG ?	?	SIG LG ?
Dir 5	60	NS ?	SIG ?	SIG +	NS+	SIG -	?	SIG LG -
Inv 3	60	NS ?	SIG -	SIG +	NS ?	SIG +	?	SIG LG +
Moderate	58	? ?	SIG -	SIG +	NS+	? ?	?	SIG ? +
Dir 7	50	? +	SIG -	SIG +	NS+	? -	QU	SIG ? +
Inv 11	61	? ?	SIG -	SIG -	NS ?	? ?	GR	SIG ? ?
Very Low	71	SIG -	? ?	SIG -	NS -	SIG +	?	SIG ? +
Dir 2	66	? +	? +	SIG -	? -	? -	DV	SIG ? ?
Inv 2	72	SIG -	? -	? -	NS ?	SIG +	?	NS SM +

Table 4.6 continued

War preceding growth (WP)

LAG LEVEL	R²	DGR	PCI	PROD	MEG	3GR	SIG	ZERO-INT
Very High	60	SIG +	? +	? ?	NS -	? -	GR SIG	SM +
Dir 7	56	SIG ?	? +	SIG ?	NS -	? -	GR SIG	SM +
Inv 3	73	NS +	SIG +	NS -	NS -	SIG ?	INT SIG	LG +
Moderate	60	SIG ?	? ?	? ?	NS +	? ?	GR ?	SM +
Dir 9	57	SIG ?	SIG +	? -	NS +	? -	GR ?	SM ?
Inv 3	71	NS -	NS ?	NS +	NS -	SIG +	INT SIG	LG +
Very Low	74	NS ?	SIG +	SIG -	NS ?	SIG -	QU SIG	? ?
Dir 2	70	NS ?	SIG +	SIG -	NS ?	SIG -	PCI SIG	? -
Inv 3	77	NS ?	SIG ?	SIG ?	NS ?	SIG -	3GR SIG	SM +

Nonwar conflict preceding growth (NWP)

LAG LEVEL	R²	DGR	PCI	PROD	MEG	3GR	SIG	ZERO-INT
Very High	58	NS +	SIG -	SIG +	NS ?	SIG -	GDP SIG	SM +
Dir 6	48	NS ?	? ?	SIG ?	NS -	SIG -	GR ?	SM ?
Inv 2	71	NS ?	? -	SIG +	NS ?	SIG ?	GDP ?	? +
Moderate	61	? ?	? -	SIG +	NS +	? -	? SIG	SM +
Dir 3	56	SIG +	NS -	SIG +	NS +	NS -	GDP SIG	SM +
Inv 10	63	? +	SIG -	SIG +	NS ?	? -	QU ?	? +
Very Low	58	SIG ?	? ?	? -	NS -	SIG ?	? SIG	? ?
Dir 4	57	? ?	? +	SIG -	NS -	SIG -	? SIG	? +
Inv 5	57	SIG -	NS ?	? -	NS +	SIG +	GR ?	SM -

The lead-and lag profile of the inverse GCR shows uniformly higher correlations than those of the direct relationship across all subsets and delays, with only three weak exceptions: NWF high leads (0.51 = 0.51); TCP high lags (0.60 = 0.60); NWP low lags (0.57 = 0.57) (see Table 4.6). The inverse relationship shows 3GR as predominantly significant, while the direct relationship shows 3GR as regularly negative, at low lags and leads, in contrast to DGR, which shows no pattern of significance or effect.

In the direct relationship, GDP is predominantly negative at low leads and lags. PCI is predominantly significant at high delays only in the inverse GCR, at moderate delays in both direct and inverse GCR, and in neither relationship at low lags and leads. Although the direct GCR shows equivocal effects, within the inverse GCR the zero-intercept is predominantly positive except in NWF (low lead), TCP (moderate lag), WP (moderate lag), and NWP (low lag). The zero-intercept is only insignificant twice in the direct GCR (TCP high lead, NWF high lead) and once in the inverse relationship (TCP low lag). The zero-intercept is large only twice in the direct GCR (NWF moderate lead, TCP high lag) and four times in the inverse GCR (TCF and TCP high delay; WP high and moderate lag).

Table 4.7 Variables and Dominance Profiles

Total conflict following growth (TCF)

DOMINANCE	R²	LEAD	DGR	PCI	PROD	MEG	3GR	ZERO-INT
Rate (13)	59	0-14;7	? +	SIG -	? ?	NS +	SIG ?	? ? +
Dir 6	52	0-14;7	? +	SIG -	SIG+	NS ?	SIG -	? ? ?
Inv 7	63	0-11;7	SIG+	SIG -	? -	NS -	SIG+	? ? +
Quant (7)	51	0-10;4	? -	SIG ?	? ?	NS +	? -	SIG ? ?
Dir 2	37	4-4; 4	? ?	SIG ?	SIG-	? ?	NS ?	SIG ? -
Inv 5	56	0-10;4	NS ?	SIG -	? -	NS +	SIG -	? SM +
Dummy (10)	47	0-11;3	? ?	? -	? +	? +	NS +	SIG ? +
Dir 5	38	0-3; 2	NS ?	NS -	? +	SIG+	NS -	? ? +
Inv 5	55	0-11;4	? ?	SIG -	? +	? +	? +	SIG LG+

Total conflict preceding growth (TCP)

DOMINANCE	R²	LEAD	DGR	PCI	PROD	MEG	3GR	ZERO-INT
Rate (11)	57	0-13;6	? +	SIG ?	SIG ?	NS+	SIG ?	? ? ?
Dir 3	64	4-13;7	SIG+	SIG ?	SIG+	NS ?	SIG -	SIG SM+
Inv 8	55	0-10;6	? ?	? -	SIG -	NS ?	SIG+	? ? ?
Quant (8)	56	3-17;10	? -	SIG ?	SIG ?	NS+	? ?	SIG ? ?
Dir 5	45	3-17;10	NS ?	SIG -	SIG+	NS+	? -	SIG ? +
Inv 3	76	5-15;9	NS -	SIG+	SIG -	NS ?	NS +	SIG SM -
Dummy (11)	63	1-13;5	NS ?	SIG -	SIG ?	NS ?	? -	SIG LG+
Dir 6	61	1-13;6	NS +	SIG -	SIG ?	? +	? -	SIG LG ?
Inv 5	65	1-10;5	? ?	SIG -	SIG+	NS ?	SIG -	SIG LG+

War following growth (WF)

DOMINANCE	R²	LEAD	DGR	PCI	PROD	MEG	3GR	ZERO-INT
Rate (6)	61	0-9; 3	SIG ?	SIG+	SIG ?	NS ?	? -	SIG SM ?
Dir 2	36	0-3; 2	? +	SIG ?	SIG ?	NS ?	SIG -	? SM ?
Inv 4	74	0-9; 3	SIG -	SIG+	SIG -	NS ?	? ?	SIG SM ?
Quant (5)	48	1-10;5	? +	SIG ?	? -	NS -	? -	SIG SM ?
Dir 3	25	1-10;5	NS +	SIG -	NS -	NS -	NS -	SIG SM +
Inv 2	82	3-6; 4	NS ?	SIG+	SIG -	NS ?	? ?	? SM ?
Dummy (16)	50	0-14;7	? ?	? -	? +	? -	NS +	SIG SM +
Dir 13	48	0-14;7	NS ?	? -	NS +	SIG-	? ?	SIG SM +
Inv 3	57	7-10;8	SIG+	SIG -	SIG +	NS -	NS +	SIG SM +

War preceding growth (WP)

DOMINANCE	R²	LEAD	DGR	PCI	PROD	MEG	3GR	ZERO-INT
Rate (12)	61	1-14; 8	SIG ?	? +	SIG ?	NS -	SIG ?	? SM ?
Dir 9	54	3-14;10	SIG+	? +	SIG -	NS -	SIG -	? SM ?
Inv 3	72	1-5; 3	SIG ?	NS ?	SIG ?	NS ?	SIG+	SIG LG+
Quant (8)	65	0-15;6	? ?	SIG+	? -	NS ?	? -	? SM -
Dir 5	58	0-9; 4	NS -	SIG+	SIG -	NS+	? -	SIG SM -
Inv 3	76	1-15;9	NS +	SIG+	NS ?	NS -	SIG-	NS SM -
Dummy (7)	64	4-15;9	? -	? ?	? +	NS -	? -	SIG SM +
Dir 4	57	5-12;9	SIG -	? -	? +	NS -	NS -	SIG ? +
Inv 3	73	4-15;9	NS -	NS ?	NS ?	NS -	SIG?	SIG SM +

Table 4.7 continued

Nonwar conflict following growth (NWF)

Rate (15)	53	0-15;5	SIG ?	? ?	SIG ?	NS+	? +	? ? ?
Par 5	41	1-14;6	? -	? -	? ?	NS+	SIG+	? ? +
Inv 10	60	0-15;4	SIG ?	? ?	SIG -	NS+	? +	? ? ?
Quant (8)	45	0-10;5	? ?	SIG ?	SIG -	NS+	? -	SIG ? ?
Dir 4	53	0-7; 4	NS ?	SIG +	SIG -	? +	NS -	SIG LG -
Inv 4	37	2-9; 5	? +	SIG ?	SIG -	NS ?	? -	SIG LG ?
Dummy (7)	45	0-11;4	? ?	? -	? +	NS+	NS+	SIG LG+
Dir 4	38	0-8; 3	NS -	NS ?	? +	NS+	NS ?	SIG ? ?
Inv 3	53	0-11;3	SIG+	SIG -	SIG+	NS ?	NS	SIG LG+

Nonwar conflict preceding growth (NWP)

Rate (11)	64	0-13;5	SIG ?	NS +	? -	NS +	SIG ?	? SM -
Dir 5	59	0-13;7	? -	? +	? ?	NS ?	SIG -	? SM -
Inv 6	68	0-8; 4	SIG -	NS +	SIG-	NS +	SIG+	? SM -
Quant (11)	51	2-15;8	NS +	SIG -	SIG+	NS ?	? -	? SM +
Dir 4	50	3-17;10	? +	SIG -	SIG+	NS ?	? -	SIG SM +
Inv 7	52	2-15;8	NS +	SIG -	SIG+	NS ?	? -	NS SM +
Dummy (8)	60	0-10;4	? +	? -	SIG ?	? -	? ?	SIG +
Dir 4	48	0-10;3	NS +	? -	SIG ?	SIG -	? +	SIG SM+
Inv 4	72	1-6; 4	SIG+	? -	SIG+	NS ?	SIG -	SIG LG+

Variables and Dominance Profiles

The fourth dimension of the GCR—variables and dominance patterns—shows several remarkable features (see Table 4.7). Not systematically related across the composite relationship to correlation or lags and leads, dominance patterns affect primarily the zero-intercept. The groupings of PCI-3GR and GDP-DGR show weak associations with the zero-intercept, suggesting that the significance of these groups may suppress the zero-intercept. Although different associations and groupings are features of both separate GCR (direct and inverse), they are not powerful or salient enough to constitute regularities. In addition, the inverse relationship seems to increase the significance of the growth variables generally, relative to that of the zero-intercept.

When growth-rate variables dominate the composite relationship, the zero-intercept loses significance, except in WF. Within the inverse GCR, however, under growth-rate dominance, the zero-intercept retains significance in both war subsets (WP, WF), while within the direct GCR, it loses significance in all sets except TCP, rather than in the war subsets. Under growth-rate dominance DGR gains significance in the inverse relationship, but *not* for the direct GCR; 3GR gains significance in both types of relationship, but its inverse effect is predominantly negative, while in the direct GCR it has a positive effect. In the direct GCR, DGR and 3GR have predominantly opposite effects; in the inverse relationship their effects are predominantly the same (NWP is the only exception to this regularity).

Under dummy-variable dominance, in the composite relationship, the zero-intercept is always significant; in the direct relationship zero-intercept is not significant in TCF. Under dummy-dominance, the inverse relationship shows significance of all growth variables more often (62%) than does the direct GCR (17%), which is dominated by ambiguous or insignificant growth variables.

Zero-intercept Dimension

The zero-intercept seems not systematically related to any individual variable, or grouping of variables, except the pairs of growth-rate variables, quantity variables, and dummy variables, in either the conjunct profile or the disjunct profiles. The zero-intercept shows a predominant size under 4 only for war following growth (WF), and a predominant size over 1 only for NWF. In the direct GCR, the zero-intercept is predominantly greater than 1 in all subsets except WP, where half of the intercepts are very small. Across all subsets, the inverse relationship shows zero-intercepts predominantly larger than 1 (see Table 4.8).

Table 4.8 Size of the Zero-intercept

	SMALL (< 1)		MODERATE (1-4)		LARGE (> 4)	
War Preceding	12	(44%)	8	(30%)	7	(26%)
18 Dir	9	(50%)	6	(33%)	3	(17%)
9 Inv	3	(33%)	2	(11%)	4	(56%)
War Following	8	(30%)	15	(55%)	4	(15%)
18 Dir	6	(33%)	9	(50%)	3	(17%)
9 Inv	2	(22%)	6	(67%)	1	(11%)
Nonwar Preceding	8	(27%)	13	(43%)	9	(30%)
13 Dir	2	(15%)	8	(61%)	3	(24%)
17 Inv	6	(35%)	5	(30%)	6	(35%)
Nonwar Following	4	(13%)	10	(33%)	16	(54%)
13 Dir	1	(08%)	5	(38%)	7	(54%)
17 Inv	3	(18%)	5	(29%)	9	(53%)
Total Preceding	7	(23%)	6	(20%)	17	(57%)
14 Dir	2	(14%)	4	(29%)	8	(57%)
16 Inv	5	(31%)	2	(13%)	9	(56%)
Total Following	6	(20%)	9	(30%)	15	(50%)
13 Dir	2	(15%)	5	(38%)	6	(47%)
17 Inv	4	(24%)	4	(24%)	9	(52%)

Regional Profiles

Each region shows at least one distinctive internal regularity: Scandinavia shows four regularities; Northeast Asia shows three; Europe, Latin America, Middle East and Africa, and Southeast Asia show two each; North America shows a single regularity.

Europe and North America show high correlations, except when war follows growth (0.53). Scandinavia and Latin America show moderate correlations except when war follows growth (Scandinavia, 0.29; Latin America, 0.12); these are the only low correlations. None of the regions show dominance of the relationship by either growth-rate or quantity variables or significance of either MEG or 3GR. Europe and Southeast Asia show no predominantly significant variables. DGR is predominantly significant only in Latin America, and PCI only in Scandinavia and North America. The zero-intercept is predominantly significant only in Europe and Northeast Asia, small only in Latin America and Southeast Asia, and positive only in Europe and Northeast Asia.

Europe shows uniformly high correlations, mixed effects, lags and leads clustered from between two and five years, uniformly significant, positive zero-intercept, and significance of none of the growth variables.

Scandinavia shows moderate correlations except when war follows growth (WF, 0.29), insignificance of DGR and MEG, and significance of both PCI and GDP except when war is the dependent variable. All Scandinavian countries show direct effects of the GCR.

North America shows high correlation except when war follows growth. PCI is significant except when war precedes growth. The United States shows an inverse relationship.

Latin America shows moderate correlation and significant positive DGR except for war following growth (0.12, NS +), and nonwar following growth, SIG ?), and small zero-intercept. All countries show direct effects.

Middle East and Africa shows high correlations when conflict precedes growth and moderate correlations when conflict follows growth, and uniform significance of GDP. All countries show inverse effects.

Northeast Asia shows high correlations in WF, WP, and NWP, and moderate correlations in TCP, TCF, and NWF. Lags and leads cluster from six to nine years. GDP is significant except when war follows growth (WF); zero-intercept is significant and positive except when nonwar is dependent (NWF shows SIG ?; NWP shows NS +). All countries show inverse relationships, except Japan, which is mixed.

Southeast Asia shows high correlations in WF, WP, and TCP, and moderate correlations in NWP, TCF, and NWF, and a small zero-intercept. Southeast Asian countries show mixed effects (see Table 4.9).

Table 4.9 Regional Profiles

Aggregate Summary Profiles

REGION R²	LEAD	DGR	PCI	PROD	MEG	3GR	SIG	ZERO-INT
Europe 0.63	2-5	? ?	? ?	? ?	? ?	? ?	?	SIG ? +
Dir 0.57	?	? ?	? ?	? ?	? ?	? -	?	? ? ?
Inv 0.67	2-5	? ?	? ?	? ?	? ?	? ?	DV	SIG ? +
Scand 0.45	?	NS ?	SIG ?	SIG ?	NS -	? ?	DV	? ? ?
Dir 0.45 0 Inv	?	NS ?	SIG ?	SIG ?	NS -	? ?	DV	? ? ?
N Amer 0.65	?	? ?	SIG ?	? ?	? ?	? ?	QU	? ? ?
Dir 0.50	?	? ?	SIG ?	? ?	NS ?	? ?	GR	? SM ?
Inv 0.80	?	? ?	SIG ?	? ?	NS ?	? ?	QU	SIG LG ?
Lat Am 0.41	?	SIG +	? ?	? ?	? ?	? ?	?	? SM ?
Dir 0.41 0 Inv	?	SIG +	? ?	? ?	? ?	? ?	?	? SM ?
ME Afr 0.54 0 Dir	?	? ?	? ?	SIG ?	NS ?	? ?	?	? ? ?
Inv 0.54	?	? ?	? ?	SIG ?	NS ?	? ?	?	? ? ?
NE Asia 0.56	6-9	? ?	? ?	SIG ?	? ?	? ?	DV	SIG ? +
Dir 0.66	?	? ?	? ?	? ?	? ?	? ?	?	SIG SM +
Inv 0.53	6-9	? ?	? ?	SIG ?	? ?	? ?	DV	
SE Asia 0.57	?	? ?	? ?	? ?	NS ?	? ?	?	? SM ?
Dir 0.51	?	? +	? ?	? ?	? ?	? ?	?	SIG ? ?
Inv 0.60	?	? ?	? ?	? ?	NS ?	? +	GR	? SM ?

Total conflict following growth (TCF)

REGION R²	LEAD	DGR	PCI	PROD	MEG	3GR	SIG	ZERO-INT
Europe 0.60	0-10;4	? ?	SIG -	? ?	? ?	? ?	?	SIG LG +
2 Dir 0.58	4-7; 5	SIG -	? +	? -	? -	NS -	?	SIG LG ?
4 Inv 0.62	0-10;3	NS ?	SIG -	? +	? ?	? +	DV	SIG LG +
Scand 0.41	0-6; 5	NS ?	SIG +	SIG +	NS -	SIG ?	?	SIG ? ?
4 Dir 0.41 0 Inv	0-6; 5	NS ?	SIG +	SIG +	NS -	SIG ?	?	SIG ? ?
N Amer 0.63	0-14;7	? ?	SIG -	? ?	? ?	? ?	?	? ? ?
1 Dir 0.45	; 14	NS +	SIG -	NS ?	NS ?	SIG +	GR	NS SM -
1 Inv 0.81	; 0	NS ?	SIG -	SIG +	SIG +	NS ?	QU	SIG LG +
Lat Am 0.44	2-8; 4	SIG+	NS -	SIG +	SIG +	NS -	MEG	? SM -
3 Dir 0.44 0 Inv	2-8; 4	SIG+	NS -	SIG +	SIG +	NS -	MEG	? SM -
ME-Afr 0.47 0 Dir	0-10;4	NS ?	SIG +	SIG -	NS ?	SIG -	?	NS ? ?
4 Inv 0.47	0-10;4	NS ?	SIG +	SIG -	NS ?	SIG -	?	NS ? ?
NE Asia 0.58 0 Dir	6-11;9	SIG+	SIG -	SIG ?	? ?	SIG +	?	SIG ? +
4 Inv 0.58	6-11;9	SIG+	SIG -	SIG ?	? ?	SIG +	?	SIG ? +
SE Asia 0.54	0-9; 5	SIG -	? -	NS ?	NS +	? ?	?	SIG SM -
3 Dir 0.36	2-9; 6	SIG+	NS -	NS +	NS +	NS -	GR	SIG LG +
4 Inv 0.63	0-9; 4	SIG -	SIG -	NS -	NS ?	SIG +	PCI	SIG SM +

Table 4.9 continued

Total conflict preceding growth (TCP)

REGION R²	LEAD	DGR	PCI	PROD	MEG	3GR	SIG	ZERO-INT
Europe 0.61	1-10;5	SIG ?	SIG -	SIG ?	NS ?	SIG ?	INT	SIG LG+
2 Dir 0.57	4-5; 4	SIG +	SIG ?	? +	NS ?	? -	GR	SIG ? +
4 Inv 0.63	1-10;5	? ?	SIG -	SIG +	NS ?	SIG -	INT	SIG LG+
Scand 0.50	1-16;7	NS -	SIG ?	SIG ?	NS +	SIG ?	?	SIG LG ?
4 Dir 0.50 0 Inv	1-19;7	NS -	SIG ?	SIG ?	NS +	SIG ?	?	SIG LG ?
N Amer 0.68	15-17;16	NS ?	SIG -	SIG +	? +	? +	GDP	SIG LG+
1 Dir 0.49	; 17	NS ?	SIG -	SIG +	SIG +	NS ?	GDP	SIG LG+
1 Inv 0.87	; 15	NS ?	SIG -	SIG +	NS ?	SIG +	GDP	SIG LG+
Lat Am 0.48	1-9; 4	SIG +	SIG -	SIG +	SIG ?	NS ?	MEG	SIG SM+
3 Dir 0.48 0 Inv	1-9; 4	SIG +	SIG -	SIG +	SIG ?	NS ?	MEG	SIG SM+
ME Afr 0.68 0 Dir	0-6; 3	? ?	SIG ?	SIG -	NS ?	SIG ?	?	? SM ?
4 Inv 0.68	0-6; 3	? ?	SIG ?	SIG -	NS ?	SIG ?	?	? SM ?
NE Asia 0.55	3-10; 6	? -	SIG ?	SIG ?	NS ?	SIG ?	?	SIG LG+
1 Dir 0.63	3-3; 3	NS ?	SIG -	SIG +	NS ?	SIG -	GDP	SIG SM+
3 Inv 0.52	3-10; 7	NS -	SIG -	SIG +	NS ?	SIG +	GR	SIG LG+
SE Asia 0.66	7-13;10	NS +	? ?	SIG ?	NS ?	SIG ?	?	SIG SM -
3 Dir 0.70	11-13;12	NS +	SIG -	SIG +	NS ?	SIG ?	INT	SIG LG+
4 Inv 0.63	7-8; 8	NS +	? +	SIG -	NS ?	? +	GR	? SM -

War following growth (WF)

REGION R²	LEAD	DGR	PCI	PROD	MEG	3GR	SIG	ZERO-INT
Europe 0.66	0-6; 2	? -	SIG +	? -	? -	? -	?	SIG SM +
3 Dir 0.53	0-5; 2	? -	SIG ?	? -	SIG -	NS -	INT	SIG SM +
3 Inv 0.80	0-6; 4	NS +	SIG +	SIG -	NS ?	SIG -	QU	SIG SM +
Scand 0.29	9-14;11	NS +	SIG -	NS +	SIG -	NS ?	DV	SIG SM +
3 Dir 0.29 0 Inv	9-14;11	NS +	SIG -	NS +	SIG -	NS ?	DV	SIG SM +
N Amer 0.53	3-9; 6	SIG ?	SIG ?	SIG ?	NS ?	NS ?	DGR	SIG ? ?
1 Dir 0.32	; 3	SIG+	SIG -	SIG +	NS ?	NS ?	DGR	SIG SM +
1 Inv 0.74	; 9	SIG -	SIG +	SIG -	NS ?	NS ?	DGR	SIG LG -
Lat Am 0.12	1-9; 5	NS +	SIG -	NS ?	NS -	NS +	INT	SIG SM +
3 Dir 0.12 0 Inv	1-9; 5	NS +	SIG -	NS ?	NS -	NS +	INT	SIG SM +
ME Afr 0.50	5-12;11	? +	SIG -	SIG +	NS ?	? ?	INT	SIG ? +
2 Dir 0.48	5-12;8	NS ?	SIG ?	SIG ?	NS ?	SIG ?	?	SIG LG ?
2 Inv 0.51	7-10;8	SIG+	SIG -	SIG +	NS ?	NS ?	INT	SIG SM +
NE Asia 0.66	0-11;7	NS ?	NS ?	NS ?	SIG -	NS +	DV	SIG ? +
3 Dir 0.66	0-11;6	NS +	? ?	? ?	SIG -	NS +	DV	SIG SM +
1 Inv 0.68	; 8	SIG -	NS ?	NS ?	SIG -	NS +	INT	SIG SM +
SE Asia 0.63	0-13;4	? ?	? -	? ?	NS -	? -	INT	SIG SM +
3 Dir 0.57	1-13;6	SIG+	NS -	NS ?	NS ?	SIG -	INT	SIG SM +
2 Inv 0.71	0-3; 2	? -	SIG ?	SIG ?	NS ?	? +	GR	SIG SM ?

Table 4.9 continued

War preceding growth (WP)

REGION R^2	LEAD	DGR	PCI	PROD	MEG	3GR	SIG	ZERO-INT
Europe 0.68	1-7; 4	SIG ?	SIG ?	? ?	NS +	SIG -	?	? ? +
3 Dir 0.62	5-7; 6	SIG+	SIG -	NS +	NS +	NS -	?	NS SM+
3 Inv 0.81	1-4; 2	NS -	SIG ?	NS -	NS ?	SIG -	?	SIG LG+
Scand 0.55	8-14;10	SIG+	NS -	SIG -	NS -	SIG+	GR	NS SM -
3 Dir 0.55	8-14;10	SIG+	NS -	SIG -	NS -	SIG+	GR	NS SM -
0 Inv								
N Amer 0.66	11-12;12	? -	SIG +	? -	NS ?	? -	?	SIG SM -
1 Dir 0.55	; 11	SIG -	SIG +	SIG -	NS ?	NS ?	DGR	SIG SM -
1 Inv 0.77	; 12	NS +	SIG +	NS ?	NS ?	SIG -	PCI	SIG LG -
Lat Am 0.42	7-14;11	SIG+	NS +	NS +	SIG ?	SIG -	3GR	SIG SM +
3 Dir 0.42	7-14;11	SIG+	NS +	NS +	SIG ?	SIG -	3GR	SIG SM +
0 Inv								
ME Afr 0.61	3-15; 7	SIG ?	? +	? ?	NS -	? ?	?	NS SM ?
2 Dir 0.54	3-5; 4	SIG ?	? +	SIG ?	NS ?	? -	?	? SM ?
2 Inv 0.67	5-15;10	SIG ?	? +	NS ?	NS -	NS +	?	NS ? ?
NE Asia 0.69	0-11; 8	? -	? +	SIG -	NS -	SIG -	INT	SIG SM +
3 Dir 0.70	0-11; 7	SIG -	SIG +	SIG -	NS -	SIG -	?	SIG SM +
1 Inv 0.66	; 9	NS ?	NS ?	SIG+	SIG -	SIG -	INT	SIG SM +
SE Asia 0.67	0-15; 7	NS ?	SIG ?	SIG ?	NS ?	? -	?	SIG ? ?
3 Dir 0.63	0-12; 7	NS +	SIG +	SIG -	NS ?	NS -	PCI	SIG LG -
2 Inv 0.72	1-15; 8	NS -	? ?	? ?	NS ?	? +	?	? SM +

Nonwar conflict following growth (NWF)

REGION R^2	LEAD	DGR	PCI	PROD	MEG	3GR	SIG	ZERO-INT
Europe 0.60	0-15; 4	? -	? ?	SIG ?	? +	? ?	?	SIG LG+
2 Dir 0.57	0-4; 2	? -	? +	? -	NS ?	? -	?	SIG ? ?
4 Inv 0.62	0-15; 5	? -	? -	SIG+	NS +	? ?	?	? LG+
Scand 0.46	3-7; 5	NS ?	SIG ?	SIG ?	NS -	? +	?	SIG LG ?
4 Dir 0.46	3-7; 5	NS ?	SIG ?	SIG ?	NS -	? +	?	SIG LG+
0 Inv								
N Amer 0.65	6-14;10	? +	NS -	? +	NS +	? +	?	? SM+
1 Dir 0.51	; 14	NS ?	NS -	NS +	NS ?	SIG+	3GR	NS SM+
1 Inv 0.78	; 6	SIG+	NS ?	SIG+	NS +	NS ?	DGR	NS SM+
Lat Am 0.41	0-2; 1	SIG ?	NS ?	SIG ?	NS +	SIG ?	?	? SM -
3 Dir 0.41	0.2; 1	SIG ?	NS ?	SIG ?	NS +	SIG ?	?	? SM -
0 Inv								
ME Afr 0.47	0-5; 2	? ?	SIG -	SIG ?	NS ?	SIG+	?	SIG ? ?
0 Dir								
4 Inv 0.47	0-5; 2	? ?	SIG -	SIG ?	NS ?	SIG+	?	SIG ? ?
NE Asia 0.48	2-11;6	SIG+	SIG ?	SIG+	NS ?	NS +	?	SIG LG ?
0 Dir								
4 Inv 0.48	2-11;6	SIG+	SIG ?	SIG+	NS ?	NS +	?	SIG LG ?
SE Asia 0.44	0-9; 5	SIG -	? ?	? -	NS +	? -	DGR	NS SM+
3 Dir 0.34	1-8; 5	SIG -	NS ?	NS ?	NS +	NS -	DGR	NS LG+
4 Inv 0.52	0-9; 4	SIG ?	SIG -	? -	NS ?	NS -	DGR	NS SM+

Table 4.9 continued

Nonwar conflict preceding growth (NWP)

REGION R²	LEAD	DGR	PCI	PROD	MEG	3GR	SIG	ZERO-INT
Europe 0.60	0-6; 3	SIG+	? +	? ?	NS ?	SIG -	?	SIG ? +
2 Dir 0.57	0-3; 2	SIG ?	NS +	? +	NS ?	SIG -	?	SM+
4 Inv 0.62	1-6; 4	SIG ?	? -	? ?	NS ?	? -	INT	SIG LG+
Scand 0.47	1-11; 8	NS ?	SIG ?	SIG -	NS -	SIG ?	?	SM ?
4 Dir 0.47	1-11; 8	NS ?	SIG ?	SIG -	NS -	SIG ?	?	SM ?
0 Inv								
N Amer 0.77	15-17	NS ?	SIG -	SIG +	NS ?	? ?	GDP	SIG ? +
1 Dir 0.70	; 17	NS ?	SIG -	SIG +	NS ?	SIG -	GDP	SIG SM+
1 Inv 0.83	; 15	NS ?	SIG -	SIG +	NS ?	SIG+	GDP	SIG GL+
Lat Am 0.56	1-9; 4	SIG+	SIG -	SIG +	SIG ?	NS ?	MEG	SIG SM+
3 Dir 0.56	1-9; 4	SIG+	SIG -	SIG +	SIG ?	NS ?	MEG	SIG SM+
0 Inv								
ME Afr 0.68	0-6; 3	? -	? ?	SIG ?	NS ?	SIG ?	?	SIG SM ?
0 Dir								
4 Inv 0.68	0-6; 3	? -	? ?	SIG ?	NS ?	SIG ?	?	SIG SM ?
NE Asia 0.61	2-15; 6	? -	? -	SIG +	SIG +	SIG -	GDP	NS SM+
0 Dir								
4 Inv 0.61	2-15; 6	? -	? -	SIG +	SIG +	SIG -	GDP	NS SM+
SE Asia 0.50	0-13; 6	? ?	NS ?	SIG ?	NS ?	? ?	?	NS SM -
3 Dir 0.46	0-13; 7	NS +	NS ?	SIG +	NS ?	SIG ?	DGR	SIG SM -
4 Inv 0.54	0-8; 5	NS +	NS ?	SIG -	NS ?	? +	GR	NS SM -

Aggregate Summary

Consolidation of dimensional subset profiles provides an image of the superordinate, universal or generic, growth-conflict relationship across the analytical subsets. In some useful sense the lawlike regularities within such a global profile constitute a paradigm of axiomatic principles of a generic growth-conflict relationship. Such a powerful result demands a more rigorous standard than that used to analyze subsets (at least two-thirds of included cases; [see previous section, "Presentation of Regularities"]). To constitute a lawlike regularity for the generic relationship, a feature of the relationship or a constellation of growth variables must obtain in five of six conflict subsets. An observation occurring regularly only in each of one pair of subsets (TCP & TCF; NWP & NWF; WP & WF; TCP & NWP & WP; TCF & NWF & WF) is a singularity at the global level. An internal regularity observed in only a single subset is an anomaly. Any set of inconsistent observations is a weakness, but may also constitute an anomaly.

A composite profile over all six observation subsets shows moderate correlation between preceding growth and following conflict, and higher correlation between preceding conflict and following growth. Lags and leads show extreme ranges, but means cluster from four to seven years. Quantity variables seem individually more often significant than do growth-rate variables, which are predominantly country-specific when related to war. The effects of PCI and GDP are generally opposite; the zero-intercept is generally positive. MEG is predominantly insignificant.

A disjunctive profile of the inverse GCR shows a predominance of this relationship in the TC and NW subsets (TCP, TCF, NWP, NWF), while the direct relationship dominates both war subsets (WF, WP). Across all six subsets mean adjusted correlations for the inverse GCR are substantially higher than those of the direct relationships. In addition to the conjunct regularity of differences in the effects of the quantity variables (PCI, GDP), the effects of the growth-rate variables (DGR, 3GR) differ notably between the direct and the inverse relationships; DGR and 3GR tend to be respectively + and - in the direct GCR, but respectively - and + in the inverse relationship. The pair of growth-rate variables is jointly most significant in the inverse relationship more often than in the direct GCR, but is predominant in neither.

Disjunction seems not to affect the extreme ranges of lags and leads, which appear in both relationships. Similarly the MEG dummy variable and the zero-intercept do not vary from their conjunct regularities in the disjunct relationships. Although disjunction resolves many instances of conjunct country-specificity or ambiguity, many remain. Some features remain ambiguous in one type of relationship, but are specific in the other. Each disjunct type of GCR is substantially better defined than is the conjunct relationship (see Tables 4.10 and 4.11).

Table 4.10 Conjunct and Disjunct Summary Profiles

	R^2	DELAY	DGR	PCI	PROD	MEG	3GR	SIG	ZERO-INT
TCF	54	0-14; 4	? ?	SIG ?	? ?	NS +	? ?	GR ?	? +
13 Dir	45	0-14; 4	? ?	? -	? +	? +	? -	GR ?	? ?
17 Inv	59	0-11; 5	? ?	SIG -	? ?	NS +	? +	GR SIG	? +
TCP	62	0-17; 7	? ?	SIG -	SIG ?	NS +	? ?	DV SIG	? +
14 Dir	56	1-17; 8	? +	SIG -	SIG +	NS +	? -	DV SIG	? +
16 Inv	62	0-15; 6	? -	SIG -	SIG ?	NS ?	SIG +	GR SIG	? +
WF	56	0-14; 6	? ?	SIG ?	? ?	? -	? ?	DV SIG	SM +
18 Dir	43	0-14; 5	? +	SIG -	? ?	? -	NS -	DV SIG	SM +
9 Inv	70	0-10; 5	SIG ?	SIG +	SIG -	NS -	NS +	GR SIG	SM +
WP	67	0-15; 7	SIG ?	? -	? ?	NS -	? -	GR ?	SM ?
18 Dir	58	0-14; 8	SIG ?	? +	SIG -	NS ?	? -	GR SIG	SM ?
9 Inv	74	1-15; 7	NS ?	? +	NS ?	NS -	SIG ?	? ?	? +
NWF	49	0-15; 5	? ?	? ?	SIG ?	NS +	? ?	GR ?	? ?
13 Dir	44	0-14; 4	? -	? +	? ?	NS +	? +	GR SIG	? ?
17 Inv	53	0-15; 5	SIG ?	SIG ?	SIG ?	NS +	? ?	GR ?	? ?
NWP	58	0-17; 6	? ?	? -	SIG ?	NS ?	? ?	? ?	SM +
13 Dir	53	0-17; 7	? +	? -	SIG ?	NS -	SIG -	GR SIG	SM +
17 Inv	62	0-15; 5	? -	? -	SIG +	NS +	SIG ?	QU ?	? ?

Table 4.11 Profiles of the Growth-conflict Relationship

	CONJUNCT	INVERSE	DIRECT
Growth—Conflict Correlation	MODERATE 0.53	Higher 0.61	Lower 0.44
Conflict—Growth Correlation	HIGH 0.62	Higher 0.66	Lower 0.56
Subset Dominance	NA	TCP, TCF NWP, NWF	WP, WF
Growth-Rate Variables	Less Often Individually Significant; Country-Specific	DGR is - 3GR is + More Often Jointly Significant	DGR is + 3GR is - Less Often Jointly Significant
Regional Dominance	NA	Middle East and Africa, Northeast Asia	Scandinavia, Latin America
Quantity Variables	More Often Individually Significant; Opposite Effects		
MEG Period	Insignificant		
Zero-Intercept	Generally Positive		
Lags and Leads	Extreme Range; Cluster 4–7 years		

REGULARITIES

The analytical results, and indeed the data, show sufficient consistency across several dimensions to indicate several lawlike regularities, the object of this study. While not individually either explanatory or predictive, these regularities provide a foundation for development of hypotheses about the growth-conflict relationship.

Growth and Conflict Tend to Be Associated

With fewer low-correlation coefficients than either moderate or high correlations, and a mean correlation level of 0.58 (median is 0.57), the independent growth variables "explain" at least half of the variation in the dependent conflict variable in all subsets except NWF (nonwar conflict following growth = 0.49). This exception persists with less prominence in the form of correlation levels lower than those for conflict preceding growth across the other subsets for conflict following growth (TCF, WF), and may reflect the relative weakness of the growth process in generating conflict at moderate leads. Other exceptions to this broad regular association between growth and conflict are few. In Scandinavia growth reflects more than half the change in conflict only when war precedes growth; Latin American mean correlations exceed 0.50 only when growth follows nonwar conflict (NWP, 0.56). Most other exceptions involve conflict that follows growth:

Moderate lags (NWP)	0.47
Very high leads (WF)	0.40
Dummy-variable dominance (TCF, NWF)	0.47, 0.45
Quantity-variable dominance (WF, NWF)	0.48, 0.45

High Lags and Leads Show Low Correlation Levels

High lags and leads (subset mean $\geq$ 6.0) occur with lower correlation levels than do low lags and leads (subset mean $\leq$ 4.6), except for nonwar conflict preceding growth (NWP: R^2 = 0.58 at both levels). Differences in correlation levels are substantial (0.11 for TCP, 0.12 for WF, 0.14 for WP, 0.16 for TCF) except for NWF (0.02).

Inverse Is More Powerful Than Direct

Across the observation sets, mean correlation levels between higher growth and lower conflict, or between lower growth and higher conflict (inverse effect) are uniformly high (0.58—0.73). Mean correlation levels between high growth and high conflict, or between low growth and low conflict (direct effect), are substantially lower (0.38—0.66). The single weak exception to this regularity is the case of regressions on total conflict preceding growth (TCP), where the mean corrected correlation coefficient for low-confidence inverse effects is 0.603, and mean correlation of low-confidence direct effects is 0.610.

For countries experiencing direct effects, correlation coefficients are below 0.60 in 74% of all GCR, and about half have low confidence (52%). Correlations are predominantly below 0.60 in all subsets except WP (predominantly < 0.65). The lowest mean correlation coefficient (0.42) is in WF, which shows predominantly low-confidence relationships. Of 23 high-correlation direct GCR, 15 are high-confidence. Of 63 low-correlation direct GCR, 37 are low-confidence.

For countries experiencing predominantly the inverse GCR, correlation coefficients are above 0.60 in 65% of all inverse GCR. Correlation coefficients are predominantly above 0.60 in predominantly high-confidence relationships between growth and war (WP, WF), and in the relationships between preceding total conflict and following growth (TCP). Of 57 high-correlation GCR, 37 are high-confidence. Of the 31 low-correlation GCR, 21 are low-confidence. In countries experiencing the inverse GCR, high growth is regularly and confidently associated with low war, and regularly associated with low total conflict. Within the direct GCR, growth cannot regularly or confidently be associated with high or low conflict. Although weaker across low-confidence effects, the regularity clearly holds for all high-confidence effects, both inverse and direct.

Conflict Operates More Slowly Than Does Growth

Across the observation sets, mean *lags* on the dependent variable (preceding conflict) are *larger* (6-7 > 4-6 years) than mean *leads* on the dependent variable (following conflict). While this may be an artifact of any simultaneous determination present (see Appendix N), the impact of international conflict seems to appear *later* in the subsequent growth-generation process than does the impact of growth in the following conflict-generation process. Although comparison of leads and lags cannot impute any sort of causality or directionality to the growth-conflict relationship, and the possibility of simultaneous determination confuses the relationship, the persistent notable difference in size suggests a possible weak lawlike regularity. The greater power of conflict, especially war, to disrupt a society and affect growth intuitively implies a longer delay in resuming (or beginning) postconflict growth. This possible regularity also warrants caution in accepting it as a legitimate regularity because of the relatively large number of exceptions that seem to be counterexamples. The most salient exceptions to this possible regularity are the cases of:

> regressions on total conflict (TC) when growth-rate variables (GR) are dominant (6 < 7); the regularity clearly holds for GR-dominated observations on war (W) (8 > 3), but is balanced for GR-dominated observations on nonwar (NW) (5 = 5);
>
> regression on total conflict (TC) with moderate leads and lags (5 < 7); the regularity holds for high and low leads and lags;
>
> regressions in Europe on nonwar conflict (NW) (3 < 4); the regularity holds for European observations on war and total conflict;
>
> regressions in Scandinavia on war (W) (10 < 11); the regularity holds for Scandinavian regressions on nonwar (NW) and total conflict (TC);
>
> regression on war (W) with low leads and lags (6 <7); the regularity holds for moderate and high leads and lags;
>
> regressions in Middle East and Africa (MEA) on total conflict (TC) (3 < 4) and on war (W) (7 < 11); the regularity holds for MEA regression on nonwar (NW) (3 > 2);
>
> regression on total conflict (TC) in Northeast Asia (NEA) (6 < 9); the regularity holds for NEA regression on war (W) (6 > 4), but is balanced for nonwar (NW) (6 = 6);
>
> regression on nonwar (NW) in Europe (3 < 4); the regularity holds for European regression on war (W) (5 > 4), and for regression on total conflict (TC) (5 > 4).

Duration of Modern Economic Growth Is Insignificant

Presence or absence of current modern economic growth (reflected in the dummy variable, MEG) seems not to be systematically related to international conflict in any of the growth-conflict relationships (composite, direct, inverse). The most salient exception to this regularity is Latin America, where MEG is insignificant only for regressions on war and nonwar following growth (WF, NWF). Indeed, in Latin America MEG is the most significant variable for total conflict (TC) and for nonwar proceeding growth (NWP). A second minor exception is in Northeast Asia for nonwar conflict preceding growth (NWP). Each of these exceptions, however, is so small (three cases, four cases) as to prevent reliable inference.

Influence and Significance of Quantity Variables Vary

Even where both are country-specific, the effects (negative, positive) of PCI and GDP operate predominantly to counteract each other. The regularity persists across the composite relationship, despite any independent variance in the nature of respective effects across countries, regions, periods, and over time. Where the effects of only one of the quantity variables are definite within an analytical subset or across a dimension, the effects of the other persist as opposite, even though not clearly predominant. The resulting joint neutral effect of the quantity-variable pair seems unrelated to the significance of either variable, or to that of the pair of variables. The few salient exceptions to this regularity at the dimensional level show the effects of both PCI and GDP as positive:

Scandinavia (TCF) +,+	Hi-Cnf Inverse (WP) +,+
Scandinavia (WP) -,-	Latin America (WP) +,+

For the composite relationship the national-product variable shows no predominant effect or pattern. The effect of absolute levels of wealth on international conflict seems to be random or influenced by some exogenous variable. It is never predominantly positive or negative, significant or insignificant across an entire subset or dimension. This regularity persists across the disjunct relationships.[71] PCI is predominantly significant at low correlations across all subsets except war preceding growth, and is insignificant at low correlations only in four countries:

New Zealand (TCF, NWF, NWP)	Finland (WF)
Thailand (NWP)	Argentina (WP)

For countries experiencing the direct growth-conflict relationship, the quantity variables (PCI, GDP) are jointly ambiguous and country-specific: significant in 52% of the GCR, and positive in only 47% of these. Both PCI and GDP are significant in 37% and insignificant in 32% of the direct relationships. For countries experiencing the inverse GCR, the quantity variables are predominantly significant in most (62%) of the growth-conflict relationships, and positive in 48% of the relationships where they are significant. Both PCI and GDP are significant in 45%, and insignificant in 20% of the inverse relationships. The aggregate effect of quantity variables in inverse GCR is a significant, but country-specific, association.

The effect of PCI in the direct GCR is ambiguous in all subsets. PCI is significant in 44 (51%) of the relationships, with eight high-confidence associations with low correlation, and seven high-confidence associations with high correlation. PCI is insignificant in 42 cases, associated with both low correlation (19 high-confidence, 14 low-confidence) and high correlation (nine high-confidence). In contrast to significance at low correlations in the composite analysis, the significance of PCI in direct GCR cannot be confidently associated with either high or low correlations; PCI cannot be used to predict or explain conflict in either the conjunct or the direct GCR.

Most (55 = 63%) of the inverse relationships show *per capita* income as significant, with seven high-confidence low-correlation associations and 20 high-confidence high-correlation associations. PCI is insignificant in 33 cases, associated both with low correlations (three high-confidence, six low-confidence) and with high correlations (17 high-confidence, seven low-confidence). In inverse relationships, PCI is predominantly significant in TCP (total conflict preceding growth) and in every subset of conflict following growth (WF, NWF, TCF). The *per capita* income is predominantly insignificant in NWP (nonwar conflict preceding growth), and ambiguous in WP (war preceding growth) (see Table 4.12).

Table 4.12 Impact and Significance of Quantity Variables

	COMPOSITE	PARALLEL	INVERSE
Aggregate	Quantity variables counteract each other in a jointly neutral influence, with no apparent systematic regularities in significance		
			Significant, country-specific
Per capita Income			Significant for conflict following growth
			Significant for total conflict preceding growth
	Significant at low correlations		Significant at high-confidence, high correlations
Gross Domestic Product		Significant for total conflict and nonwar conflict preceding growth	

Growth-rate Variables Are Country-specific

Across the observation sets, the indicators of growth-rates (DGR, 3GR) show no notable propensity to be significant or insignificant, positive or negative. The few salient definite impacts of the individual growth-rate variables in deviation from this regularity include:

DGR		3GR	
Very high lags and leads	SIG or NS +	Very high lags and leads	SIG
Very low lags and leads	SIG or NS	Quantity variable dominance	-
Scandinavia	NS	Dummy variable dominance	+ or -
Latin America	SIG +	Low R^2	NS

Growth-rate Variables Dominate High-confidence Effects

Across the subsets, one of the growth-rate variables (DGR, 3GR) dominates in some of the country observations in every subset. The pair of growth-rate variables dominates in observations showing either high-confidence inverse effects or high-confidence direct effects in every subset. Only the pair of growth-rate variables shows dominance in every subset, at each level of confidence, and for each effect.

For countries experiencing the direct GCR, the growth-rate variables are individually significant in only 43% of the growth-conflict relationships, and positive in only 44% of the relationships where they are significant. Even when significant, the aggregate effect of the individual growth-rate variables is ambiguous. The growth-rate variables are predominantly insignificant in the direct relationships between preceding growth and following conflict.

For countries experiencing direct GCR, the decadal growth-rate is predominantly significant only between preceding war and following growth. The decadal growth rate is insignificant in each of WF, NWF, and TCF, and the tridecadal growth rate is insignificant in WF and ambiguous in NWF and TCF.

For countries experiencing the inverse GCR, the growth rate variables (DGR, 3GR) are predominantly significant in most (54%) of the growth-conflict relationships, and positive in 48% of the relationships where they are significant. The aggregate effect of the growth-rate variables is a weak association between high growth and low conflict, and between low growth and high conflict.

For countries experiencing the inverse GCR, the decadal growth rate is predominantly significant between growth and following total conflict. The tridecadal growth rate is predominantly significant in the inverse relationships between preceding conflict and following growth (see Table 4.13).

Table 4.13 Impact and Significance of Growth-rate Variables

	CONJUNCT	DIRECT	INVERSE
Aggregate	Growth-rate variables show pervasive dominance of GCR of both types in all subsets		
	The pair of growth-rate variables shows predominant dominance of high-confidence relationships		
	Ambiguous country-specific	Ambiguous country-specific	Weakly positive and significant
Decadal Growth-rate		Significant for war preceding growth	Significant for total conflict following growth
Tridecadal Growth-rate		Ambiguous or insignificant	Significant for conflict preceding growth

SINGULARITIES AND IRREGULARITIES

The observed relationships show notable singularities in several sets and subsets of observations. Also, several features of the growth-conflict relationships, not sufficiently pronounced to constitute rigorously defined anomalies, appear as pervasive irregularities across the universe of observations. Each of the regional regularities (see previous section, "Regional Profiles") constitutes a singularity at the global level.

Classical historians cavalierly dismiss singularities as simple violations of *ceteris paribus*. Orthodox theory accepts that singularities and irregularities are artifacts of structure and policy, and contentedly imposes structural, functional, or other typologies to deal with them.[72] A refined approach would also investigate a possibility of misformulation, since qualitatively different growth processes may be operating in different countries at different times.

Zero-intercept Shows Several Singularities

The zero-intercept is predominantly positive at high lags and leads. Broadly significant, especially at extreme lags and leads, across all observation subsets, the zero-intercept is predominantly significant when quantity variables are dominant.

Especially in observations of lagged total conflict (TCP) subsets, the zero-intercept is often very large relative to the dependent variable. In seven of the

TCP and four of the NWF dimensional profiles the zero-intercept is predominantly large. The zero-intercept also tends to be large and significant for observations with low-confidence effects in all sets (TC, W, NW).

The zero-intercept is predominantly significant in direct GCR, almost never insignificant, and most often significant at low lags and leads. It is generally positive, predominantly larger than 1, usually larger than the mean of the dependent conflict variable, but only rarely predominantly large. Inverse relationship generally show lower significance for the zero-intercept, which is predominantly less significant under dominance of growth-rate variables. The zero-intercept is predominantly significant and positive in high-confidence direct GCR, significant in low-confidence inverse GCR, and small in high-confidence inverse growth-relationships.

The zero-intercept has a large, positive impact on conflict through the direct relationship, and a smaller impact under either growth-rate-variable dominance or in the inverse relationship. Any set of exogenous, missing factors integrated into the zero-intercept is most significant in the direct relationship and tends toward associating high conflict with high growth. Under growth-rate-variable dominance and the inverse relationships the exogenous factors lose significance, and do not show a predominant effect.

Growth Variables Predict Only Disjunct Effects

The set of lawlike regularities draws some powerful general predictions and explanations from the undifferentiated growth-conflict relationship itself. With finer resolution, the separate disjunct relationships allow specific predictions related to specific growth variables and to particular conflict types. Particularly for countries experiencing inverse relationships, individual growth variables show high-confidence significant associations with all types of conflict.

Within the direct GCR, neither growth rates nor PCI can be used to predict either low or high conflict after either low or high growth. Nor can GDP be used to predict war. However, the significance of GDP for the TCP subset allows a period of high nonwar conflict or total conflict for a country experiencing the direct GCR to be a predictor of a high national product a few years after the war. The singular significance of DGR in direct WP relationships suggests that a period of high war for a country experiencing the direct GCR is a predictor of a high decadal growth rate a few years after the war. Since the mean lag for war in this sample is less than 9 years, the implication is that the war itself would have occurred early in the period of high growth that generated the later high decadal growth rate.

The high significance of PCI for inverse TCP relationships makes high total conflict, *but not nonwar conflict or war alone*, for a country experiencing the inverse GCR, a predictor of a low *per capita* income a few years after the conflict. In contrast to the ambiguous role of PCI in the composite and direct analyses, the statistical significance of PCI within the inverse GCR is confidently associated with high correlation coefficients, although the specific influence is country-specific.   Predominantly significant in all inverse relationships for following conflict (WF, NWF, TCF) a high *per capita* income is, for a country experiencing the inverse GCR, a predictor of low conflict of any sort for a few years. A period of high growth with a significant DGR for a country experiencing the inverse GCR is a predictor of a period of low total conflict (TCF) for a few years after the growth period. The significance of 3GR in all inverse relationships with preceding conflict (WP, NWP, TCP) allows high conflict of any sort for a country experiencing the inverse GCR to predict a low 30-year growth rate a few years after the conflict. Since the mean lag for conflict in this sample is less than 6 years, the implication is that the conflict would have occurred at the end of a long period of low growth (see Tables 4.14 and 4.15).

Table 4.14 "Predictions" of Quantity Variables

		Preceding	Predictor	Following
CONJUNCT GCR		No significant Associations or Predictors		
DIRECT GCR		High Growth	Significant High GDP	High Total and Nonwar Conflict
		Low Growth	Significant Low GDP	Low Total and Nonwar Conflict
		Hi-Lo Total and Nonwar Conflict	Significant Association	Hi-Lo GDP
INVERSE GCR		Hi-Lo Total Conflict	Significant Association	Lo-Hi PCI
		Hi-Lo PCI	Significant Association	Lo-Hi Conflict
		High Growth	Significant High PCI	Low Conflict
		Low Growth	Significant Low PCI	High Conflict

Table 4.15 "Predictions" of Growth-rate Variables

	Preceding	Predictor	Following
CONJUNCT GCR	No Significant Associations or Predictors		
DIRECT GCR	Hi-Lo War	Significant Association	Hi-Lo DGR
INVERSE GCR	Hi-Lo Growth	Significant DGR	Lo-Hi Total Conflict
	Hi-Lo Conflict	Significant 3GR	Lo-Hi Growth
	Hi-Lo Conflict after Long Lo-Hi Growth	Significant Association	Lo-Hi 3GR

AN ANOMALY

Across the observation sets, the growth-rate variables jointly dominate the inverse relationship. The quantity variables are individually, however, more often significant than are individual growth-rate variables, the zero-intercept or the dummy variable. It is clear that profiles may show two or all three variable pairs with at least one individual variable significant, but that only one pair can dominate the observation. Thus, figures indicating individual variable significance are not mutually exclusive parts of a whole. This statistical artifact cannot, however, explain the anomaly that shows growth-rate variables jointly dominant in composite GCR nearly three-quarters as often as they are individually significant, while quantity and dummy variables are jointly dominant only one-third and one-half as often as they are significant. Nor does methodology account for another persistent weak "dominance anomaly" in inverse relationships, where growth-rate variables are jointly dominant about two-thirds (67%) as often as they are significant, while quantity variables are jointly dominant about two-fifths (39%) and dummy variables about two-thirds (68%) as often as they are respectively significant.

In contrast to the composite and inverse "dominance anomaly," the direct GCR shows a "dominance regularity" (within the 95% range of statistical confidence) that allows growth-rate variables to be jointly dominant about four-fifths (81%) as often as they are significant, while quantity and dummy variables are jointly dominant about two-thirds (68%) and nine-tenth (92%) as often as they are respectively significant.

Table 4.16 Significance and Dominance: Conjunct GCR

Conjunct GCR	SIGNIFICANCE	DOMINANCE
QUANTITY VARIABLES	86 of 108 (0.80)	47 of 174 (0.27)
DUMMY VARIABLES	74 of 108 (0.69)	59 of 174 (0.34)
GROWTH-RATE VARIABLES	58 of 108 (0.54)	68 of 174 (0.39)

Of the 108 dimensional profiles of the composite GCR (9 lag, 9 lead, 18 dominance, 18 correlation, 12 effects, 42 regional) over the six subsets, 86 show at least one of the quantity variables (PCI, GDP) as predominantly significant, yet the pair of quantity variables jointly dominates only 47 of the 174 observations. Of the 108 dimensional profiles, 72 show the zero-intercept as significant, and eight show MEG as significant (six show both MEG and the zero-intercept as significant), yet this pair of variables dominates only 59 of the 174 observations. In contrast to both of these pairs of variables, only 58 of the 108 dimensional profiles, however, show at least one growth-rate variable (DGR, 3GR) as predominantly significant, yet the pair of growth-rate variables dominates 68 of the 174 observations (see Table 4.16).

Of the 108 dimensional profiles of the direct GCR, 69 show at least one of the quantity variables (PCI, GDP) as predominantly significant, and the pair of quantity variables jointly dominates only 47 of the 174 observations. Of the direct-relationship profiles, 62 show the zero-intercept as significant, and 13 show MEG as significant (11 show both MEG and zero-intercept as significant); this pair of variables dominates only 59 observations. Of the 108 direct dimensional profiles, 52 show at least one growth-rate variable (DGR, 3GR) as predominantly significant, and the pair of growth-rate variables dominates 68 of the 174 observations (see Table 4.17).

Table 4.17 Significance and Dominance: Direct GCR

Direct GCR		SIGNIFICANCE	DOMINANCE
QUANTITY VARIABLES	68%	69 of 108 (0.64)	47 of 174 (0.27)
DUMMY VARIABLES	92%	64 of 108 (0.59)	59 of 174 (0.34)
GROWTH-RATE VARIABLES	81%	52 of 108 (0.48)	68 of 174 (0.39)

Table 4.18 Significance and Dominance: Inverse GCR

Inverse GCR		SIGNIFICANCE	DOMINANCE
QUANTITY VARIABLES	39%	75 of 108 (0.69)	47 of 174 (0.27)
DUMMY VARIABLES	68%	54 of 108 (0.50)	59 of 174 (0.34)
GROWTH-RATE VARIABLES	57%	63 of 108 (0.58)	68 of 174 (0.39)

Of the 108 dimensional profiles of the inverse GCR, 75 show at least one quantity variable (PCI, GDP) as predominantly significant; 53 profiles show the zero-intercept as significant, and four show MEG as significant (three show both MEG and the zero-intercept); 63 inverse dimensional profiles show at least one growth-rate variable (DGR, 3GR) as predominantly significant (see Table 4.18).

In a context of disjunction, the dominance anomaly resolves into a definitive singularity of the inverse GCR, with a weak reflection in the direct (possibly a statistical artifact). For countries experiencing the inverse relationship, the *pair* of growth-rate variables dominates, *despite* individual salience of quantity variables and the prominence of other factors (reflected in a persistently significant and dominant zero-intercept, with implication of exogenous processes or missing variables).

This clear anomaly in combination with the set of pervasive regularities exposes the ingenuous weakness of this simple model of the growth-conflict relationship. Misformulation of the regression model may be masking a process or structure that could force the *pair of growth-rate variables, but not necessarily the individual variables*, to dominate the relationship. Also probable is that misformulation might have created the anomaly as an artifact of inappropriate premises or assumptions about the independent variable. Immediately suspect as a misformulation is the aggregation of economic growth into a simple set of growth indicators. Of the initial assumptions, the least viable is that of the homogeneity of the growth process over time and across countries.

A "SPECULATIVE" PROFILE OF GROWTH AND CONFLICT

Several of the regularities are strong and empirically robust, while others are weaker and rely on inference from empirical results. Even, however, after consideration of their imperfections, these significant relationships between growth and conflict critically weaken the realist assertion of their irrelevance to each other. Nations that experience rapid economic growth must expect their involvements with international conflict to be related to their growth in one, or both, of two ways: direct-positive or inverse-negative. The direct relationship is weaker of the two and involves complex linkages between levels of *per capita* income (PCI) and gross domestic product (GDP) and international conflict, which tend to associate high growth with high conflict. The stronger inverse relationship stresses linkages between growth-rates of PCI and conflict, with higher growth rates associated with lower conflict. Even in the presence of an anomaly, the set of lawlike regularities provides a useful profile of the growth-conflict relationship.

Growth and Conflict Tend to Be Associated in Two Ways: Direct and Inverse. While lawlike regularities do not assign causality, it is clear that growth and conflict occur more often together than either occurs alone. In most countries, most of the time, growth variables "explain" much of the country's conflict. Although not the only, or primary, variable associated with conflict, growth clearly exerts significant influence on international conflict.

The Inverse Relationship Is More Powerful Than the Direct Relationship. Pervasive differences in correlation levels leave no doubt that high growth is closer associated with low than with high conflict, and that high conflict is closer associated with low than with high growth.

Growth-rate Variables Dominate the Inverse Relationship and All High-confidence Effects. It is clear that the growth-rate variables affect the relationships far more than the individual significances and influences suggest. All high-confidence relationships and all inverse relationships clearly depend on the growth-rate variables for much of their power.

High Lags and Leads Show Low Correlation Levels. Clear decreases in correlations for delayed effects imply that the power of the growth-conflict relationship deteriorates over time.

Individual Growth Variables Are Broadly Country-specific, and Weakly Predictive Only in the Disjunct Relationships. Pervasive ambiguity and country-specificity in both significance and effects of the individual growth variables do little to explain the growth-conflict relationships.

The Zero-intercept is Pervasively Powerful, but Shows No Regularities in Significance, Size, or Effects. Although the zero-intercept involves several powerful singularities, none are extensive enough to constitute a regularity. While growth is clearly a primary determinant of the relationship between growth and conflict, it is assuredly not the only significant influence on international conflict.

A critical element of any growth-related explanation or prediction about conflict is clearly the type of growth-conflict relationship predominant in a nation. The type of relationship determines the risk of growth-related conflict, its timing, its kind (war or nonwar), which growth variables most influence its occurrence, and the relative strength of any exogenous factors in generating or inhibiting conflict. Collectively the lawlike regularities form a powerful set that can be a solid foundation for both policy making and further investigation and analysis.

NOTES

1. The possibility of simultaneous determination and "feedback" between growth and conflict, as well as the plausible argument of multiple causes, prevent any reliance on *post hoc, ergo propter hoc* logic. Particularly in relationships involving prior conflict and subsequent growth, these possibilities weaken any conclusions, including identification of apparent regularities (see Appendix N).

2. An alternative method is the LOGIT regression process. Since, however, the dependent-variable conflict data are not binary, and are indeed cardinal, the WOLS method is appropriate.

3. Louis Kreisberg, *International Conflict Resolution* (New Haven, Connecticut: Yale University Press, 1992), 5-6.

4. Louis Kreisberg, "Interlocking Conflicts in the Middle East," in Louis Kreisberg, ed., *Research in Social Movements, Conflicts and Change* (Greenwich, Connecticut: JAI Press, 1980), Vol 3: 99-118; Richard E. Neustadt & Ernest R. May, *Thinking in Time: The Uses of History for Decision-Makers* (New York: Free Press, 1986).

5. C. S. Gochman & Z. Maoz, "Militarized Interstate Disputes 1816-1976: Procedures, Patterns, and Insights," *Journal of Conflict Resolution* 28 (1984), 585-616; Melvin Small & J. David Singer, *Resort to Arms: International and Civil Wars: 1816-1980* (Beverly Hills, California: Sage Publications, 1982).

6. Quincy Wright, *A Study of War*, 2d ed. (Chicago: University of Chicago Press, 1965), 636.

7. Lewis Richardson, *Statistics of Deadly Quarrels* (Pittsburgh: Boxwood Press, 1960).

8. Michael D. Wallace, "Arms Races and Escalation: Some New Evidence," *Journal of Conflict Resolution* 23 (March 1979), 3-16; J. David Singer, ed., *Explaining War: Selected Papers From the Correlates of War Project* (Beverly Hills, California: Sage Publications, 1979); J. David Singer & Melvin Small, *The Wages of War, 1816-1965: A Statistical Handbook* (New York: John Wiley, 1972).

9. Jack Levy, *War in the Modern Great Power System: 1495-1975* (Lexington: University Press of Kentucky, 1983), 51.

10. Small & Singer, *Resort to Arms: International and Civil Wars: 1816-1980*, 38.

11. Edward D. Mansfield, *Power, Trade, and War* (Princeton, New Jersey: Princeton University Press, 1994), 39.

12. Mansfield, *Power, Trade, and War*, 44-47.

13. Charles A. McClelland, "International Interaction Analysis: Basic Research and Some Practical Applications," *World Event/Interaction Survey Technical Report 2*, November 1968 (Los Angeles: University of Southern California, 1968).

14. Philip M. Burgess & Raymond W. Lawton, *Indicators of International Behavior: An Assessment of Events Data Research* (Beverly Hills, California: Sage Publications, 1972), 10-11.

15. Bernard C. Cohen, *The Press and Foreign Policy* (Princeton, New Jersey: Princeton University Press, 1963).

16. Harold D. Lasswell, "The Structure and Function of Communication in Society," in L. Bryson, ed., *The Communication of Ideas* (New York: Harper, 1948).

17. Charles A. McClelland & R. A. Young, "World Event/Interaction Survey Handbook and Codebook," *World Event/Interaction Survey Technical Report 1*, January 1969 (Los Angeles: University of Southern California, 1969).

18. Rudolph J. Rummel "Testing Some Possible Predictors of Conflict Behavior Within and Between Nations," in *Papers I*, Chicago Conference, Peace Research Society (Chicago: Peace Research Society, 1963), 79-111; Rudolph J. Rummel "Dimensions of Conflict Behavior Within and Between Nations," in *General Systems: Yearbook of the Society for General Systems Research*, Vol. VIII (Society for General Systems Research, 1963), 1-50.

19. Edward E. Azar, "The Analysis of International Events," *Peace Research Review* 4 (November 1970): 1-106; Edward E. Azar & Joseph D. Ben-Dak, eds. *Theory and Practice of Events Research* (New York: Gordon and Breach Science Publishers, 1975); Edward E. Azar & Thomas J. Sloan, *Dimensions of Interaction: A Source Book for the Study of the Behavior of 31 Nations from 1948 through 1973* (Philadelphia: University of Pennsylvania Press, 1975).

20. Charles F. Hermann, Maurice A. East, Margaret G. Hermann, Barbara G. Salmore & Stephen A. Salmore, *CREON: A Foreign Events Data Set* (Beverly Hills, California: Sage Publications, 1973).

21. Richard N. Rosecrance, "Bipolarity, Multipolarity, and the Future," in J. N. Rosenau, ed. *International Politics and Foreign Policy* (New York: Free Press, 1969).

22. R. J. Leng & J. David Singer, *Toward a Multi-theoretical Typology of International Behavior*, Paper presented at the Event Data Conference, April 1970 (East Lansing: University of Michigan, 1970).

23. Walter H. Corson, *Conflict and Cooperation in East-West Crises: Measurement and Explanations*, Paper presented at the American Political Science Association Annual Meeting, September 1970 (Los Angeles: American Political Science Association, 1971).

24. Robert Burrowes, "Mirror, Mirror on the Wall: A Comparison of Sources of External Events Data," in James N. Rosenau, ed. *Comparing Foreign Policies: Theories, Findings, and Methods* (Beverly Hills, California: Sage Publications, 1974), 383-406.

25. J. Wilkenfeld, "Domestic and Foreign Conflict Behavior of Nations," *Journal of Peace Research* 5 (1968): 56-69; J. Wilkenfeld, "Some Further Findings Regarding the Domestic and Foreign Conflict Behavior of Nations," *Journal of Peace Research* 6 (1969): 147-156; J. Wilkenfeld, ed., *Conflict Behavior and Linkage Politics* (New York: McKay, 1973).

26. Patrick J. McGowan, *Dimensions of African Foreign Policy Behavior*, Paper presented at the Canadian Association of African Studies Annual Meeting (Montreal: Canadian Association of African Studies, 1973).

27. Vernard Lanphier, *Foreign Relations Indicator Project*, Paper presented at the International Studies Association Annual Meeting, March 1972 (Dallas: International Studies Association, 1972); McClelland, "International Interaction Analysis: Basic Research and some Practical Applications"; Kenneth N. Waltz, "International Structure, National Force, and the Balance of World Power," in James N. Rosenau, ed., *International Politics and Foreign Policy* (New York: Free Press, 1969).

28. Simon Kuznets, "Characteristics of Modern Economic Growth," in his *Postwar Economic Growth: Four Lectures* (Cambridge, Massachusetts: Belknap Press of Harvard University Press, 1964).

29. Lloyd G. Reynolds, *Economic Growth in the Third World, 1950-1980* (New Haven, Connecticut: Yale University Press, 1985), 6-7.

30. Simon Kuznets, "Characteristics of Growth," 37; Moshe Syrquin, "Patterns of Structural Change," in Hollis B. Chenery & T. N. Srinivasan, eds., *Handbook of Development Economics*, Vol. 1 (Amsterdam: Elsevier Science Publishers, 1988), 223-224. From his analysis of growth after 1816, Kuznets has indicated that decadal rates of

growth in PCI are "well above 10 per cent" for countries experiencing modern economic growth, and assumes "15 percent per decade as a typically low limit." Simon Kuznets, *Modern Economic Growth*, (New Haven, Connecticut: Yale University Press, 1966), p. 67. Available information and data about ancient civilizations, as well as projections of modern data into the past, suggest that these sorts of growth rates are large multiples of ancient and premodern rates.

31. With respective average annual growth rates of output at 2.6% and 1.5%, Britain's *per capita* output rose by 1.3% annually while France's rose 1.2%. These results rely on estimates for Britain by P. Deane & W. A. Cole, *British Economic Growth 1688-1959*, (Cambridge: Cambridge University Press, 1969), which are not universally accepted. Other estimates place Britain's position closer to France by the time of the French Revolution, and imply a less startling divergence in growth after Waterloo: P. K. O'Brien & C. Keyder, *Economic Growth in Britain and France 1780-1914* (London: G. Allen & Unwin, 1976), esp. pp. 57-62; N. Crafts, "British Economic Growth, 1700-1831: A Review of the Evidence," *Economic History in Review* 36 (1983): 84. Maxine Berg's more recent analysis acknowledges Deane and Cole's estimates as high, and suggests not only that population growth is independent of modern economic growth, but that the origins of an initial period of MEG are as far as two generations before its start: Maxine Berg, *The Age of Manufactures: 1700-1820* (New York: Oxford University Press, 1985), 25-27.

32. Reynolds, *Economic Growth in the Third World, 1950-1980*, 413.

33. Kuznets, *Modern Economic Growth*, 67-68.

34. After a century of annual growth at about 0.3%, from 1780 Britain took 58 years to double real income *per capita*, and led the Industrial Revolution (1830-1910) with annual growth of about 1.2%. In 1820, before industrial expansion, U.S. GDP *per capita* was about three-quarters that of Britain. U.S. annual growth from 1830 to 1910 was about 1.6% (GDP grew at 4.2%, but population also grew rapidly). From 1839 the U.S. took only 39 years to double income *per capita* at about 1.8% annually, and by the 1890s was the world's richest country in *per capita* income. After the Meiji reforms, from 1885 Japan took 34 years to double GDP *per capita* at an annual rate of about 2%. From 1966 South Korea took only 11 years to double GDP *per capita* at about 6.3% annual growth.

35. Karl Marx, *Capital, A Critique of Political Economy, 3 Volumes*, Vol. I (Harmondsworth: Penguin/New Left Books, 1976-1981), 489-490.

36. Berg, *The Age of Manufactures: 1700-1820*, 44.

37. Kuznets, "Characteristics of Modern Economic Growth," 39-40.

38. See Moses Abramovitz, "Resource and Output Trends in the United States since 1870," *Occasional Paper 52* (New York: National Bureau of Economic Research, 1956); Robert M. Solow "Technical Change and the Aggregate Production Function." *Review of Economics and Statistics* 39 (August 1957): 312-320; Odd Aukrust & Juul Bjerke, "Real Capital and Economic Growth in Norway, 1900-56," in [Raymond Goldsmith & Christopher Saunders, eds., *The Measurement of National Wealth*, International Association for Research in Income and Wealth, Income and Wealth, Series VIII (Chicago: Quadrangle Books, 1959), 80-118]; Edward F. Denison *The Sources of Economic Growth in the United States and the Alternatives Before Us*, CED Supplementary Paper No. 13 (New York: Council on Economic Development, 1960); John W. Kendrick, *Productivity Trends in the United States* (Princeton, New Jersey: National Bureau of Economic Research, 1961); World Bank, *The East Asian Miracle*

(New York: Oxford University Press, 1993). But see also Angus Maddison, *Economic Growth in the West* (New York: The Twentieth Century Fund, 1964) for a dissenting view. Maddison (p. 88) suggests that "in modern conditions there cannot be widely varying degrees of technical advance due to differences in technical knowledge." Variations in growth are due to more or less capital per employee and differing age structure of capital. In analyzing the period 1870-1933, when US advantage was in superior natural resources and rapid population growth, Maddison (pp. 88-90) argues that from about 1913, European investment was reduced due to World War I and its consequences. Variations in growth occurred because assets have a longer life where relative labor costs are rising more slowly. Differences in European and American growth were determined by macroeconomic circumstances affecting entrepreneurial attitudes toward risk, and reinforced by the momentum of the economy. Government policy was primarily responsible for setting this momentum.

39. R. DuPlessis & M. C. Howell, "Reconsidering the Early Modern Urban Economy: The Cases of Leiden and Lille," *Past and Present* 94 (1982): 84.

40. In the context of modern economic growth, Adam Smith's accomplishment was to formulate distinct principles of production within a teleological structure of economic growth. Smith analyzed and explained the effects of division of labor and specialization, which generated gains in productivity; and the emergence and performance of various forms of industrial organizations, which affected productivity in various ways. Smith argued that both division of labor and technological changes depended on development of markets and capital accumulation, which also both affected productivity. The extent of specialization, Smith argued, was also constrained by the absolute size and rate of growth of capital.

In Book III Smith brought his ideas together in a dynamic model of what was then modern economic growth. Perhaps overwhelmed by contemporary salience of the problems of labor, Smith argued a "natural" progress for economic development from agriculture to manufactures to international trade, which he regretfully noted did not reflect history, except in a few isolated English counties. In his disparagement of those merchants and artificers who "in pursuit of their own peddlar principle of turning a penny wherever a penny was to be got" reversed the terms of trade in favor of towns, he seems, albeit unwittingly, to have predicted the essence of the set of innovations that brings subsequent MEG: what has come to be known as entrepreneurship. Adam Smith, *An Inquiry into the Nature and Causes of the Wealth of Nations* (New York: Modern Library, [1776] 1937).

41. Berg, *The Age of Manufactures: 1700-1820*, 80; Franklin F. Mendels & Pierre Deyon, "Proto-industrialization: Theory and Reality," in *Proto-industrialization: Proceedings of the Eighth International Congress of Economic History in Budapest, 1982*, Section A-2, (Lille: Université des arts, lettres et sciences humaines de Lille, 1982); D. C. Coleman, "Proto-industrialization: A Concept Too Many," *Economic History in Review* 36 (1983): 435-448.

42. Kuznets, *Modern Economic Growth*, 498.

43. Simon Kuznets, "Findings and Questions," in *Postwar Economic Growth: Four Lectures, Simon Kuznets* (Cambridge, Massachusetts: Belknap Press of Harvard University Press, 1964), 120.

44. Terry J. Collingsworth, William Goold, & Pharis J. Harvey, "Time for a Global New Deal," *Foreign Affairs* 73 (January/February 1994), 11.

45. Simon Kuznets, *Six Lectures on Economic Growth* (New York: Free Press, 1959), 15.

46. Kuznets, *Modern Economic Growth*.

47. The historical scale of the postwar boom may be appreciated by attempting to form estimates or guesses of modern economic growth. British and European output probably grew at about 2.5% *per decade* in the early eighteenth century, while gross world product may have grown by as much as 1.5% *per annum* during the previous period of expansion from the 1860s until World War I. Simon Kuznets, *Economic Growth and Structure* (New York: W. W. Norton, 1965), esp. 13.

48. Gunnar Myrdal, *Economic Theory and Underdeveloped Regions* (London: G. Duckworth, 1957); Gunnar Myrdal, *Asian Drama: An Inquiry into the Poverty of Nations* (New York: Pantheon, 1968).

49. Absence, and weakness, of very long time series has encouraged use of cross-country comparisons and studies to identify differences in economic or political structures. Invaluable insight provided by these studies has generated robust structural theoretical approaches to both economic growth and international relations. They are not, however, wholly satisfactory substitutes for robust longitudinal studies. In addition to technical difficulties (exchange rates, national cultures and value systems, political systems, differences in the meanings of regression coefficients, *etc.*), contemporary cross-country analysis precludes any estimate of causality. It cannot explain why countries behave as they do, or why growth rates differ, or whether growth is linked to conflict. Nor can it clarify qualitative changes in national institutions that accompany growth and affect conflict. "Each country is a historically unique individual whose growth experience will not be replicated precisely by any other country. This sense of identity is lost when Ghana becomes simply X_{33} in a supposedly homogeneous universe" (Reynolds, *Economic Growth in the Third World*, 14).

50. Reynolds, *Economic Growth in the Third World*, 389.

51. In this sense, reference to an annual rise in GNP as "growth" is at best misleading: a single annual change cannot distinguish movement along a long-term growth line from a cyclical shift away from equilibrium. See Kuznets, "Findings and Questions," 105-106.

52. Especially for early periods, GDP measurements are simply not available. In such cases, reports of GNP, Net National Product, or other measures of aggregate production must be the basis of analysis.

53. Kuznets, *Modern Economic Growth*, 70-71.

54. Reynolds, *Economic Growth in the Third World*, 8; Kuznets, *Modern Economic Growth*, 26-28.

55. Stanley Hoffmann, *Janus and Minerva: Essays in the Theory and Practice of International Politics* (Boulder, Colorado: Westview Press, 1987), 15.

56. Kenneth N. Waltz, *Theory of International Politics* (Reading: Massachusetts: Addison-Wesley, 1979), 18.

57. David S. Yost, "Political Philosophy and the Theory of International Relations," *International Affairs* 70 (1994): 289.

58. See Hoffmann, *Janus and Minerva: Essays in the Theory and Practice of International Politics*.

59. Hedley Bull, *The Anarchical Society: A Study of Order in World Politics* (London: Macmillan, 1977), 249.

60. Yost, "Political Philosophy and the Theory of International Relations," 281.

61. Initial regression analysis determined that annual growth rate (AGR) is only related to international conflict by coincidence, and at random. Indeed, both AGR and the incidence of war may follow the Poisson distribution. High volatility and narrow range around a mean close to zero of AGR obviate its utility as a long time series.

62. Values for time series reflect both observation and calculation:

- Gross domestic product (GDP) = Direct observations
- *Per capita* income (PCI) = GDP/population
- Decadal growth rate in *per capita* income

$$DGR = (PCI_t - PCI_{t-10})/PCI_{t-10}$$

- Tridecadal growth rate in *per capita* income

$$3GR = (PCI_t - PCI_{t-30})/PCI_{t-30}$$

- Modern economic growth condition (quadrivariate, discrete, discontinuous); value is 0 for years when country is not experiencing MEG; 1 during the first MEG period; 2 during the second period; 3 during the third period.

63. It is possible and plausible that some or all of the independent growth variables may be "endogenous" variables that are determined by, or at least correlated with, the dependent conflict variables. The extent of "feedback" involved in such simultaneity would generate some indeterminate amount of inconsistency and bias in the OLS estimators. In such a case the growth-conflict relationship would be best presented as a complex set of simultaneous-equation models, each with multiple endogenous variables simultaneously determined by an interrelated series of equations:

$$W = F(DGR, PCI, GDP, MEG, 3GR);$$
$$DGR = f(W); PCI = g(W); GDP = h(W); MEG = i(W); 3GR = j(W).$$

Analogous models would specify each of the other conflict variables (NW and TC) also. OLS parameters would be inconsistent as estimators for the models, and an instrumental-variables technique, such as two-stage least squares, would be appropriate. Even, however, where local simultaneity can be clearly shown, the Ando-Fisher theorem allows use of the OLS technique, *as if simultaneity were not present,* and *if the "feedback" is sufficiently small,* with only minor loss of information or introduction of error. The Ando-Fisher theorem is, however, only an "existence" theorem that does not establish tests for "sufficient smallness" of feedback. Since this investigation does not seek a deterministic result, and since calculation of the extent and sufficient smallness of simultaneous "feedback" is beyond the scope and purpose of the immediate argument, analysis *as if* simultaneity is not present seems justifiable.

64. A statistical test inherent in the regression procedure computes the ratio of a regression coefficient to its standard error: the *t-statistic* (t-stat). If the t-stat exceeds 2 in absolute (+ or -) magnitude, it is more than 95% likely that the coefficient is not zero, and the probability is very small that the observed magnitude of the coefficient is due to pure chance. The size of the t-stat, thus, indicates the significance of a coefficient in influencing the dependent variable.

65. The possibility of simultaneous determination between the growth-rate variables (DGR, 3GR) and the conflict variables, especially war, prevents drawing any conclusions about directionality or causality between prior conflict and following growth. The relationships between prior growth and subsequent conflict seem free from this sort of simultaneity.

66. Since the search for lawlike regularities is not deterministic, the actual value of the coefficient of an independent variable is less informative than its significance (t-stat) and effect (positive or negative). Since they are not normalized for differences in currency or inflation, growth variables' coefficients cannot be compared across countries or over time.

67. Parallel presentation of each subset would also show five profiles of the same 30 (or 27) observations. To avoid redundancy, this study presents only the six subset profiles along each of the five dimensions.

68. The perhaps arbitrary choice of DGR to represent growth in this comparison reflects the observation that both AGR and 3GR are generally less significant and less powerful in influencing conflict than is DGR; DGR is, by definition, derived from PCI, which is derived from GDP. Thus, although statistical rigor might suggest another formulation of the comparison, use of DGR as a proxy for aggregate growth is a plausible and convenient technique in the search for lawlike regularities.

69. Use of the term "direct" in this context to characterize a particular effect of the growth-conflict relationship does not imply the absence of intervening or additional contributing variables that may also be influencing the dependent conflict variable. Reference is only to the relative parallel movements and concurrently high or low values of the independent growth variable and the dependent conflict variable.

70. While sharpening contrasts within direct or inverse relationships, estimating a GCR confidence level denies much meaning to a relationship that offers only low confidence. Thus, for the sake of clarity and concision in presentation, only the "effects" profiles separate the GCR into these four confidence-level subprofiles. The other dimensional profiles present only the composite profile of 174 undifferentiated GCR, and the two disjoined profiles of inverse GCR and direct GCR, without reference to confidence levels.

71. National product (GDP) is predominantly significant only between preceding total conflict and nonwar conflict and growth for countries experiencing the direct GCR. Since possible simultaneity prevents reliance on even this result, the analysis can say nothing about GDP.

72. Hollis B. Chenery & Moshe Syrquin, *Patterns of Development, 1950 to 1983* (Washington, D. C.: The World Bank, 1989).

5

A Quandary and a Conjecture

Crude analysis of the empirical record confirms the existence and power of the conjunct growth-conflict relationship, and indicates some significant regularities about its nature along several dimensions. The disjoined relationships show significantly finer resolution and more details, especially along the "effects" dimension. In disclosing a large portion of the political-economic theory of the dynamics between economic growth and international conflict, which is the object of this study, disjunction, however, creates its own dilemma of determining which growth-conflict relationship is relevant, why it is active, and what to do about it.

The puzzling near-equal salience (89 direct and 85 inverse) and confidence (2.7% high-direct, 26.4% low-direct, 26.4% high-inverse, 22.4% low-inverse) for each of the two distinct effects (see Table 4.2) seems to imply almost random selection of inverse or direct effects of growth. The inherent power of the growth-conflict relationship (mean correlation coefficient is 0.58), however, drastically weakens this conclusion. In combination with this quandary, the pervasive dominance of the relationship by the pair of growth-rate variables suggests that the dual growth-conflict relationships arise from separate sources: two fundamentally different types of growth (see Appendix M).

The premise for disjunction of the growth process is that the two different effects observed (direct, inverse) are not simply dimensional aspects, or randomly selected results, of a simple homogeneous growth process. Rather, they arise from separate growth-conflict relationships, each the result of a distinct associated type of growth. Recognition of two types of growth allows association of each through only one GCR either directly to a positive effect or inversely to a negative effect. Intuitively, disjunction of the growth process would seem useful, not only in strengthening the regression model, but, most importantly, in completing the logical syllogism involving growth and conflict by linking an identifiable cause with a distinct effect.[1] This syllogism supports a hypothesis that countries experiencing one type of growth have a GCR with direct-positive effects, and that countries experiencing the other type of growth show inverse-negative effects. A corollary would predict that the growth types are not mutually exclusive, but that a single country could experience both simultaneously or sequentially. This simultaneous occurrence of each type of growth could explain the prevalence of ambiguous results in both history and theory, since countries would show both direct and inverse effects of growth, either simultaneously or with different lags and leads.

Verification of this hypothesis as a lawlike regularity requires differentiation between types of growth without reference to effects of the observed growth-conflict relationship. Relying solely on the growth variables and factors missing from the regression specification, the hypothesis must describe both types of growth and their respective operating variables, determine which countries have experienced each, and demonstrate close association between growth types and GCR effects.

TYPES OF GROWTH

Properly skeptical about combining cross-country results into any analysis of change over time, Kuznets suggested that differences across countries and over time, when they are more than incidental or cyclical, reflected cardinal differences in quality and type of national economies, their underlying societies and polities, and their particular growth processes. Kuznets further suggested that persistent decadal rates of growth in *per capita* income of 10% - 20% (a definitive feature of modern economic growth) are enough to signify major, profound changes in structures and patterns of national economies, societies, polities, growth processes and international relationships.[2]

Although Kuznets' temporal analysis did not develop his insight much beyond informed speculation, his results implied some systematic relationships between growth and structural change. His early intimations of changes in type of growth over time reappeared a generation later in structural analyses of growth across countries, which began with his implicit prediction of structural change associated with growth.[3] Development economists have noted clear differences in both economic structures and growth processes across the spectrum of what has come to be known as national development or modernization (see Appendix I).

Changes in Growth Over Time

Modern economic growth has seemed to commence in established countries with a period of acceleration in the rates of growth for population, GDP, and PCI. Countries that were well-populated and politically stable before the nineteenth century experienced an initial long period of acceleration of low growth rates to much higher rates in a following period of constancy, and then a period of retard to lower growth rates. Available records suggest that in the acceleration period (not later than about 1780-1820 for Britain, 1810-1860 in the United States, 1820-1870 in Germany, 1840-1880 in Sweden) population growth began earlier than did growth in PCI.

During early acceleration, increase in GDP balanced population growth as technology began to increase production. National economies began to shift from agricultural dominance toward industrial salience, new technology diffused through the society, and social, economic, and political institutions began to adjust to new conditions of living and working. Early acceleration brought a sort of "static" growth, whereby PCI remained relatively constant even as GDP increased. During midacceleration, governments and societies reacted to the pressures of static growth with secular decisions and policy development that affected rates and patterns of both the growth process and the directions of political and social development. After some lag until population growth stabilized and industrialization began to affect productivity, PCI began to grow significantly only in late acceleration, when static growth induced "dynamic" growth that actually improved living conditions of the entire society by increasing PCI even as population also grew.

The most prominent feature of the acceleration period in mature countries was the indigenous transition to a modern industrial system of production. It involved powerful domestic strains and pressures as traditional balances between population, technology, work, and wealth yielded to new uncomfortable situations, even to the point of revolution (France), civil war (United States) or coalescence (Germany). Unfamiliar international relationships of both conflict and cooperation reflected shifts in relative economic position, national power, and roles in the international political-economy, themselves artifacts of changing national growth processes. The following constancy and retard periods may have reflected societies' needs to acclimate themselves to the new worlds they had made for themselves.

Countries that only appeared in modern times (United States, Canada, Australia, Latin American countries, etc.) also experienced dramatic increases in PCI, but not necessarily smooth acceleration in population and GDP growth. These countries experienced truncated, rather than accelerating, growth of population and GDP, since rates of population growth reflected immigration, rather than indigenous fecundity, and increases in production often relied on importation of technology and labor. After an initial burst of immigration and technology transfers, high rates of static growth continued with little acceleration into a period of constancy, and eventual retard. In parallel, or with a relatively short lag, growth rates of PCI, like those of older countries, went through a complete cycle of slow acceleration, constancy, and retard, as industrialization began, well after growth of population and GDP, to generate dynamic growth.

The most prominent feature of the acceleration period for younger countries was the brevity of population growth. Nor did younger nations experience either the wrenching effects of indigenous technology development and diffusion or the traumatic transition to a modern industrial system of production: their immigrating populations brought technology and industry with them. They also brought a familiar set of international relationships, with some intent simply to append their new countries to an existing world structure.

Each group of countries experienced both static and dynamic growth; each shifted from static to dynamic growth with industrialization after a period of slow acceleration or a brief burst and constancy; each showed subsequent periods of constancy and retard. Older countries developed technologies indigenously and adapted political-economic institutions slowly during early acceleration; modern countries imported technologies and brought institutions with immigrating populations. Upon completion of preparatory periods of static growth, both groups shifted into dynamic growth, and progressed into a period of constant high growth rates, which eventually deteriorated into lower growth rates.

Modern economic growth (criterion for inclusion in the analytical universe) begins abruptly with a notable increase in annual production growth rates. After what has historically been a very long period of slow premodern growth, MEG progresses through an initial period of static growth, which introduces dynamic growth, which may eventually dominate aggregate growth. In the process, a national political-economy undergoes several specific transformations before it progresses further. In parallel with the transformations, the nature and composition of a nation's aggregate growth shift from predominance of static growth through mixed static and dynamic growth, to prominence of dynamic growth. Conveniently termed revolutions, these transformations seem necessary for sustained growth—and also for national development (see Appendix I). Historically showing a trend from static toward dynamic growth they include:

> a political revolution that makes political decision-making responsive to popular domestic economic influences (it may also increase the influences of other aspects of national life, including social, cultural, and populist forces); this transformation has historically accompanied acceleration of static growth;
>
> a social revolution that loosens traditional linkages between political status, social position, economic wealth, and personal attributes; this transformation creates the potential for dynamic growth by linking knowledge to wealth and power; and
>
> a series of economic revolutions that (1) distribute productive labor across a population, rather than within individuals or families (distribution of labor); (2) increase the intensities of capital and technology, and decrease that of labor, in a nation's production function; (3) shift the intensity of a nation's production from physical resources to intellectual capital.[4]

Nothing inherent in MEG suggests inevitability of a shift from static to dynamic growth, or a decline in growth rates (except perhaps in some bromidic sense that nothing can accelerate forever). Nor does the mechanism seem implacably irreversible. The MEG process itself includes a real possibility of alternative decisions, policies, or approaches, or the intrusion of other sets of exogenous factors, which may divert, terminate, or reinforce growth. Periods of acceleration, constancy, and retard commence and end —and probably can be ended by human intervention—for some reason or at some particular set of circumstances. Industrialization in late acceleration seems historically to initiate dynamic growth and constancy, which leads to retard. Some—but not all—nations, however, resume MEG after this hiatus.[5]

Differences in Growth Across Countries

The dramatic surge of growth in recent generations has prompted analysis of why and how some countries enter modern economic growth while others do not. Chenery, Syrquin, Srinavasan, Kubo, Robinson, Pack, and others have introduced similar concepts in cross-country input-output models and temporal recursive models of national economic growth. Most input-output models have incorporated static concepts of growth analysis to compare analogous features of several economies at the same time. Recursive models involving dynamic growth analyze a single economy over time, and allow transition from one "state" of an economy to another, although common recursive models tend to be unclear about differences between states and the processes that move an economy from one state to another.

While input-output models have relied primarily on economic variables, recursive models have introduced additional noneconomic variables (political, ideological, psychological, *etc.*), as well as changes in economic structures and processes. Investigating variations in structural correlates of growth (implicitly a dynamic sort), Chenery and Syrquin posited a set of fundamental "growth processes" that interact uniquely in different national or regional growth mechanisms (see Appendix I). Especially in analyzing economic structures, development economists have also observed distinctive features across countries in different stages of development, which suggest the static-dynamic growth dichotomy. "A major difference between the LDCs [less developed countries] and the DCs [developed countries] seems to be that growth in the former is largely accounted for by the accumulation of inputs rather than growing efficiency in their deployment."[6]

Static and Dynamic Growth

Disjunction of generic economic growth into two types—static and dynamic—not only suits the Kuznetsian view of long-term MEG, but accommodates modern concepts of national development (see Appendix I). The direct-inverse, positive-negative duality of the growth-conflict relationship also suggests abandoning the initial simple assumption of a homogeneous growth process for a hypothesis of disjunction into static and dynamic growth.

The two distinct sets of effects would seem to result from two different types of growth. Disjunction of the independent variable (aggregate economic growth) into its static and dynamic components offers an explanation both for divergence of orthodox theoretical conclusions about the growth-conflict relationship, and for variability in empirical observations of it. Differences not only in the composition of the independent variable (static or dynamic growth) across countries, but in the respective influences of static and dynamic growth on conflict, could generate the observed disparate and equivocal results. When both types of growth are operating, the resultant composite growth-conflict relationship could have both positive and negative components, weighted perhaps in accordance with the salience of each type of growth.

Static Growth

Microeconomic orthodoxy has historically "explained" growth of aggregate economic output in any country or period as a result of increases in raw materials, or in intensity of at least one factor of production (labor, capital, technology), and enlargement of markets for increasing production. Any extraneous growth not explained by the talisman of more resources and high investment is implicitly the result of a vague "residual."[7] At a macroeconomic level growth has been attributed to correct growth-inducing policies, including market capitalism, free trade, liberal investment policy, state intervention to "get the prices right" and ensure efficient allocation of resources.[8] This sort of growth relies completely on exploitation and manipulation of economic resources; it is "resource-based growth."

Orthodox explanations of growth have arisen, almost intuitively, from comparative analysis—intertemporal and cross-country—of national input-output accounts, which provide useful profiles of national wealth at various points in time and space (see Appendix J). Implicit in stationary comparative analysis are the assumption of homogeneous growth and the condition that the nature of the growth process remain resource-based, or static, across and between various profiles (that they are indeed comparable). The result of this passive analysis, begun and ended with stationary observations of static growth, is a compelling, if incomplete, strategic concept for controlled modernization through planned industrialization.

> The standard neoclassical prescription of "getting the prices right" and bringing them in line with international prices, even though desirable in many cases, is not a necessary, and certainly not a sufficient, condition for successful industrialization. . . . It is now well known that the favorite neoclassical showcase of South Korea is not predominantly one of market liberalism but of aggressive and judiciously selective state intervention.[9]

Kuznets' work has suggested that MEG begins in a premodern economy as static growth, with its engine of increasing resources, more inputs, more outputs, and expansion. Prominent in any simple pre-MEG economy

—growing or stagnant—have been shortages of capital, technology, and skilled labor (trained, educated, experienced in industry), and only a narrow range of raw materials limited to national resources. Unskilled labor has been excess; agriculture could not efficiently absorb more labor, despite low productivity. An obvious growth strategy has been to match factor intensity with factor availability by husbanding scarce resources (capital, technology, and skilled labor), increasing intensity of excess resources (unskilled labor), and using more raw materials. In premodern conditions, an economy deliberately seeking growth must stress unskilled-labor-intensive production that requires little capital or technology, and expansion of domestic sources for raw materials. The result has historically been a hesitant start of initial acceleration into a Kuznetsian process of MEG.

Necessarily, goods produced by such economies soon saturate a slow-growing domestic market. Further growth requires one or both of two alternatives:

expanding into foreign markets for both goods and raw materials, to sustain further increases in inputs and resource-based growth;[10] or

shifting the economy to capital-intensive, skill-intensive, or technology-intensive production for the domestic market.

In modern economies, where a capitalistic market allocates resources, expansion through trade has been most common, although military conquest has not been unknown. Saturation of the domestic market has encouraged labor-intensive manufactured exports. Since costs of capital, skilled labor, and technology have been high (they were scarce), and cost of unskilled labor has been low (it was abundant), rational commercial and industrial entrepreneurs have pursued profit by husbanding costly factors, exploiting low-cost unskilled labor, and expanding foreign markets (often with active political-military state support). Availabilities of foreign supplies of scarce domestic resources and foreign markets for abundant domestic goods accelerated international flows of resources and products. The result has been continuing accelerating labor-intensive, resource-based, "zero-sum," static growth. Victorian England is a historic example, and Hong Kong, a prime modern case of this sort of growth.[11]

In the colonial variation of this approach, some countries were able to increase both production and consumption by adding the resources of other economies to their own. Even in absence of empire, until the modern economic era, statically growing societies had most often increased their absolute wealth through conquest, trade, diplomatic-political expansion, and sporadic investment in foreign projects. In proper combinations with domestic factors of production and controlled colonial commerce, more foreign resources—capital, materials, labor—could bring greater aggregate production, reduced risks of instability in the home society, and may even have increased productivity of domestic resources. With final closure of the world's unclaimed lands, modern economies have been forced toward the more difficult techniques of using existing capital efficiently, shifting factor intensities, and mobilizing unused capital.

Planned economies have tended to prefer the latter approach, and to eschew the vagaries of international capitalism. Shifting factor intensities, however, eventually led to declining efficiency as an economy approached the limits of national resources. So long as economic planners can continue to increase allocations of *both* resources *and* raw materials, static resource-based growth can continue. When quantity, quality, or political power to allocate resources deteriorate, static growth with no inherent economic engine grinds to a halt. The Union of Soviet Socialist Republics and its network of related economies are obvious examples of this approach.

A third alternative, combination of expansion and shifting, has been less common. Shifts in factor intensities have occurred, in parallel with expansion of trade, in response to foreign or political influences, rather than to domestic market features. Some economically exogenous (ideology, politics, morality, *etc.*) or structural (corporate organization, sectoral composition, state regulatory, *etc.*) factors may have influenced the economic rationalities involved in allocating resources. Economies on this path of mixed growth have overcome factor shortages in capital and technology through foreign investment and technology transfer, rather than a narrow focus on labor intensitivity. The result has often been a rapid shift from static to dynamic growth. (The obvious examples of this growth pattern have been the United States, and more recently Japan and Southeast Asia.)

Static growth has been common over time and across countries. It is based on increases of inputs, or shifts in factor intensity, in an otherwise unchanging national aggregate production function. Static growth does not inherently affect productivity or *per capita* wealth of society (although it generally improves both incidentally), since it has no necessary relationship with either work or population, and includes labor as one among several static factors of production. It increases national wealth, but not necessarily quality of life or productivity.

Static growth can sustain itself only by acquiring ever more physical resources for allocation to production and consumption, or continuing increases in discrete factor intensities. It is "zero-sum," in that it converts a quantity of economic inputs into the same quantity of different economic outputs, and in the sense that additional inputs must be outputs from some other economy. Its primary engine is resources. The direct-positive growth-conflict relationship, associating high growth with high conflict, and low growth with low conflict, arises from static resource-based growth. The primary vehicle for expansion of a statically growing economy is trade.

Static growth is what Kuznets, Kennedy, and Kindleberger saw in Europe before World War I.[12] It is this sort of growth that remains the foundation of mercantilism, provides one rationale for conflict in a classical realist world, and has invited both aggression and invasion since Gilgamesh fought history's first (recorded) resource-based war.

Orthodoxy prescribes policy actions and structural changes to initiate and accelerate static growth, and to sustain it with ever-increasing foreign trade with a permanently positive balance-of-trade. Aggregate output (GDP) is an intuitive macroeconomic index of static growth; trade is an analogous microeconomic index.

Dynamic Growth

Generated itself by dramatic increases in static resource-based growth, the Industrial Revolution introduced technology as a novel factor of production, created by humans from new knowledge.[13] Individuals, firms, and governments in industrializing economies applied technology to production, consumption, and welfare, and induced yet more growth. Technology diffused through societies that were rapidly gaining knowledge, brought second-order effects, increases in productivity, and sociopolitical change, and eventually became an additional existing resource available as a factor of production (see note 7 at the end of this chapter). Static resource-based growth continued, even accelerated, despite high costs of capital, physical constraints on materials, and demographic limits on labor. Technology-intensive operations replaced capital- or labor-intensive production, and eventually technology became the growth-limiting resource.

Dramatically different from premodern growth, this sort of technology-based growth is also subtly different from static resource-based growth. It involves not only increases in output and production (GDP), but also real dynamic improvements in standards of living (PCI). It is qualitatively different, in that it contains the germ of a powerful dynamic sort of growth that is neither "zero-sum" nor resource-intensive nor even technology-intensive, need not capture markets, exploit resources, or transfer technology from other nations, and does not tend toward international conflict.

While enjoying high rates of static growth in Kuznets' constancy periods, industrializing nations were also incubating in "high-tech industries" the neonatal precursors of dynamic growth that would mature in the twentieth century. The blend of accelerating static growth and emerging dynamic growth generated high aggregate growth rates that declined only when the predominant static growth began to lose momentum as economies approached the limits of physical resources.

In considering growth over two-and-a-half centuries, Kuznets deemphasized traditional factors of production (including technology), and stressed innovation, the creation of new knowledge. For Kuznets, it was intuitively clear that parallel processes of population growth and increase of wealth, which he measured, were mutually and self-reinforcing. Further, both are intimately related to the growth of new knowledge.[14] Kuznets surmised a basic force of innovation increasing the stocks of human knowledge, which energized MEG. "[T]he scientific base of technological innovation underlying modern economic growth has provided an *accelerated* [emphasis in original] potential, making possible the increasing rates of growth per capita despite the decline in input of man-hours per capita."[15]

This dynamic sort of growth that intrigued Kuznets is based not on exploitation of economic resources, but on application and creation of human knowledge; it is "knowledge-based growth." It is growth that explains the "residual" of neoclassical growth theory, the human enrichment embodied in technological progress, and the "total factor productivity" of development economics. Paul Romer formally introduced knowledge into the production function in 1983 in his doctoral thesis at the University of Chicago on "Dynamic Competitive Equilibria with Externalities, Increasing Returns, and Unbounded Growth." The change is not just one of semantics—knowledge is not the same thing as either technological progress or total factor productivity. Knowledge of how to do things, how to apply technology, how to make things, or of how to decide what to do, raises the return on an investment and affects market allocation of resources. Knowledge creates more wealth with the same amounts of capital, labor, and technology by using them in innovative ways or in doing different things. This simple concept —Knowledge-based Dynamic Growth—explains increasing rates of return over time, nonconvergence of growth rates among countries, and increasing returns to scale (all anomalies in neoclassical models).[16]

Dynamic growth is a modern anomaly both over time and across countries. Unlike static growth, which has emerged repeatedly in reaction to purely economic pressures, dynamic growth seems to require a substantial base of human knowledge, which has come to exist only in modern times, and in a few places. It is based on flat, or even decreasing, levels of physical inputs in a changing national aggregate production function. This sort of growth creates new resources, instead of simply acquiring existing wealth. Transfers of technology, expertise, training, education, or even example, as well as indigenous innovation, generate dynamic growth, which operates the inverse-negative relationship between growth and conflict.

Dynamic growth is what the trade liberals of the Manchester School glimpsed in David Ricardo's theories about comparative advantage. It is the sort of growth that changes the nature of Organski and Kugler's power resources from political-military to socioeconomic. This is the sort of dynamic growth missing from Solow's formulation, suggested by Rosenberg and Birdzell, implied by Gilpin's concepts of interdependence, assumed by Chenery and Syrquin, and generalized by Paul Romer into a larger economic concept.[17] It is what Kenichi Ohmae has in mind when he describes the process of globalization.[18] This is the dynamic growth that improves the quality of living through increasing productivity and product without a corresponding increase in physical resources devoted to production.

In contrast to the informed self-interest that energizes static growth with an incentive to trade, the motive force of dynamic growth is diffusion of knowledge with an incentive to learn. Involving increases in stocks of knowledge and intellectual capital, "dynamic" knowledge-based growth enhances the functional or productive capacities of an individual, society, polity, economy, region, or even of the entire world. Dynamic growth is self-sustaining, creating its own demand through continual creation of new intellectual capital without "zero-sum,"acquisition of more physical resources.[19] It is "positive-sum," in that it converts noneconomic inputs into economic outputs, and in the sense that additional inputs are not outputs from some other economy. Not limited by availability of physical resources, this sort of growth seems, in principle, limited only by the capacities of human intellect.

Dynamic growth strategies prescribe policy actions and structural changes for such things as primary education, research and development, trade reform, intellectual property, and basic knowledge of how to do things, and deemphasize manufacturing, business, inflation, exchange rates, and orthodox economic, industrial, or commercial issues. The primary structural changes involved in generating dynamic growth involve not a nation's economy or its polity, but its people, their knowledge, and their ways of thinking. These sorts of changes are the results less of economic investment or political commitment than of learning, of mastering the arts of innovation and creativity, and of diffusing knowledge through an entire society. The engines of such change are education, training, technology transfer, and establishment of knowledge-sensitive national infrastructures. In the absence of spontaneous emergence of motivation and innovation, the primary vehicle for this sort of change has been foreign direct investment with its payload of knowledge, expertise, and experience.[20]

For an economy experiencing dynamic growth, industrialization, modernization, expansion, and improvement of living standards rely not on allocating more existing resources to production, but instead on creation of new intellectual resources and innovation of new production functions. Expansion of a dynamically growing economy relies less on trade or transfers of goods and resources, more on transfers of capital, and most on transfers of knowledge, often through foreign direct investment. Dynamic growth affects productivity and *per capita* wealth of society. It is intimately related to both work and population, and includes unskilled labor only as one static factor of production among other more dynamic factors. Knowledge-based dynamic growth relates high growth to low conflict, and low growth to high conflict, in the inverse-negative growth-conflict relationship. *Per capita* income is an intuitive macroeconomic index of dynamic growth; foreign direct investment (FDI) is an analogous microeconomic index.

MIXED AND SHIFTING GROWTH AND CONFLICT

It is historically clear that national economies rarely enter modern economic growth simultaneously: periods of acceleration, constancy, and retard occur at different times, as do national political-economic revolutions. By the late nineteenth century, the industrializing economies were experiencing both static and dynamic growth at various rates, and under various political-economic regimes. While European national economies were experiencing dramatic—sometimes traumatic—internal restructuring conducive to dynamic growth, the world economy settled into an early period of slow static interdependent acceleration around

> an elaborate division of labor among industrial and non-industrial economies based on specialization. Secondly, interdependence involved unprecedented flows of goods and factors of production (capital, technology, and labor) among national economies. . . . international economic interdependence was based on a hierarchy of world markets which ultimately culminated in London.[21]

The hierarchy, implicitly reflecting dissimilar national growth experiences, was always pregnant with political effects, strife, and strains. Separate times for initial acceleration, different durations of phases, and shifting relative rates of growth of population and wealth brought continuing changes in relative economic position. Human progress created a volatile international brew of uneven static and dynamic growth, of some nations seeking additional resources and markets, and others seeking to learn-by-doing. The result can readily generate international conflict.

As uneven mixed growth adjusts relative national capabilities, options for influencing other nations, and for changing the national position in the international hierarchy, shift in parallel. Insofar as capabilities depend on attributes, changes in attributes—especially through economic growth—powerfully affect international behavior. Kuznets, and later structuralists, saw this constant—and for them apparently unpredictable—shifting of the balance, or hierarchy, of power as the static-growth-related engine of conflict: the direct growth-conflict relationship. Both insight and analysis have characterized resource-based growth as arising from increase or expansion of national factors-of-production, usually through trade, migration, or capital transfers. These processes stimulate static growth, and operate the direct growth-conflict relationship. Whether in seeking additional resources or in exercising its new international prestige, a growing nation would inevitably come into conflict with some other nation trying to protect its resources and position.

Another view is that static-growth-related expansion is the primary source of conflict. Various combinations of growing population, growing wealth, and advancing technology multiply demands upon domestic resources. To meet these demands for sustained static growth, societies have tended to develop specialized production capabilities, expand their Ricardian trade, and extend their interests into the rest of the world as wealth and power increase. In the "zero-sum" world of static growth, conflict is the result. "The greater the unsatisfied demands and needs in a society and the greater the capabilities, the higher is the likelihood that national activities will be extended outside territorial boundaries."[22]

Neither pressures of domestic growth nor shifts in balance-of-power necessarily and always lead to conflict or war.   Nations can ameliorate domestic pressures, project influence into foreign areas, and adjust international relations in many ways, including trade, investment, war, migration, isolation, charity and foreign aid, diplomacy, sanctions and rewards.   History seems equivocal concerning national sources of domestic conflict. It is clear, however, that international conflict has tended to develop when a country with high, growing capabilities and unsatisfied domestic demands begins to extend its interests and influence, to develop feelings that its interests outside its borders should be protected, or to exchange positions on the international hierarchy with another nation.[23] This is the direct growth-conflict relationship between static growth and international conflict.

Both history and theory suggest that the static growth that initially accelerates a nation into MEG has only slight impact on conflict until it generates domestic pressures, and national capability, to expand.   In an initial acceleration period, trade provides additional resources, production is labor-intensive, capital is accumulating from increasing returns to domestic investment, national capabilities do not threaten, growth is focused internally; growth-related conflict is still rare, although conflict may arise from purely political issues.   These sorts of conditions—typifying early MEG—suggest an operationally separate commercial liberal approach to economics and a realist approach to politics. International relations are predominantly political. Static growth continues until constrained by resources: the direct growth-conflict relationship is not yet active.

At this point a growing nation must determine how to continue (or in principle to abandon) further growth.   The critical selection of either the path from growth toward conflict or that toward cooperation occurs when a nation both determines to extend its capabilities further outside its own boundaries, and selects a mode or style of international behavior for doing so.   The primarily political determination of whether and how to confront the rest of the world is conditioned by internal economic demands (for resources, markets, prestige, jobs, etc.) and by national capabilities (more or less relative to another nation than in the past), which are both consequences of growth. The strength of domestic linkages (interest groups, elites, etc.) between populations and the different domestic effects of static or dynamic growth acts as a particularly powerful weight in selecting cooperative or confrontational modes of national expansion and international behavior.[24]   This political decision, albeit indirectly and perhaps unknowingly to decision-makers, contains the economic consequence of entraining static or dynamic growth (or both), and activating the associated growth-conflict relationship(s).

From this point, continued static growth through trade or conquest increases probabilities of conflict as the economy expands in competition with other nations.   Well into Kuznets' constancy period or even retard, the combination of domestic pressures to expand and national capabilities to do so makes conflict a viable policy option. These sorts of conditions—typifying an industrializing national political-economy—suggest a power-based structuralist approach to both economics and international relations, and a focus on national attributes (trade balances, aggregate production, national power, *etc.*), competitiveness, and national interests: international relations are both political and economic; the direct growth-conflict relationship is active and gaining power.   For nations with sufficiently powerful capabilities to obtain foreign resources, static growth can continue, albeit accompanied by international conflict. Nations without much national power resort to various political stratagems for surviving or avoiding conflict, or fall into economic recession or domestic turmoil.

Nations that have managed to go through the initial political-economic transformations may shift to the dynamic-growth path.   With lower requirements for additional resources, dynamic growth carries a lower probability (but not zero) of conflict: the inverse growth-conflict relationship emerges. Shifting the intensities of production from resources and unskilled labor to technology and ideas allows a nation to generate new factors of production without obtaining more physical resources. Static growth continues, but loses its urgency as dynamic growth accelerates to maintain high aggregate growth rates. Efficient trade continues to provide enough resources; intensity of production shifts from muscle power to "human capital"; returns to capital increase even though amounts of capital may not; national capabilities can easily become threatening; political conflict remains a possibility. These sorts of conditions—suggesting a "postindustrial" political-economy—support a liberal approach to economics and international relations with a focus on processes (trade, improvements in productivity, *etc.*), interdependence, and common international interests. The inverse growth-conflict relationship has become active, and is supplanting the direct relationship.

In a context of parallel disjunction of *both* growth *and* the growth-conflict relationship, growth *does* lead to war, when it is based on "zero-sum," resource-based expansion and accumulation of resources as national wealth. This is static growth operating through the direct growth-conflict relationship. In this context growth can also help *prevent* war, if it involves "positive-sum" knowledge-based increases in intellectual capital and its innovative application to productivity.   This is dynamic growth operating through the inverse growth-conflict relationship.

Uneven across both time and space, dynamic and static growth are not contradictory, mutually exclusive, or even competitive in any sense. They have different effects on international conflict, have different sources and engines, and operate in different ways through different economic variables and processes.   In most modern countries they usually coexist as major components of aggregate growth and interact powerfully with each other, each exerting its particular influence on international conflict.   Occurring simultaneously or sequentially, either can, but need not, generate the other.

As a nation's mixture of static and dynamic growth varies, so also vary the salience of each type of growth-conflict relationship and the combined effects of aggregate growth on conflict.

DISTINGUISHING BETWEEN STATIC AND DYNAMIC GROWTH

At a macroeconomic level it may not be possible to distinguish between the two growth processes, since both affect the same indicators.   At the microeconomic level, however, they have decidedly different effects.   Static growth leads to accumulation of physical resources.   Dynamic growth generates intellectual capital, either through spontaneous indigenous innovation or from foreign sources.   This difference in microeconomic cause and effect allows statistical disjunction of the conjunct growth process, estimation of the salience of static and dynamic growth in each country, and comparison of countries by predominant type of growth.

In modern times the primary method for accumulating physical resources in static growth is trade: buying and selling, exchanging money for goods and services, and even barter.   A nation's trade balance (money difference between exports and imports) reflects its success in accumulating resources and goods; its trade level (money sum of exports and imports) analogously reflects its efforts to accumulate resources in pursuit of static growth.   The effects of trade in generating static growth are not long delayed and are best reflected in annual growth rates.

With parallel logic, the difference and sum of inward and outward foreign direct investment (FDI) may act as idioms for national success in obtaining new knowledge from foreign sources, and national dedication to pursuing dynamic growth.[25]   FDI is the primary indicator, as well as the modern engine and vehicle, of dynamic growth, which increases rates of PCI growth. Completion of the syllogism gives to FDI the critical role not only as the engine of dynamic growth, but, by extension, also as the progenitor of the inverse growth-conflict relationship, which associates low conflict with high growth.[26]   Modern multinational enterprise (MNE) and foreign direct investment, and the dynamic growth that they have brought, are the systemic differences in the international political-economy that account for substantial differences in the processes of growth and development in Western Europe, Latin America, Africa, Northeast Asia, and Southeast Asia.

In contrast to the relatively quick effects of trade on static growth through changes in stocks of physical resources, the results of foreign direct investment in changing national stocks of human capital through increases in knowledge are ponderously slow, best reflected in decadal (or even longer) growth rates. The uncomplicated result of this approach is a simple equation:

PCI Decadal Growth = *F(Trade-Level Decadal Growth, FDI-Level Decadal Growth)*,

or

PCIDGR = *F(TrdDGR, FDIDGR)*.

The regression significances (t-stat) of trade and FDI growth rates reflect their respective influences on the aggregate growth rate, and hence suggest the salience of each in the national growth process. The Kuznetsian concept of shifting growth patterns over time would predict predominance of trade growth rates through an acceleration period dominated by static growth, with a high t-stat for trade growth rate only. As an economy shifted toward dynamic growth, the significance of FDI would begin to rise, while trade would remain prominent; trade growth rate could have a high t-stat, and FDI growth rate would show an increasing t-stat over time. At some point the growth rate of FDI would become highly and confidently significant, and the country could be said to be experiencing significant dynamic, as well as static growth: both trade growth and FDI growth would be highly significant. In principle, the shift could continue with trade growth losing salience and FDI growth coming to dominate the growth process.

This schema offers a binary gauge for distinguishing dynamically growing countries from those dominated by static growth: significant FDI growth rate (t-stat > 2), with a moderate or high correlation coefficient ($R^2 > 0.40$), for a time-series regression of aggregate growth rate on growth rates of its trade and FDI levels. Aggregate growth, *regardless of aggregate growth rate*, in regressions showing less significant FDI growth or lower correlation would be dominated by static growth.

Using this FDI-based criterion to sort the universe of 30 countries experiencing modern economic growth according to the predominant type of growth in each produces three groups of countries. Five countries' data do not reflect enough FDI to generate viable decadal time-series country-regressions: Russia (two observations), China (four observations), Taiwan (four observations), Iran (zero observations on eight years of FDI data), Iraq (zero observations on six years of FDI data).

Twelve countries have experienced predominantly dynamic growth; thirteen show predominantly static growth (see Table 5.1). Although the observations suggest many additional interesting features about both the growth processes and the growth-conflict relationship, they clearly establish a dichotomy between dynamically growing countries and those experiencing static growth.

The evident contrasts between static resource-based growth and dynamic knowledge-based growth mimic—or perhaps reflect—the equally evident and powerful differences in the pair of growth-conflict relationships—direct-positive and inverse-negative. Exploiting this mimicry to juxtapose the results of disjunction of growth-conflict relationships with those of disjunction of growth creates a simple two-dimensional pairing for each country in the MEG universe. This perspective reveals not merely the linkage between growth and conflict, but exposes the underlying connection between growth and the growth-conflict relationship. The four possibilities are static-direct, static-inverse, dynamic-direct, dynamic-inverse (see Table 5.2).

Table 5.1 Significance of FDI Level and Growth Type

DYNAMIC GROWTH			STATIC GROWTH		
Country	|t-stat|	R^2	Country	|t-stat|	R^2
United Kingdom	2.21	0.38	Netherlands	0.397	0.72
France	2.01	0.88	Italy	1.18	0.19
United States	2.61	0.71	Germany	0.11	0.60
Brazil	5.46	0.69	Canada	1.28	0.26
South Korea	4.05	0.52	Mexico	1.86	0.84
Australia	4.14	0.69	Argentina	0.46	0.42
Malaysia	2.17	0.85	Japan	1.09	0.24
Thailand	3.15	0.91	New Zealand	0.33	0.09
Philippines	2.16	0.53	Indonesia	1.68	0.47
Singapore	2.02	0.89	Finland	0.598	0.05
Norway	3.89	0.44	Denmark	0.08	0.38
Nigeria	2.37	0.48	Sweden	1.49	0.33
			Israel	0.09	0.07

Of 25 countries in the universe whose data allow determination, 21 (84%) show either the static-direct pairing (12 countries) or the dynamic-inverse pairing (nine countries). Only four countries show anomalous pairings inconsistent with the hypothesis: Australia, Brazil, and Norway show the dynamic-direct pairing; Israel shows static-inverse (see Table 5.2).

Table 5.2 Growth-conflict Pairing

DYNAMIC-INVERSE		STATIC-DIRECT		ANOMALOUS
France	Singapore	Netherlands	Finland	Norway
United Kingdom	South Korea	Italy	Sweden	Australia
United States	Nigeria	Germany	New Zealand	Brazil
Thailand	Philippines	Canada	Indonesia	Israel
Malaysia		Mexico	Japan	
Philippines		Denmark	Argentina	

The conjectural hypothesis predicted that countries experiencing predominantly static growth will have a GCR with direct effects (static-direct), and that countries experiencing primarily dynamic growth will show inverse effects (dynamic-inverse), and that few (if any) countries would show anomalous pairings. This result, a convincing, moderately powerful, lawlike regularity in solid support of the hypothesis, is the object that this investigation has sought. It expands and refines the results of Chapter 4, and solidifies the conclusion that it is the type of growth, and not simply growth itself, that determines the nature, timing, and levels of international conflict. It is clear that a powerful dual relationship links economic growth and conflict, and that the type of growth determines which aspect of that dual relationship is active and operating.   It is also apparent that foreign direct investment is a critical independent variable that can determine both the type of growth and, through the associated growth-conflict relationship, the nature and level of international conflict.

It seems intuitively possible to do something about foreign direct investment, and thereby to influence both growth and conflict. While many nations have done something about FDI, the actions of the nations of the Association of Southeast Asian Nations (ASEAN) are particularly instructive, since they have also experienced both peace and prosperity.

NOTES

1. Structural work of Chenery and Syrquin at the national level implies that growth decomposition would be a sound basis for dealing with growth in any analytical context: Hollis B. Chenery & Moshe Syrquin, *Patterns of Development, 1950-1970* (London: Oxford University Press, 1975); Hollis B. Chenery & Moshe Syrquin, *Patterns of Development, 1950 to 1983* (Washington, D. C.: The World Bank, 1989).

2. Simon Kuznets, *Economic Growth and Structure* (New York: W. W. Norton, 1965), 16-23.

3. Chenery and Syrquin showed that the benefits of ample uniform data include an ability to compare cross-country and time-series relationships involving growth, and the possibility of identifying relationships between them (*Patterns of Development, 1950-1970*, 2).

4. In Europe the political, social, and first economic revolutions occurred in the seventeenth, eighteenth and early nineteenth centuries; the second economic revolution occurred as the Industrial Revolution in the nineteenth century, and the third economic revolution began in the last half of the twentieth century. In North America, these same transformations began a few generations later than in Europe, but proceeded rather faster.   Uncolonized Asia (Japan, Thailand, China) began even later in the nineteenth century, and has suffered several major interruptions. Colonial Asia, Africa, and Latin America were powerfully focused in their beginnings of growth by their various metropoles (Britain, France, Netherlands, Belgium, Portugal, the United States), and have stalled or accelerated accordingly. See Rudolf von Albertini, *Decolonization: The Administration and Future of the Colonies, 1919-1960* (London: Holmes & Meier, 1982), for lucid discussions of their respective fates without the expected burden of polemic.

5. Since about 1700 Britain and France have each experienced three periods of modern economic growth; Germany, Canada, the United States, Japan, Taiwan, Finland, Norway, and Denmark have experienced two periods.   Sweden and the Netherlands probably experienced their first MEG periods in the sixteenth and

seventeenth centuries with second periods in the nineteenth and twentieth centuries. China seems to have experienced an even longer series of MEG periods with one ending in about the fifteenth century, another ending with the fall of the empire in the late nineteenth and early twentieth centuries, and the current MEG beginning about midcentury.

6. Howard Pack, "Industrialization and Trade," in Hollis B. Chenery & T. N. Srinivasan, *Handbook of Development Economics*, Vol. 1 (Amsterdam: Elsevier Science Publishers, 1988), 352.

7. The basic theory of long-term growth was devised in the 1950s by Robert Solow. Much modified and improved since its original exposition, Solow's neoclassical theory used an algebraic equation—the production function—that relates the output of an economy to the amounts of capital and labor used in that economy. Robert M. Solow, "Technical Change and the Aggregate Production Function," *Review of Economics and Statistics* 39 (August 1957): 312-320. Theory assumes constant returns to scale and diminishing returns (plausible and reasonable in a closed world of Smithian perfect competition). Although Solow's original production function included only two discrete factors of production (capital and labor), neoclassical orthodoxy has accepted technology as a third discrete factor. A mystery variable, called the residual, completes the equation, and "explains" any growth not "explained" by the other discrete factors of production. Extensive application of the theory has shown that changes in capital and labor generate less than half of the observed changes in output. The rest is attributed collectively to the residual, to technological progress, or to another elusive concept, "total factor productivity."

8. World Bank, *The East Asian Miracle* (New York: Oxford University Press, 1993).

9. Pranab Bardhan, "Alternative Approaches to Development Economics," in Hollis B. Chenery & T. N. Srinivasan, eds. *Handbook of Development Economics*, Vol. 1 (Amsterdam: Elsevier Science Publishers, 1988), 62; L. P. Jones & I. Sakong, *Government Business and Entrepreneurship in Economic Development: The Korean Case* (Cambridge, Massachusetts: Harvard University Press, 1980); Howard Pack & L. E. Westphal, "Industrial Strategy and Technological Change: Theory versus Reality," *Journal of Development Economics* 22 (June 1986): 87-128.

10. Economic inputs for a home economy would necessarily be outputs from a foreign economy. Resources transferred from foreign economies, whether through conquest or trade, are not available as inputs for growth in the foreign economy. A paradox of Ricardian comparative advantage obviates sustained resource-based growth, even while maximizing current, static welfare in both countries. Only where two economies are fully complementary in their respective resource requirements (inputs) and products (outputs), and remain complementary through parallel and even growth, would Smithian or Ricardian trade or other transfer of resources sustain "zero-sum" resource-based growth in each country.

11. From the mid-eighteenth century through the nineteenth century, Britain was the leading European country experiencing growth. During this period Britain extended its power to embrace a global empire and enforce a Pax Britannica through much of the world. The United States, as it grew in the nineteenth century, extended its markets and resource base by purchase of contiguous territory, by minor foreign military ventures, forcible military and commercial penetration of Japan with the Perry mission, acquisition of the Philippines and domination of Cuba and Central America through victorious war. Japan extended itself through military occupations on

mainland East Asia and extension of military and commercial dominance into Oceania and Southeast Asia. Germany deliberately used small wars as instruments of coagulation into a single political entity, and expansion into the rest of the world.

Simon Kuznets was able to infer from these experiences that beyond some minimal level of population, GDP, and PCI, and perhaps of geographic size, at least for these growing nations, "extension into 'empty' contiguous territory or the imposition of open-door arrangements upon a 'backward' country is a positive function at the economic level" (Kuznets, *Economic Growth and Structure*, 51).

Since the examples occurred during periods of home-country static growth, this association suggests compulsive, or inherent, features of static growth beyond some threshold minimum that tend toward international expansion, and possibly conflict.

12. Although Kuznets recognized the ability of innovation to accelerate growth, it was only in the 1980s that the concept of "decomposition" of growth into resource-based and knowledge-based components emerged. Rosenberg and Birdzell differentiated between "growth associated with an expansion of trade and economic resources and economic growth primarily attributable to innovation." Nathan Rosenberg & L. E. Birdzell, *How the West Grew Rich* (New York: Basic Books, 1986, 328.

13. In a strictly economic sense, technology is useful or productive knowledge. Although it includes the ability to put abstract, scientific knowledge to practical human use, technology is itself a discrete and quantitative resource: a factor of production. The existence of a technology, or of an ability to apply knowledge to human needs, does not imply that it is profitable, or even commercially viable. Technology can be, and frequently is, a commercial commodity: it can be bought and sold, transferred from one person or organization to another. Van R. Whiting, Jr., *The Political Economy of Foreign Investment in Mexico* (Baltimore: Johns Hopkins University Press, 1992), 108-109.

14. Kuznets reasoned that population increases had arisen from solutions to problems of health, and from technological prolongation of human life, and had generated ever more contributors to the stocks of useful human knowledge. Increases in wealth had emerged from increases either in factors of production through discovery of new sources, or in productivity through inventing or discovering more efficient techniques or combinations of resources.

15. Simon Kuznets, "Findings and Questions," in *Postwar Economic Growth: Four Lectures, Simon Kuznets* (Cambridge, Massachusetts: Belknap Press of Harvard University Press, 1964), 109.

16. Dr. Romer elaborated the concept of knowledge-based growth to include four discrete factors of production: economic capital, unskilled labor, human capital, and intellectual capital. The theory included a spiral of unbounded growth in which capital investment elicits or generates new knowledge, which increases productivity, which reduces risk of greater investment. The implication is that sustained investment can lead to sustained growth, with knowledge as the dynamic mediator between capital, labor, and output. The Romer model incorporates international knowledge transmission into explanations of different growth rates in different countries: *ceteris paribus*, closed national economies grow more slowly than open ones. It also predicts that lack of human capital (education, innovation, intellectual freedom, etc.) could prevent growth even with heavy investment in physical capital. Paul Romer, "Endogenous Technical Change," *Journal of Political Economy* 98 (1990): S71-S102; Paul Romer, *Are Nonconvexities Important for Understanding Growth?* (Cambridge, Massachusetts: National Bureau of Economic Research, 1990).

Refinement of Romer's theory suggests that the rate of growth of knowledge is a critical determinant of an economy's growth rate. Where population growth is faster than growth of knowledge, demands for consumption, energy, and resources increase apace population, but enhancements to national capacities to meet demand are constrained by lagging knowledge. Such an economy must rely on increases of its factors of production (exploration, conquest, trade, economies of scale, fiscal policy, *etc.*) to meet demand. When knowledge expands faster than population, enhancements to national capacities proliferate, availabilities of resources, energy, and goods for consumption increase beyond the demands of society. Increases in productivity (invention, innovation, rationalization, *etc.*) increase the aggregate and *per capita* wealth of society.

17. Solow, "Technical Change and the Aggregate Production Function"; Rosenberg & Birdzell, *How the West Grew Rich*; Robert Gilpin, *The Political Economy of International Relations* (Princeton, New Jersey: Princeton University Press, 1987); Chenery & Syrquin, *Patterns of Development, 1950 to 1983*; Romer, "Endogenous Technical Change,"; Romer, *Are Nonconvexities Important for Understanding Growth?*

18. Kenichi Ohmae, *The Borderless World* (New York: HarperCollins, 1990), esp. pp. 30-31 and chapter 8.

19. Chenery and Syrquin showed an interesting pseudo-orthodox economic relationship between the growth of intellectual capital implicit in dynamic growth, domestic demand, the pattern of a nation's trade, and further dynamic growth. Thus, where intellectual capital increases rapidly as income increases, the shifting pattern of domestic demand generates domestic manufacturing capacity. In addition to effects of Engel's Law in raising nonfood consumption, rising levels of income bring changes in factor intensities due to growth of financial and intellectual capital relative to population and labor force. These eventually become a comparative advantage in exports, which shifts the pattern of exports from primary goods to manufactures in parallel with, albeit lagged behind, the shift from primary production to manufacturing. The result is sustained dynamic growth. "The transformation of trade normally takes place much later in the transition [to an industrial economy] . . . [although] there is great variability in the timing of this aspect of the transition" (Chenery & Syrquin, *Patterns of Development, 1950-1970*, 42).

20. Imports of high technology modern goods with extensive "embedded" technology, or of modern goods that "embody" high-technology, may lead to creation of new knowledge through "reverse-engineering." The arcane definitional discussion of whether any growth thereby generated is static or dynamic is both irrelevant to the current analysis and beyond the crude resolution of this study.

21. Robert Gilpin, "Economic Interdependence and National Security in Historical Perspective," in Klaus Knorr & Frank N. Trager, *Economic Issues and National Security* (New York: National Security Education Program of New York University, 1977), 38; see also J. A. Hobson, *Imperialism: A Study*, 3d ed. revised (London: G. Allen & Unwin, 1938), esp. 57.

22. Nazli Choucri & Robert C. North, "In Search of Peace Systems: Scandinavia and the Netherlands; 1870-1970," in Bruce M. Russett, ed., *Peace, War, and Numbers* (Beverly Hills, California: Sage Publications, 1972), 241.

23. Choucri and North have combined this observation with both structural analysis and the expansionist position, and argued that wars arise in two stages: (1) the rise of either internal pressures or a perceived need to expand interests, activities, and

influence; (2) cross-country comparison, challenge, rivalry, and conflict on some salient dimension or attribute.

Nazli Choucri & Robert C. North, "Dynamics of International Conflict: Some Policy Implications of Population, Resources, and Technology," *World Politics* 24 supplementary issue (Spring 1972): 80-122.

24. Choucri & North, "In Search of Peace Systems: Scandinavia and the Netherlands," 255-257.

25. This uncomplicated approach assumes that spontaneous indigenous innovation is not a modern growing nation's largest source of new knowledge. Countries with large components of indigenous knowledge would have accordingly large zero-intercepts in a bivariate regression.

26. Application of the syllogism relies ultimately on the block recursiveness of the growth-conflict relationship within the international political-economy, as established under the Ando-Fisher theorem of decomposability (see Appendix N).

6

What It All Means

In seeking to explain the absence of conflict as modern countries experienced sustained rapid aggregate economic growth, history had little to offer beyond broad anecdotes suggesting that over decades or centuries growth and conflict had been known to occur together. Theory showed far more variety, and offered several explanations for several sorts of growth-conflict relationships. Many were trade-related, and the most sophisticated included both growth and conflict among larger sets of independent and dependent variables. All considered economic growth as a homogeneous, aggregate process, affecting and affected by many other political and economic variables. The reality, power, and dual nature of the growth-conflict relationship, about which so many historians and theoreticians have speculated, became clearer with some nomothetic analysis of the empirical record (see section "A 'Speculative' Profile of Growth and Conflict" in chapter 4).

THE DUAL GROWTH-CONFLICT RELATIONSHIP

Despite the ambiguity of both history and theory about any relationships between growth and conflict, analysis of the empirical data has clearly shown that growth and conflict occur more often together than either occurs alone. Equally clear are the reality and power of two distinct growth-conflict relationships: direct and inverse. Even though the characteristics of aggregate growth and the nature of conflict vary across countries and over time, the dual effects on international conflict of the growth process itself seem regular and powerful. Slightly more powerful, and somewhat slower, are the dual effects of conflict on growth. Although not the only influence, economic growth clearly exerts significant inverse-negative pressure on international conflict, primarily through *rates* of growth. Paradoxically, however, growth can also exert a somewhat weaker direct-positive stimulus on conflict through *levels* of wealth. The dual nature of the growth-conflict relationship prevents, however, a deterministic prediction about the particular effects of growth on conflict, or the consequences of conflict for growth. It is also necessary to know *which growth-conflict relationship is operating* in a particular country or circumstance. The simple observation of aggregate growth and generic conflict do not allow this determination.

THE DUALITY OF GROWTH

Disjunction of growth provided the necessary key for determining which growth-conflict relationship governs the effects of economic growth: each relationship is associated with a different type of growth: static and dynamic. It is the type of growth and its associated growth-conflict relationship that determine the effects of growth and conflict on each other. Resource-based static growth associates high growth with high conflict, and low growth with low conflict, in a direct-positive relationship. Knowledge-based dynamic growth associates high growth with low conflict, and low growth with high conflict, in an inverse-negative relationship.

Each type of growth seems to occur independently, with static usually preceding dynamic growth. Although static growth can be both rapid and intense for brief periods, sustained growth has seemed to involve a shift from static toward dynamic growth. The shift occurs with enough consistency to form notable patterns of change in type and frequency of conflict, as the nature of growth shifts over time. Each type of growth appears with sufficient likeness across countries to show regular patterns of differences and similarities in national conflict experiences consistent with differences in the nature of growth. To explain the effects of growth and conflict on each other, it seems enough to determine *which type of growth is predominant* in a particular case.

DUAL ENGINES OF GROWTH

In disjoining the growth process, Chapter 5 explained static growth as arising from incremental increase or expansion of national factors of production, usually through trade, migration, or capital transfers. These processes act as engines of static growth, and establish the direct growth-conflict relationship. Trade emerges as a convenient indicator of static growth, and an apparently primary precursor of the direct growth-conflict relationship. Involving, in contrast, increases in knowledge and intellectual capital, dynamic growth enhances the functional or productive capacities of an individual, society, polity, economy, region, or even of the entire world, through transfers of technology or expertise, training and education, or even example. Completing the syllogism gives to foreign direct investment a critical role not only as the engine of dynamic growth, but, by extension, also as the progenitor of the inverse growth-conflict relationship, which associates low conflict with high growth. In analogy with trade, FDI is a convenient indicator of dynamic growth.

THE POLITICAL-ECONOMIC IMPORTANCE OF FDI

Identification of FDI as a critical discriminator between static and dynamic growth demands recognition of both FDI and its parent, multinational enterprise, as powerful features of modern international political-economy. Neither existed, even in prenatal form, when modern economic growth appeared in Renaissance Europe. In the premodern international system faced by the developing European nations, each nation had to provide its own internal engine of growth, since the system itself was fully occupied in managing the Hobbesian, realist international world of all against all. Except when constrained by an international security regime, nations followed their own inclinations (euphemistically known as interests), and endured frequent conflict with other nations. The various classic liberal models (Jefferson, Hamilton, Kant, Rousseau, Locke, *etc.*) provided this internal engine separately in each nation through nationalism and liberal political-economic features. The realist international political system, with its various international security regimes, insulated these national economic engines from each other, kept their workings self-reliant, and transformed uneven economic growth into international conflict.

The introduction of other sorts of entities into international relations in the late nineteenth century began to reduce the salience of an international security regime in guiding or constraining international behaviors. Domestic political expectations of continuing economic growth increased the influences of external economic processes on international relations. Within the far different international system faced by post-1945 nations within a rigid Cold War security regime operated by a hegemon, a nation could easily rely on an external engine of growth, provided by foreign direct investment and technology transfer from multinational enterprises (or in principle, by official state aid from one of the protagonists of the Cold War). The new ability to generate domestic economic growth from foreign sources confounded both realism and liberalism and brought a flurry of new research into national development and a profusion of interesting "neo"-concepts.

The twentieth century has brought several salient periods of what Richard Haass has called "international deregulation," during which the international system has restructured itself around "new players, new capabilities, and new alignments—but, no new rules."[1] Across these successive deregulations the maturation of multinational enterprise, with its powerful dynamic of foreign direct investment, has gradually brought these unique entities into increasing prominence as legitimate "players" in an international political-economy —fundamentally different from that in which Europe developed—with both sovereign national states and multinational organizations having and exercising political and economic power.

Familiar linkages between international conflict and uneven or trade-related economic growth, changes in distributions of power, status inconsistencies, and even some of Lenin's "contradictions," remain firm. The modern international political-economy, however, involves an additional set of actors—multinational enterprises—an additional dynamic—FDI—and a powerful growth-conflict relationship—inverse—that did not yet exist when orthodoxy was still radical. Further, the persistent intrusion of commerce and economics into the classical model of predominantly political-military international relations has recast national power as a political-economic attribute. No longer is its exercise an exclusive prerogative of the state; industrial might can be more relevant and influential than military force structures or diplomatic skill in asserting national interests.

Multinational enterprise and transnational financial institutions using FDI have established networks of labor and capital that transcend national boundaries—and may even be nonnational—in broad disregard for orthodox notions of power. National states are losing historic primacy as economic units as physical resources lose salience as stores of wealth, and information, knowledge, and skills emerge as currencies of power. As Geoffrey Stern has noted, however, states remain dominant political entities and provide a legal structure for the global economy (see Appendix K). They also remain a significant political-economic feature of global affairs in their persistent preparation for international conflict and war.[2]

Multinational enterprise and foreign direct investment, and the relatively new kind of growth that they can bring, are novel systemic features of the modern international political-economy that account for substantial differences in the processes of growth and development in Western Europe, Latin America, Africa, Northeast Asia, and Southeast Asia. These unique entities with this powerful dynamic not only have redefined power resources and distribution of power, but have operationally disjoined both growth and the growth-conflict relationship. They have made anachronisms of orthodox realist, liberal, or radical approaches to conflict. International relations no longer involves only, or even primarily, war, diplomacy, and trade. Indeed, in a fashionable oxymoron, international relations no longer involves primarily nations, or even states. Nor are traditional Jeffersonian export-promotion or Hamiltonian import-substitution approaches to national development fully relevant to modern political-economic realities. The result is a powerful inverse relationship between growth and conflict, and the splendid paradox that the source of high economic growth and general prosperity may be the same as the source of low international conflict and relative peace.

An uncomplicated conclusion from the transformation of the international political-economy, attractive to both development economists and political scientists, might be that FDI would bring prosperity and peace to both host nations and home countries. Notwithstanding several formidable *caveats* to this wonderful generalization, the special importance of FDI—as well as trade— implied by the disjunction of growth, to growing nations is clear.[3] Whether a national goal is to increase aggregate growth or to reduce international conflict (or both), FDI seems to provide a powerful stimulus for acceleration of the shift toward dynamic growth. Relying solely on indigenous innovation, creativity, and inspiration to increase knowledge and apply it to productivity, early modern economic growth in Europe spanned decades and even centuries, with growth rates that would be considered disastrously low by modern standards.[4] For modern nations separated from other advanced nations by a "development gap," FDI can compress the Kuznetsian evolutionary pattern of slow shift from static to dynamic growth to a single-generation revolution by transferring technology and knowledge to backward nations. The result of FDI-related compression is a dramatically rapid increase in aggregate growth rate, even though as nations grow and "close the gap," their annual growth rates seem to fall from very high to average. The ASEAN experience in active management of FDI through normal sovereign legal powers clearly shows that modern countries with very low initial production *per capita* can use trade *in combination with FDI* to "close the gap more quickly (the advantage of backwardness). The more backward a country, the greater its scope for fast growth by copying the leaders."[5]

Confounding both realism and liberalism, FDI has become one of the salient features of the international political-economy in the half-century after World War II. In all countries for which data are available, both flows and stocks of FDI have a larger, and increasing, role in national politics and economics than in the prewar era. Generally ignored over the centuries in which trade dominated considerations of international economics, FDI was simply missing from orthodox international political-economic analysis. By the 1980s FDI had attained such stature as to incite the inclusion of a specific negotiating agenda on Trade-Related Investment Measures (TRIM) in the Uruguay Round of negotiations under the General Agreement on Tariffs and Trade, although the principles behind the TRIM negotiations remained focused on trade. It is increasingly clear that any orthodox analysis of the international political-economy that omits some consideration of FDI suffers inherently from incompleteness.

The inescapable conclusion is that neither host nations nor home countries can afford—politically or economically—not to manage FDI actively. The national mix of FDI and trade, and the legislative-diplomatic recipe for it, may be even more critical than the traditional balance of political-military-diplomatic power in achieving and maintaining acceptable national levels of peace and prosperity.

SOME PRACTICAL CONNECTIONS

In some useful sense the regularities identified in Chapters 4 and 5 at a global level constitute a paradigm of axiomatic principles establishing a generic growth-conflict relationship expected to be operating across all countries. Although the analysis above does not penetrate the regional level very deeply, it is not unreasonable to expect the generic relationship to persist, albeit with some characteristic idiosyncrasies, also at a regional level.

Growth and Conflict in Southeast Asia

It is well-known that the nations of Southeast Asia (excluding Indochina) have experienced both rapid growth and relatively peaceful international relations for several decades since World War II.[6] Common commercial wisdom, most policy, and much political-economic theory associate their growth with the large flows of foreign investment into the region, although the effect of FDI on international conflict is less than clear. What is less widely understood is the extent to which their peace and prosperity have been accompanied by a consistent regional pattern of developing legal and diplomatic systems that has suggested active national management of some of the variables within the growth-conflict relationship. Host national legislative and international diplomatic approaches to management of foreign direct investment reflect a consistency that, even if not deliberate or intentional, is remarkable.

For most of this period the five founder states of the Association of Southeast Asian Nations (ASEAN) formed a cohesive regional political and economic entity. These countries (Indonesia, Malaysia, the Philippines, Singapore, and Thailand) share several characteristics that make them an intuitively reasonable set for evaluating the hypothesis that the analytical results of Chapters 4 and 5 in fact comprise a set of lawlike regularities. They share a common heritage of culture, ethnicity, and socioeconomics.[7] They all began deliberate modernization and development efforts as independent nation-states between 1945 and 1960. These generic similarities tend to damp the differences in FDI flows and growth that might be attributable to noneconomic factors, and to minimize exogenous influences on international conflict.

Each of the ASEAN nations, like many other countries, adopted a domestic approach of patronal authoritative economic guidance, limited government economic intervention, and gradual restructuring, within a capitalistic political-economic structure. The ASEAN nations fit loosely into the international political networks of patron-client dependency operated by the superpowers, within which orthodoxy predicts no systematic relationships between growth and conflict (irrelevance due to patronal insulation). The ASEAN approach to the international economy differed from those of most other countries (notably Japan, South Korea, China, India, and the countries of Indochina) in at least three features: ASEAN focus on inward foreign direct investment; ASEAN tendencies to marginalize government-directed industrial policy; and ASEAN preferences for equity industrial financing—foreign and domestic.

In contrast to their similarities, the ASEAN countries showed distinctly different levels and rates of development—very high (Singapore), moderate (Malaysia and Thailand), low (Indonesia and Philippines)—although none have failed to grow or develop. The incidence of international conflict also varies considerably across the five countries with Singapore not experiencing enough war to generate a viable regression, and Thailand showing multiple military conflicts in nearly every year since World War II.[8]

The ASEAN Growth-Conflict Relationships

The six subset profiles of the ASEAN growth-conflict relationship comprise 28 observations (Singapore's dearth of war precludes viable Singaporean series for WP and WF). They are broadly comparable to the global profiles, but show some notable regional features (see Table 6.1). In parallel with the global profile, the composite ASEAN profiles show moderate correlations between prior growth and subsequent conflict (WF, NWF, TCF), and higher correlations between prior conflict and subsequent growth for both war and nonwar conflict (WP, NWP). The Total Conflict subset, however, shows the reverse relationship (TCF @ 0.57 > TCP @ 0.56), which may be a statistical artifact of the small sample size.

Table 6.1 ASEAN Regional Summary Profiles

GCR	R^2	LEAD	DGR	PCI	PROD	MEG	3GR	SIG	ZERO-INT
Generic composite relationship (28 observations)									
ASEAN 0.55	0-15;6	? ?	? ?	? ?	NS ?	? ?	?	?	SM ?
8 Dir 0.63	1-13;8	? ?	? ?	? ?	? ?	SIG -	?	SIG	SM ?
20 Inv 0.55	0-15;5	? ?	? ?	? ?	NS ?	? +	?	?	SM ?
Total conflict following growth (TCF) (5 observations)									
ASEAN 0.57	0-9; 5	SIG -	SIG -	NS -	NS ?	SIG ?	?	SIG	SM+
1 Dir 0.68	; 7	SIG -	NS ?	NS ?	SIG+	SIG -	DGR	SIG	SM+
4 Inv 0.54	0-9; 4	SIG -	SIG -	NS -	NS ?	SIG +	PCI	SIG	SM+
Total conflict preceding growth (TCP) (5 observations)									
ASEAN 0.56	7-13;9	NS +	NS ?	SIG ?	NS ?	SIG ?	GR	SIG	SM -
1 Dir 0.72	; 13	SIG+	NS ?	SIG +	NS ?	SIG -	DGR	SIG	SM -
4 Inv 0.52	7-8; 8	NS +	? +	SIG -	NS ?	? +	GR	?	SM -
War following growth (WF) (4 observations)									
ASEAN 0.50	0-4; 2	? -	SIG ?	? ?	NS -	SIG -	?	SIG	SM+
2 Dir 0.57	1-4; 2	? -	? ?	? -	? -	SIG -	INT	SIG	SM+
2 Inv 0.44	0-3; 2	? ?	SIG ?	SIG ?	NS ?	? +	GR	SIG	SM ?
War preceding growth (WP) (4 observations)									
ASEAN 0.51	1-15;9	NS ?	SIG ?	SIG ?	NS ?	NS ?	?	SIG	LG+
2 Dir 0.49	9-12;10	? +	SIG ?	SIG ?	NS ?	NS -	?	SIG	LG ?
2 Inv 0.52	1-15;8	NS -	? ?	? ?	NS ?	? +	?	NS	? +
Nonwar following growth (NWF) (5 observations)									
ASEAN 0.55	0-9; 5	SIG -	SIG -	NS -	NS +	NS -	DGR	NS	SM+
1 Dir 0.68	; 7	SIG -	NS ?	NS ?	SIG+	SIG -	DGR	NS	SM+
4 Inv 0.52	0-9; 4	SIG ?	SIG -	NS -	NS ?	NS -	DGR	NS	SM+
Nonwar preceding growth (NWP) (5 observations)									
ASEAN 0.59	0-13;6	SIG+	NS ?	SIG -	NS ?	SIG+	DGR	NS	SM -
1 Dir 0.81	; 13	SIG+	NS ?	SIG+	NS ?	SIG -	DGR	SIG	SM -
4 Inv 0.54	0-8; 5	NS +	NS ?	SIG -	NS ?	? +	GR	NS	SM -

Lags and leads show extreme ranges, but means cluster at five years. The effect of the zero-intercept is generally positive, and its value is predominantly small. MEG is almost uniformly insignificant (MEG is significant only occasionally in Indonesia).

Notable singularities in the ASEAN profile are the uniform significance of DGR and 3GR for subset TCF, the significance and predominance of DGR in NWF, and the high salience of the growth-rate variables across all subsets except WP. Variations from the global profiles are minor:

> Individual quantity variables (PCI and GDP) seem significant slightly less frequently (rather than more often in the global profile) than do growth-rate variables (DGR and 3GR).
>
> The effects of PCI and GDP are not as predominantly opposite as they are in the global profile.
>
> While GDP is uniformly significant for subsets TCP and NWP, both quantity variables seem relatively less significant in the ASEAN profile than in the global profile.

A discrete profile of the inverse GCR in ASEAN shows a large (4:1) predominance of this relationship in the TC and NW subsets (TCP, TCF, NWP, NWF), while both war subsets (WF, WP) show a balance between direct and inverse relationships.[9] In contrast to the global profile, across all ASEAN subsets except WP mean correlations for the inverse GCR are substantially *lower* than those of direct relationships. As in the global profile, the effects of 3GR differ between the direct and the inverse GCR, tending to be negative in the direct GCR, but positive in the inverse relationship; unlike the global regularity, DGR tends to have the same effect in each GCR.

The pair of growth-rate variables is most significant in the inverse relationship (70%), and in half of the direct relationships. Disjunction of the GCR seems not to affect the extreme ranges of lags and leads, which appear in both relationships in each profile. Similarly the MEG dummy variable and the zero-intercept do not vary from their composite regularities in the discrete relationships. The zero-intercept is generally significant, small, and positive in direct GCR, and small in inverse GCR. As in the world profile, each discrete type of GCR is more clearly defined in the ASEAN profile than is the composite relationship.

Separating the ASEAN countries according to predominant type of GCR (direct or inverse) shows only *Indonesia* in each subset experiencing a direct GCR—weakly correlated (R^2 = 0.47) and less than highly reliable (t-stat = 1.68)—associating low growth with low conflict, and high growth with high conflict. The four other countries experienced a predominantly inverse GCR showing notable—strong, consistent, and reliable—associations between low growth and high conflict, and between high growth and low conflict: *Malaysia and the Philippines in all subsets; Singapore and Thailand in nonwar and total conflict subsets* (see Table 6.2).

Table 6.2 Types of Growth

DYNAMIC GROWTH			STATIC GROWTH		
Country	|t-stat|	R^2	Country	|t-stat|	R^2
Malaysia	2.17	0.85	Indonesia	1.68	0.47
Thailand	3.15	0.91			
Philippines	2.16	0.53			
Singapore	2.02	0.89			

Sorting the ASEAN countries according to the predominant type of growth in each (as indicated by the relative significance of FDI and trade in generating growth) shows that four countries have experienced predominantly dynamic growth: *Malaysia, Philippines, Singapore, Thailand*. Only *Indonesia* has shown predominantly static growth. As at the global level, the trade-FDI regressions clearly establish a dichotomy between dynamically growing countries and those experiencing primarily static growth.

The major hypothesis emerging from the global analysis above predicts that countries experiencing predominantly static growth will have a GCR with direct effects (static-direct), that countries experiencing primarily dynamic growth will show inverse effects (dynamic-inverse), and that only a few countries will show anomalous pairings. As hypothesized, all ASEAN countries show either the static-direct pairing (*Indonesia*) or the dynamic-inverse pairing (*Malaysia, Philippines, Singapore, Thailand*).[10] This regional result, a powerful, convincing, lawlike regularity in solid support of the hypothesis, verifies the concept of a dual growth-conflict relationship, and solidifies the conclusion that it is the type of growth, and not simply growth itself, that affects international conflict.

The clear dual relationships between FDI and trade, dynamic and static growth, and their inverse and direct effects on conflict make it clear that any analysis of the international political-economy that omits consideration of FDI suffers inherently from incompleteness. Exposure of a single critical variable in FDI places the ability to guide a nation's development toward *both* peace *and* prosperity unequivocally within the capabilities of an informed national government.

Doing Something About It

Simple extensions of the lawlike regularities of the inverse and direct growth-conflict relationships through the dual processes of dynamic and static growth link conflict to their respective engines and sources. As intervening, dependent variables, *both* FDI flows, *and* trade levels, seem to be separately associated with international conflict. FDI would seem to be associated through dynamic growth to the inverse relationship; trade, through static growth to the direct relationship. It then becomes interesting, if not critical, to understand what actually *does* influence FDI, and how to manage FDI flows into a country.

The nations of Southeast Asia, like many others, recognized, or at least came to believe, that FDI could make substantial contributions to national development. Facing a world in which MNEs from a few industrial nations were the major investors, many infant nations adopted an uncritical policy of attracting as much FDI as possible, but gave little thought to managing it or to any effects on international politics. By the third wave of FDI in the late 1960s, clashes between host nations and corporate investors were becoming intense.[11] To control MNEs and FDI, some host countries enacted specific statutes; others developed policies or imposed regulations; most relied on *ad hoc* negotiations.[12] Frustration with other efforts (the failed New International Economic Order of the 1970s) led the Southeast Asian nations (and a few others) into deliberate efforts to manage FDI through domestic legal techniques. ASEAN governments methodically used laws and legal-economic structures in creating institutions to attract FDI and to channel any economic surpluses toward development. They have all stressed foreign investment legislation and investment incentives, and have given a large role to FDI in generating economic growth. In notable contrast, establishment and development of political institutions in and among ASEAN countries seem to have been less obviously linked to FDI.

Virtually all governments that have used FDI successfully in achieving economic development have relied, like Southeast Asians, on their domestic legal systems to control, or manage, foreign direct investment. Some have established financial incentives through foreign investment legislation to obtain large flows and stocks of FDI and a wide range of economic benefits (Singapore—$45.8 bn; Brazil—$33.6 bn; Malaysia—$29.1 bn, *etc.*). Others have relied on restrictions and regulations to gain a focused set of specific economic benefits that complemented other developmental efforts with relatively small amounts of actual FDI (India—$1.1 bn; Venezuela—$3.3 bn; the Philippines —$4.5 bn; South Korea—$7.2 bn; Japan—$8.9 bn, *etc.*).[13] Regardless of the particular benefits that they expected from FDI, ASEAN host nations have also oriented active diplomacy and international legal participation toward comfortable relationships with individual home countries. Each ASEAN government has approached FDI not simply as a source of funds to be manipulated within the national economy, but as an element of the nation's international political existence.

Less successful nations' bad or costly experiences have almost uniformly reflected strategies inconsistent with attracting and managing the investment required for achieving development goals (Egypt, Yugoslavia, China, *etc.*). These nations seem to have limited their approaches to FDI to a purely domestic focus on maximizing capital flows and jobs, and more recently on technology transfer. Even though not absent, their diplomatic efforts to manage FDI have not been prominent.

Although hindsight tempts analysts to impute intentions that reflect results to erstwhile policy-makers, it is unlikely that any of the early ASEAN national leaders launched their countries into development or modernizations with a coherent strategy for management of either growth or investment. Each country's development, however, has seemed to fit a common pattern. Legal management of FDI has complemented of rapid economic growth based on industrialization, and a rapid shift from static to dynamic growth. Flexible development of both economic and political institutions has recognized the international political relevance of FDI, but has stressed its domestic impacts (see Appendix L). For each nation, specific domestic legislation has been a primary management technique; international law and diplomacy have been powerful complements.

Historical Evolution

After World War II Southeast Asians recognized the power of foreign investment as an engine of growth, and saw manufacturing as a vehicle of economic development. The ASEAN governments acted through foreign investment laws to stimulate FDI, particularly from former metropoles, into manufacturing sectors. Economic activity began to surpass that of the 1930s in the 1950s, as new investment in food processing and light manufacturing began to generate rapid growth.

In the 1960s the ASEAN nations adopted ambitious development plans, emphasizing manufacturing for domestic markets under import-substitution and protectionist industrialization strategies. Foreigners still preferred to invest in natural resource extraction, trading, and banking, which grew rapidly with more economic activity. As the 1960s became the 1970s, host nations shifted import-substitution tactics to export promotion strategies, while foreign investors began to use ASEAN economies as export platforms, and to increase their FDI accordingly.

Unlike massive nineteenth-century migrations of labor to sources of capital to build heavy European manufacturing enterprises, capital moved to Southeast Asia's labor in the 1970s and 1980s to build export-oriented light manufacturing enterprises. Southeast Asia's low labor costs, especially in Singapore and Malaysia, attracted direct investment, in some contrast to the high returns promised by large European portfolio investments in development of American resources and infrastructures. In further contrast to the American experience, FDI initially dominated the Southeast Asian industrialization process, and began to shift it away from manufacturing toward higher-profit industries. Tourism, services, and agricultural processing became targets for foreign direct investors, although host government planners continued to stress export-oriented light manufacturing.

Legislative Management of FDI

ASEAN governments gradually learned to use the legal powers of sovereignty to manage investment. They used three techniques to attract foreign direct investment, to control its effects, and to channel any surpluses toward development: foreign investment legislation, bilateral investment treaties, and multilateral investment agreements. In addition to legislative restrictions and incentives, governments used fiscal and economic techniques to provide a better investment climate to attract foreign direct investment. Active diplomacy supported domestic policy through negotiation of international investment agreements.

Domestic Foreign Investment Law. Each country began with a basic investment law to attract foreign direct investment, supplemented legislation with political assurances that investments would be safe from expropriation or nationalization, and negotiated repatriation of profit. As development strategies crystallized into legal institutions, governments enacted complementary legislation to diffuse foreign direct investment benefits through their economies, and specialized law to deal with sensitive issues.[14]

ASEAN governments routinely used investment incentives to counterbalance poor infrastructure, small domestic demand, and unskilled workforces inherent in their underdeveloped economies. They have generally legislated incentives through tariff codes and tax provisions enacted within a basic foreign investment law.[15] Incentives were available to "pioneer" firms or "essential" industries with particular roles in the national development plan. Postcolonial nationalist fears of foreign domination generally balanced incentives with restrictions on extent of foreign ownership of equity or land, employment of foreign staff, and repatriation of profits. Every nation used foreign investment legislation to emphasize changes in development strategy as growth shifted quickly from static to dynamic: from economic stabilization to import substitution (static growth) to export promotion and industrialization (mixed growth) to technology transfer and diversification (predominantly dynamic growth).

1. *First Generation Protection*: Early foreign investment law included parallel approaches of protection for infant industries, FDI monopolies, and controlled entry. In the 1950s direct investment was primarily in branches or wholly owned subsidiaries of foreign firms, with negligible local equity participation. In political response to domestic pressure for more home control of foreign direct investment operations, governments legislated ownership requirements in accordance with countries' development plans. By the 1970s the bulk of new FDI had at least 10% local ownership. This change accelerated transfers of knowledge and the shift to dynamic growth.

2. *Second Generation Restriction*: Second generation foreign investment law diversified FDI sources, and increased local participation in FDI projects and commercial relationships. Restrictive and protective legislation focused FDI into particular sectors. Host countries set criteria and priorities for FDI and

enforced them through approval or licensing. Other commercial laws affected FDI indirectly through trade barriers, exchange controls, export subsidies, credit support, and various preferences for firms with high local equity. Restrictive socioeconomic legislation also increased long-term costs through fragmentation of production in small protected national markets, dissipation of economies of scale through market distortions, low productivity, and high overheads, and increasing requirements for using, training, and supporting particular segments of domestic labor forces. While FDI firms absorbed such costs globally, local firms required protection or subsidization to survive.

3. *Third Generation Interdependence*: Many Asian—and some other—countries have developed to the point where protection is necessary to prevent failure of domestic firms, rather than to promote growth and attract foreign investment. Torn between the domestic pressure to continue growth with self-sufficiency, and the attractions of modernization and interdependence, Indonesia and the Philippines continue to struggle with this dilemma. Stability, direction, and cautious political-economic openness were enough to bring growth in first and second generation economies, whose primary problems were unemployment, prices, and national savings. To shift definitely to dynamic growth, third generation investment laws must encourage technology-intensive high-productivity FDI by reducing the cost of equipment (special credit terms, subsidies, tax provisions, *etc.*) as labor costs rise and production functions intensify the salience of technology. As social demands of modernizing societies increase, countries must rely more on the bonds of interdependence, and less on national resources to meet them. In practice, some successful countries have adopted third generation investment laws that lead to an open economy (Singapore, Hong Kong) with no bias against, and no preference for, exporting or foreign ownership. Others have legislated toward bureaucratic subsidy regimes that can offset the protectionist bias (Korea, Taiwan, Malaysia) of traditional import-substitution strategies. Although it is too early to draw definitive conclusions about either, both patterns seem to show sustained high flows of FDI, salience of dynamic growth, and high rates of aggregate growth.

Complementary Domestic Legislation. To maintain national momentum along the path toward dynamic growth, third generation investment legislation—whether liberal or authoritarian—must be accompanied by parallel social and economic development legislation. Complementary legislation requires a politically powerful combination of authoritarianism, legitimacy, and liberalism that few governments have. The most successful countries have accompanied investment laws with legislation affecting education (to create a skilled workforce) and labor (to ensure that wage growth sustains domestic demand, and to guarantee a responsive, productive workforce for FDI firms); and with active collaboration with foreign investors (rather than domination, dependence, or conflict). A notable observation—perhaps coincidence—is the high official interest in, and legislation addressing, what has come to be known as "science and technology infrastructure" (universities, technology parks, government research establishments) in some third generation countries (Taiwan, Korea, Malaysia, Japan).[16]

Specialized Investment Law. Each of the ASEAN countries has established an area of specialized law around foreign direct investment in industries based on continuing and increasing exploitation of resources. These primary sectors remain potent sources of controversy, conflict, and instability, both in ASEAN and throughout the world. Although they are powerful engines of economic growth, they show little shift toward industrialization. Three major problems of foreign investment in these sectors create particular legal concerns that have not been readily amenable to stable legislative solutions:

> fear that multinational investors will exploit concessions in accordance with their own perspectives of markets and profits, rather than with consideration for the host country's developmental preferences;
> concerns that foreign investors will systematically capture revenues due to domestic owners, operators, investors, workers, government, and other parties, which are often ambiguous and negotiable at best; and
> anxiety and confusion about responsibilities for investment in infrastructure to support operations to extract resources.

Since these concerns change continually, the formal legislative process has often been too cumbersome to deal synoptically with them. Primary-sector investment legislation has tended to be broad, vague, and flexible, with considerable discretion reserved to government officials. Implementing regulations to deal with particular situations or circumstances have sometimes accumulated to levels of complexity that make them unworkable, and even self-contradictory. Each problem tends to be solved by specific negotiations, which place governments at a disadvantage. Partly, perhaps, because of the inherent inability to legislate efficiently and effectively in these areas, ASEAN countries tolerated official corruption, MNE exploitation, project inefficiency, and simple crime in these critical sectors. The primary sectors remain powerful sources of international conflict both in ASEAN and throughout the world, as well as of economic growth, which is essentially all static and resource-based. Perhaps the inherent difficulty of progress toward dynamic growth in these sectors has led most developing nations (including the ASEAN countries) to prefer manufacturing and "high-tech" sectors for modernization and development.

Treaty Management of FDI

Each ASEAN country has signed bilateral investment treaties and acceded to various multilateral investment agreements. None of the countries seem to have related the timing of treaties and agreements either to foreign investment legislation or to particular phases of national development plans. Initiatives seemed, rather, to arise in investor countries.

Bilateral Investment Treaties. While all countries included some industry-specific provisions in some bilateral investment treaties, only Indonesia tried actively to use bilateral investment treaties to focus FDI on economic development goals. Most bilateral investment treaties are virtually pro forma versions of the standard bilateral investment treaty text adopted by an investor government for all of its investment treaties across the world.[17] Many investor governments (United States, United Kingdom, France, Japan, *etc.*) actively use investment treaties to support their MNE in a standard policy approach. Host governments (including all ASEAN governments), in contrast, seemed content to accept an investor government's standard bilateral investment treaty provisions with only minor variations or additions, which seemed more to reflect current political issues than actual development plans.

High correspondence between implementation of bilateral investment treaties and increases in FDI flows may be attributed to investor government initiatives. ASEAN host governments have focused attentions on foreign investment legislation and complementary domestic legal institutions, and seemed almost to accept bilateral investment treaties as a welcome, and beneficial, diplomatic adjunct to development.

Multilateral Investment Agreements. A country's accession to multilateral investment agreements does not seem systematically related to its development plans or current stage of development. Indonesia and Thailand acceded to their first agreements well before they established formal or deliberate approaches to development.[18] A second spurt of multilateral investment agreements came in the late 1960s, under American domination of Southeast Asia in connection with the war in Vietnam, when Indonesia, Malaysia, and Singapore acceded to the Washington Convention on Settlement of Investment Disputes Between States and Nationals of Other States, and the Philippines acceded to the New York Convention on Recognition and Enforcement of Foreign Arbitral Awards. Regional multilateral investment agreements appeared only in the 1980s, as primarily political arrangements, when all five ASEAN nations created the Basic Agreement on ASEAN Industrial Joint Ventures (1983) and the Agreement for the Promotion and Protection of Investments (1987).

Since the Cold War, multilateral investment agreements seem incidental adjuncts to multilateral relationships or anomalous additions to political arrangements about trade. Motivations for accessions to multilateral investment agreements seem to have arisen neither internally as part of a development strategy, nor among investor nations. The ASEAN nations seem to have used multilateral investment agreements more as political instruments of international relations, than as economic instruments of national development. Although multilateral investment agreements assuredly influenced foreign direct investment flows, the economic benefits, like those of bilateral investment treaties, were probably serendipitous.

LAWLIKE REGULARITIES IN THE ASEAN EXPERIENCE

Intuition and history suggest the presence of some uniform relationships involving foreign direct investment (FDI), foreign investment laws (FIL), bilateral investment treaties (BIT), and multilateral investment agreements (MIA) in ASEAN development. Expectation that such uniformities are not purely coincidental, but reflect some sort of lawlike regularity, forms a foundation for an initial test hypothesis. The premise that use of these legal-diplomatic instruments (FIL, BIT, MIA) by ASEAN nations was related to foreign direct investment, when quantified, becomes the initial test equation. Least-squares regression techniques with distributed-lag time series forecasting estimate relationships between FDI flows and the independent variables measure their explanatory power, and allow comparison across countries. Refinement of any uniformities among the relationships, and determination of their scope and limitations, provide a clear analytical basis for identifying lawlike regularities around an appropriate theory that explains the relationship and the observed uniformities.

The Model

Governments seem implicitly to have expected that their legal and diplomatic actions would influence, or even determine, the behaviors of foreign direct investors and the flows of investment (the critical variable in shifting from static to dynamic growth, and from the direct to the inverse growth-conflict relationship). The simplest of expectations seems to have been that their uses of these legal-diplomatic instruments—foreign investment law, bilateral investment treaties, multilateral investment agreements—would affect the flows of foreign direct investment into their nations: that FDI depends in some way on FIL, BIT, and MIA.

Any "ASEAN Model," then, would simply be the way in which ASEAN countries seem to have managed these legal-diplomatic variables and the ways in which foreign direct investment affected their shifts from static to dynamic growth. Its parameters would include the sets of lawlike regularities that identify the inverse and direct growth-conflict relationships and the lawlike regularities surrounding static and dynamic growth. In addition to the global generalities, however, it would also include the set of lawlike regularities that characterize the ASEAN relationship between FIL, BIT, MIA, and FDI.

Generalization of the "ASEAN Model" would refine these sets of lawlike regularities into a specification of an observable relationship involving international conflict as a dependent variable, type of growth as a dependent intervening variable, and the set of legal-diplomatic variables used by the ASEAN countries as an independent variable. The final set of lawlike regularities across this double relationship would complete the syllogism by providing a single engine of both growth and conflict, which people can manage or manipulate.

In beginning a statistical search for uniformities, the lawlike regularities of the ASEAN relationship between FIL, BIT, MIA, and FDI become independent variables, which governments might manipulate to influence FDI, the single dependent variable, in a general functional relationship of the form:

$$FDI = f(FIL, BIT, MIA).$$

In statistical notation, this function becomes:

$$FDI = \alpha FIL + \gamma BIT + \delta MIA + \zeta(other\ factors) + \epsilon$$

where   FDI, the dependent variable, is annual flow of new-equity foreign direct investment into each country, with negative or positive values;[19]

FIL is a discrete independent variable in the form of an index for foreign investment legislation;

BIT is a discrete independent variable in the form of an index for bilateral investment treaties;

MIA is a discrete independent variable in the form of an index for multilateral investment agreements;[20] and

(other factors) is the set of continuous "control variables" that reflects the aggregate of other factors affecting FDI flows; for this study, GDP per capita, its annual growth rate, and an index of international conflict serve to isolate the effects of the diplomatic-legislative variables of the hypothesis;

ϵ is residual error term, approaching zero in a robust regression estimate; and

the coefficients, α, γ, δ, and ζ represent the respective influences of each legal-diplomatic and control variable on FDI.

A logical syllogism extended from this equation, which would seem to explain the occurrence of both high growth and low conflict in ASEAN, would be represented by a simple flow diagram:

FIL
BIT ⇒ FDI ⇒ HIGH DYNAMIC GROWTH ⇒ INVERSE GCR ⇒ LOW CONFLICT
MIA

The Variables

A country's implementation of bilateral investment treaties and multilateral investment agreements changes its investment climate in a fundamentally stable way. Since contents of treaties and agreements are broadly similar across countries and over time, analysis can conveniently avoid coding problems by increasing the variables BIT and MIA by 1 for each new BIT or MIA in force. Thus, the BIT variable is 0 until a country signs its first BIT; thereafter BIT could assume any value between 0 and 12 (Malaysia had signed 12 bilateral investment treaties prior to 1993). Similarly MIA could assume any value between 0 and 6 (Indonesia has signed all 6 multilateral investment agreements).

In recognizing their greater variability and volatility, the FIL variable addresses four distinct effects of foreign investment legislation on FDI—three stable, long-term consequences (FIL1, FIL2, FIL3) and one volatile, short-term result (FIL4):

FIL1:   The first stable effect is whether a country has any foreign investment legislation at all, which at least provides some form of basic property rights for foreign investors; FIL1 would be 0 for each annual observation of a country until it enacts the first FIL and 1 thereafter;

FIL2:   The second stable effect is whether foreign investment legislation contains seven provisions relevant to the investment decision of an investor:

absence of ownership restrictions	rights to transfer capital
tax incentives	exemption from import duties
guarantees against expropriation or nationalization	protection against competing imports incentives to export

Since each provision of FIL2 can be either present [1] or absent [0], the possible values of FIL2 range from 0 to 7; each annual observation of each country's FIL2 is the sum of the presence or absence in its current foreign investment legislation of these seven provisions.

FIL3:   The third stable effect of foreign investment legislation is through imposition of 6 sorts of performance requirements on FDI projects:

employment of local workers	local content in manufactured goods
operation of training programs	operations only in specified sectors
export requirements	location restrictions

Since each requirement can be either present [1] or absent [0] in national investment law, possible values of FIL3 range from 0 to 6 for each country; each annual observation of a country's FIL3 is the sum of the presence or absence of these requirements.

The presence or absence of the foreign investment law (FIL1), each of the seven provisions (FIL2), and each of the six performance requirements (FIL3) could be treated as 14 separate discrete variables. It is statistically convenient, however, to aggregate them in a single discrete index variable for each country—FIL123. The intuitively expected positive effects of FIL1 and FIL2 and negative effect of FIL3 combine in a composite discrete variable:

$$FIL123 = FIL1 + FIL2 - FIL3.^{21}$$

Because the fourth effect of foreign investment law is short-term and volatile, it cannot readily be aggregated with long-term effects, and is better treated separately:

FIL4:   The fourth volatile effect of foreign investment legislation is stability of host country legislation and regulations over time; the variable has high value for periods of stable law, and low value for unpredictability; FIL4 assumes value 0 for the year in which FIL was initially established, increases by 1 for each succeeding year in which no change occurs, and decreases by 1 for each year in which legal changes occur; FIL4 may assume either negative or positive values; each annual observation of FIL4 is the cumulation of changes to foreign investment legislation.

Commercial-financial wisdom and practice suggests that economic growth should encourage FDI. Two convenient indices of host nation growth, which are suitable as control variables, are *per capita* Income (PCI), and its annual growth rate (AGR):

PCI: Measured as real (GDP) per capita for each host nation, PCI is a continuous control variable that reflects both general economic growth and purchasing power of any host national target market;[22]
AGR: The annual growth rate of PCI is a continuous control variable reflecting host national economic trends and the expectations of foreign investors.

A third control variable, international conflict (CNF), serves to isolate the legal-diplomatic independent variables from political effects of international conflict between the host nation and the rest of the world:

CNF: Defined as the sum of host national involvements in interstate war and incidence of host national nonwar interstate conflict in a single year, the CNF control variable has a minimum value of 0, and assumes higher positive values as a host nation engages in more international conflicts.[23]

Introduction of a fourth control variable, time trend (TREND), accommodates any broad tendencies over time or hysteresis in FDI flows. TREND assumes a value of 0 in year 0 of a time series, and increases by 1 in each successive year. The time-trend variable tests the hypothesis that the dependent variable is affected simply by the passage of time.

The Regressions

Using continuous FDI as the dependent variable, discrete values of FIL (FIL123 and FIL4), BIT, and MIA as independent variables, and continuous values of PCI, AGR, and CNF as control variables, the test hypothesis becomes the test regression equation:

$$FDI = \alpha FIL123 + \beta FIL4 + \gamma BIT + \delta MIA + \zeta PCI + \eta AGR + \theta CNF + \iota TREND + \epsilon.$$

The values of the coefficients α, β, γ, δ, ζ, η, θ, and ι, with ϵ as close to 0 as possible, indicate the sensitivity of FDI flows to each of the independent and control variables. As the variables have been constructed, intuition would expect the coefficient of FIL123 to be positive or negative, those of FIL4, BIT, MIA, PCI, and AGR to be positive, and that of CNF to be negative.

Two sets of time-series regressions (unlagged and lagged) for each country (annual observations of each of the variables from 1957 to 1989), and a pooled regression of cross-country data (33 annual comparisons of the observations of each country's eight variables) estimate separate equations relating independent and control variables to FDI. The estimated coefficients for these equations indicate sensitivity of FDI to each variable, and may suggest techniques for manipulating and predicting FDI flows, with the related effect of influencing both growth and conflict. Results of time-series regressions indicate the respective influences of the independent and control variables on amounts of FDI flows; the cross-country pooled regression indicates their influences on direction of flow.[24]

Basic Unlagged Time Series Equations

Country-specific time-series regressions relate current FDI flows to current values of independent and control variables. Few coefficients are statistically significant (95%),[25] although goodness-of-fit $(\overline{R}^2)$ is high.[26] Equation (1) for each country presents the best regression estimates for coefficients of the significant independent and control variables, while omitting those variables that do not significantly affect FDI flows.

INDONESIA
$$FDI = -0.5 - 31.0(FIL4) + 50.7(BIT) + 1.5(PCI) + 29.5(CNF) - 26.1(TREND) \tag{1}$$
Adjusted goodness of fit is 80%.

MALAYSIA
$$FDI = -336.4 - 64.3(FIL4) + 0.5(PCI) - 71.8(TREND) \tag{1}$$
Adjusted goodness of fit is 73%.

PHILIPPINES
$$FDI = -6.43 - 39.3(FIL4) + 174.4(BIT) + 111.8(MIA) \tag{1}$$
Adjusted goodness of fit is 63%.

SINGAPORE
$$FDI = -1096.6 - 132.4(BIT) + 0.2(PCI) + 3173.1(AGR) \tag{1}$$
Adjusted goodness of fit is 83%.

THAILAND
$$FDI = -94.2 - 259.5(BIT) + 68.6(PCI) + 842.0(AGR) \tag{1}$$
Adjusted goodness of fit is 77%.

Results of the basic unlagged regressions, summarized in Table 6.3, confute the intuitive positive relationship between FIL and FDI and indicate that the content of FIL (FIL123) is not a significant influence on FDI flows.

Table 6.3 Basic Time-series Regression Coefficients

	INDONESIA	MALAYSIA	PHILIPPINES	SINGAPORE	THAILAND
FIL123	NS	NS	NS	NS	NS
FIL4	-31.04 (12.4)	-64.3 (27.6)	-39.3 (11.6)	NS	NS
BIT	50.7 (17.8)	NS	174.4 (74.3)	-132.4 (82.9)	-259.5 (55.1)
MIA	NS	NS	111.8 (31.7)	NS	NS
PCI	1.54 (0.3)	0.55 (0.14)	NS	0.23 (0.04)	68.6 (8.8)
AGR	NS	NS	NS	3173.1 (1564.9)	842.0 (393.1)
CNF	29.5 (10.7)	NS	NS	NS	NS
TREND	-26.1 (10.9)	-71.8 (32.3)	NS	NS	NS
$\bar{R}^2$	0.804 (102.9)	0.728 (255.4)	0.632 (114.1)	0.827 (431.5)	0.775 (157.3)

NS = Variable is insignificant at the 95% level
(.) = Standard error of coefficient; standard error of regression with $\bar{R}^2$

Results for BIT and MIA show inconclusive support for a hypothesis that BIT and MIA are associated with higher flows of FDI. While PCI has an obvious positive effect on FDI flows, and CNF is generally insignificant, AGR and TREND suggest no uniformities. It is notable that only in Indonesia and Philippines are both FIL4 and BIT significant; further, only in Philippines are only the legal-diplomatic variables significant. Beyond noting that either FIL4 or BIT has significant influence on FDI flows and that FIL123 has no significant influence, no clear patterns, uniformities, or substantive conclusions emerge from these basic unlagged regression results. Each country seems to be unique in its basic, unlagged relationships between FDI, FIL, BIT, MIA, PCI, CNF, and AGR.

Lagged and Differenced Time Series Equations

Equations (1) above reflect current effects of current values of FIL, BIT, MIA, PCI, CNF, and AGR on current flows of FDI. Foreign investors, however, often take considerable time, and analyze historical investment data, to make new investment decisions.   Since the independent and control variables operate on FDI only through the long investment decision-making process of multinational investors, their effects can be expected to appear in FDI flows only after some delay, or lag.   The long decision-making process distributes the stable effects of enacting FIL, signing BIT, and acceding to MIA, over several years: variously lagged values of each independent and control variable could be expected to have the most significant influences on FDI flows.   The delay involved—between occurrence of changes in independent variables and their effects on FDI flows—suggests that lagging may be an important factor in the relationship.

The response of FDI to changes in BIT and MIA, and to long-term effects of FIL, intuitively fits the Geometric Model of Lag.[27] In some contrast, annual changes in FIL4, PCI, CNF, and AGR, are not permanent, but instead generate an expectation that any trend will persist, as in the Adaptive Expectations Model of Lag.[28] Both lag models recognize the effect of prior FDI flows on current flows of FDI; thus, the lagged FDI variable itself may act as a predictor, with an assumption that the significance of past flows of FDI will decrease over time.[29] Since the two models of lag are statistically equivalent, estimation of the dependent variable through lagged-variable regression is reduced to a single time series regression for each country:

$$FDI = C + \alpha(FDI_{t-1}) + \beta(FIL123_{t-k}) + \gamma(FIL4_{t-l}) + \gamma(BIT_{t-m}) + \delta(MIA_{t-n})$$
$$+ \zeta(PCI_{t-o}) + \eta(AGR_{t-p}) + \theta(CNF_{t-q}) + \iota(TREND) + \epsilon,$$

where   lagged values for a variable are indicated by the subscript $_{t-n}$, which indicates that the value of that variable n years before the relevant FDI flow acts as the most significant predictor. Lags for different variables, and for different countries, may be of different lengths.

Since accessions to bilateral investment treaties or multilateral international agreements do not occur every year, the time series for BIT and MIA are erratic with sporadic large changes in values.   Because of the nature of their implementation, the decisive factor in changing a country's investment climate is its accession to a new treaty or agreement, rather than the number of them that it has accumulated.   Thus, the difference between the current value of each relevant variable (BIT or MIA) and the previous year's value of the same variable (first difference), instead of the actual numbers or provisions of treaties and agreements, is the relevant variable.   Applying simplified lag models and first differencing refines the basic time-series regression equation to:

$$FDI = C + \alpha(FDI_{t-1}) + \beta(FIL123_{t-k}) + \gamma(FIL4_{t-l}) + \gamma(\Delta BIT_{t-m}) + \delta(\Delta MIA_{t-n})$$
$$+ \zeta(PCI_{t-o}) + \eta(AGR_{t-p}) + \theta(CNF_{t-q}) + \iota(TREND) + \epsilon,$$

where   first differences of BIT and MIA variables are indicated by the prefix Δ.

Since FDI flows were initially small, if the model is robust, α should be between 0 and $\pm$ 1; lags on FIL4 should be small (1—3 years); lags on ΔBIT and ΔMIA could be larger (6—8 years). Equation (2) for each country indicates a combination of lags that best fits observed data (high correlation coefficient, at least two significant (95%) independent or control variables, and compliance with technical criteria for robustness).

INDONESIA

$$FDI = -21.1 + 0.6(FDI_{t-1}) - 23.1(FIL4) + 77.4(\Delta BIT_{t-7}) + 253(\Delta MIA_{t-7}) + 0.8(PCI_{t-2}) \qquad (2)$$

Goodness of fit is improved to 92%. The coefficient of lagged FDI is less than 1 as expected. Neither BIT nor MIA affect FDI flows quickly (lags of seven years), although both are strong influences. Stability of FIL has significant effect but its coefficient is unexpectedly negative; FIL123 is insignificant. PCI is the only significant control variable.

MALAYSIA

$$FDI = -91.7 + 0.6(FDI_{t-1}) + 276.1(\Delta BIT_{t-2}) - 314.4(\Delta MIA_{t-1}) + 0.1(PCI) \qquad (2)$$

Goodness of fit improves to 84%. The coefficient of lagged FDI is less than 1 as expected. Both BIT and MIA affect FDI flows after only one or two years. The FIL variables are insignificant at all lags. PCI is the only significant control variable.

PHILIPPINES

$$FDI = -59.9 - 58.6(FIL4_{t-3}) + 227.6(\Delta BIT_{t-7}) + 130.1(PCI_{t-3}) \qquad (2)$$

Goodness of fit improves to 75%. All coefficients are large, although the effect of FIL4 is unexpectedly negative. Each variable operates slowly, with delays of three to seven years. Lagged FDI, FIL123 and MIA are not significant. PCI is the only significant control variable.

SINGAPORE

$$FDI = -395.0 - 142.6(FIL4_{t-1}) + 288.2(\Delta BIT_{t-6}) + 509.5(\Delta MIA_{t-6}) - 567.6(CNF_{t-4}) + 0.3(PCI_{t-6}) \qquad (2)$$

Goodness of fit improves to 94%. Neither BIT nor MIA affect FDI flows quickly (lags of six years), while stability of FIL has a significant effect on FDI within one year; Lagged FDI and FIL123 variables are insignificant. Both PCI and CNF are significant control variables.

THAILAND

$$FDI = -55.7 + 115.1(FIL4_{t-4}) + 234.5(\Delta BIT_{t-4}) + 264.2(\Delta MIA_{t-6}) + 13.3(PCI) \qquad (2)$$

Goodness of fit improves to 80%. FIL4 operates to establish credibility after four years. Signature of a BIT is reflected four years later, while MIA has a six-year delay. Lagged FDI and FIL123 are insignificant. PCI is the only significant control variable.

The lagged and differenced regressions [equations (2)], summarized in Table 6.4, confute the intuitive positive relationship between FIL and FDI, and confirm that the content of FIL (FIL123) is not a significant influence on FDI flows.

Table 6.4 Lagged and Differenced Time-series Regression Coefficients

	INDONESIA	MALAYSIA	PHILIPPINES	SINGAPORE	THAILAND
FDI	Lag: 1 0.55 (0.11)	Lag: 1 0.55 (0.16)	NS	NS	NS
FIL123	NS	NS	NS	NS	NS
FIL4	Lag: 0 -23.1 (8.9)	NS	Lag: 3 -58.6 (14.0)	Lag: 1 -142.6 (46.2)	Lag: 4 115.1 (34.9)
ΔBIT	Lag: 7 77.4 (24.2)	Lag: 2 276.1 (89.0)	Lag: 7 227.6 (77.4)	Lag: 6 288.2 (110.4)	Lag: 4 234.5 (89.6)
ΔMIA	Lag: 7 253.3 (48.1)	Lag: 1 -314.4 (120.4)	NS	Lag: 6 509.5 (197.5)	Lag: 6 264.2 (125.1)
PCI	Lag: 2 0.78 (0.21)	Lag: 0 0.11 (0.04)	Lag: 3 130.0 (23.6)	Lag: 6 0.34 (0.04)	Lag: 0 13.3 (5.2)
AGR	NS	NS	NS	NS	NS
CNF	NS	NS	NS	Lag: 4 -597.6 (165.4)	NS
TREND	NS	NS	NS	NS	NS
$\overline{R}^2$	0.921 (66.1)	0.848 (186.5)	0.754 (94.8)	0.940 (251.7)	0.804 (146.9)

NS = Variable is Insignificant for All Lags at the 95% level
(.) = Standard Error of Coefficient; Standard Error of Regression with $\overline{R}^2$

The results suggest some regular lawlike relationships across the ASEAN countries between FDI flows and the independent legal-diplomatic variables FIL4, MIA, and BIT, and confirm the expected positive influence of PCI on FDI flows. In all countries annual increases in BIT have a significant positive association with FDI flows, after delays of two to seven years. In all countries except the Philippines, increases in MIA have significant influence on FDI, although effects vary. In all countries except Malaysia, FIL4 has significant influence on FDI, although effects vary. All of these legal-diplomatic variables (FIL4, ΔBIT, ΔMIA) have significant influence in three countries: Indonesia, Singapore, Thailand. Delays in effects of ΔBIT (mean = 5.1 years) and ΔMIA (mean = 5.0 years) are predominantly longer than those in the effects of FIL4 (mean = 2.0 years).

Although coefficients are positive and less than 1 as expected, lagged FDI flows have only a weak influence on current flows of investment; this occurs in only two countries. The only control variable that is uniformly significant is PCI, although its lags vary, and coefficients are small except in the Philippines. Goodness-of-fit (R^2) of lagged and differenced relationships is uniformly better than those of basic current relationships.

The Cross-Country Structural Equation

Annual observations from 1957 to 1989 of the variables across the five ASEAN countries provided data in time series for a single cross-country regression equation that captures influences of both country-specific and regional effects. Since neither lagged nor differenced values are used in the cross-country procedure, the functional equation is simply the original representation for the current year:

$$FDI = \alpha FIL123 + \beta FIL4 + \gamma BIT + \delta MIA + \zeta PCI + \eta AGR + \theta CNF + \iota TREND + \epsilon.$$

The best estimate of the cross-country regression equation, including only variables that are significant at the 95% level, is:

$$FDI = -137.6 - 20.1(FIL4) + 175.9(MIA) + 0.1(PCI)$$

Goodness of fit is 74%. Standard errors of regression coefficients are FIL4 = 6.9; MIA = 23.9; PCI = 0.005; Regression = 282.8.

The counterintuitive effect of FIL4 is negative and significant as in regressions on current time series and lagged, differenced time series. The influence of PCI is again positive, but small. The cross-country influence of MIA is large and positive, as in the lagged, differenced time-series regressions. Like the time-series regressions, FIL123 is not significant; nor, however, is BIT significant, in contrast to the time-series regressions. As in the time-series regressions, PCI is the only significant control variable.

Statistical Conclusions

In all five countries, the lagged, differenced equations are noticeably better (with higher correlations and lower standard errors) reflections of actual data observations than are the basic current-year cross-country relationships. The lagged, differenced time series regressions show powerful relationships between FDI and changes in FIL4, MIA, and BIT.[30] The cross-country regression also shows the same powerful relationships between FDI and changes in MIA and

FIL4, which are significant predictors. In addition, PCI is also a positive predictor in the cross-country regression. These results suggest several lawlike regularities about the relationships between these legal-diplomatic variables and international conflict:

> in all relationships, the coefficient of ΔBIT is large and positive; ΔBIT exerts a strong influence on FDI flows, with country-specific delays;
>
> in all relationships, FIL123 is insignificant;
>
> in most (three of five significant) relationships, FIL4 shows a significant counterintuitive *negative* influence on FDI flows; lags on FIL4 are noticeably shorter than those on ΔBIT and on ΔMIA;
>
> in most (three of five significant) relationships, ΔMIA shows a significant positive influence after a long delay (six or seven years); and
>
> of the control variables, only PCI shows uniform significant influence, always positive, with country-specific delays; levels of prior year's FDI had a significant, positive influence on current flows of FDI only in Indonesia and Malaysia.

Foreign Investment Legislation

As noteworthy, perhaps, as the predictive-explanatory power of some variables, is the insignificance or absence of other variables. None of the variables FIL1, FIL2, FIL3—or their composite FIL123—seem to be good predictors, or even to exert significant influences on FDI flows in the country-specific time-series regressions. Indeed, inclusion of any combinations of these variables in the regressions reduces the power of any estimate of the equation coefficients and weakens the relationship. It seems clear that among the countries of ASEAN, country-specific FDI flows over time are *not* significantly affected by the simple existence of foreign investment laws, by their particular incentives, or by their deterrent provisions.

The only significant effect of the individual FIL-content variables (FIL1, FIL2, FIL3) seems to be across countries, as a discriminator for steering foreign direct investment into one country or another within ASEAN. Best estimates of the cross-country relationship with the four individual FIL variables forced into it are overwhelmingly dominated by PCI as the single most significant factor. Incentives (FIL2) have the expected positive effect, although FIL1 and FIL3 seem to exert perverse effects, while FIL4 and BIT lose their significance:

$$FDI = -85 - 713FIL1 + 46FIL2 + 225FIL3 + 114MIA + 0.1PCI. \tag{A}$$

Goodness of fit is 76%, with a regression standard error of 270. Coefficient standard errors are: FIL1 = 168; FIL2 = 21; FIL3 = 43; MIA = 6; PCI = 0.006.

When the dominance of the control variable (PCI) is absent, BIT replaces MIA as the only significant diplomatic factor, and FIL4 remains insignificant. Individual FIL-content variables, even when significant, show poor correlation with FDI flows; FIL2 is positive and FIL3 is negative as expected; the influence of FIL1, however unexpectedly varies:

$$FDI = -19 - 125FIL1 + 63FIL2 - 123FIL3 + 132BIT. \tag{B}$$
Goodness of fit is only 42%, with a regression standard error of 419. Coefficient standard errors are: FIL1 = 246; FIL2 = 34; FIL3 = 58; BIT = 14.

$$FDI = -29 + 49FIL2 - 140FIL3 + 129BIT \tag{C}$$
Goodness of fit is only 42%, with a regression standard error of 418. Coefficient standard errors are: FIL2 = 18; FIL3 = 48; BIT = 12.

$$FDI = -21 - 418FIL1 + 77FIL2 + 130BIT \tag{D}$$
Goodness of fit is only 40%, with a regression standard error of 423. Coefficient standard errors are: FIL1 = 205; FIL3 = 34; BIT = 14

Investment Agreements and Treaties

In each country-specific time series, the pair of variables MIA and BIT jointly has a notably large influence on FDI. The bilateral investment treaty seems to be the most powerful of the legal instruments available to host governments. Bilateral investment treaties influence FDI only after a delay, but their weight in determining flows is large. Although treaty provisions are often incorporated into foreign investment law, it may be that MNE are more comfortable in relying on international law, and on the treaty-enforcement power of home governments for guarantees and rights, than on host national law. While these speculations can only be tentative, they are neither counterintuitive nor in conflict with available evidence.

In the cross-country regression, the coefficient of MIA is positive and large, while BIT is insignificant. This unexpected anomaly suggests that MIA may be a discriminator among countries, while also a positive determinant of FDI flows into the region. Another possibility is that multinational enterprises give different weight to different multilateral investment agreements (this study accords equal weight to each). Accession to some MIA may be a prerequisite for substantial FDI flows into any country. Since this effect is permanent, additional MIA become redundant in an investment decision, once a target country has been identified, and simply increase the correlation by coincidence. It may also be that the signals sent by exclusively regional MIA, which granted preferences to local competitors of extraregional investors, were discouraging to multinational sources of FDI.[31]

Previous Flows of FDI

While this variable could not be tested in the cross-country procedure, in the time-series, lagged FDI had a weak positive effect. Previous levels of FDI were a significant influence on current FDI flows only in the regression estimates for Indonesia and Malaysia. Elsewhere lagged FDI did not influence current flows significantly. This equivocal result does not allow a strong conclusion about any hysteresis, or "follow-the-leader" effect involving FDI. Nor does the *assumption* of geometrically declining effects of previous FDI flows over time allow a conclusion that high FDI flows in one year will affect flows in the next year. While this equivocal result may arise from assumptions and technical idiosyncrasies of the study, it is, however, intuitively comfortable, economically rational, and politically realistic to expect that multinational investment decisions include considerations of previous FDI.

Some Implications of the ASEAN Experience

Foreign investment laws have operated as instruments for managing foreign direct investment within the development strategies of the ASEAN countries. These countries have generally accepted bilateral investment treaties initiated by investor countries, and appear to have used multilateral investment agreements as political instruments of foreign policy. Consistent with practices of other host nations, this pattern may have been conditioned by the pervasive networks of patron-client dependencies operated by the superpowers during the Cold War. Acceptance of "client" status may have reduced the salience of international relations, and (as Mullins speculated) focused leaders' attention on domestic development. Profound structural changes undoubtedly occurred, as predicted by both Kuznets and Chenery and Syrquin (see Appendix I), although this analysis can only speculate about the relative impacts of FDI, "client status," and domestic decisions. By accepting a "client" status that reduced the salience of international relations and the urgency of national security (as Mullins speculated[32]), leaders of the ASEAN countries seem to have been able to focus their attention primarily on managing the development process.

As orthodoxy would expect, foreign direct investment in the ASEAN countries has been clearly affected by legislative stability and change in foreign investment law, although the negative influence of legislative stability is unexpected, and opens new questions for further work. The most powerful influence seems to have been a supportive relationship between host nation and home country (manifested in bilateral investment treaties). A third influence has been national acceptance of international legal norms in multilateral investment agreements, which seem to be important in determining amounts and directions of foreign direct investment flows. Further, as expected, previous levels of foreign direct investment may operate in some countries—possibly through adaptive expectations—to influence current and future flows.

Contrary to popular wisdom, neither the provisions of foreign investment laws nor various sets of investment incentives seem to affect country-specific foreign direct investment flows significantly. Also unexpected is the apparent influence that multilateral investment agreements may exert on investors' decisions to direct foreign direct investment flows toward one country or another.   The relationship between foreign investment law, bilateral investment treaties, and multilateral investment agreements seems far from simple, and deserves further sophisticated investigation. Analysis of foreign investment legislative provisions and interpretation of signals sent by foreign investment legislation and multilateral investment agreements, as received by multinational investors, seem to warrant particular attention.

It is not enough for developing nations simply to want the economic benefits of foreign investment and enact a basic foreign investment law. Chapters 4 and 5 have shown the elemental political-economic relationships between foreign investment, growth, and international conflict. The ASEAN countries' experience has shown powerful—although probably not deliberate, planned, or intended—linkages between host national legislation, diplomacy, and management of foreign direct investment. These linkages, in recursive extension of the lawlike regularities identified in Chapters 4 and 5, show clearly that the effects of host national legislative-diplomatic management of FDI are not limited to accelerating aggregate growth, but operate, as well, to influence international conflict.

The clear implication is the importance of a broad range of changing, flexible policies consistent with both development objectives and international political-economic conditions, as well as some effort at coordinating development strategy with foreign policy.[33] The prosaic domestic routines of drafting and passing legislation, and negotiating investment agreements, have contributed to regional political stability and relative peace among ASEAN nations over the last half-century. Generalization of this narrow result to other regions and countries can suggest a means for virtually every sovereign nation to manage flows of inward foreign direct investment in ways most suitable for its stage of economic development, national purposes, and international political situation. Legislative-diplomatic management of FDI can be a powerful instrument of both national growth and international responsibility: a tool of both peace and prosperity.

SOME THEORETICAL IMPLICATIONS OF THE RESULTS

Each of the orthodox theoretical approaches deserves the respect that it has earned through its service in understanding international relations. The disparity between the lawlike regularities discovered here and the tenets of orthodoxy suggests examining views about the original concepts behind them. Critical reexamination may find that current debates—in ministries and in universities—involve the deaf in one such "unreal" world and the blind in another, both perceiving the "real" world about which they are deeply concerned as if it were that in which their respective orthodoxies were developed. Of particular stridency are the real differences between a world with multinational enterprises that dwarf many sovereign states and another in which several political empires embrace the entire globe. In the latter, war and international conflict were the predominant international processes; they deserved and got theoretical and pragmatic attention.   In another more peaceful world, trade and commercial alternatives to war and conflict deserve similar attention, and usually receive it.

Assault on Orthodoxy

Orthodoxy offers a solid analytical, pedagogical, pragmatic foundation that places thought and debate about policy, international order, economic development, and business firmly into historical and philosophical perspective. Each theoretical approach can rest, however, only on its own premises; when those premises fail or weaken, the approach loses relevance. Its conclusions become increasingly incongruous with experience as both theory and practice struggle to explain anomalies as "special cases."   Multinational enterprise, foreign direct investment, and the salience of dynamic growth present a growing constellation of anomalies that lie beyond the premises of classical orthodoxy.

The clear relationships between FDI, dynamic growth, and their inverse effects on conflict, and between trade, static growth, and their direct effects on conflict lead to a set of propositions that refine Russett's seminal concepts of attributes and total national capabilities (see section "Change in National Attributes" in chapter 3), and distil Mansfield's murky blend of nondeterministic dualism. Expanding Russett's concepts about changes in national attributes into an inchoate operational principle of national choice with dual foci of growth and conflict leads to a multidisciplinary hyphenated political-economic alternative to the traditionally separate orthodoxies of economics and of political science:

> The genesis of international conflict lies in the distribution of attributes and derived capabilities of individual nations, which determines national rank in some international hierarchy and conditions national behaviors.
> Crucial attributes whose variation forcefully affects international conflict include (but are not limited to) growth of population and levels of physical, financial, and technological resources; level of trade in resources and goods and its influence in generating aggregate national growth; rates of increase of knowledge and skills within the society, both through indigenous processes and from foreign sources, and their power to generate aggregate national growth; relative growth in levels of resource-related trade and in knowledge-related FDI with other nations.
> A distinctive, manipulable national pattern of these conflict-related attributes determines the configuration and calculus of domestic political and economic pressures;   mediated by varying blends of static and dynamic economic growth, various combinations of attributes bring different national profiles and different patterns of international behavior.
> The dependence of external national behavior on internal national attributes is neither monotonic nor direct; nor is it uniquely or directly causal; it is a powerful conditioner that may be reinforced, weakened, or canceled by other variables, including human decision-making.

The propositions are inconsistent with classical realism's premise that conflict is inherent and endemic in an anarchic international system. The results in Chapter 4 and the explanations presented in Chapter 5 reject realist notions of a global system comprising predominantly relations among uniform sovereign national states.   An uncomfortable implication exposes the weaknesses in analyses of international relations without reference to the natures of those national states, or accounting for transnational entities. These results overturn the monistic level-of-analysis principle of realism, which weds effects at any level to causes at the same level, by associating systemic effects (international conflict) with national phenomena (growth).[34]   The clear influences of the type of national growth on international conflict and the recursive role of foreign direct investment in dynamic growth compromise the realist notion of simplistic, monistic causality, and mortally wound the realist "billiard-ball-model" of the international political-economy.[35]

In addition to their assaults on classical realism, these results are also generally   incompatible   with   Marxism-Leninism,   and   the   derivative revolutionary approaches to international relations, except perhaps in primitive and preindustrial conditions. They seem broadly inconsistent with views that deemphasize growth-conflict relationships as "by-products" of something else,[36] and reveal status theory,[37] like liberalism, as incomplete.

The propositions are weakly consistent with the classical liberal assertion (revealed as incomplete, but not wrong) that international conflict is inversely related to international economic relationships. The set of propositions rejects the determinism of mercantilism and orthodox liberalism, and even the mechanical spontaneity of Norman Angell or Woodrow Wilson. While not denying idealistic possibilities that man can change reality, disjunction of growth refines the nondeterministic dualism of interdependence theory into a clear, definitive feature of the international political-economy.[38] States can choose their paths for political-economic development, balance costs and benefits, violate the law of uneven growth,[39] and choose between the logic of the trading state[40] and the imperatives of the territorial state. Incorporating the conclusions of Chapters 4 and 5, the propositions seem fully consistent with redefinition of power resources,[41] as well as with most of the various structural[42] and interdependency[43] arguments.

In the context of disjoined growth, dualism, nondeterministic national choice, and hyphenated political-economy, the growth-conflict relationship loses some of its anomalous mystery. The monistic level-of-analysis principle can be retired gracefully, as humanity settles comfortably into the broader relationships linking national attributes and capabilities with international behavior (long a central theme in theory and literature of international relations).[44] Economic growth, however, must be assessed as *two* processes —static and dynamic. In addition to—or possibly instead of—the sorts of political-economic-demographic attributes used by Galtung, Rosenau, Rummel, Russett, and others, the predominant *type* of growth occurring in a country, with the relative salience of its precursor trade or FDI, is a distinctive, critical attribute of any modern nation, with a clear link to international conflict, and probably also to other international behaviors.

The lawlike regularities discovered in this study have sufficient salience in international affairs—whether political or economic—that they can no longer be dismissed as anomalies. They are well on the way to establishing a new "real-world" orthodoxy in which classical realism and liberalism, as well as the traditional "radical" approaches and many of the "neo"-approaches are anomalous. Policy science and historians can choose to deal with the new "real" world in a journalistic sort of crisis management. Theory cannot long do so; it needs a new orthodoxy without anomalies.

Some New Concerns

A fundamental premise of classical realism, as well as "Waltzian" neorealism, was that only sovereign national states were involved politically, and that cross-border economic transactions occurred at the sufferance of national states.[45] Even liberal systems allow only Westphalian states, although many of the "neo"-schools recognize that other entities have legitimate roles. While recognizing the significance of cooperation and commerce, orthodoxy accepted that the essentially conflictual, or competitive, relationships between national states are regulated ultimately by national political-military power. In a more mellow "interdependency" approach, Robert Gilpin echoes Organski and Kugler, as well as Kuznets, and other analysts, in noting that even in the orthodox realist world, national power rests ultimately on each nation's separate industrial and economic base. The results of this study, in contrast to both orthodoxy and interdependency, imply a significant influence not only for national economic power, but for a nation's *type of growth*, and a significant role for FDI, in international relationships, *which may be independent of national political-military power*. By introducing powerful interdependence among heterogeneous nation-states and nonsovereign multinational enterprises, dynamic growth severely weakens the realist paradigm of homogeneous nation-states in an eternal struggle for survival.

Enriching the orthodox conceptual models of economic growth as a homogeneous dependent variable, and reformulating the growth-conflict relationship along dual paths, allow refinement of orthodoxy into a powerful notion of understanding growth and conflict. Perhaps most critical is understanding dynamic growth, mediated by foreign direct investment, as a major political-economic force. Dynamic growth, which need not rely on an indigenous engine, extends the international liberal paradigm to include developmental market capitalism and hierarchic, paternal government, with significant state intervention in economic planning and transactions. For dependency theory the transition to dynamic growth explains how to replace inevitable conflict and permanent exploitation with a real possibility for growth out of dependency. Dynamic growth and interdependence obviate many of the cumbersome structural typologies invented by development economics to rationalize differences in patterns of growth and conflict over time and across countries.

In addition to inconsistency with orthodox concepts of national power, these results have a profound, if subtle, effect on theories of interdependence in a puzzling paradox, reminiscent of Raymond Vernon's "obsolescing bargain" argument.[46]   As modern industrial core nations have expanded into agrarian periphery nations, the latter have developed industrial bases, which increased their national political power, but also bound home countries, through transnational networks of FDI and trade, in economic interdependence with host nations.   The process also creates a new sort of dependency of multinational enterprises—and core investors—on host governments for earnings, resources, and any other benefits involved.

The gradual shifts in the balances of power and the deepening of interdependence, as FDI animated host nation growth, have created new types of vulnerabilities in core states, in addition to those always felt by periphery states.   Although ultimately related to growth—or its absence—these can exacerbate any noneconomic international tensions, stimulate competition, and possibly lead to conflict.   Foreign direct investment is not, of course, the primary cause of this shift in the balance (or imbalance) of power—either among nations or from core to periphery—but it "both accelerates this tendency and tends to abort any effort to reinvigorate the core's industrial base."[47]

Competition among governments has historically been a prominent precursor to international conflict.   Just as governments have historically competed, and even gone to war, about trade, they are learning to compete both for and about FDI.   Trade competition has involved import barriers, subsidies, industrial policies, imitation of successful policies, and other clever techniques to distort commercial competition to the advantage of one country. Investment competition involves clear analogues in foreign investment laws and treaties, preferential or prejudicial taxation, aggressive privatization, structural impediments, deregulation, and even inaction.

Interstate competition for FDI leads governments to monitor, imitate, and refine successful policies of other countries.   Indeed, use of imported ideas for manipulation of policies and regulatory environments as incentives to foreign investors has become a preferred form of intergovernmental competition.[48] Virtually all national states encourage inward investment and location of production facilities within their borders.

Direct investment has made this competition more immediate.   A country which does not enact business-friendly policies risks losing its firms to locations elsewhere through an exodus of direct investment.   Similarly, countries that do not compete actively to attract investment may deprive themselves of vital technologies as well as management and marketing skills.[49]

Robert Reich has suggested that this new sort of FDI-related interstate competition operates within an expanding paradigm of transnational production by multinational enterprises. Reich postulates that a global production model is replacing that of the national economic base,[50] and implies that autonomous multinational enterprises are replacing national corporate "champions" as relevant objects for national policy.

A Refined Image

While Kenneth Waltz's three images of international relations probably reflected the world as it existed and operated in the early and mid-twentieth century, the lawlike regularities discovered in this study suggest a different —perhaps a fourth—image for the international political-economy of the twenty-first century. In addition to man, the state, and the system, the world now responds to a powerful market, with its own actors—firms, corporations, multinational enterprises—that involve, affect, include, and exclude the actors and processes in each of Waltz's images. The most powerful of these new actors—the multinational enterprises—and the process that can accompany them—dynamic growth—are exogenous to, yet penetrate into, each of the three "Waltzian images." Nor is war still the most significant relationship among global actors; economic growth has assumed primacy for many actors in each of Waltz's images, and for all actors in a putative fourth market-based image.

Whether the lawlike regularities presented here are a fourth Waltzian image or a version of what James Rosenau has called "postinternational politics,"[51] they demand understanding by scholars, politicians, officials, and business executives. Both politics and economics color this image. Modern economic growth comprises traditional static elements that favor conflict, and modern dynamic elements that inhibit conflict. National socio-political-economic transformations change the contributions of each to aggregate growth. Although noneconomic sources of conflict persist in the presence of either type of growth, nations experiencing increasing proportions of dynamic growth to aggregate growth have lower incentives to enter conflict, and less need for international security regimes to control conflict. It is not unreasonable to speculate, however, a corresponding and increasing requirement for international commercial regimes, not limited to sovereign national states, to manage it.

Countries rely on static growth to accumulate existing economic resources—including in modern economies the resource of information—through trade, commerce, or other voluntary exchanges, and potentially through theft, conquest, or coercive transfers. Static growth increases absolute wealth, measured by GDP; trade and conquest sustain those increases by obtaining additional resources. Redistributions of resources and wealth, and ensuing changes in relative power among nations, are explicit sources of international conflict.

Dynamic growth entails creation and application of new, additional knowledge—not just accumulation of more information—which inhibits conflict by expanding limits on physical factors of production, and by creating robust reciprocal political-economic interdependence. It increases standards of living, measured by PCI; foreign direct investment sustains those increases by broadening national capabilities to create new intellectual capital. Diffusion of knowledge, and potential convergence of standards-of-living, tend to inhibit international conflict.

In contrast to the engine of static growth—more resources—the fundamental engines of modern dynamic growth—knowledge and innovation—are no longer purely national resources as they have historically been in the orthodox realist-referent model, which favored static growth. Knowledge has become a global resource, and innovation, a global dynamic, diffused and mediated primarily by multinational enterprises through foreign direct investment. While static growth is primarily a national phenomenon, dynamic growth is becoming an international phenomenon in an increasingly diverse international political-economy.

Simultaneous experiences of static and dynamic growth—not merely differences in aggregate growth rates—in different countries exacerbated differences in national attributes and induced conflict in a Kuznetsian, classical, homogeneous world system. Their effects in a heterogenous, interdependent system are dramatically different. While static growth retains many of its conflictual features, dynamic growth allows nations to migrate from the *inter*national system to the *trans*national (or Rosenau's *post*international[52]) system. As knowledge-based growth gains prominence over resource-based growth diminishes, its positive-sum tendencies toward convergence reduce the resource-based urgencies and conflictual effects of static growth. As the relationships of national states expand to involve other types of systemic actors, the dual focus of governments on *inter*national affairs (diplomacy, war) and *non*national business (trade, litigation) broadens to include *trans*- and *extra*national relationships that are closely related to purely national concerns. Foreign direct investment between national states and multinational firms epitomizes the former; interfirm strategic alliances exemplify the latter. In this emerging system of diverse relationships among heterogeneous actors, international conflict depends not simply on the incidence or rate of growth, but on the type of growth, as well as any exogenous political stimuli or security regimes.

The growth-conflict relationship necessarily varies over time, as a single country progresses along its growth path. It differs dramatically at any single time across countries at different points on their separate growth paths. In the modern interdependent world, it is probably not possible—and certainly not prudent—for a country to seek only one sort of growth. It seems to be the ability to shift from one sort to the other that allows nations to determine whether peace or prosperity—or neither or both—will occur. The duality of the relationship itself, and of the growth process that originates it, creates and resolves the paradox that confounds orthodoxy: growth can both induce and inhibit conflict.

Although this study can offer only an image of the vastly complex growth-conflict relationship, some specific propositions and corollaries about the relationship include:[53]

> The contribution of dynamic growth to aggregate growth influences the national level of international conflict.
>> Where dynamic growth is low, even if static growth and trading interdependence are high, conflict is probable; a robust international security regime is necessary to minimize international conflict.
>> Where dynamic growth is high, conflict is improbable; political-economic interdependence minimizes international conflict, even in absence of an international security regime.
> Levels of international trade can reflect the contribution of static growth to aggregate growth.
>> Trade levels reflect the urgency of national need to continue aggregate growth beyond levels that can be sustained by domestic resources.
> Types, flows and stocks of foreign direct investment can determine the contribution of dynamic growth to aggregate growth.
>> Host nation policies and choices affect levels of foreign direct investment within parameters set in home countries and the global economy.

SOME FINAL THOUGHTS

This study has raised, suggested, and perhaps ignored as many questions and issues as it has addressed. Identifying the powerful lawlike regularity relating economic growth to international conflict, exposing the complex dualities of the growth-conflict relationship and of the growth process, and revealing the criticality of FDI have made it clear that neither economics nor political science, nor even business or commerce, can continue to ignore that relationship. It is real. It is powerful. It is persistent and pervasive. It extends beyond both political science and economics, and intrudes deeply into business theory and policy-making. It involves diplomacy, commerce, law, and war. But most important, it lies well within the combined capabilities of economists, political scientists, politicians, and industrialists to manage, to control, and even to exploit it. Economics, political science, international relations, and business theory must recognize the growth-conflict relationship as a prominent dynamic of the "real" international political-economy in which policy-makers operate, with possibly more relevance to the future of humanity than growth, conflict, profit, or markets, as individual phenomena.

The ASEAN results confirm the criticality and power of FDI in development and growth processes. Effective management of FDI seems able to accelerate the shift from static toward dynamic growth with its accompanying inverse growth-conflict relationship. In the amazing world of *both* multinationals and countries sharing both power and wealth, this unique political-economic process may be at least a part of the key to sustained prosperity and general peace.

Collaboration, in addition to competition, among and between national states and multinational enterprises can bring the full potential of national and multinational power to bear not only on national interests and corporate profits, but on the host of insistent problems that continue to vex mankind. Deliberate management of foreign direct investment by *both* government and industry, with deepening political-economic awareness of its effects on *both* growth and conflict, may provide the key to the sustainable peace and prosperity that neither has been able to bring alone.

NOTES

1. Richard N. Haass, "Paradigm Lost," *Foreign Affairs* 74 (January/February 1995): 43.

2. See M. Castells, "High Technology, Economic Restructuring, and the Urban-regional Process in the United States," *High Technology, Space and Society* (Urban Affairs Annual Reviews), 28 (1985): 11-40.

3. The universe of modern economic growth is barely a sixth of the world's countries; these results say nothing at all about most of the world's countries and peoples. The mean correlations presented in Chapter 4 imply only that conflict and growth are related more often than not; any linkage between them is associational, not causal. The relationship between types of growth and types of relationships shown in Chapter 4 is a lawlike regularity, not a law.

4. It is easy to forget that annual growth of 0.8% was seen as virtually impossible in the seventeenth century. Historical comparisons suggest that countries that began modern economic growth in the presence of other countries that had already grown, have grown faster than their predecessors. The first country to experience MEG, Britain shifted toward dynamic growth over more than two centuries. After a century of annual growth at about 0.3%, from 1780 Britain took 58 years to double real income *per capita*, and led the Industrial Revolution (1830-1910) with annual growth of about 1.2%. In 1820, as the United States was entering MEG before industrial expansion, GDP *per capita* in the United States was about three-quarters that of Britain. Annual growth of the American economy from 1830 to 1910 was about 1.6% (GDP grew at 4.2%, but population also grew rapidly). From 1839 the United States took only 39 years to double income *per capita* at about 1.8% annually, and by the 1890s was the world's richest country. After the Meiji reforms, from 1885, with increasing influences from the advanced countries of the time, Japan took 34 years to double GDP *per capita* at an annual rate of about 2%. From 1966 South Korea, with deliberate solicitation of FDI, took 11 years to double GDP *per capita* at about 6.3% annual growth.

5. "When Nations Play Leapfrog," *The Economist*, 329 (16 October 1993): 84.

6. In recognizing the separate results of Cattell and Rummel (see section on "Status-field Theory, Chapter 3) as mutually supporting, the analysis accepts the premise that domestic conflict is not a significant explanation for international conflict, and may confidently be omitted from statistical consideration.
Raymond B. Cattell, "The Dimensions of Cultural Patterns by Factorization of National Characters," *Journal of Abnormal and Social Psychology* 64 (1949): 443-469;

Rudolph J. Rummel, "Dimensions of Domestic Conflict Behavior: Review of Findings," in Dean Pruitt & Robert Snyder, eds., *Theories of International Conflict* (Englewood Cliffs, New Jersey: Prentice-Hall, 1969).

7. Within a broadly heterogeneous regional culture, they all have a single dominant ethnic group and several minority groups. They all began the postwar period with large unskilled labor forces, low costs of production, and significant stocks of historic foreign direct investment. Each inherited an aging infrastructure from a dominant preindependence (prewar for historically independent Thailand) metropolitan source.

8. Although this study does not focus narrowly on either economic growth or international conflict, this spectrum of both variables across the regional sample could lend some generality to regional findings.

9. These anomalies may be statistical artifacts reflecting the absence of viable war regressions for Singapore, and the relatively small size of the sample.

10. Of the 30 countries in the universe of MEG, 21 showed the expected pairings (static-parallel; dynamic-inverse).

11. Most early clashes arose over "concession agreements" allowing MNEs to exploit natural resources, which were particularly distressing to host countries. For a pointed legal analysis of these so-called economic development agreements, see Lord McNair's summary opinion: D. P. O'Connell, *The Law of State Succession* (Cambridge: Cambridge University Press, 1956). In their seminal political-economic study, Thomas Gladwin and Ingo Walter analyzed over 650 conflicts involving foreign direct investment by only five multinational investors (Dow Chemical, Gulf Oil, International Telephone & Telegraph, F. Hoffman-La Roche, and Rio Tinto-Zinc) over a decade. The authors conclude that such conflict is complex, diverse, pervasive, increasing, and particularly subject to escalation and mismanagement. Thomas Gladwin & Ingo Walter *Multinationals Under Fire* (New York: John Wiley, 1980).

12. See Raymond Vernon, *Sovereignty at Bay* (New York: Basic Books, 1971); Raymond Vernon, "The Obsolescing Bargain: A Key Factor in Political Risk," in Mark B. Winchester, *The International Essays for Business Decision Makers*, Vol. 5 (Houston: Center for International Business, 1980); Theodore H. Moran, *Multinational Corporations and the Politics of Dependence* (Princeton, New Jersey: Princeton University Press, 1974).

13. Data are cumulative inflows of foreign direct investment in constant American dollars over the period 1970-1989. International Monetary Fund, *International Financial Statistics Yearbook* (Washington, D.C.: International Monetary Fund, 1994).

14. Texts of foreign investment laws and related legislation for the ASEAN countries are in: International Centre for the Settlement of Investment Disputes, "Individual Country Supplements," in *Investment Laws of the World* (Dobbs Ferry, New York: Oceana Publications, 1991).

15. Indonesia has historically stressed tax incentives through exemptions and reductions for FDI projects provided by amendments to the Foreign Capital Investment Law (1967) and the Corporate Tax Law (1925); in 1986 Indonesia exempted imported capital items and inputs for FDI projects. In its Investment Incentives Act (1968), as amended, Malaysia emphasizes tax relief as its primary investment incentive, although various laws also provide for free trade zones, accelerated depreciation, and investment tax credits. The Philippines Promotion of Investments Act (1968) provides a host of tax credits and exemptions to FDI projects, including exemptions on imported capital equipment. Singapore does not distinguish between FDI and domestic investment, but

provides tax incentives to all "pioneer industries"; Singapore has eliminated tariffs on nearly all items. Thailand's revisions of the Industrial Investment Act (1960) provide both tax benefits and exemptions from import duties on capital goods and raw input materials.

16. Perhaps most ambitious of third generation countries is Taiwan with its "Plan to Develop Taiwan as an Asia-Pacific Regional Operations Center" involving legislative revision of regulations and incentives to create incentives for research, develop selected "high-tech" and "high-value-added" industries, establish 20-30 "intelligent industrial parks," expand functions of export processing zones, restructure the Chung Shan Institute of Science and Technology, commercialize defense technology, consolidate technical investment management, and promote large industrial investment projects. Chi-Ming Yin, "Industry in the Republic of China: A Tale of Transformation," *Scientific American* 273(4) (October 1995): T24-T26. Singapore has found the concept so successful that it has adopted legislation to export scientific-industrial parks to China, India, Indonesia, and Vietnam, on the model of the Batamindo Industrial Estate, its joint venture industrial park with Indonesia. Louis Kraar, "Need a Friend in Asia? Try the Singapore Connection," *Fortune*, 133(4) (4 March 1996): 172-183.

17. Texts of the Bilateral Investment Treaties of the ASEAN countries are in respective country sections of International Centre for the Settlement of Investment Disputes, "Investment Promotion and Protection Treaties," in *Investment Laws of the World* (New York: Oceana Publications, 1991).

18. Indonesia acceded to the Paris Convention for the Protection of Industrial Property in 1950; only in 1967 did the New Order Government recognize economic development as a national goal. Although the Royal Thai government had promoted economic development and implemented various development policies well before World War II, these efforts were not coordinated in a formal national development plan. Thailand acceded to the New York Convention on Recognition and Enforcement of Foreign Arbitral Awards in 1959, and introduced the First National Economic Development Plan in 1961.

19. Annual FDI data, continuous in millions of American real dollars, are available in annual editions of International Monetary Fund, *International Financial Statistics Yearbook*.

20. Definition and coding of these variables (part of the "specification" of the regression) are technically parts of the test hypothesis. Results of the regression process may either confirm or refute these definitions and the coding processes.

21. Adoption of this intuitive aggregation is technically a part of the test hypothesis to be confirmed or refuted by the regression process.

22. Like FDI data, annual PCI data are available directly in annual editions of International Monetary Fund, *International Financial Statistics Yearbook*.

23. Because FDI investors are not expected to have access to host-national diplomatic or military documents of state, data for the CNF variable are coded from open sources and reflect journalistic reports of international events. Summaries of press coverage of wars and nonwar conflicts are in annual volumes of *New York Times Index*, *Keesing's Contemporary Archives*, *Facts on File*, *Deadline Data*, etc. It is clear that domestic host-nation conflict and specific bilateral conflicts between home countries may affect FDI decisions by affected firms. At this initial level of broad analytical generality in seeking lawlike regularities, rather than explanations, the specificity of these types of conflicts to particular FDI decisions and projects limits their relevance. Each of these types of

conflict, as well as investor access to privileged information, deserves full analysis in case studies of particular projects, nations, or investors.

24. Nothing in lawlike regularity or the regression process assigns causality. These results do *not* say that FIL, BIT, or MIA caused FDI to occur, prevented its occurrence, or even that ASEAN governments intended to influence FDI. The analytical processes demonstrate only the existence of relationships between legal-diplomatic variables and FDI.

25. A statistically significant coefficient is at least twice as large as its standard error. The probability (determined through the ordinary least-squares regression procedure) that the relationship between it and the dependent variable (FDI flow) is not due to chance is greater than 95%. An independent variable is significant in a regression equation, and exerts a significant influence on the dependent variable, if its coefficient is statistically significant.

26. The correlation coefficient (R^2) measures the goodness of fit between the estimated equation and the observed data, as the proportion (from 0 to 1) of the variance in FDI that is explained by the independent variables. A low value of a correlation coefficient ($R^2 < 0.4$) indicates a weak relationship between the variables; a high correlation ($R^2 > 0.6$) indicates a strong relationship.

27. The Geometric Model of Lag associates change in a dependent variable with unit change in an independent variable. Changes in independent variables are permanent. Weights of lagged independent variables are all positive, less than 1, and decline geometrically with time.

28. The Adaptive Expectations Model uses the ratio of expected change in the relevant independent variable (FIL4 in this case) to its actual change (designated as θ) to weight its own coefficient (by multiplying), and the coefficient of the lagged dependent variable (FDI_{t-1}) (multiplying by [1-θ]). This weighting factor is also, along with the "other factors," incorporated into the regression as an additional predictor, usually represented by the letter C in a regression equation.

29. This assumption allows aggregation of the effects of all previous flows into those of last year's flows in FDI_{t-1}.

30. The coefficients of changes in these variables are at least twice as large as their standard errors, and the probability that the relationship is not due to chance is greater than 95%.

31. The ASEAN nations created the Basic Agreement on ASEAN Industrial Joint Ventures (1983) and the Agreement for Promotion and Protection of Investments (1987). These regional MIA tacitly exclude non-ASEAN firms from their terms.

32. A. F. Mullins, Jr., *Born Arming: Development and Military Power in New States* (Stanford, California: Stanford University Press, 1987).

33. The evolution of development strategies and foreign-investment-legislative styles through a series of stages, as reflected in changes in the legal-diplomatic variables over time (Maurice Flory, *Droit international du développement* [Paris: Presses Universitaires, 1977]), seems an additional critical national developmental process that is clearly linked to flows of foreign direct investment.

34. Kenneth Waltz's "neo"-concept of realism recognizes this weakness. He concludes that "so fundamental are man, the state, and the state system in any attempt to understand international relations that seldom does an analyst, however wedded to one image, entirely overlook the other two." Kenneth N. Waltz, *Man, the State and War: A Theoretical Analysis* (New York: Columbia University Press, 1954), 160.

35. Jürg Martin Gabriel, *Worldviews and Theories of International Relations* (New York: St. Martin's Press, 1994), 7.

36. Edward D. Mansfield, *Power, Trade, and War* (Princeton, New Jersey: Princeton University Press, 1994), 232.

37. Johann Galtung, "A Structural Theory of Aggression," *Journal of Peace Research* 1(2) (1964): 95-119; Rudolph J. Rummel "US Foreign Relations: Conflict, Cooperation, and Attribute Distances," in Bruce M. Russett, ed., *Peace, War, and Numbers* (Beverly Hills, California: Sage Publications, 1972).

38. Interdependence theory holds that *both* the distribution of political-military capabilities *and* trade explain the incidence of conflict, and that the relationship between trade and the frequency of war is inverse. See Mansfield, *Power, Trade, and War*, esp. 233; see also Jacob Viner, "Peace as an Economic Problem," in Jacob Viner, *International Economics* (Glencoe, Illinois: Free Press, 1991); Robert O. Keohane & Joseph S. Nye, Jr., *Power and Interdependence: World Politics in Transition* (Boston: Little, Brown, 1977); Robert O. Keohane & Joseph S. Nye, Jr., "*Power and Interdependence* Revisited," *International Organization* 41 (1987): 725-753; Richard N. Rosecrance, *The Rise of the Trading State: Commerce and Conquest in the Modern world* (New York: Basic Books, 1986); Joseph S. Nye, Jr., "Neorealism and Neoliberalism," *World Politics* 40 (1988): 235-251; and James N. Rosenau, "Global Changes and Theoretical Challenges: Toward a Postinternational Politics for the 1990s," in Ernst-Otto Czempiel & James N. Rosenau, eds., *Global Changes and Theoretical Challenges: Approaches to World Politics for the 1990s* (Lexington, Massachusetts: Lexington Books, 1989), esp. 2.

39. Simon Kuznets, *Modern Economic Growth* (New Haven, Connecticut: Yale University Press, 1966); Robert Gilpin, *War and Change in World Politics* (Cambridge: Cambridge University Press, 1981).

40. Rosecrance, *The Rise of the Trading State*.

41. Norman Angell, *The Great Illusion: A Study of the Relationship of Military Power in Nations to Their Economic and Social Advantage* (London: Weidenfeld & Nicholson, 1910); Nazli Choucri & Robert C. North, *Nations in Conflict* (San Francisco: W.H. Freeman, 1974); A.F.K. Organski & Jacek Kugler, *The War Ledger* (Chicago: University of Chicago Press, 1980).

42. Kenneth N. Waltz, *Theory of International Politics* (Reading: Massachusetts: Addison-Wesley, 1979); Rummel, "US Foreign Relations: Conflict, Cooperation, and Attribute Distances."

43. Robert Gilpin, *The Political Economy of International Relations* (Princeton, New Jersey: Princeton University Press, 1987); Keohane & Nye, "*Power and Interdependence* Revisited"; Mansfield, *Power, Trade, and War*.

44. Raymond Aron, *Peace and War* (New York: Frederick A. Praeger, 1967); A.F.K. Organski, *World Politics*, 2d ed. (New York: Alfred A. Knopf, 1968); P. Renouvin & J. B. Duroselle, *Introduction to the History of International Relations* (New York: Frederick A. Praeger, 1967); Richard N. Rosecrance, *Action and Reaction in World Politics* (Boston: Little, Brown, 1963); Quincy Wright, *A Study of War*, 2d ed. (Chicago: University of Chicago Press, 1965).

45. Orthodox political science respects generally the realist model of international relations, in which political conflict and war are the central issues between sovereign nation-states. The primary purpose of international relations and diplomacy is, thus, to maintain order in the relations between states. See Hedley Bull, *The Anarchical*

Society: A Study of Order in World Politics (London: Macmillan, 1977); Bruce Miller, *The World of States* (London: Croom Helm, 1981); Joseph Frankel, *International Politics, Conflict and Harmony* (London: Penguin, 1969). The basic unit of analysis is the sovereign nation-state, and the purpose of analysis is to study the behaviors of states and determine the results of their behavior for the states: more or less wealth, more or less powerful, more or less secure.

46. Vernon, *Sovereignty at Bay*, 47; see also Vernon, "The Obsolescing Bargain: A Key Factor in Political Risk." Progressive obsolescence of the FDI bargain between a multinational enterprise (MNE) and a host-national (HN) government reduces the benefits of the FDI project for the HN and increases the costs. Fixed capital becomes "sunk" and hostage to the HN government. As risk of research, development, or exploration decreases when production begins, and the technology involved matures, becomes available on the open market, and loses value, power begins to shift to the host nation. The HN gains technological and managerial skills that reduce the relative values of those of the MNE. The MNE bargaining power decreases significantly as management of the enterprise by host country nationals becomes practicable. "The number of readily available alternative sources [of technology, capital, or other resources] increases and there is a direct transfer and diffusion of technology and management to host country nationals."
Stephen J. Kobrin, "Foreign Enterprise and Forced Divestment in LDCs," in Benjamin Gomes-Casseres & David B. Yoffie, eds., *The International Political Economy of Direct Foreign Investment*, Vol. II (Brookfield, Vermont: Edward Elgar, 1993), 112.

"[T]he country starts to move up a learning curve that leads from monitoring industry behavior to replicating complicated corporate functions."
Moran, *Multinational Corporations and the Politics of Dependence*, 164.

47. Robert Gilpin, "The Political Economy of Foreign Investment," in Robert Gilpin, *US Power and the Multinational Corporation* (New York: Basic Books, 1975), reprinted in Gomes-Casseres & Yoffie, eds., *The International Political Economy of Direct Foreign Investment*, 274.

48. Thomsen and Woolcock have, however, found surprising evidence that "the role of policies is often exaggerated. Firms are not so much engaging in regulatory arbitrage as responding to the competitors' actions": Stephen Thomsen & Stephen Woolcock, *Direct Investment and European Integration: Competition Among Firms and Governments* (London: Pinter Publishers for the Royal Institute of International Affairs, 1993), 99. Only areas that affect size and structure of capital markets showed any correlation of policies with flows of foreign investment.

49. Thomsen & Woolcock, *Direct Investment and European Integration: Competition Among Firms and Governments*, 8.

50. Robert Reich, "Who is 'Them'?," *Harvard Business Review* (March-April 1991): 77-88.

51. Rosenau, "Global Changes and Theoretical Challenges: Toward a Postinternational Politics for the 1990s," 2.

52. Rosenau, "Global Changes and Theoretical Challenges: Toward a Postinternational Politics for the 1990s," 2.

53. An additional corollary about a domestic polity is indirectly related to the growth-conflict relationship. In a heterogeneous international political-economy, a liberal democratic domestic polity is sufficient, but not necessary, and some form of market capitalism is necessary, but not sufficient, to generate dynamic growth. A stable combination of political and economic liberalism can generate dynamic growth.

A national emphasis on liberal democracy probably has much value for addressing political and ideological sources of international conflict exogenous to the growth-conflict relationship.   Its primary relevance for economic growth-related sources of international conflict lies in its historic power to energize the slow acceleration of growth rates as a society creates its own indigenous, novel base of knowledge and technology for transition to dynamic growth.   The only modern nations that have followed this path are Britain, France, and perhaps Sweden or the Netherlands. Ancient Greece, China, Zimbabwe, and the Meso-American civilizations may have experienced variations of this effect.   Importation of knowledge and technology bases by other modern nations beginning modern economic growth obviated their economic need for liberal democracy.

Appendix A: On Economic Stagnation

In his formidable 1942 *A Study of War*, Quincy Wright noticed that states with high standards of living seemed somewhat less likely than poor states to initiate war.[1] Nearly 40 years later Ruth Leger Sivard made a similar observation in noting that of more than 120 cases of armed conflict between 1955 and 1979, all but six involved poor states.[2] These observations, and other anecdotal coincidences, have suggested that economic stagnation, or negative growth, may generate international conflict as governments deliberately go to war to distract dissatisfied populations from domestic economic torpor.

Another suggestion is that economic recession or depression may lead populations to impute their economic difficulties to foreign sources, and into war or conflict in an effort to remove those foreign causes, or to revenge them.[3] Still another persuasive assertion is that the political instability induced by economic poverty is the necessary condition awaiting sufficient excuse to go to war—either civil, revolutionary, or interstate. While these, and other similar, propositions may appeal to public intuition and some ideologies, the dearth of historical evidence, and the obvious expenses of war and international conflict, combine to discredit the suggestion that sustained international conflict is systematically linked to economic stagnation, or depression.[4]

It may indeed be heuristic to investigate the proposition that economic stagnation is related to international conflict. A systematic relationship, however, between economic growth and conflict seems not only more relevant to apparent global trends, but more useful in identifying manipulable factors that decision-makers can use to pursue the goals of avoiding conflict while encouraging growth. In addition, it seems plausible to consider cases of recession, depression, and stagnation simply as instances of "negative" or "zero" growth, which would be included in any lawlike generality about growth and conflict.

NOTES

1. Quincy Wright, *A Study of War* (Chicago: University of Chicago Press, 1942).

2. Ruth Leger Sivard, *World Military and Social Expenditures 1979* (Leesburg, Virginia: World Priorities, 1979).

3. Robert Gilpin, *The Political Economy of International Relations* (Princeton, New Jersey: Princeton University Press, 1987), 57; see also G. Lagos, *International Stratification and Underdeveloped Countries* (Chapel Hill: University of North Carolina Press, 1963).

4. Simon Kuznets, *Modern Economic Growth* (New Haven, Connecticut: Yale University Press, 1966), 344-345; Raymond Aron, *The Century of Total War* (Boston: Beacon Press, 1955), 17-22; See also Samuel P. Huntington, "Arms Races: Prerequisites and Results," in Robert J. Art & Kenneth N. Waltz, eds., *The Use of Force: Military Power and International Politics*, 3d ed. (Lanham, Maryland: University Press of America, 1988), 637-670; Rudolph J. Rummel, *The Dimensions of Nations* (Beverly Hills, California: Sage Publications, 1972); A.F.K. Organski & Jacek Kugler, *The War Ledger* (Chicago: University of Chicago Press, 1980); Nazli Choucri & Robert C. North *Nations in Conflict* (San Francisco: W.H. Freeman, 1974), 26-43.

Appendix B: On the Three Traditions

Martin Wight identified three main historical approaches to thinking about international relations: realism, rationalism, and revolutionism. He classified their respective ideas, notions, and concepts into three distinct "traditions," each with its distinctive political and economic aspects[1]:

> Realists, or Machiavellians [Bacon, Hobbes, Richelieu, Frederick the Great, Napoleon, Bismarck, E. H. Carr], who emphasize the anarchical aspects of international politics: "sovereign states acknowledging no political superior, whose relationships are ultimately regulated by war."
>
> Rationalists, or Grotians [Aristotle, Acquinas, Locke, Burke, Madison, de Tocqueville, Gladstone, Lincoln, Churchill], who stress "diplomacy and commerce" and institutions for "continuous and organized intercourse between these sovereign states."
>
> Revolutionists, or Kantians [Rousseau, Kant, Mazzini, Wilson, Cobden, Bright, Marx, Mao], who rely on a "concept of a society of states, or family of nations," in pursuit of an imperative vision of the unity of mankind.[2]

To be faithful to history, Wight recognized several subcategories, and even noted some anomalies. He distinguished "soft" revolutionaries, with some sort of gradual, legal, peaceful approach to revolution (Kant, Wilson, Mazzini), from "hard" revolutionaries committed to violence and destruction (the Jacobins, Marxist-Leninists).

Wight also discussed a fourth anomalous sort of thinking, with which he never seemed really comfortable, and did not classify as a separate "tradition." This was the approach taken by a less salient group of thinkers that he called "inverted revolutionists"—"of whom pacifists are the chief, although not the only, example."[3] Intent, like the Quaker religion, on "evoking the latent power of love in all people, and transforming the world by the transformation of souls,"[4] "it is 'inverted' because it repudiates the use of power altogether. It is 'Revolutionist' because it sees this repudiation as a principle of universal validity, and energetically promotes its acceptance."[5]

Wight's triad, unlike Kenneth Waltz's "Three Images,"[6] included war as an ineradicable element in international society within each "tradition." Differences lay in how humanity and nations should deal with it. Waltz, and others[7] have organized alternative taxonomies around the question, "What are the causes of war?" and have deemphasized economic concerns.

NOTES

1. Martin Wight, *International Theory: The Three Traditions*, Gabriele Wight & Brian Porter, eds., (Leicester: Leicester University Press for the Royal Institute of International Affairs, 1991), esp. 7-8, 46-47, 254, 257, 267.

2. Wight, *International Theory: The Three Traditions*, 7-8.

3. Wight, *International Theory: The Three Traditions*, 254.

4. Wight, *International Theory: The Three Traditions*, 257.

5. Wight, *International Theory: The Three Traditions*, 108.

6. Kenneth N. Waltz, *Man, the State and War: A Theoretical Analysis* (New York: Columbia University Press, 1954).

7. Michael Donelan, *Elements of International Political Theory* (Oxford: Clarendon Press, 1990), esp. 1-2; Martin Ceadel, *Thinking About Peace and War* (Oxford: Oxford University Press, 1987, esp. 19, 193-194).

Appendix C: On Long Waves

In the 1930s, N.D. Kondratieff published an analysis of long economic waves of growth and decline.[1] These "Kondratieff Series" focused on British, French, German, and American prices, production, and consumption. The most systematic evidence was associated with his price series, which suggested three long waves:

Rise from about 1780 to 1810-1817; fall from 1810-1817 through 1844-1851;

Rise from 1844-1851 to 1870-1875; fall from 1870-75 through 1890-1896;

Rise from 1890-1896 to 1914-1920; fall beginning in 1914-1920.

Kondratieff indicated several regularities in these waves, which he insisted were effects not causes of the long waves:

Downswing-Fall = Years of depression dominate; agriculture suffers pronounced and long depression; unusually many technical discoveries and inventions are made but not applied until the beginning of the next upswing-rise.

Upswing-Rise = Years of prosperity are relatively more frequent; at the beginning, production grows and world markets assimilate new territories; the most disastrous and extensive wars and revolutions occur (this particular regularity has come to be known as "The Kondratieff War Generalization").

Kondratieff identified seven wars that began in a downswing-fall:

1823 Franco-Spanish	1877 Russo-Turkish	1884 Sino-French
1827 Navarino Bay	1879 Pacific	1885 Central American
1828 Russo-Turkish.		

The twenty-eight wars that began in an upswing-rise include:

1846 Mexican-American	1860 Italo-Roman	1898 Spanish-American
1848 Austro-Sardinian	1862 Franco-Mexican	1904 Russo-Japanese
1848 1st Schleswig-Holstein	1863 Ecuadorian-Colombian	1906 Central American
1849 Roman Republic	1864 2nd Schleswig-Holstein	1907 Central American
1851 La Plata	1865 Spanish-Chilean	1909 Spanish-Moroccan
1853 Crimean	1866 Seven Weeks	1911 Italo-Turkish
1856 Anglo-Persian	1870 Franco-Prussian	1912 First Balkan
1859 Italian Unification	1894 Sino-Japanese	1913 Second Balkan
1859 Spanish-Moroccan	1897 Greco-Turkish	1914 World War I
1860 Italo-Sicilian.		

In expanding Kondratieff's work beyond economics, Pitirim Sorokin presented in 1937 perhaps the first empirical evidence for theories of periodicity, hysteresis, or trends linking growth and conflict.[2] Sorokin did little with his data, however, and "rather apologetically reports that his only finding is that states are involved in larger and more frequent wars in periods of greater economic strength."[3] Kuznets refers to Kondratieff's work in developing his own hypothesis that world war at the end of economic growth cycles serves to confirm change in international power structures.

Fernand Braudel's greatest work is his powerful reformulation of history over very long time spans, of the *longue durée*.[4] Although Braudel's work and concepts are not limited to economic growth or international relations, and explore the depths and heights of human existence, he recognizes both growth and conflict as major phenomena in human affairs. In Volume III, *Le Temps du Monde*, Braudel extends Kondratieff's arguments and incorporates Kondratieff waves into secular trends of more than a century, which show explosive world growth from the mid-eighteenth century through at least the 1970s.[5] In parallel the modern age had brought fierce international conflict to all corners of the world. In cataclysmically relating growth and conflict, Braudel concludes that

> the history of the world between about 1400 and 1850-1950 is one of an ancient [political-economic] parity [between Europe and Asia] collapsing under the weight of a multisecular distortion, whose beginnings go back to the late fifteenth century. . . . [The] machine revolution [was] not merely an instrument of competition, [but] a weapon of domination and destruction of foreign competition.[6]

Both the Kondratieff war generalization and Braudel's analysis remain controversial, and the only credible evidence of any historical periodicity at all about the incidence of war. They are strongly complementary, and provide powerful mutual support for each other. Each argues a strong, positive, direct relationship between growth and conflict, with implications of some historic force (analogous to Marx's materialistic forces of production) that may be beyond human control. Although he does not refer to Braudel's work, William Thompson concludes, after reviewing various subsequent analyses and arguments about Kondratieff long waves and international conflict, that

> [T]he empirical evidence on the relationships between Kondratieffs and major-power warfare suggests the advisability of remaining agnostic about the historical existence of Kondratieff's long waves and their hypothesized effects on conflict. By "agnostic" I merely mean to suggest that we should leave the question open to further theoretical and empirical enquiry.[7]

NOTES

1. Nicolai D. Kondratieff, "The Long Waves in Economic Life," *Review of Economic Statistics* 17 (November 1935): 105-115; reprinted as Nicolai D. Kondratieff, "The Long Waves in Economic Life," *Review* 2 (Spring 1979): 519-562.

2. Pitirim Sorokin, *Social and Cultural Dynamics*, Vol. 3 (New York: American Book Company, 1937).

3. Dean G. Pruitt & Richard C. Snyder, eds., *Theory and Research on the Causes of War* (Englewood Cliffs, New Jersey: Prentice-Hall, 1969), 217-218.

4. Fernand Braudel, *Civilization and Capitalism, 15th-18th Century*, 3 vols. (New York: Harper & Row, 1981-1984) (Revised French edition, *Civilisation, Materielle, Economie et Capitalisme: XVé-XVIIIé Siecle* [Paris: Libraire Armand Colin, 1979] was preceded by an earlier edition that began to appear in 1967.)

5. Braudel, *Civilization and Capitalism, 15th-18th Century*, Vol. 3, 71-88.

6. Braudel, *Civilization and Capitalism, 15th-18th Century*, Vol. 3, 534.

7. William R. Thompson, *On Global War: Historical-Structural Approaches to World Politics* (Columbia: University of South Carolina Press, 1988), 195.

Appendix D: On Foreign Investment

For early liberals, foreign investment was primarily bonds issued by governments to foreign banks, other governments, and wealthy foreign citizens. They did not envisage the paradoxically growth-related sources of conflict in large flows of technology, capital, and production, carried by modern foreign direct investment as practiced by multinational enterprises.

Modern corporate forms of foreign direct investment involve direct relationships between host-nation governments and investor multinational enterprises, which may be either competitive or cooperative. Economic growth in the host nation increases the power of the host-nation government in its relationships with foreign investors. As relative bargaining power shifts to the host nation government (Vernon's "Obsolescing Bargain"[1]), in parallel investors' incentives increase to appeal to home-country governments for support, which can easily escalate into overt international conflict.

Intense competitive pressures force multinational enterprises to find the least costly, most efficient, production sites; the resulting migration of production capabilities carries much of the energy and capability that generate economic growth. Successful direct investment eventually brings some growth to the host nation, which increases host nation national power. Consequent changes in the international distribution of power activate the realist or structuralist mechanism for international conflict.

Investment and technology transfer, especially since World War II, have established many poor countries as cost-efficient, competitive producers for world markets. Such uneven "supply-side" growth of technology and capability, however, without complementary "demand-side" growth of domestic markets, creates a volatile source of international conflict. Persistent low levels of *per capita* income prevent many high-tech, industrializing, host countries from increasing consumption significantly. The only markets able to absorb their increasing production are those of already wealthy home countries. While these are increasingly flooded with inexpensive, high-quality imports from industrializing countries, their own producers must wait until economic growth generates export markets in poorer countries for their own more costly products. This paradox of modern trade and investment leads to powerful domestic pressures—in both host and home countries—that can readily lead to international conflict.

The combined effect of these processes can be a powerful vortex pulling host nations into conflict with home-countries, even within the powerful liberal free trade and investment regime.

NOTE

1. Raymond Vernon, "The Obsolescing Bargain: A Key Factor in Political Risk," in Mark B. Winchester, ed., *The International Essays for Business Decision Makers*, Vol. 5 (Houston: Center for International Business, 1980).

Appendix E: On Division of Labor

Marxist theory presented division of labor and specialization of "manufactures" as an initial innovation in organization that transferred control of product from worker to capitalist.   The subsequent technological innovation of "modern machine production" in the factory system and capitalization of production transferred control over the production process itself.   Marx recognized the criticality of shifting the intensity of production from labor to capital, but saw technology primarily as a vehicle for institutionalizing the division of labor, rather than as a continuing, powerful force of innovation.[1]

What Marx actually intended to include in the "manufactures" stage and what, in the "modern machine production" stage, remains a matter of debate. He dealt with two forms of manufacturing: heterogeneous, the mechanical assembly of components made elsewhere; and organic, a series of connected processes that converted raw materials into a final product.   He applied Charles Babbage's ideal ratio between size of groups of workers and each special function[2] to his own ideal model of a single-function "manufactures" workshop controlled by a single capitalist. Marx also, however, referred in the same context to centralized factory-style manufacturing with "modern machines," and to traditional domestic "putting-out" production by artisans,[3] the former possibly a subsequent stage, and the former probably prior to his "manufactures" stage. His original intent about identifying stages of industrial development seems to have been obscured in his concerns about social and economic "contradictions" and inequities.

NOTES

1. Stephen A. Marglin, "What Do Bosses Do? The Origins and Functions of Hierarchy in Capitalist Production," *Review of Radical Political Economy* 6 (Summer 1974), 60-112; Maxine Berg, *Technology and Toil in Nineteenth Century Britain* (London: CSE Books, 1979).

2. The Babbage Principle was that "by dividing work into several processes of different degrees of skill and strength, a manufacturer can purchase *exactly* the precise quantities of each needed for the work; thus, the total labor required would necessarily be less than that needed in a single workman that must possess sufficient skill and sufficient strength for all component tasks" (Babbage, cited in Maxine Berg, *The Machinery Question and the Making of Political Economy 1815-1848* (Cambridge: Cambridge University Press, 1980), 182-189).

3. Karl Marx, *Capital, A Critique of Political Economy, 3 Volumes,* Vol. I (Harmondsworth: Penguin/New Left Books, 1976-1981), esp. 465; Karl Marx, *Die Grundrisse (Foundations of the Critique of Political Economy),* trans. and ed. by M. Nicholaus (Harmondsworth: Penguin/New Left Books, 1973), 510-511.

Appendix F: On Alternative Economies

In her detailed case studies of the English textile industry over the course of the Industrial Revolution, Maxine Berg explores the sorts of institutional rigidities around which alternative economic systems developed. She argues that invoking the concept of Ricardian comparative advantage (to credit liberal economics with providing the engine of growth in these economies) only explains any transition to MEG tautologically by demonstrating the result.[1] She dismisses any suggestion that these sorts of rigid institutions operated merely—or cleanly and discretely—to create alternative economies able to generate sustained growth. Rather than emerging through human practice and custom, many were established to accomplish some particular ideological or political purpose, or to demonstrate a socioeconomic theory of human behavior. With thinly veiled disapproval of the illiberal politics common in many of her examples, she implies that several common institutions of alternative economies, in particular, actually did much to inhibit the emergence of modern economic growth:

> restrictions on capital and entrepreneurship, preferential terms, availability, and conditions of credit imposed by nonmarket criteria;
> high and inflexible wage rates enforced by government, organized labor, or communal consensus to nonmarket levels;
> artificially low wage rates brought by high population growth and poor quality of the products of unskilled workers; low wages often led to sabotage, embezzlement, shoddy work, and other frauds by workers against employers;
> "polarity of master and man" in class-conscious communities in contrast to the socially uniform communities that emerged through modern economic growth;
> social divisions that grew parallel with division of labor, restricted socioeconomic mobility, inhibited enterprise, and nurtured antagonism to technical and organizational change;

failure to develop local industries to exploit newly discovered local resources that threatened to disrupt traditional work and economic patterns; abortive industrial development also occurred where expensive technology-based increases in productivity displaced small local investors;[2]

high dependence on business and trade cycles or export markets with no strong, stable home market; depressions (late 1730s–1740s) and numerous eighteenth-century wars brought traumatic, brief declines in growth that vulnerable industries could not survive;[3]

traditions of high capital volatility through flexible, dynamic investment portfolios; investment decisions to cross sectors and industries in response to short-term trade cycles brought dramatic shifts of capital and emphasis; investors sought short-term gain rather than long-term growth;

socio-cultural limits on entrepreneurship, exemplified in Josiah Tucker's comparison of English West Country (stagnant) and Yorkshire (dynamic)[4]; and

ineffective techniques of Marketing, Sales, and Distribution that were not responsive to the dynamics of an export market-economy.[5]

NOTES

1. Maxine Berg, *The Age of Manufactures: 1700-1820* (New York: Oxford University Press, 1985), 118.

2. Such abortive industrial developments in eighteenth-century England occurred in Cornwall (tin, copper), Shropshire (pottery, glass, chemicals), Staffordshire (glass, engineering, armaments), North Wales (iron, copper, brick, lime, textiles, rope), Derbyshire (textiles, lead), Ireland (cotton). Sidney Pollard, *Peaceful Conquest* (Oxford: Oxford University Press, 1981), 14-16.

3. P. Deane and W. A. Cole found unambiguous (although not universally recognized) decline in British and European economic growth, in both output and incomes, beginning in the 1740's, after the agricultural depression of the earlier decade. P. Deane & W. A. Cole, *British Economic Growth 1688-1959* (Cambridge: Cambridge University Press, 1969). The effects of war were probably felt most in industrial production; most eighteenth-century wars affected the belligerents' home markets more than their international trade. W. A. Cole, "Factors in Demand," in R. Floud & D. McCloskey, eds., *The Economic History of Britain Since 1700, Vol. I 1700-1860* (Cambridge: Cambridge University Press, 1981), esp. 53.

4. Journeymen in Yorkshire,

being so little removed from the Degree and Condition of their masters, and likely to set up for themselves by the Industry and Frugality of a few years . . . thus it is, that the working people are generally Moral, Sober and Industrious; that the goods are well made, and exceedingly cheap.

In the West Country,

The Motives to Industry, Frugality and Sobriety are all subverted to this one consideration viz. that they shall always be chained to the same Oar (the Clothier), and shall never be but journeymen. . . . Is it little wonder that the trade in Yorkshire should flourish, or the trade in Somersetshire, Wiltshire, and Gloucestershire should be found declining every Day?

Josiah Tucker, *A Brief Essay on the Advantages and Disadvantage which Respectively Attend France and Great Britain with Regard to Trade* (London: N.P., [1749, 1757], cited in R. G. Wilson, "The Supremacy of the Yorkshire Cloth Industry in the Eighteenth Century," in N. B. Harte & K. G. Ponting, *Textile History and Economic History* (Manchester: Manchester University Press, 1973), 238.

5. Wilson's analysis of Josiah Tucker's descriptions of the profound differences between Yorkshire and the West Country again provide the best example:

> The difference between the ways in which the West Riding trade was handled by the active [specialist] merchants of Leeds, Wakefield (and eventually Halifax) and the exports of every other production area from Norwich down, which were all monopolized by non-specialist London traders often working within the restrictions of the trading companies themselves, accounts in good measure for Yorkshire's growing supremacy in the eighteenth century.

Wilson, "The Supremacy of the Yorkshire Cloth Industry in the Eighteenth Century," 241.

Appendix G: On Protoindustrialization

Drawing on nineteenth-century German and English economic historians, Franklin Mendels formalized a theory of "protoindustrialization" around economic growth as it occurred in eighteenth-century England and France.[1] Economic activity concentrated in growing cities at regional, subnational levels as supplies of labor migrated toward both work and markets; manufacturing and agriculture shared a single unskilled labor force that was the primary engine of growth; the major markets for both agricultural produce and industrial goods were international; technological innovations affected both agriculture and manufacturing. During early protoindustrial growth, Mendels theorized, rapid rates of innovation and change would have little macroeconomic effect beyond a local "spurt" of rapid growth as increasing incomes based on a brief competitive advantage brought population increases that broke the historic balance between labor supply and subsistence wages. After a lag of one–two generations, however, this imbalance would become the labor surplus to drive sustained growth in the Industrial Revolution. Thus the result of Mendels' theory was the need for continuing rapid technological innovation and economic change to sustain a permanent imbalance between labor supply and wages. Self-sustaining growth was only possible *after* a long period of permanent economic instability and social turmoil.

Mendels did not theorize at the microeconomic level explored by Maxine Berg, and thus missed the powerful effects of these changes on

> productivity and output in individual industries, establishing above all a trend of improvement in each sector. But the experience in the eighteenth century was of a secret but gathering force. And the change it made to the economy as a whole, though delayed, was ultimately marked and abrupt. The technological spurt and organizational changes of the eighteenth century did not make their mark on the wider economy until the decades of the 1820s to the 1840s.[2]

Like Daniel Defoe, and later Marx, Mendels was powerfully impressed with the constellation of related innovations that emerged in eighteenth-century economies just emerging from mature mercantilism:

division of labor and specialization which appeared in England and
    France about a half century after the Treaty of Westphalia;
labor-saving technical devices that came into common industrial usage
    especially after about 1720 (Defoe sets 1680 as the start of "a
    projecting age in which men set their heads to designing Engines
    and Mechanical Motion");[3] and
expansion of markets beyond national political borders.

It was the combined effects of these three profound innovations that turned the engine of economic growth in early protoindustrial economies in Europe and England.   Mendels' original theory of protoindustrialization included several predictions that anticipated subsequent industrialization and further modern economic growth:

protoindustrial population growth ultimately brought diminishing
    returns for both agriculture and industry; political pressures of a
    growing population prompted organizational and technological
    innovation in both sectors, which led to the factory system and
    industrialization, and to increasing pressures for continued
    expansion of national economies;
protoindustrialization concentrated economic profits and wealth in
    merchants, landlords, commercial farmers, and manufacturers; this
    was the "Accumulation of Capital" that stimulated Marx's analyses;
protoindustry required and generated new knowledge of industrial
    organization, commercial management, and work skills, as well as
    technologies and mechanical devices; these matured into the
    innovations that enervated full industrialization; and
protoindustrialization required and generated regional, technical, and
    industrial specializations that reflected both comparative advantage
    and noneconomic, political motivations, which generated political
    pressures on government for protection and support of specialist
    industries, and even individual firms.

NOTES

1. Franklin Mendels, "Proto-industrialization: The First Phase of the Process of Industrialization." *Journal of Economic History* 32 (1972).

2. Maxine Berg, *The Age of Manufactures: 1700-1820* (New York: Oxford University Press, 1985), 46-47.

3. Daniel Defoe, *A Tour Through the Whole Island of Great Britain* (Harmondsworth: Penguin Books, [1720] 1971), 156-170.

Appendix H: On Confidence Levels

The Ordinary Least Squares regression process minimizes the sum of the squares of deviations of actual data from the curve of a fitted equation by estimating an unconstrained zero-intercept and the coefficients of each independent variable. A powerful regression explains most of the variance of the dependent variable and shows only small unexplained residual variation of the dependent variable (the Error Sum of Squares). A weak regression explains little variance of the dependent variable, has a high Error Sum of Squares, and shows a low correlation coefficient. The correlation coefficient (R^2) measures the proportion of the total variation in the dependent variable that is "explained" by the regression equation. The adjusted correlation coefficient, which is used in this analysis, improves the measure of "goodness of fit" to the data for the regression equation by accounting for degrees of freedom of the equation and minimizing the residual variance (rather than the variation) of the dependent variable.

A high adjusted correlation coefficient means that the unexplained variance (the difference between the actual data and the data predicted or explained by the regression equation) is small, and that the independent variables explain most of the variance of the dependent variable from predicted values. If the data include sufficient observations of independent variables that are near zero to allow statistically meaningful results, the zero-intercept can be interpreted directly as a reasonable estimate of the dependent variable when the independent variables are all zero. In such a regression, high "goodness of fit" should mean that the zero-intercept is comparable to the mean of the dependent variable.

In absence of sufficient observations of zero for the independent variables, the zero-intercept can only be interpreted in conjunction with the goodness of fit of the regression. It is easily shown[1] that the best estimate of the zero-intercept is the difference between the mean of the dependent variable (actual data) and the sum of the products of the estimated coefficients and the means of their respective variables (predicted data):

$$Z_e = CNF_m \cdot (\alpha_{1e} V_{1m} + \ldots \alpha_{ne} V_{nm}).$$

Thus, a high adjusted correlation coefficient leads to the result that the zero-intercept (unexplained difference between means of actual data and predicted data) should also be small. Similarly a low correlation coefficient should reflect a large zero-intercept, since the unexplained variance is large. A regression showing a high correlation coefficient *and* a low zero-intercept provides high confidence in the regression specification. Similarly, a regression with low correlation *and* high zero-intercept provides high confidence. Where correlation and zero-intercept are *both* high or *both* low, the specification offers only low confidence.

NOTE

1. Robert S. Pindyck & Daniel L. Rubinfeld, *Econometric Models and Economic Forecasts*, 3d ed. (New York: McGraw-Hill, 1991), App. 4.1, 91-92.

Appendix I: On Growth Processes

Many modern economists and officials, and some political analysts, use interchangeably the terms "growth" and "development" to refer not only to any increase in national wealth or income (economic growth), but also to technological progress, improvements in productivity, spread of industrialization, changes in economic structure, or socio-political shifts toward liberal democracy (development). More or less of any of these attributes can position a country, economy, or polity in some hierarchy or typology of modernity as more or less developed. A more analytical style restricts the term *growth* to an economic context in referring to "incremental increases (or expansions) in the levels, quantities, or sizes of particular variables relevant to the processes, issues, and outcomes under scrutiny."[1]   Thus, in the conventional context of national development, static growth would reflect increases in economic variables with little or no related national development; dynamic growth would involve increases in economic variables with significant parallel development. In a context of development economics, the hypothesis of disjunction of growth would suggest differences in levels of international conflict with some relationship to differences in national development.

In developing a structural model of the growth process, Hollis Chenery and Moises Syrquin expanded Kuznets' insight about a relationship between economic growth and structural change. Using their multidimensional approach to structural analysis they analyzed the process of growth across countries and over time. Chenery and Syrquin achieved results that replicated Kuznets' observations indicating "a period of accelerated structural change . . . followed by a deceleration,"[2] and introduced trade and human capital as objective, analytic elements of growth.[3]

Expanding Kuznets' earlier concepts they used the term "development" to encompass the two processes of economic growth and structural change operating in parallel. Predicting that growth brought structural change (which could readily be measured with well-known demographic and economic techniques), Chenery and Syrquin advanced 10 measurable growth processes that "describe different dimensions of the overall structural transformation of a poor country into a rich one"[4]:

ACCUMULATION PROCESSES
Investment, saving, and capital inflow as percent of GDP;
Government revenues as percent of GDP;
Education as percent of GDP, and school enrollment;

RESOURCE ALLOCATION AND DISTRIBUTION PROCESSES
Domestic demand components as percent of GDP;
Production components as percent of GDP;
Trade components as percent of GDP;
Labor allocation by sector;
Income distribution as shares of GDP;

DEMOGRAPHIC PROCESSES
Urbanization as percent of population;
Demographic birth and death rates.[5]

NOTES

1. Nazli Choucri & Robert C. North "Growth, Development, and Environmental Sustainability: Profiles and Paradox" in Nazli Choucri, ed., *Global Accord: Environmental Challenges and International Responses* (Cambridge, Massachusetts: MIT Press, 1993), 67.

2. Chenery & Syrquin *Patterns of Development*, 25.

3. Chenery & Syrquin *Patterns of Development*, 32-40.

4. Hollis B. Chenery & Moshe Syrquin *Patterns of Development, 1950-1970* (London: Oxford University Press, 1975), 8.

5. Chenery & Syrquin *Patterns of Development*, 9.

Appendix J: On Static Models

Kubo, Robinson, and Syrquin use this approach in developing a generic "Static Input-Output Model," which decomposes and relates national output and economic structure. They recognize the limitations of the model, specifically for dealing with investment and changes in productivity, and note that the effect of technological change on productivity is "quite different from that captured by changes in input-output coefficients, although the effects may be related. . . . No explanation of the source of such changes in labor productivity is offered [by the static model]."[1]

Comparative static analysis does not account for forces that may be not only shifting the economic structure of a nation, but altering the growth processes operating within that structure. Analysis of this sort of growth requires a dynamic analytical model that considers both quantitative input-output relationships and qualitative aspects of economic growth.

The computable general equilibrium (CGE) model developed by Kubo, Robinson, and Syrquin expands the static model to nonlinear functions; simulates operations of markets for labor, goods, and foreign exchange; introduces behavioral and technological assumptions; and incorporates a recursive mechanism for dealing with intertemporality. This basic CGE model eventually converges to a "growth path with equilibrium characteristics."[2]

An alternative extension of the static input-output model incorporates capital accumulation, but omits incentives and market dynamics.[3] While static models can be both arcane and sophisticated, they seem inherently unable to deal well with qualitative or subjective variables, such as technology, knowledge, innovation, or productivity.[4]

NOTES

1. Yuji Kubo, Sherman Robinson & Moshe Syrquin, "The Methodology of Multisector Comparative Analysis," in Hollis B. Chenery, Sherman Robinson & Moshe Syrquin, eds., *Industrialization and Growth* (New York: Oxford University Press for

the World Bank, 1986), 143.

2. Kubo, Robinson & Syrquin, "The Methodology of Multisector Comparative Analysis," 145.

3. See K. Dervis, J. de Melo & Sherman Robinson, *General Equilibrium Models for Development Policy* (Cambridge: Cambridge University Press, 1982), chapter 2; Yuji Kubo, Sherman Robinson & S. Urata, *The Impact of Alternative Development Strategies: Simulations with a Dynamic Input-Output Model* (Berkeley: Department of Agricultural and Resource Economics, University of California, Berkeley, 1986).

4. For surveys of early efforts to extend the static input-output growth model by expanding parameters, see C. R. Blitzer, P. B. Clark & L. J. Taylor, *Economy-Wide Models and Development Planning* (London: Oxford University Press, 1975), and Sherman Robinson, *Multisectoral Models of Developing Countries: A Survey*, Working Paper 401 (Berkeley: Department of Agricultural and Resource Economics, University of California, Berkeley, 1986).

Appendix K: On Defense of Realism

Realist Geoffrey Stern recognizes reasonable, fashionable arguments that the state's primacy as sole actor in world affairs has eroded, but finds them fatally flawed. In an interesting defense of realism, he argues that "since the exact legal status of nonstate actors is mired in controversy, . . . they cannot be said to have destroyed its legal primacy.[1]

In response to globalist doubts about the continued relevance of the sovereign state in a tightening "high-tech" tangle of transnational forces, common markets, global ideologies, and international organizations, Stern delicately suggests that although the very concept of sovereignty may never have been much more than a legal fiction anyway,

> [i]n political terms . . . even if nonstate actors are increasingly making their presence felt, in many parts of the world the role of the state may be said to have been growing in parallel. . . .
>   Second, whereas before the twentieth-century governments tended to leave such matters as international trade and commerce, migration, sport, and ideological or religious orientation to the individual, these have now tended to become increasingly subject to government regulation.[2]

Nor have the political allures of sovereign statehood and ever-increasing government power lost their appeal. In addition to continuing nationalistic concerns in mature states about "competitiveness" and "national interests," the strident demands of Palestinians, Kurds, Kashmiris, Chechens, Karens, Bosnians, Croats, Tibetans, *Quebecois*, Basques, Scots, and a host of other emerging nations, suggest that neither the sovereign state nor realist politics have become obsolete. A plethora of unsatisfied peoples insisting on self-determination and a sovereign homeland—even though the entire territory of the earth has already come within the jurisdiction of some existing sovereign state—seems not only to promise continuing conflict in a realist world, but to confirm Stern's observation that "the sovereign principle is often as much cherished by those who have it . . . as by those who seek it.[3]

Stern clearly appreciates that the nature of sovereignty, and even some of the premises of realism, have changed as the nature of power has shifted from exclusive reliance on political-military power resources to include a modern obsession with economic resources and market power. He does not quibble about degrees or levels—or even about definitions—but realistically recognizes that states have become interdependent, and that nonstate actors have become politically important. He does not accept, however, that either trend marks the end of sovereignty, or even transfer of sovereignty to international organizations.

> [Many liberals and globalists may argue on the one hand that] the thickening web of international economic institutions, common markets, and specialized agencies further limits the ability of states to chart their own destinies. On the other hand, it can be contended that such organizations as the EU [European Union], the World Bank, and the International Monetary Fund (IMF) may enhance the ability of states to exercise sovereign power by providing the instruments of collaboration by which participants may secure their individual objectives. . . . it is still governments that determine the shape of international politics. . . . whenever governments resort to economic sanctions in support of political objectives, they underline the pre-eminence of politics.[4]

In expanding his conservative realism to embrace much of the change that he has observed in his long scholarly career, Stern implicitly (if also parenthetically) recognizes the salience of knowledge and skill in exercising power, and in expanding the study of international relations beyond pure politics to embrace at least economics.

> What has to change, however, is the traditional emphasis on measurable military capability. . . . any realistic account of the capacity of states to outwit, outmaneuver or defeat their rivals nowadays has to be based on a range of diplomatic, economic, political, and other considerations, including the skill of leaders in being able to choose the appropriate pressure for the ends in view. . . . this has meant placing much greater emphasis than hitherto on the intricacies of the international political economy and on technological, demographic, and environmental factors.[5]

NOTES

1. Geoffrey Stern, "International Relations in a Changing World: Bucking the Trendies." *The World Today* 51 (July 1995): 149.
2. Stern, "International Relations in a Changing World," 149-150.
3. Stern, "International Relations in a Changing World," 150.
4. Stern, "International Relations in a Changing World," 149-150.
5. Stern, "International Relations in a Changing World," 150-151.

Appendix L: On Growth Strategies

Static growth strategies stress unskilled-labor-intensive production that requires little capital or technology, and expansion of domestic sources for raw materials. Such strategies have encouraged rapid growth of labor-intensive manufactured exports. Since costs of capital, skilled labor, and technology have been high (they are scarce), and cost of unskilled labor has been low (it is abundant), rational commercial and industrial entrepreneurs pursued profit by husbanding costly factors, exploiting low-cost unskilled labor, and expanding markets. Even in the absence of empire or hegemony, until the modern era, statically growing societies had most often expanded their absolute wealth through conquest, aggressive trade, diplomatic-political expansion, and sporadic investment in foreign projects. In proper combinations with domestic factors of production and controlled colonial commerce, additional foreign resources—capital, materials, labor—brought greater aggregate production, reduced risks and increased wealth in the home society, and may even have increased domestic productivity.

Dynamic growth strategies prescribe policy actions and structural changes for such things as primary education, research and development, trade reform, intellectual property, and basic knowledge of how to do things. They deemphasize manufacturing, business, inflation, exchange rates, and orthodox economic, industrial, or commercial issues. These sorts of changes are the results less of economic investment or political commitment than of learning, of mastering the arts of innovation and creativity, and of diffusing knowledge through an entire society. The engines of such change are education, training, innovation, technology transfer, and establishment of knowledge-sensitive infrastructures. For an economy experiencing dynamic growth, modernization, industrialization, expansion, and improvement of living standards rely not simply on allocating additional already existing resources to production, but instead on creation of new intellectual and technological resources and innovation of new production functions.

Appendix M: On Dualism and Growth

The origins of the concept of dual growth are obscure, although its cognitive roots may be somewhere in David Hume's articulation of "the rich country —poor country problem."[1] While he seems to have envisaged some division along lines of comparative advantage, Hume indicated that nations could move from "courser" to "more elaborate" manufactures and industries over time.[2] Hume's failure to consider cognitive innovation or technological progress as sources of growth clearly imposed limits to a single type of growth—static: "The growth of everything, both in arts and nature, at last checks itself."[3]

Thomas Malthus stressed natural limits for a single type of resource-based growth in economies operating under a low-income ceiling, possibly imposed by slow technological progress.[4] The distinguished Malthusian interpreter, Emmanual LeRoy Ladurie, however, considered the real ceiling on growth of *per capita* income to be stagnant technology, rather than shortages of land or resources. His conclusions imply that innovation might raise, or remove, that ceiling, but he did not suggest that growth above the resource ceiling would be of a different sort.[5]

Nor was Adam Smith able to conceive that innovation might generate a sustained flow of inventions that could remove the barriers to infinite static growth inherent in expansion of capital stock.   For Smith steady-state stagnation was a probable result, should a nation ever confront those resource-based barriers. For Smith the only alternative was expansion through trade. Like Hume, Smith did not conceive an alternative to static growth. Explicitly acknowledging a finite limit on real output, Smith concluded that

> [i]n a country which had acquired the full complement of riches which the nature of its soil and climate, and its situation with respect to other countries, allowed it to acquire, . . . fully peopled in proportion to what either its territory could maintain or its stock employ, . . . fully stocked in proportion to all the business it had to transact, . . . the ordinary profit [would be] as low as possible.[6]

Smith did not stress any differences between growth arising from technical progress and the benefits accruing from economies of scale. He was more intent on approaching the high-income frontier (about $440 annually per person in the Netherlands) with existing technology, than on any opportunities for further progress. Smith's rough dichotomy between countries with high potential growth and others reflected physical differences in constraints imposed by natural resources, and in the effectiveness of policy in managing economic affairs. He stressed removing economic backwardness, and largely ignored innovation as a creative economic process.

The work of David Ricardo stimulated development of two-sector models and theories with resource-based constraints on a single kind of accumulation of capital (static growth) that could occur in all sectors at all times. Ricardian emphasis on the industrial sector as the locus of rapid technological change implicitly linked growth to structural change, introduced the notion of technology as a discrete factor of production, and confused current concepts about limits of growth.

Karl Marx speculated about some limits to capitalistic growth imposed by the difficulty of sustaining technical progress, and, presumably, would have expected some complementary growth to arise from technical progress, in addition to capital accumulation as the primary form of growth. The nature of growth did not assume much relevance, however, in his primarily sociopolitical analysis, and he was not at all concerned about shifting from one type of growth to another.

Alfred Marshall may have glimpsed the radiance of dynamic growth when he found the genius of French, German, and American industrialization in "fine goods, embodying some artistic feeling and individual judgment"; . . . [industries that can be nurtured by] "academic training and laboratory work" . . . [or even innovative] "massive multiform standardization."[7] Marshall recommended to Britain a prescription that would shift the country into dynamic growth: expansion and improvement of popular education and university education for "the well-to-do classes"; expansion of training in science and engineering; allocation of public funds to scientific research laboratories; and even innovative modern market research techniques and radical forms of industrial financing.[8]

In contrast to Malthus and Ricardo, and to Marx, Joseph Schumpeter rejected resource-based constraints on growth, stressed the role of technical progress, and deemphasized the role of capital accumulation as an engine of growth. His provocative approach placed enterprise and the entrepreneur in the central role of capturing the transient and sporadic benefits of innovation, and transmuting them into opportunistic growth. Schumpeter concluded that since innovation seemed to occur discontinuously over time and space (in "swarms" or "constellations") growth occurs in a series of innovation-led cycles. Surely Schumpeter recognized that the growth arising from the efforts of entrepreneurs in capturing the benefits of innovation was qualitatively different from that occurring routinely in what he characterized as a "circular flow" of static technology and exchanges of economic resources. His later attempts to institutionalize innovation suggest that he did recognize his discovery of dynamic growth, but may not have been able to do much with it.[9]

W.E.G. Salter's concept of "embodiment" of technical progress in capital stock allowed him to make a sharp distinction between growth arising from simple Smithian economies of scale, and that initiated by technical progress. Salter's explanation of growth in terms of labor productivity, rather than as an accumulation of capital or an increase in total factor productivity, relied explicitly on a "different" sort of growth: dynamic.[10] Schultz's introduction of the concept of "human capital" crystallized Marshall's insight about education, although the idea had been adumbrated by Adam Smith (and neglected by Ricardo, Marx, and Schumpeter).[11]

Walt Rostow's dual concepts of "takeoff" and the "drive to technological maturity" as stages of growth were a seminal explication of the duality of the growth process.[12] His observation of dramatic increase in levels of higher education in both "lower middle-income" and "upper middle-income" countries after about 1960, as well as a "radical shift toward science and engineering," prompted him to christen the phenomenon "a virtually unnoticed revolution." In recommending, like Marshall, that growing countries shift to dynamic growth through emphasis on education, Rostow pointedly recognized the need to "develop an ability to create and maintain effective and flexible partnerships among scientists, entrepreneurs, and the working force."[13]

In contrast to Rostow's concept that economies, in general, progressed from one stage to another, the *corpus* of "development economics" established a dichotomy between rich, successful, "advanced" countries and poor, backward, "undeveloped" countries. Rather than implying any duality in the growth process as nations progress toward wealth, development economics offers explanations for economic backwardness, and prescribes (like Adam Smith) strategies for overcoming it. Four broad types of explanations have been offered: (1) an unfavorable institutional setting; (2) colonialism and plunder; (3) population pressures on natural resources; (4) diversion of national savings away from economic growth. Immanuel Wallerstein's Modern World System is perhaps the archetype of these explanations. Wallerstein's core-periphery dichotomy is based on economic functions inherited through diverse historical patterns. Core states exercise those functions that generate large rewards for accumulated capital, while periphery states perform less-well-rewarded tasks. The core-periphery dichotomy necessarily includes quantitatively different compensation for the different economic tasks performed. It does not, however, involve any qualitative differences in the type of growth experienced as regions change their structural roles in the world economy; core nations simply receive higher rewards. Wallersteinian "development" involves far more than simply economic growth. As the loci of economic activities change over time, some areas experience "progress" or growth, *but others must accept "regression."* "This is not quite a zero-sum game, but it is also inconceivable that all elements in a capitalist world-economy shift their values in a given direction simultaneously."[14]

In parallel to Rostow's concept of temporal progress through stages of growth, E. F. Denison has probably been most ambitious in "partitioning" aggregate growth into "factors" by giving weights to various components of growth, although he deals explicitly with only a single aggregate kind of growth. Adjusting labor for differences in education (*à la* Marshall and Schultz), and ignoring Salter and Schumpeter, he allows for Smithian economies of scale, Ricardian shifts in production structure, specialization, and disembodied technical progress. Denison's "total factor productivity" with its implicit several types of growth, however, still does not explain *all* of aggregate growth; he is left with an unexplained "residual."[15]

Since the emergence of economics as a legitimate intellectual pursuit, and the rise of their interest in economic growth, economists have resisted any notion that growth might not be homogeneous.[16] Classical economics created taxonomies based on such discriminators as physical resources, policy environments, or historical experiences. Radicals relied on social structures, modes of production, or economic functions, and even on race, culture, and climate, to account for disparities in growth, growth rates, and the effects of growth. Like Marshal and Schumpeter, neither Salter nor Schultz, however, nor even Denison nor Rostow, conceived explicitly that they were dealing with a "different" type of growth. Even development economics generally accepted that growth depended on physical resources and how they were distributed. As recently as 1982 (just as Paul Romer was introducing knowledge-based growth) Angus Maddison, in discussing education, could only "acknowledge this factor as one that has obviously facilitated economic growth, but whose precise role cannot be identified, probably because a shortage of educated people has never been a serious drag on growth in advanced capitalist countries."[17]

Only a few, perhaps particularly prescient or perceptive, analysts glimpsed the profound differences between resource-based growth and knowledge-based growth, or the dramatic contrast in their social and political consequences.

NOTES

1. See notably Istvan Hont's account of the early debate on the issue in Istvan Hont, "The 'rich country—poor country' Debate in Scottish Classical Political Economy," chap. 11 in Istvan Hont & Michael Ignatieff, eds., *Wealth and Virtue: The Shaping of Political Economy in the Scottish Enlightenment* (Cambridge: University Press, 1983).

2. Eugene Rotwein, ed., *David Hume: Writings on Economics* (Madison: University of Wisconsin Press, 1955), esp. 200.

3. Rotwein, *David Hume: Writings on Economics*, 198.

4. Thomas R. Malthus, *First Essay on Population 1798* (London: Macmillan, 1966).

5. Emmanual LeRoy Ladurie, "*Les Masses Profondes: La Paysannerie*," in Fernand Braudel & E. Larousse, eds., *Histoire Économique et Sociale de la France*, part I, vol. 2 (Paris: Presses Universitaires de la France, 1977).

6. Adam Smith, *An Inquiry into the Nature and Causes of the Wealth of Nations*, ed. Edwin Cannan. (New York: Random House, [1776] 1937), 94-95.

7. Alfred Marshall, *Industry and Trade* (London: Macmillan, 1919). Reprinted in *Reprints of Economic Classics*, Chapters 3-5, 32-106 (New York: Augustus M. Kelley, 1970).

8. Marshall, *Industry and Trade*, 95-103.

9. Joseph A. Schumpeter, *The Theory of Economic Development* (New York: Oxford University Press, 1961); see also Joseph A. Schumpeter, *Business Cycles* (New York: McGraw-Hill, 1939).

10. W.E.G. Salter, *Productivity and Technical Change* (Cambridge: Cambridge University Press, 1960).

11. T. W. Schultz, "Investment in Human Capital," *American Economic Review* (March 1961).

12. W. W. Rostow, *Stages of Economic Growth* (Cambridge: University Press, 1960, 1971).

13. W. W. Rostow, *Rich Countries and Poor Countries* (Boulder, Colorado: Westview Press, 1987).

14. Immanuel Wallerstein, *The Modern World-system* (New York: Academic Press, 1974), 356; see also Immanuel Wallerstein, "The Present State of the Debate on World Inequality," chapter in Immanuel Wallerstein, ed., *World Inequality: Origins and Perspectives on the World System* (Montréal: Black Rose Books, 1975), 12-28.

15. E. F. Denison & J. P. Poullier, *Why Growth Rates Differ* (Washington, D.C.: Brookings Institution, 1967).

16. For a critical survey of the major theories of growth, see the final chapter of J. D. Gould, *Economic Growth in History: Survey and Analysis* (London: Methuen, 1972), 378-446.

17. Angus Maddison, *Phases of Capitalist Development* (New York: Oxford University Press, 1982), 23; see also Angus Maddison, "What Is Education For?" *Lloyds Bank Review* (April 1974).

Appendix N: On Lawlike Regularities

Ubiquitous in natural science, and remarkable in their simplicity, physical laws rely on a few independent variables in relationships that explain behaviors of complex systems.   Formulation of laws involves making simplifying assumptions, finding limiting conditions under which they hold, and recognizing cases where they do not hold. Somewhat less rigorous than pure law, a "lawlike regularity" must regularly provide a "reasonably good" explication of the evidence. While laws reflect accurately a specific system's behavior, the utility of a lawlike regularity lies in the variety of cases to which it applies, rather than precision of fit to any particular case.

Awareness of how a lawlike relationship fits into other available information outside the regularity is as important as discovery of the regularity itself. Additional information may have great theoretical and empirical importance, or lead to refinements of the lawlike relationship.   A regular relationship cannot be said to describe the lawlike aspects of a process unless there exists a viable theoretical explanation of why the observed relationship is what it is.   Without a theoretical model of the process underlying a regularity, its worth as a lawlike relationship cannot be determined. Moreover, the operation of such a model must be verifiable independently of the regularity itself.   As in the physical sciences, explanations of social scientific systems need not be complicated, complex, or even profound.

Neither laws nor lawlike relationships are necessarily causal; indeed they may originate in the coincidence of chance with purpose. Specification of causal ordering suffers from each of two contradictory weaknesses:

> Because models can at best approximate reality, some variables are always excluded from any equation; it is therefore not possible to establish clear causality among several interrelated variables.
> Reality does not consist of simultaneous causal dependencies, but rather of recursive, hierarchical relationships; it is therefore, possible to determine clear causal relations.

A plausible reconciliation of these disparate views recognizes local simultaneity and hierarchy within some specific subdomain of a system—a specific event-interaction, a particular issue area, a definite geographic region, a defined decision sequence, or a finite time series—but suggests that its influence on the system itself diminishes as generality expands through the system and congeals into a law-lie regularity. Thus, at a general level the world—and each of the component systems that it comprises—is more nearly block recursive than either simultaneous or hierarchical.[1]

The explanatory variables that contribute to understanding a relationship may be themselves dependent variables in a hierarchic dependency, exogenous variables taken as "givens" for the relationship, or endogenous "manipulables" determined by policy-makers or influenced by "givens" or by other "manipulables." It is clear that the policy-related utility of any model based on lawlike regularities depends on the "manipulability" of its independent variables. After specifying the dependent and independent variables, a first effort is to establish as clearly as possible an observable relationship between them. This is often in the form of an equation that explains behavior of the dependent variable in terms of the independent variables. The second task is to collect useful observations of the relationship, and identify across a large population of cases any regularities in relationships that fit the evidence reasonably well. A next task is to determine the scope of these relationships: limiting conditions under which they hold and the variety of cases to which they apply. A theory begins to emerge as the scope and limits of the relationships become apparent. Finally the most important task is to develop a sound theoretical explanation of why the relationships fit the data. Only sound theory of the origin of the relationship can lead to any probabilistic model that can be substantiated.

Discovery of lawlike regularities, and their accompanying propositions, are probabilistic and not deterministic. Any determinism that may be operating, specifically in the social sciences, is the result of human decision, habit, irrationality, and freedom of choice. Despite the unpredictability of individual human actions, however, the concept of lawlike regularities rests on the belief that "many perseverant behavior patterns — for example, many patterns of cooperation, organization, conflict, and resort to violence — make certain outcomes *highly probably* [italics in original]."[2]

Traditional statistical-scientific approaches to problem-solving, relying on the "scientific method" borrowed from physical science, differ from the search for lawlike regularities in their focus on testing an initial specific hypothesis, and accumulating results that expand and refine the hypothesis with increasing generality and precision. They are often concerned with the choice of one from a set of credible, adequate, or alternative hypotheses on the basis of goodness of fit with observed data or experimental results. Search for lawlike relationships, in contrast, is concerned with identifying and formulating simple relationships observed within the data, without the benefit of a formal initial hypothesis to focus the search. The test, then, is in determining whether these relationships hold for some useful varieties of data, and the research task emphasizes refining and determining the scope of both data and regularities into a single hypothesis, with a focus on some manipulable independent variable. Whereas the scientific method begins with at least one deterministic hypothesis, the search for regularities culminates with a single probabilistic hypothesis, but does not attempt to verify or prove it in any deterministic way. Despite nondeterminism and lack of "proof," the value of simple lawlike regularities is not a peculiar feature of complex systems in the physical sciences, but seems particularly useful to social scientific analyses.

NOTES

1. Franklin M. Fisher, "On the Cost of Approximate Specification in Simultaneous Equation Estimation," in Albert Ando, Franklin M. Fisher & Herbert A. Simon, eds., *Essays on the Structure of Social Science Models* (Cambridge, Massachusetts: MIT Press, 1963), 32-63. This position is supported by the theorem that if a system is near-decomposable with only small "feedbacks" relative to primary influences, system-level analysis may plausibly proceed *as if* it were completely decomposable (partitioned, recursive, and epistemologically hierarchic), with only minor short-run cognitive or epistemic costs at subsystem levels. The Ando-Fisher theorem is, however, only an "existence" theorem that does not establish tests for "sufficient smallness" of feedback. Despite this weakness, aggregation and partition will, over the general system, "be at worst trivially possible and at best quite helpful." Albert Ando & Franklin M. Fisher, "Near-Decomposability, Partition and Aggregation, and the Relevance of Stability Discussions," in Ando, Fisher & Simon, *Essays on the Structure of Social Science Models*, 92-106; 100.

2. Nazli Choucri & Robert C. North, "Dynamics of International Conflict: Some Policy Implications of Population, Resources, and Technology," *World Politics* 24 supplementary issue (Spring 1972): 97.

Bibliography

Abramovitz, Moses. *Resource and Output Trends in the United States since 1870*, Occasional Paper 52. New York: National Bureau of Economic Research, 1956.

Adams, R.E.W., ed. *The Origins of Maya Civilization*. Albuquerque: University of New Mexico Press, 1977.

Ando, Albert & Franklin M. Fisher. "Near-Decomposability, Partition and Aggregation, and the Relevance of Stability Discussions." In *Essays on the Structure of Social Science Models*, eds., Albert Ando, Franklin M. Fisher & Herbert A. Simon, 92-106. Cambridge, Massachusetts: MIT Press, 1963.

Ando, Albert, Franklin M. Fisher & Herbert A. Simon, eds. *Essays on the Structure of Social Science Models*. Cambridge, Massachusetts: MIT Press, 1963.

Angell, Norman. *The Great Illusion: A Study of the Relationship of Military Power in Nations to Their Economic and Social Advantage*. London: Weidenfeld & Nicholson, 1910.

Angell, R. C., V. S. Dunham & J. D. Singer. "Social Values and Foreign Policy Attitudes of Soviet and American Elites." *Journal of Conflict Resolution* 8 (1964): 329-491.

Aron, Raymond. *The Century of Total War*. Boston: Beacon Press, 1955.

Aron, Raymond. *Peace and War*. New York: Frederick A. Praeger, 1967.

Art, Robert J. & Kenneth N. Waltz, eds. *The Use of Force: Military Power and International Politics*, 3d ed. Lanham, Maryland: University Press of America, 1988.

Ashley, Richard. "The Poverty of Neorealism." *International Organization* 38 (Spring 1984).

Ashton, Thomas S. *An Economic History of England: The 18th Century*. London: Barnes & Noble, 1955.

Aukrust, Odd & Juul Bjerke. "Real Capital and Economic Growth in Norway, 1900-56." In *The Measurement of National Wealth*, International Association for Research in Income and Wealth, Income and Wealth, Series VIII, eds. Raymond Goldsmith & Christopher Saunders, 80-118. Chicago: Quadrangle Books, 1959.

Azar, Edward E. "The Analysis of International Events." *Peace Research Review* 4 (November 1970): 1-106.

Azar, Edward E. & Joseph D. Ben-Dak, eds. *Theory and Practice of Events Research.* New York: Gordon and Breach Science Publishers, 1975.

Azar, Edward E. & Thomas J. Sloan. *Dimensions of Interaction: A Source Book for the Study of the Behavior of 31 Nations from 1948 through 1973.* Philadelphia: University of Pennsylvania Press, 1975.

Balick, Michael J. & Paul Alan Cox. *Plants, People, and Culture.* New York: Scientific American Library, 1996.

Bardhan, Pranab. "Alternative Approaches to Development Economics." In *Handbook of Development Economics*, Vol. 1., eds. Hollis B. Chenery & T. N. Srinivasan. Amsterdam: Elsevier Science Publishers, 1988, 39-71

Becker, Bertha K. & Claudio A. G. Egler. *Brazil: A New Regional Power in the World-Economy.* Cambridge: Cambridge University Press, 1992.

Berg, Maxine. *The Age of Manufactures: 1700-1820.* New York: Oxford University Press, 1985.

Berg, Maxine. *The Machinery Question and the Making of Political Economy 1815-1848.* Cambridge: Cambridge University Press, 1980.

Berg, Maxine. *Technology and Toil in Nineteenth Century Britain.* London: CSE Books, 1979.

Berger, J. *et al. Sociological Theories in Progress*, Vol. I. Boston: Houghton Mifflin, 1966.

Berry, Brian J. L. "An Inductive Approach to the Regionalization of Economic Development." In *Essays on Geography and Economic Development*, Department of Geography, Research Paper No. 62, ed. Norton Ginsburg, 78-107. Chicago: University of Chicago Press, 1960.

Black, Eugene R. "Profit-Making Foreign Aid." From "One Type of Foreign Aid That Makes a Profit," address by Eugene R. Black, President of the World Bank, before the Connecticut Chamber of Commerce (Hartford, 8 May 1956). Text from *U.S. News & World Report*, 22 June 1956, 104-106. In *US Foreign Aid* The Reference Shelf, Vol. 29, No. 5, ed. Grant S. McClellan 90-96. New York: The H.W. Wilson Company, 1957.

Blitzer, C. R., P. B. Clark & L. J. Taylor. *Economy-Wide Models and Development Planning.* London: Oxford University Press, 1975.

Bobrow, D. B. & J. L. Schwarz, eds. *Computers and the Policy-Making Community.* Englewood Cliffs, New Jersey: Prentice-Hall, 1968.

Booth, Ken. "Human Wrongs and International Relations." *International Affairs* 71 (January 1995): 103-126.

Braudel, Fernand. *Civilization and Capitalism, 15th-18th Century*, 3 vols. New York: Harper & Row, 1981-1984. (Revised French edition *Civilisation, Materielle, Economie et Capitalisme: XVé-XVIIIé Siecle.* Paris: Libraire Armand Colin, 1979, was preceded by an earlier edition that began to appear in 1967.)

Bryson, L., ed. *The Communication of Ideas.* New York: Harper, 1948.

Bueno de Mesquita, Bruce. *The War Trap.* New Haven, Connecticut: Yale University Press, 1981.

Bull, Hedley. *The Anarchical Society: A Study of Order in World Politics.* London: Macmillan, 1977.

Burgess, Philip M. & Raymond W. Lawton. *Indicators of International Behavior: An Assessment of Events Data Research*. Beverly Hills, California: Sage Publications, 1972.

Burns, Edward McNall. *Western Civilizations*, 7th ed. New York: W. W. Norton, 1969.

Burrowes, Robert. "Mirror, Mirror on the Wall: A Comparison of Sources of External Events Data." In *Comparing Foreign Policies: Theories, Findings, and Methods*, ed. J. N. Rosenau, 383-406. Beverly Hills, California: Sage Publications, 1974.

Butterworth, Raymond Lyle. *Managing Interstate Conflict, 1945-1974: Data With Synopses*. Pittsburgh: University Center for International Studies, University of Pittsburgh, 1976.

Buzan, Barry. "Economic Structure and International Security: The Limits of the Liberal Case." *International Organization* 38 (1985): 597-624.

Cable, Vincent. "What Is International Economic Security?" *International Affairs* 71(2) (April 1995): 305-324.

Caraley, Demetrios & Cerentha Harris. *New World Politics: Power, Ethnicity, and Democracy*. New York: Academy of Political Science, 1993.

Carroll, Lewis. *Through the Looking Glass and What Alice Found There*. New York: Random House, 1946.

Carus-Wilson, E. M., ed. *Essays in Economic History*. London: Edward Arnold, 1954.

Castells, M. "High Technology, Economic Restructuring, and the Urban-regional Process in the United States." *High Technology, Space and Society* (Urban Affairs Annual Reviews) 28 (1985): 11-40.

Cattell, Raymond B. "The Dimensions of Cultural Patterns by Factorization of National Characters." *Journal of Abnormal and Social Psychology* 64 (1949): 443-469.

Cattell, Raymond B., B. H. Bruel & H. P. Hartman. "An Attempt at More Refined Definitions of the Cultural Dimensions of Syntality in Modern Nations." *American Sociological Review* 17 (1951): 408-421.

Cattell, Raymond B. & Richard L. Gorsuch. "The Definition and Measurement of National Morale and Morality." *Journal of Social Psychology* 67 (1965): 77-96.

Ceadel, Martin. *Thinking About Peace and War*. Oxford: Oxford University Press, 1987.

Chenery, Hollis B., Sherman Robinson & Moshe Syrquin. *Industrialization and Growth*. New York: Oxford University Press for the World Bank, 1986.

Chenery, Hollis B. & T. N. Srinivasan, eds. *Handbook of Development Economics*, Vol. 1. Amsterdam: Elsevier Science Publishers, 1988.

Chenery, Hollis B. & Moshe Syrquin. *Patterns of Development, 1950 to 1983*. Washington, D. C.: The World Bank, 1989.

Chenery, Hollis B. & Moshe Syrquin. *Patterns of Development, 1950-1970*. London: Oxford University Press, 1975.

Choucri, Nazli, ed. *Global Accord: Environmental Challenges and International Responses*. Cambridge, Massachusetts: MIT Press, 1993.

Choucri, Nazli. "Multinational Corporations and the Global Environment." In *Global Accord: Environmental Challenges and International Responses*, ed. Nazli Choucri, 205-254. Cambridge, Massachusetts: MIT Press, 1993.

Choucri, Nazli & Robert C. North. "Dynamics of International Conflict: Some Policy Implications of Population, Resources, and Technology." *World Politics* 24 supplementary issue (Spring 1972): 80-122.

Choucri, Nazli & Robert C. North. "Growth, Development, and Environmental Sustainability: Profiles and Paradox." In *Global Accord: Environmental Challenges and International Responses*, ed. Nazli Choucri, 67-132. Cambridge, Massachusetts: MIT Press, 1993.

Choucri, Nazli & Robert C. North. "In Search of Peace Systems: Scandinavia and the Netherlands; 1870-1970." In *Peace, War, and Numbers*, ed. Bruce M. Russett, 239-274. Beverly Hills, California: Sage Publications, 1972.

Choucri, Nazli & Robert C. North. *Nations in Conflict*. San Francisco: W.H. Freeman, 1974.

Choucri, Nazli & Robert C. North. *Nations in Conflict: National Growth and International Violence*. San Francisco: W. H. Freeman, 1975.

Clapham, J. H. *An Economic History of Modern Britain*, 3 vols. Cambridge: The University Press, 1938.

Cobden, Richard. *The Political Writings of Richard Cobden*, Vol. I. London: William Ridgway, 1868.

Cohen, Bernard C. *The Press and Foreign Policy*. Princeton, New Jersey: Princeton University Press, 1963.

Cole, W. A. "Factors in Demand." In *The Economic History of Britain Since 1700, Vol. I 1700-1860*, eds., R. Floud & D. McCloskey, 36-65. Cambridge: Cambridge University Press, 1981.

Coleman, D. C. "Colbertism." In *Problems of the Planned Economy*, eds. John Eatwell, Murray Milgate & Peter Newman, 51-53. New York: W. W. Norton, 1990.

Coleman, D. C. "Proto-industrialization: A Concept Too Many." *Economic History in Review* 36 (1983): 435-448.

Coleman, D. C., ed. *Revisions in Mercantilism*. London: Methuen, 1969.

Collingsworth, Terry, J., William Goold & Pharis J. Harvey. "Time for a Global New Deal." *Foreign Affairs* 73 (January/February 1994): 8-13.

Condliffe, John. *The Commerce of Nations*. New York: W. W. Norton, 1950.

Corson, Walter H. *Conflict and Cooperation in East-West Crises: Measurement and Explanations*. Paper presented at the American Political Science Association Annual Meeting, September 1970. Los Angeles: American Political Science Association, 1971.

Crafts, N. "British Economic Growth, 1700-1831: A Review of the Evidence." *Economic History in Review* 36 (1983).

Cunningham, W. *The Growth of English Industry and Commerce*, 3 vols. Cambridge: Cambridge University Press, 1907.

Deane, P. & W. A. Cole. *British Economic Growth 1688-1959*. Cambridge: Cambridge University Press, 1969.

Defoe, Daniel. *A Tour Through the Whole Island of Great Britain*. Harmondsworth: Penguin Books, [1720] 1971.

Denison, Edward F. *The Sources of Economic Growth in the United States and the Alternatives Before Us*, CED Supplementary Paper 13. New York: Council on Economic Development, 1960.

Denison, Edward F. & J. P. Poullier. *Why Growth Rates Differ*. Washington, D.C.: Brookings Institution, 1967.

Dervis, K., J. de Melo & Sherman Robinson. *General Equilibrium Models for Development Policy*. Cambridge: Cambridge University Press, 1982.

Desai, Meghnad. "Vladimir Ilyich Lenin." In *Problems of the Planned Economy*, eds. John Eatwell, Murray Milgate & Peter Newman, 151-154. New York: W. W. Norton, 1990.

Deutsch, Morton. "Field Theory." In *International Encyclopedia of the Social Sciences*, ed. David L. Sills, Vol. 5, 407-417. New York: Macmillan and Free Press, 1972.

Donelan, Michael. *Elements of International Political Theory*. Oxford: Clarendon Press, 1990.

DuPlessis, R. & M. C. Howell. "Reconsidering the Early Modern Urban Economy: The Cases of Leiden and Lille." *Past and Present* 94 (1982): 49-84.

Durant, Will. *The Age of Faith*. New York: Simon & Schuster, 1950.

Durant, Will. *The Reformation*. New York: Simon & Schuster, 1957.

Earle, Edward Meade. "Adam Smith, Alexander Hamilton, Friedrich List: The Economic Foundations of Military Power." In *Makers of Modern Strategy: From Machiavelli to the Nuclear Age*, ed. Peter Paret, 217-261. Princeton, New Jersey: Princeton University Press, 1986.

East, Maurice & Charles F. Hermann. "Do Nation-Types Account for Foreign Policy Behavior?" In *Comparing Foreign Policies*, ed. James N. Rosenau, 269-303. Beverly Hills, California: Sage Publications, 1974.

Easton, David. *The Political System: An Inquiry Into the State of Political Science*. New York: Alfred A. Knopf, 1953.

Eatwell, John, Murray Milgate & Peter Newman, eds. *Problems of the Planned Economy*. New York: W. W. Norton, 1990.

Engels, Freidrich. *The Peasant War in Germany*. New York: International Publishers, [1850] 1926.

Ethier, Wilfred. *Modern International Economics*. New York: W. W. Norton, 1983.

Farrell, R. B., ed. *Approaches to Comparative and International Politics*. Evanston, Illinois: Northwestern University Press, 1966.

Fei Xin. *Xing cha sheng lan (Triumphant Tour of the Star Raft)*, edited by Feng Chengjun. Peking: Zhonghua Shuju (China Bookshop), [1436] 1954.

Finer, Samuel. "State- and Nation-Building in Europe: The Role of the Military." In *The Formation of National States in Western Europe*, ed. Charles Tilly, 84-163. Princeton, New Jersey: Princeton University Press, 1975.

Fisher, Franklin M. "On the Cost of Approximate Specification in Simultaneous Equation Estimation." In *Essays on the Structure of Social Science Models*, eds., Albert Ando, Franklin M. Fisher & Herbert A. Simon, 32-63. Cambridge, Massachusetts: MIT Press, 1963.

Flory, Maurice. *Droit international du développement*. Paris: Presses Universitaires, 1977.

Frankel, Joseph. *International Politics, Conflict and Harmony*. London: Penguin, 1969.

Frei, Daniel. *Managing International Crises*. Beverly Hills, California: Sage Publications, 1982.

Gabriel, Jürg Martin. *Worldviews and Theories of International Relations*. New York: St. Martin's Press, 1994.

Galtung, Johann. "Rank and Social Integration: A Multidimensional Approach." In *Sociological Theories in Progress*, Vol. I, eds. Joseph Berger, Morris Zelditch & Bo Anderson, 145-198. Boston: Houghton Mifflin, 1966.

Galtung, Johann. "A Structural Theory of Aggression." *Journal of Peace Research* 1(2) (1964): 95-119.

Gann, Thomas & J. Eric S. Thompson. *The History of the Maya from the Earliest Time to the Present Day*. New York: Scribner's, 1931.

Garst, Daniel. "Thucydides and Neorealism." *International Studies Quarterly* 33 (March 1989).

George, A. L. "Prediction of Political Action by Means of Propaganda Analysis." *Public Opinion Quarterly* 20 (November 1960): 334-345.

Gilpin, Robert. "Economic Interdependence and National Security in Historical Perspective." In *Economic Issues and National Security*, eds. Klaus Knorr & Frank N. Trager, 19-66. New York: National Security Education Program of New York University, 1977.

Gilpin, Robert. "The Political Economy of Foreign Investment" (originally published in Robert Gilpin, *US Power and the Multinational Corporation*. New York: Basic Books, 1975). In *The International Political Economy of Direct Foreign Investment* Vol. II, eds. Benjamin Gomes-Casseres & David B. Yoffie, 241-275. Brookfield, Vermont: Edward Elgar, 1993.

Gilpin, Robert. *The Political Economy of International Relations*. Princeton, New Jersey: Princeton University Press, 1987.

Gilpin, Robert. *U.S. Power and the Multinational Corporation: The Political Economy of Foreign Direct Investment*. New York: Basic Books, 1975.

Gilpin, Robert. *War and Change in World Politics*. Cambridge: Cambridge University Press, 1981.

Ginsburg, Norton, ed. *Essays on Geography and Economic Development, Department of Geography Research, Paper No. 62*. Chicago: University of Chicago Press, 1960.

Gladwin, Thomas & Ingo Walter. *Multinationals Under Fire*. New York: John Wiley, 1980.

Gochman, C. S. & Z. Maoz. "Militarized Interstate Disputes 1816-1976: Procedures, Patterns, and Insights." *Journal of Conflict Resolution* 28 (1984): 585-616.

Gochman, Charles S. & Alan Ned Sabrosky, eds. *Prisoners of War? Nation-States in the Modern Era*. Lexington, Massachusetts.: Lexington Books, 1990.

Goldstein, Morris & Mohsin S. Khan. "Income and Price Effects in Foreign Trade." In *Handbook of International Economics*, Vol. II, eds. Ronald. W. Jones & Peter B. Kenen, 1041-1105. Amsterdam: North-Holland, 1984.

Gomes-Casseres, Benjamin & David B. Yoffie, eds. *The International Political Economy of Direct Foreign Investment* Vol. II. Brookfield, Vermont: Edward Elgar, 1993.

Gordon, Donald. *The Moment of Power: Britain's Imperial Epoch*. Englewood Cliffs, New Jersey: Prentice-Hall, 1970.

Gould, J. D. *Economic Growth in History: Survey and Analysis*. London: Methuen, 1972.

Guilmartin, J. *Gunpowder and Galleys: Changing Technology and Mediterranean Warfare in the Sixteenth Century*. London: Cambridge University Press, 1974.

Haass, Richard N. "Paradigm Lost." *Foreign Affairs* 74 (January/February 1995): 43-58.

Hamilton, Peter. "The Enlightenment and the Birth of Social Science." In *Formations of Modernity*, eds. Stuart Hall & Bram Gieben, 18-58. Oxford: Polity, 1992.

Harris, William V. *War and Imperialism in Republican Rome: 327-70 BC.* New York: Oxford University Press, 1979.

Harte, N. B. & K. G. Ponting. *Textile History and Economic History.* Manchester: Manchester University Press, 1973.

Healey, Denis. "The Sputnik and Western Defence." *International Affairs* 34(2) (April 1958): 145-156.

Hermann, Charles. F. & Margaret G. Hermann. *Validation Studies of Inter-Nation Simulation.* China Lake, California: U. S. Naval Test Station, 1963.

Hermann, Charles F., Maurice A. East, Margaret G. Hermann, Barbara G. Salmore & Stephen A. Salmore. *CREON: A Foreign Events Data Set.* Beverly Hills, California: Sage Publications, 1973.

Herz, John H. *Political Realism and Political Idealism.* Chicago: University of Chicago Press, 1951.

Hirschman, Albert O. *National Power and the Structure of Foreign Trade.* Berkeley: University of California Press, [1945] 1980.

Hobson, J. A. *Imperialism: A Study,* 3d ed. revised. London: G. Allen & Unwin, 1938.

Hoffmann, Stanley. *Janus and Minerva: Essays in the Theory and Practice of International Politics.* Boulder, Colorado: Westview Press, 1987.

Holsti, Ole R. "Content Analysis in Political Research." In *Computers and the Policy-Making Community,* eds., Davis B. Bobrow & Judah L. Schwarz, 111-153. Englewood Cliffs, New Jersey: Prentice-Hall, 1968.

Holsti, Ole R., R. Brody & R. North. "Measuring Affect and Action in International Reaction Models: Empirical Materials from the 1962 Cuban Missile Crisis." *Journal of Peace Research* 1 (1964): 170-189.

Hont, Istvan & Michael Ignatieff, eds. *Wealth and Virtue: The Shaping of Political Economy in the Scottish Enlightenment.* Cambridge: University Press, 1983.

Hughes, Helen & You Poh Seng. *Foreign Investment and Industrialization in Singapore.* Madison: University of Wisconsin Press, 1969.

Huntington, Samuel P. "Arms Races: Prerequisites and Results." In *The Use of Force: Military Power and International Politics,* 3d ed., eds. Robert J. Art & Kenneth N. Waltz, 637-670. Lanham, Maryland: University Press of America, 1988.

International Centre for the Settlement of Investment Disputes. "Individual Country Supplements." In *Investment Laws of the World.* Dobbs Ferry, New York: Oceana Publications, 1991.

International Centre for the Settlement of Investment Disputes. "Investment Promotion and Protection Treaties." In *Investment Laws of the World.* Dobbs Ferry, New York: Oceana Publications, 1991.

International Monetary Fund. *International Financial Statistics Yearbook.* Washington, D.C.: International Monetary Fund, 1962-1994.

Jones, L. P. & I. Sakong. *Government Business and Entrepreneurship in Economic Development: The Korean Case.* Cambridge, Massachusetts: Harvard University Press, 1980.

Jones, R. W. & P. B. Kenen, eds. *Handbook of International Economics.* Amsterdam: North-Holland, 1984.

Kean, James & Patrick J. McGowan. "National Attributes and Foreign Policy Participation: A Path Analysis." In *Sage International Yearbook of Foreign Policy Studies*, ed. Patrick J. McGowan, Vol. 1. Beverly Hills, California: Sage Publications, 1973.

Keegan, John. *A History of Warfare*. New York: Alfred A. Knopf, 1994.

Kegley, Charles W., Jr. & Eugene R. Wittkopf. *World Politics: Trend and Transformation*, 5th ed. New York: St. Martin's Press, 1993.

Kendrick, John W. *Productivity Trends in the United States*. Princeton, New Jersey: National Bureau of Economic Research, 1961.

Kennedy, Paul M. *The Rise and Fall of the Great Powers: Economic Change and Military Conflict from 1500 to 2000*. New York: Random House, 1987.

Keohane, Robert O. & Joseph S. Nye, Jr. *Power and Interdependence: World Politics in Transition*. Boston: Little, Brown, 1977.

Keohane, Robert O. & Joseph S. Nye, Jr. "*Power and Interdependence* Revisited." *International Organization*, 41 (1987): 725-753.

Keynes, John Maynard. *The General Theory of Employment, Interest, and Money*. New York: Harcourt Brace Jovanovich, [1935] 1964.

Kindleberger, Charles P. *Foreign Trade and the National Economy*. New Haven, Connecticut: Yale University Press, 1966.

Kindleberger, Charles P., ed. *The Multinational Corporation*. Cambridge, Massachusetts: MIT Press, 1970.

Kissinger, Henry A. *A World Restored: Metternich, Castlereagh, and the Problems of Peace, 1812-1822*. New York: Grosset & Dunlap, 1964.

Knorr, Klaus. *The Power of Nations: The Political Economy of International Relations*. New York: Basic Books, 1975.

Knorr, Klaus & Frank N. Trager. *Economic Issues and National Security*. New York: National Security Education Program of the New York University, 1977.

Kobrin, Stephen J. "Foreign Enterprise and Forced Divestment in LDCs." In *The International Political Economy of Direct Foreign Investment*, Vol. II, eds. Benjamin Gomes-Casseres & David B. Yoffie, 107-130. Brookfield, Vermont: Edward Elgar, 1993.

Kondratieff, Nicolai D. "The Long Waves in Economic Life." *Review of Economic Statistics* 17 (November 1935): 105-115.

Kondratieff, Nicolai D. "The Long Waves in Economic Life." *Review* 2 (Spring 1979): 519-562.

Kraar, Louis. "Need a Friend in Asia? Try the Singapore Connection." *Fortune* 133(4) (4 March 1996): 172-183.

Krasner, Stephen D. *Defending the National Interest*. Princeton, New Jersey: Princeton University Press, 1978.

Krasner, Stephen D. "State Power and the Structure of International Trade." *World Politics* 28 (1976): 317-347.

Kreisberg, Louis. "Interlocking Conflicts in the Middle East." In *Research in Social Movements, Conflicts and Change*, Vol. 3, ed. Louis Kreisberg, 99-118. Greenwich, Connecticut: JAI Press, 1980.

Kreisberg, Louis. *International Conflict Resolution*. New Haven, Connecticut: Yale University Press, 1992.

Kreisberg, Louis, ed. *Research in Social Movements, Conflicts and Change*, Vol. 3. Greenwich, Connecticut: JAI Press, 1980.

Krugman, Paul. "Competitiveness: A Dangerous Obsession." *Foreign Affairs* 73(2) (March/April 1994): 40-41.

Kubo, Yuji, Sherman Robinson & Moshe Syrquin. "The Methodology of Multisector Comparative Analysis." In *Industrialization and Growth*, eds. Hollis B. Chenery, Sherman Robinson & Moshe Syrquin, 121-147. New York: Oxford University Press for the World Bank, 1986.

Kubo, Yuji, Sherman Robinson & S. Urata. *The Impact of Alternative Development Strategies: Simulations with a Dynamic Input-Output Model.* Berkeley, California: Department of Agricultural and Resource Economics, University of California, Berkeley, 1986.

Kuznets, Simon. "Characteristics of Modern Economic Growth." In *Postwar Economic Growth: Four Lectures*, Simon Kuznets, 36-68. Cambridge, Massachusetts: Belknap Press of Harvard University Press, 1964.

Kuznets, Simon. *Economic Growth and Structure.* New York: W. W. Norton, 1965.

Kuznets, Simon. *Modern Economic Growth.* New Haven, Connecticut: Yale University Press, 1966.

Kuznets, Simon. "Postwar Economic Growth: Findings and Questions." In *Postwar Economic Growth: Four Lectures*, Simon Kuznets, 96-143. Cambridge, Massachusetts: Belknap Press of Harvard University Press, 1964.

Kuznets, Simon. *Six Lectures on Economic Growth.* New York: Free Press, 1959.

Kuznets, Simon. "World Economic Structure: Diversity and Interdependence." In *Postwar Economic Growth: Four Lectures*, Simon Kuznets, 3-35. Cambridge, Massachusetts: Belknap Press of Harvard University Press, 1964.

Ladurie, Emmanual LeRoy. "*Les Masses Profondes: La Paysannerie.*" In *Histoire Économique et Sociale de la France*, eds. Fernand Braudel & E. Larousse, part I, Vol. 2. Paris: Presses Universitaires de la France, 1977.

Lagos, G. *International Stratification and Underdeveloped Countries.* Chapel Hill: University of North Carolina Press, 1963.

Landes, D. *The Unbound Prometheus. Technological Change and Industrial Development in Western Europe from 1750 to the Present.* London: Cambridge University Press, 1969.

Lanphier, Vernard. *Foreign Relations Indicator Project*, Paper presented at the International Studies Association Annual Meeting, March 1972. Dallas, Texas: International Studies Association, 1972.

Lasswell, Harold D. "The Politically Significant Content of the Press: Coding Procedures." *Journalism Quarterly* 19 (1942): 12-23.

Lasswell, Harold D. "The Structure and Function of Communication in Society." In *The Communication of Ideas*, ed. L. Bryson, 37-51. New York: Harper, 1948.

Lasswell, Harold D. & A. Kaplan. *Power and Society: A Framework for Political Inquiry.* New Haven, Connecticut: Yale University Press, 1950.

Leamer, Edward E. & Robert M. Stern. *Quantitative International Economics.* Boston: Allyn & Bacon, 1970.

Leng, R. J. & J. D. Singer. *Toward a Multi-theoretical Typology of International Behavior*, Paper presented at the Event Data Conference, April 1970. East Lansing: University of Michigan, 1970.

Lerche, Charles O. & Abdul A. Said. *Concepts of International Politics.* Englewood Cliffs, New Jersey: Prentice Hall, 1963.

Levy, Jack. *War in the Modern Great Power System: 1495-1975*. Lexington: University
    Press of Kentucky, 1983.
Lewin, Kurt. *A Dynamic Theory of Personality*. New York: McGraw-Hill, 1935.
Lewin, Kurt. *Field Theory in Social Science*. New York: Harper & Row, 1951.
Lind, Michael. "Hamilton's Legacy" *Wilson Quarterly* 18 (Summer 1994): 40-52.
List, Friedrich. *National System of Political Economy*. London: Longmans, Green, 1928.

Maddison, Angus. *Economic Growth in the West*. New York: The Twentieth Century
    Fund, 1964.
Maddison, Angus. *Phases of Capitalist Development*. New York: Oxford University
    Press, 1982.
Maddison, Angus. "What Is Education For?" *Lloyds Bank Review* (April 1974)
Malthus, Thomas R. *First Essay on Population 1798*. London: Macmillan, 1966.
Mansbach, Richard W. & John A Vasquez. *In Search of Theory. A New Paradigm for
    Global Politics*. New York: Columbia University Press, 1981.
Mansfield, Edward D. *Power, Trade, and War*. Princeton, New Jersey: Princeton
    University Press, 1994.
Mantoux, P. *The Industrial Revolution in the Eighteenth Century: An Outline of the
    Beginnings of the Modern Factory System in England*, rev. ed. Methuen, New
    Jersey: University Paperbacks, 1964.
Marglin, Stephen A. "What Do Bosses Do? The Origins and Functions of Hierarchy
    in Capitalist Production." *Review of Radical Political Economy* 6 (Summer
    1974): 60-112.
Marshall, Alfred. *Industry and Trade*. London: Macmillan, 1919. Reprinted in *Reprints
    of Economic Classics*, Chapters 3-5, 32-106. New York: Augustus M. Kelley,
    1970.
Marx, Karl. *Capital, A Critique of Political Economy, 3 Vols*, Vol. I. Harmondsworth:
    Penguin/New Left Books, 1976-1981.
Marx, Karl. *Die Grundrisse (Foundations of the Critique of Political Economy)*. Translated
    & edited by M. Nicholaus. Harmondsworth: Penguin/New Left Books, 1973.
Mathias, Peter. *The First Industrial Nation: An Economic History of Britain 1700-1914*.
    London: Methuen, 1969.
McClellan, Grant S., ed. *US Foreign Aid*, The Reference Shelf, Vol. 29, No. 5. New
    York: The H.W. Wilson Company, 1957.
McClelland, Charles A. "International Interaction Analysis: Basic Research and Some
    Practical Applications." *World Event/Interaction Survey Technical Report 2*,
    November 1968. Los Angeles: University of Southern California, 1968.
McClelland, Charles A. & R. A. Young. "World Event/Interaction Survey Handbook
    and Codebook." *World Event/Interaction Survey Technical Report 1*, January
    1969. Los Angeles: University of Southern California, 1969.
McGowan, Patrick J. *Dimensions of African Foreign Policy Behavior*, Paper presented at
    the Canadian Association of African Studies Annual Meeting. Montreal:
    Canadian Association of African Studies, 1973.
McNeill, William H. *The Pursuit of Power: Technology, Armed Force, and Society Since
    A.D. 1000*. Chicago: University of Chicago Press, 1982.
McNeill, William H. *A World History*. New York: Oxford University Press, 1961.
Mendels, Franklin F. "Proto-industrialization: The First Phase of the Process of
    Industrialization." *Journal of Economic History* 37 (1972).

Mendels, Franklin F. & Pierre Deyon. "Proto-industrialization: Theory and Reality." In *Proto-industrialization: Proceedings of the Eighth International Congress of Economic History in Budapest, 1982*, Section A-2. Lille: Université des arts, lettres et sciences humaines de Lille, 1982.

Midgley, Mary. *Wisdom, Information and Wonder: What is Knowledge For?* London: Routledge, 1989.

Miller, Bruce. *The World of States*. London: Croom Helm, 1981.

Mitrany, David. *The Functional Theory of Politics*. London & New York: St. Martin's Press, 1975.

Moran, Theodore H. *Multinational Corporations and the Politics of Dependence*. Princeton, New Jersey: Princeton University Press, 1974.

Morgenthau, Hans J. *Politics Among Nations*, 4th ed. New York: Alfred A. Knopf, 1967.

Morgenthau, Hans J. & Kenneth W. Thompson. *Politics Among Nations: The Struggle for Power and Peace*, 6th ed. New York: Alfred A. Knopf, 1985.

Mueller, John. *Retreat From Doomsday: The Obsolescence of Major War*. New York: Basic Books, 1989.

Mullins, A. F., Jr. *Born Arming: Development and Military Power in New States*. Stanford, California: Stanford University Press, 1987.

Myrdal, Gunnar. *Asian Drama: An Inquiry into the Poverty of Nations*. New York: Pantheon, 1968.

Myrdal, Gunnar. *Economic Theory and Underdeveloped Regions*. London: G. Duckworth, 1957.

Namenwirth, J. Z. & T. L. Brewer. "Elite Editorial Comment on European and Atlantic Communities in Four Countries." In *The General Inquirer: A Computer Approach to Content Analysis in the Behavioral Sciences*, eds. P. J. Stone *et al.*, 401-427. Cambridge, Massachusetts: MIT Press, 1966.

Nef, J. U. "The Progress of Technology and the Growth of Large Scale Industry in Great Britain, 1540-1640" & "Prices and Industrial Capitalism in France and England, 1540-1640." In *Essays in Economic History*, ed. E. M. Carus-Wilson, 88-134. London: Edward Arnold, 1954.

Neustadt, Richard E. & Ernest R. May. *Thinking in Time: The Uses of History for Decision-Makers*. New York: Free Press, 1986.

Nicholson, Michael. *Conflict Analysis*. London: Oxford University Press, 1970.

Niebuhr, Reinhold J. *Beyond Tragedy: Essays on the Christian Interpretation of History*. New York: Charles Scribner's Sons, 1937.

North, Robert C., Richard A. Brody & Ole R. Holsti. "Some Empirical Data on the Conflict Spiral." In Peace Research Society, *Papers I*, Chicago Conference. 1-14. Chicago: Peace Research Society, 1964.

North, Robert C., C. O. Holsti, M. G. Zaninovich & Dina A. Zinnes, eds. *Content Analysis: A Handbook with Application for the Study of International Crises*. Evanston, Illinois: Northwestern University Press, 1963.

Nye, Joseph S., Jr. "The Changing Nature of World Power." In *New World Politics: Power, Ethnicity and Democracy*, eds. Demetrios Caraley & Cerentha Harris, 39-54. New York: Academy of Political Science, 1993.

Nye, Joseph S., Jr. "Neorealism and Neoliberalism." *World Politics* 40 (1988): 235-251.

O'Brien, P. K. & C. Keyder. *Economic Growth in Britain and France 1780-1914*. London: G. Allen & Unwin, 1976.

O'Connell, D. P. *The Law of State Succession*. Cambridge: Cambridge University Press, 1956.

Ohmae, Kenichi. *The Borderless World*. New York: HarperCollins, 1990.

Olson, Mancur, Jr. "Rapid Growth as a Destabilizing Force." *Journal of Economic History* 23(4) (December 1963): 529-552.

Organization for Economic Cooperation and Development *Investment Incentives and Disincentives and the International Investment Process*. Paris: OECD, 1983.

Organski, A.F.K. *World Politics*, 2d ed. New York: Alfred A. Knopf, 1968.

Organski, A.F.K. & Jacek Kugler. *The War Ledger*. Chicago: University of Chicago Press, 1980.

Pack, Howard. "Industrialization and Trade." In *Handbook of Development Ecomomics*, eds. Hollis B. Chenery & T. N. Srinivasan, 333-380. Amsterdam: Elsevier Science Publishers, 1988.

Pack, Howard & L. E. Westphal. "Industrial Strategy and Technological Change: Theory versus Reality." *Journal of Development Economics* 22 (June 1986): 87-128.

Paret, Peter, ed. *Makers of Modern Strategy: From Machiavelli to the Nuclear Age*. Princeton, New Jersey: Princeton University Press, 1986.

Pindyck, Robert S. & Daniel L. Rubinfeld. *Econometric Models & Economic Forecasts*, 3d ed. New York: McGraw-Hill, 1991.

Plato. *The Dialogues of Plato*, translated by J. Harward. Chicago: Encyclopedia Britannica, 1952.

Pollard, S. *Peaceful Conquest*. Oxford: Oxford University Press, 1981.

Pool, Ithiel de Sola. *Symbols of Internationalism*. Stanford, California: Stanford University Press, 1951.

Porter, Bruce F. *War and the Rise of the State*. New York: The Free Press, 1994.

Pruitt, Dean G & Richard C. Snyder, eds. *Theory & Research on the Causes of War*. Englewood Cliffs, New Jersey: Prentice-Hall, 1969.

Rangarajan, L. N. *The Limitation of Conflict*. New York: St. Martin's Press, 1985.

Rapoport, Anatol. *Fights, Games, and Debates*. Ann Arbor: The University of Michigan Press, 1960.

Reich, Robert. "Who is 'Them'?" *Harvard Business Review* (March-April 1991): 77-88.

Renouvin, P. & J. B. Duroselle. *Introduction to the History of International Relations*. New York: Frederick A. Praeger, 1967.

Research Working Group on Cyclical Rhythms and Secular Trends. "Cyclical Rhythms and Secular Trends of the Capitalist World-Economy: Some Premises, Hypotheses, and Questions." *Review* 2 (Spring 1979): 483-500.

Reynolds, Lloyd G. *Economic Growth in the Third World, 1950-1980*. New Haven, Connecticut: Yale University Press, 1985.

Rhee, Sang-Woo. "China's Cooperation, Conflict and Interaction Behavior Viewed from Rummel's Field Theory Perspective." In *Field Theory Evolving*, ed. Rudolph J. Rummel, 371-403. Beverly Hills, California: Sage Publications, 1977.

Richardson, Lewis. *Statistics of Deadly Quarrels*. Pittsburgh: Boxwood Press, 1960.

Robinson, James H. *The Mind in the Making*. New York: Harper & Brothers, 1939.

Robinson, Sherman. *Multisectoral Models of Developing Countries: A Survey*, Working Paper 401. Berkeley: Department of Agricultural and Resource Economics, University of California, Berkeley, 1986.

Romer, Paul. *Are Nonconvexities Important for Understanding Growth?* Cambridge: National Bureau of Economic Research, 1990b.

Romer, Paul. "Endogenous Technical Change." *Journal of Political Economy* 98 (1990a): S71-S102.

Rosecrance, Richard N. *Action and Reaction in World Politics*. Boston: Little, Brown, 1963.

Rosecrance, Richard N. "Bipolarity, Multipolarity, and the Future." In *International Politics and Foreign Policy*, ed. James N. Rosenau, 325-335. New York: Free Press, 1969.

Rosecrance, Richard N. *The Rise of the Trading State: Commerce and Conquest in the Modern World*. New York: Basic Books, 1986.

Rosenau, James N., ed. *Comparing Foreign Policies: Theories, Findings, and Methods*. Beverly Hills, California: Sage Publications, 1974.

Rosenau, James N. "Global Changes and Theoretical Challenges: Toward a Postinternational Politics for the 1990s." In *Global Changes and Theoretical Challenges: Approaches to World Politics for the 1990s*, eds. Ernst-Otto Czempiel & James N. Rosenau, 1-20. Lexington, Massachusetts: Lexington Books, 1989.

Rosenau, James N., ed. *International Politics and Foreign Policy*. New York: Free Press, 1969.

Rosenau, James N. "Pre-Theories and Theories of Foreign Policy." In *Approaches to Comparative and International Politics*, ed. R. B. Farrell, 27-92. Evanston, Illinois: Northwestern University Press, 1966.

Rosenau, James N. & Gary Hoggard. "Foreign Policy Behavior in Dyadic Relationships: Testing a Pre-Theoretical Extension." In *Comparing Foreign Policies*, ed. James N. Rosenau, 117-151. Beverly Hills, California: Sage Publications, 1974.

Rosenberg, Nathan & L. E. Birdzell. *How the West Grew Rich*. New York: Basic Books, 1986.

Rostow, Walt W. *Rich Countries and Poor Countries*. Boulder, Colorado: Westview Press, 1987.

Rostow, Walt W. *Stages of Economic Growth*. Cambridge: University Press, 1960, 1971.

Rotwein, Eugene, ed. *David Hume: Writings on Economics*. Madison: University of Wisconsin Press, 1955.

Rummel, Rudolph J. "Dimensions of Conflict Behavior Within and Between Nations." In *General Systems: Yearbook of the Society for General Systems Research*, Vol. VIII. 1-50. Society for General Systems Research, 1963.

Rummel, Rudolph J. "Dimensions of Foreign and Domestic Conflict Behavior: A Review of Findings." In *Theory and Research on the Causes of War*, eds. Dean G. Pruitt & Richard C. Snyder, 219-228. Englewood Cliffs, New Jersey: Prentice-Hall, 1969.

Rummel, Rudolph J. *The Dimensions of Nations*. Beverly Hills, California: Sage Publications, 1972.

Rummel, Rudolph J. "A Status Field Theory of International Relations." In *Dimensionality of Nations Project Report No. 50*. Honolulu: Dimensionality of Nations Project, 1971.

Rummel, Rudolph J. "A Status-Field Theory of International Relations." In *Field Theory Evolving*, ed. Rudolph J. Rummel, 199-255. Beverly Hills, California: Sage Publications, 1977.

Rummel, Rudolph J. "Testing Some Possible Predictors of Conflict Behavior Within and Between Nations." In *Papers I*, Chicago Conference, Peace Research Society, 79-111. Chicago: Peace Research Society, 1963.

Rummel, Rudolph J. "US Foreign Relations: Conflict, Cooperation, and Attribute Distances." In *Peace, War, and Numbers*, ed. Bruce M. Russett, 71-113. Beverly Hills, California: Sage Publications, 1972.

Russett, Bruce M. *Community and Contention*. Cambridge, Massachusetts: MIT Press, 1963.

Russett, Bruce M. "Economic Decline, Electoral Pressure, and the Initiation of Interstate Conflict." In *Prisoners of War? Nation-States in the Modern Era*, eds. Charles S. Gochman & Alan Ned Sabrosky, 123-140. Lexington, Massachusetts: Lexington Books, 1990.

Russett, Bruce M., ed. *Peace, War, and Numbers*. Beverly Hills, California: Sage Publications, 1972.

Sabloff, Jeremy A. *The New Archaeology and the Ancient Maya*. New York: Scientific American Library, 1990.

Salter, W.E.G. *Productivity and Technical Change*. Cambridge: Cambridge University Press, 1960.

Schultz, T. W. "Investment in Human Capital." *American Economic Review* (March 1961).

Schumpeter, Joseph A. *Business Cycles*. New York: McGraw-Hill, 1939.

Schumpeter, Joseph A. *The Theory of Economic Development*. New York: Oxford University Press, 1961.

Seabury, Paul. "Realism and Idealism." In *Encyclopedia of American Foreign Policy: Studies of the Principal Movements and Ideas*, Vol. III, ed. Alexander DeConde, 856-866. New York: Scribner's, 1978.

Shelley, Percy Bysshe. *Queen Mab 1813*. Oxford: Woodstock Books, [1813] 1990.

Singer, J. David, ed. *Explaining War: Selected Papers From the Correlates of War Project*. Beverly Hills, California: Sage Publications, 1979.

Singer, J. David, Stuart Bremer, & John Stuckey. "Capability Distribution, Uncertainty and Major Power War, 1820-1965." In *Peace, War, and Numbers*, ed. Bruce M. Russett, 25-26. Beverly Hills, California: Sage Publications, 1972.

Singer, J. David & Melvin Small. "The Composition and Status Ordering of the International System, 1815-1940." *World Politics* 18(2) (January 1966): 236-282.

Singer, J. David & Melvin Small. *The Wages of War, 1816-1965: A Statistical Handbook*. New York: John Wiley, 1972.

Sivard, Ruth Leger. *World Military and Social Expenditures 1979*. Leesburg, Virginia: World Priorities, 1979.

Small, Melvin & J. David Singer. *Resort to Arms: International and Civil Wars: 1816-1980*. Beverly Hills, California: Sage Publications, 1982.

Smith, Adam. *An Inquiry into the Nature and Causes of the Wealth of Nations*, ed. Edwin Cannan. New York: Random House, [1776] 1937.

Smoker, Paul A. "A Mathematical Study of the Present Arms Race." In *General Systems: Yearbook of the Society for General Systems Research*, Vol. VIII. 51-59. Society for General Systems Research, 1963.

Smoker, Paul A. "A Pilot Study of the Present Arms Race." In *General Systems: Yearbook of the Society for General Systems Research*, Vol. VIII. 61-76. Society for General Systems Research, 1963.

Snow, Philip. *The Star Raft, China's Encounter With Africa*. London: Weidenfeld and Nicholson, 1988.

Solow, Robert M. "Technical Change and the Aggregate Production Function." *Review of Economics and Statistics* 39 (August 1957): 312-320.

Sorokin, Pitirim. *Social and Cultural Dynamics*, Vol. 3. New York: American Book Company, 1937.

Stern, Geoffrey. "International Relations in a Changing World: Bucking the Trendies." *The World Today* 51 (July 1995): 148-151.

Stone, P. J. *et al. The General Inquirer: A Computer Approach to Content Analysis in the Behavioral Sciences*. Cambridge, Massachusetts: MIT Press, 1966.

Syrquin, Moshe. "Patterns of Structural Change." In *Handbook of Development Economics*, Vol. 1, eds. Hollis B. Chenery & T. N. Srinivasan, 203-273. Amsterdam: Elsevier Science Publishers, 1988.

Tanter, Raymond. "Dimensions of Conflict Behavior Within and Between Nations, 1958-1960." *Journal of Conflict Resolution* 10(1) (March 1966): 41-64.

Thompson, William R. *On Global War: Historical-Structural Approaches to World Politics*. Columbia: University of South Carolina Press, 1988.

Thomsen, Stephen & Stephen Woolcock. *Direct Investment and European Integration: Competition Among Firms and Governments*. London: Pinter Publishers for the Royal Institute of International Affairs, 1993.

Tilly, Charles, ed. *The Formation of National States in Western Europe*. Princeton, New Jersey: Princeton University Press, 1975.

Toynbee, Arnold. *Lectures on the Industrial Revolution in England*. Boston: Beacon Press [1884] 1961.

Tucker, Josiah. *A Brief Essay on the Advantages and Disadvantage which Respectively Attend France and Great Britain with Regard to Trade*. London: n.p., [1749, 1757].

United Nations. *World Investment Report 1992, Transnational Corporations as Engines of Growth*. New York: United Nations, 1992.

United Nations Centre on Transnational Corporations. *World Investment Directory 1992, Volume I: Asia and The Pacific*. New York: United Nations, 1992.

United Nations Centre on Transnational Corporations. *World Investment Report 1991: The Triad in Foreign Direct Investment*, 84-91. New York: United Nations, 1991.

Usher, A. P. *An Introduction to the Industrial History of England*. London: G. G. Harrap, 1921.

Vayrynen, Raimo. "Economic Cycles, Power Transitions, Political Management and Wars Between Major Powers." *International Studies Quarterly* 27 (December 1983): 398-418.

Verba, Sidney & Norman H. Nie. *Participation in America.* New York: Harper & Row, 1972.

Vernon, Raymond. "The Obsolescing Bargain: A Key Factor in Political Risk." In *The International Essays for Business Decision Makers*, Vol. 5, ed. Mark B. Winchester, 281-286. Houston: Center for International Business, 1980.

Vernon, Raymond. *Sovereignty at Bay.* New York: Basic Books, 1971.

Viner, Jacob, ed. *International Economics.* Glencoe, Illinois: Free Press, 1951.

Viner, Jacob. "Peace as an Economic Problem." In Jacob Viner, ed. *International Economics.* Glencoe, Illinois: Free Press, 1951.

Viner, Jacob. "Power versus Plenty as Objectives of Foreign Policy in the Seventeenth and Eighteenth Centuries." *World Politics* 1 (1948): 1-29.

von Albertini, Rudolf. *Decolonization: The Administration and Future of the Colonies, 1919-1960.* London: Holmes & Meier, 1982.

von Gierke, Otto. *Natural Law and the Theory of Society 1500 to 1800.* Translated by Ernest Barker. Cambridge: Cambridge University Press, [1913, 1934] 1950.

Wallace, Michael D. "Arms Races and Escalation: Some New Evidence." *Journal of Conflict Resolution* 23 (March 1979): 3-16.

Wallace, Michael D. "Status, Formal Organization, and Arms Levels as Factors Leading to the Onset of War, 1820-1964." In *Peace, War, and Numbers*, ed. Bruce M. Russett, 49-70. Beverly Hills, California: Sage Publications, 1972.

Wallerstein, Immanuel. *The Modern World-system.* New York: Academic Press, 1974.

Wallerstein, Immanuel. "The Present State of the Debate on World Inequality." In *World Inequality: Origins and Perspectives on the World System*, ed. Immanuel Wallerstein, 12-28. Montréal: Black Rose Books, 1975.

Wallich, Paul & Elizabeth Corcoran. "The Analytical Economist, Don't Write Off Marx." *Scientific American* 264 (February 1991): 135.

Waltz, Kenneth N. "International Structure, National Force, and the Balance of World Power." In *International Politics and Foreign Policy*, ed. James N. Rosenau, 304-314. New York: Free Press, 1969.

Waltz, Kenneth N. *Man, the State and War: A Theoretical Analysis.* New York: Columbia University Press, 1954.

Waltz, Kenneth N. "The Myth of National Interdependence." In *The Multinational Corporation*, ed. Charles P. Kindleberger, 205-223. Cambridge, Massachusetts: MIT Press, 1970.

Waltz, Kenneth N. *Theory of International Politics.* Reading: Massachusetts: Addison-Wesley, 1979.

Webster, David L. "Warfare and the Evolution of Maya Civilization." In *The Origins of Maya Civilization*, ed. R. E. W. Adams, 335-372. Albuquerque: University of New Mexico Press, 1977.

Weigel, Dale R. "Investment in LDCs: The Debate Continues." *Columbia Journal of World Business*, vol. 23, no. 1, Spring 1988, 5-8.

"When Nations Play Leapfrog." *The Economist*, 329 (16 October 1993): 84.

Whiting, Van R., Jr. *The Political Economy of Foreign Investment in Mexico.* Baltimore: Johns Hopkins University Press, 1992.

Wight, Martin. *International Theory: The Three Traditions*. Edited by Gabriele Wight & Brian Porter. Leicester & London: Leicester University Press for the Royal Institute of International Affairs, 1991.

Wilkenfeld, J., ed. *Conflict Behavior and Linkage Politics*. New York: McKay, 1973.

Wilkenfeld, J. "Domestic and Foreign Conflict Behavior of Nations." *Journal of Peace Research* 5 (1968): 56-69.

Wilkenfeld, J. "Some Further Findings Regarding the Domestic and Foreign Conflict Behavior of Nations." *Journal of Peace Research* 6 (1969): 147-156.

Wilson, C. "The Other Face of Mercantilism." In *Revisions in Mercantilism*, ed. D. C. Coleman. London: Methuen, 1969.

Wilson, R. G. "The Supremacy of the Yorkshire Cloth Industry in the Eighteenth Century." In *Textile History and Economic History*, eds. N. B. Harte & K. G. Ponting. Manchester: Manchester University Press, 1973.

Winchester, Mark B. *The International Essays for Business Decision Makers*, Vol. 5. Houston: Center for International Business, 1980.

Wolf, Martin. "Cooperation or Conflict? The European Union in a Liberal Global Economy," *International Affairs* 71(2) (April 1995): 329.

World Bank. *The East Asian Miracle*. New York: Oxford University Press, 1993.

Wright, Quincy. "Development of A General Theory of International Relations." In *The Role of Theory in International Relations*, ed. Horace V. Harrison. Princeton, New Jersey: Van Nostrand, 1964.

Wright, Quincy. *The Study of International Relations*. New York: Appleton-Century-Crofts, 1955.

Wright, Quincy. *A Study of War*. Chicago: University of Chicago Press, 1942.

Wright, Quincy. *A Study of War*, 2d ed. Chicago: University of Chicago Press, 1965.

Yang, Yoonsae. "Foreign Investment in Developing Countries: Korea." In *Direct Foreign Investment in Asia and the Pacific*, ed. Peter Drysdale. Toronto: University of Toronto Press, 1972.

Yin, Chi-Ming. "Industry in the Republic of China: A Tale of Transformation," *Scientific American* 273(4) (October 1995): T24-T26.

Yost, David S. "Political Philosophy and the Theory of International Relations." *International Affairs* 70 (1994): 263-290.

Zinnes, Dina A. "A Comparison of Hostile Behavior of Decision Makers in Simulate and Historical Data." *World Politics* 18 (April 1966): 457-502.

Zinnes, Dina A. "Expression and Perception of Hostility in Inter-State Relations." Ph.D. diss. Stanford University, 1963.

Author Index

Subject Index

About the Author

WILLIAM H. MOTT IV has explored and exposed the complex interactions between economic growth, multinational enterprise, and international conflict during 25 years of interdisciplinary research, experience, and analysis. As a senior U.S. Army officer he served as Chief of the U.S. Office of Defense Cooperation in London. He has lectured at the Royal Military College of Science, taught at Gonzaga University and Salem State College, and is a frequent contributor to American, European, and Asian professional journals.

ISBN 0-313-30366-5

HARDCOVER BAR CODE